Capitalism and Social Progress

Also by Phillip Brown

BEYOND THATCHERISM: Social Policy, Politics and Society (*co-editor with Richard Sparks*)

ECONOMIC RESTRUCTURING AND SOCIAL EXCLUSION (*co-editor with Rosemary Crompton*)

EDUCATION, CULTURE, ECONOMY AND SOCIETY (*co-editor with A. H. Halsey, Hugh Lauder and Amy Stuart Wells*)

EDUCATION FOR ECONOMIC SURVIVAL: From Fordism to Post-Fordism? (*co-editor with Hugh Lauder*)

EDUCATION IN SEARCH OF A FUTURE (*co-editor with Hugh Lauder*)

EDUCATION, UNEMPLOYMENT AND LABOUR MARKETS

HIGHER EDUCATION AND CORPORATE REALITIES (*with Richard Scase*)

POOR WORK: Disadvantage and the Division of Labour (*co-editor with Richard Scase*)

SCHOOLING ORDINARY KIDS: Inequality, Unemployment and the New Vocationalism

Also by Hugh Lauder

EDUCATION, CULTURE, ECONOMY AND SOCIETY (*co-editor with A. H. Halsey, Phillip Brown and Amy Stuart Wells*)

EDUCATION FOR ECONOMIC SURVIVAL: From Fordism to Post-Fordism? (*co-editor with Phillip Brown*)

EDUCATION IN SEARCH OF A FUTURE (*co-editor with Phillip Brown*)

TOWARDS SUCCESSFUL SCHOOLING

TRADING IN FUTURES: Why Markets in Education Don't Work (*with David Hughes*)

Capitalism and Social Progress

The Future of Society in a Global Economy

Phillip Brown
Research Professor
The School of Social Sciences
Cardiff University

and

Hugh Lauder
Professor of Education and Political Economy
University of Bath

Foreword by

A. H. Halsey
Emeritus Professor of Sociology
University of Oxford

palgrave

First published 2001 by
PALGRAVE
Houndmills, Basingstoke, Hampshire RG21 6XS and
175 Fifth Avenue, New York, N. Y. 10010
Companies and representatives throughout the world

PALGRAVE is the new global academic imprint of
St. Martin's Press LLC Scholarly and Reference Division and
Palgrave Publishers Ltd (formerly Macmillan Press Ltd).

ISBN 0–333–92295–6 hardback
ISBN 0–333–92291–3 paperback

This book is printed on paper suitable for recycling and
made from fully managed and sustained forest sources.

A catalogue record for this book is available
from the British Library.

Library of Congress Cataloging-in-Publication Data
Brown, Phillip, 1957–
    Capitalism and social progress : the future of society in a global
    economy / Phillip Brown and Hugh Lauder ; foreword by A.H. Halsey.
        p. cm.
    Includes bibliographical references and index.
    ISBN 0–333–92295–6 — ISBN 0–333–92291–3 (pbk.)
        1. Social problems—United States. 2. Capitalism—United States. 3.
    Social problems—Great Britain. 4. Capitalism—Great Britain. I. Lauder,
    Hugh. II. Title.
    HN59.2 .B76 2000
    361.6'1'0973—dc21
                                                                00–048331

10   9   8   7   6   5   4   3   2   1
10   09 08 07 06 05 04 03 02 01

Printed and bound in Great Britain by
Antony Rowe Ltd, Chippenham, Wiltshire

Phil Brown   : *To Liz and our children, Max, George and Olivia*
Hugh Lauder : *To Karen, Jimmy and Kate;*
                          Trix Worrall and Jai Singh (i.m.), an
                          inspirational teacher

Contents

List of Tables

List of Figures

Foreword

To live in North America or in northern and western Europe at the dawn of the third millennium is to live in a world of historically unprecedented prosperity and of expectation at birth of an average length of life thirty years longer than that of our grandparents. During the twentieth century this advanced one-third of the world lived out two contending political agendas inherited from the nineteenth century – two competing projects for the transformation of society along the lines of prosperity and progress. They were Liberalism and Marxism. In retrospect we now see them as having shared historicist features – the abolition of the working class and the liberation of humankind from 'the kingdom of necessity' into 'the kingdom of light'; the lifting of 'the curse of Adam' and the attainment by all of an educated share in an enlightened democracy.

What my younger colleagues, Phil Brown and Hugh Lauder, present to us in this book is a sober analysis of the successes and failures of this inherited economic, social, and political agenda and an inspiring guide to further progress in the twenty-first century.

In an earlier work published in 2000 by Macmillan I tried to sum up British social trends in the twentieth century:

> It has been an eventful century of progress and barbarism throughout the world, with paradoxical movements towards both a longer and fuller life and towards unprecedented genocide and slaughter, towards democracy and towards dictatorship. For the aristocrat perhaps a century of dispossession. For the old and the ill, perhaps a rather more comfortable hundred years. For the homeless and dispossessed, a time of persistent degradation accentuated by surrounding opulence. For women, the young, and the fit and ordinary citizens, perhaps the greatest century in the whole history of humankind.[1]

In the Soviet Union the Marxist version of the project had failed in both its economic and especially its political aspects. In America and Britain the liberal version had been apparently triumphant. And yet, as A.B. Atkinson pointed out,[2] the distribution of income and wealth, having shown a tendency towards less inequality for the first three-quarters of the century, widened again in the final decades. The latest survey[3] indeed confirms that poverty rates have risen sharply. In 1983 14 per cent of households lacked three or more necessities because they could not afford them. That proportion had increased to 21 per cent in 1990 and to over 24 per cent by 1999. Items defined as necessities are those that more than 50 per cent of the population believes all adults should be able to afford and which they should not have to do without. Meanwhile at the other end of the economic spectrum what Robert Reich calls the symbolic analysts, an emerging class of the rich in a globalized economy, congregate in 'ghettoes of affluence' complete with burglar alarms and hired protectors for their social exlcusion, and feel little or no responsibility for the poor in neighbouring communities.

So what happened to the liberal version of freedom with richer? Of course it resulted in the post-Second World War welfare state but that, argue Brown and Lauder, was based on economic nationalism now threatened by the rise of the multinational companies. Politically, the oil crises apart, what happened was a return to the primitive form of liberalism – the idea that market individualism must rule, must be the measure of an individual's worth, must be promoted by competition. The other face of liberalism, the new liberalism of the turn of the nineteenth and twentieth centuries, faded in the 1970s along with its emphasis on equality, its concern for high quality public services and its *use of the nation state* for the purposes of wealth redistribution (through progressive direct taxation and inheritance taxes), social cohesion and cooperation, class abatement, and the fostering of the spirit of public service. All of these features of modernity which flowered so vigorously during the Second World War and the Attlean post-war government and were confidently called socialism, suffered horrendous reverses in the tumult of propaganda against state interference with the magic of the market, the vilification of the state and the glorification of greed. Not only did Keynesian macro-management and the historical class compromise between employers and Trade Unions crumble but there was also widespread deregulation of finance, de-nationalization and tax reduction as governments like those of Reagan in the US and Thatcher in UK dismantled the state apparatus and promoted the private sector, including the multinational (becoming global) corporations.

Brown and Lauder insist however that there is no necessary logic in global capitalism, no good reason why nation states cannot pursue both economic growth and social fairness, both prosperity and progress, both entrepreneurship and security. They consider the alternative of new left modernization. They reject the 'third way' advocated by the moderni-zers now firmly established around Tony Blair and occupying No. 10 Downing Street. Their purpose is to expose the flaws of the modernizing approach and to 'set the scene for a more radical and thorough debate about social justice, economic efficiency and social cohesion in the early decades of the twenty-first century'.

Their argued alternative turns on the concept of *collective intelligence.* The era of market individual industrialism has systematically ignored and in part destroyed the growth potential of each and every human being to develop and share a multiple sensitivity and skill in social institutions other than the market place. The need now is to pool intelligence, to cooperate, and to trust. They show that 'the struggle for collective intelligence involves more than changing the way we think about our own capacities and our relationship to society, it also includes weaving the principles of collective intelligence into the very fabric of society.'

Just as Durkheim wanted to mobilize the 'conscience collective' through education in the Third French Republic so now we are urged to reform twenty-first century society to a higher level of both efficiency and solidarity through the transformed up-bringing and adult life of a new socially enlightened citizenry. A new era of collective intelligence is thus the key to a richer and happier society.

We are indebted to Phil Brown and Hugh Lauder in the lead they have given in the analysis of the fundamental problems we confront in the twenty-first century.

A. H. HALSEY
Nuffield College
Oxford

Notes

1   A. H. Halsey 'Introduction: Twentieth-Century Britain', in A. H. Halsey with Josephine Webb (eds) *Twentieth Century British Social Trends*, London: Macmillan Press – now Palgrave, 2000, P.22.
2   A. B. Atkinson 'Distribution of Income and Wealth' in A. H. Halsey and J. Webb, (eds), *Twentieth Century British Social Trends*.
3   *Poverty and social exclusion in Britain*, David Gordon et al. Joseph Rowntree Foundation, 2000.

Acknowledgements

We are greatly indebted to Nicola Kerry, Jackie Swift, Christine Eagle, Matthew David, Frank Furedi, Krishan Kumar, Sarah Cant, Tim Fox, Rosemary Crompton, Andy Green, Ralph Fevre, Chris Harris, Joan Wills, Martin Thrupp, John Davies, Jane Millar, Ian Gough, Henry Levin, Martin Carnoy and Eileen Appelbaum, who commented on or helped prepare parts of the book.

We have both moved universities since the beginning of this project and we are very appreciative of the support we received at the University of Kent (UK) and at the Victoria University of Wellington (NZ) to develop our understanding of the broad range of issues the book covers. We would also acknowledge the support and interest shown by our current institutions, Cardiff University and the University of Bath and especially to Ian Jamieson, Jeff Thompson, and Bill Scott at Bath and Sara Delamont and Gareth Rees at Cardiff.

A special mention must go to Chelly Halsey at Nuffield College, Oxford for his encouragement, support and advice; to Karen Brazier, Heather Gibson, and Josie Dixon at Palgrave for their determination to give this book a public airing; and finally to Liz and Karen, our partners, who have endured the highs, lows, and several years of 'it's nearly finished'. They have demonstrated the love, understanding and endurance which gives us hope of achieving social progress.

This book would not have been completed without the support of Francis King, OBE, and the British Council and of the Victoria University of Wellington from which Hugh Lauder was granted sabbatical leave in 1994/5 to work on the book. The New Right revolution of the eighties and nineties in New Zealand was a powerful motivator behind its writing for Hugh Lauder because of the poverty, injustice and questionable economic performance it created. There are many in Aotearoa/New Zealand to whom he is indebted including his long-standing collaborator David Hughes; those in the education policy field who provided such strong criticism of New Right policies, including Ivan Snook, John Codd, Dick Harker, Roger Dale, Susan Robertson, John Freeman-Moir, Alan Scott, Mark Olssen, Michael Peters, Jim Marshall, Cathy Wylie, and Sue Watson; and Maori colleagues, Kath Irwin, Linda and Graham Smith and Trish Maringi Johnston, who provided another way of understanding education.

1
Introduction

Have not all our efforts and hopes been directed toward greater freedom, justice, and prosperity? If the outcome is so different from our aims – if, instead of freedom and prosperity, bondage and misery stare us in the face – is it not clear that sinister forces must have foiled our intentions, that we are the victims of some evil power which must be conquered before we can resume the road to better things?

Friedrich A. Hayek

Constant revolutionising of production, uninterrupted disturbance of all social conditions, everlasting uncertainty and agitation distinguish the bourgeois epoch from all earlier ones...all that is solid melts into air.

Karl Marx

1

Western nations are richer than they have ever been. Yet the social progress which was the dream of the great social thinkers of the late nineteenth and early twentieth century has eluded us. The social bargain by which workers and their families enjoyed greater prosperity through a national commitment to economic growth at mid-century has been destroyed. In America the top five per cent gain over 21 per cent of all household income, while the bottom fifth receive less than four per cent between them.[1] In Britain the gap between the rich and poor is greater than at any time since the late nineteenth century. For many-middle class families the dream of stable career progression and of their children achieving the same middle-class lifestyles has been crossed by the shadow of job insecurity. At the same time, the price of failure has increased. Since the early 1970s, high-school-educated males in America are the first generation since World War II to experience a lower standard of living than their fathers, and welfare provision for the working poor and unemployed has been stripped away.[2]

If economic growth no longer holds out the prospect of prosperity to all, the material route to human happiness also rings hollow in the face of new uncertainties. There are no doubt a small proportion of wealthy Americans and Europeans who can insulate themselves from the risks confronting the rest of society. But this is clearly not the case for the vast majority of middle-class wage earners. They are having to earn more to stand still as rising educational and health insurance costs are compounded by 'defensive' expenditure in the form of rising property insurance, burglar alarms, bars on windows, therapeutic services for stress, drug abuse and mental illness, along with all the other symptoms of disintegrating societies. One of the great paradoxes of the age is that at the very moment when choice and individual responsibility are the keynotes of nearly all political rhetoric, individuals feel increasingly powerless to influence their lives. It is for these reasons that the question of how to reconcile the goals of economic competitiveness, social justice, human freedom and security in post-industrial societies defines the subject of this book.

There is a desperate search to find solutions to the question of how nations can compete successfully in the new global competition while improving the quality of life for all their citizens. Similar questions occupied the minds of philosophers and social scientists in the nineteenth century in their efforts to describe and shape the direction of the industrial revolution. They asked how social justice could be reconciled with the extremes of inequality; how social solidarity could be maintained in the face of the centrifugal forces of the market; how human freedom could be realized in the face of alienation at work; and how society could progress when confronted with slowing economic growth. What all the great writers of that time – Durkheim, Marshall, Marx, Mill, Veblen and Weber – had in common was a concern with the central paradox of how industrial capitalism could deliver unimagined wealth only to benefit an elite at the expense of the majority. The great question of the age then, as it is today, is how the excesses of western capitalism can be controlled or transformed to benefit society as a whole.

In our own century, answers to these questions can only be found if we have a proper understanding of how social and economic life has changed. This book will argue that the scale of change has ruled out any possibility of recreating the post-war 'Golden era' of western capitalism. The Golden era was built on 'walled' economies of mass-produced goods and services which offered the prospect of a decent family wage to low-skilled workers. Large national corporations expanded to meet the insatiable demand for new consumer durables such as automobiles, televisions, radios and refrigerators. These corporations, along with the exponential growth in the public sector, played a decisive role in the creation of vast armies of white-collar workers, which offered career ladders to the sons (and gradually the daughters) of the middle class, as well as to a minority of those from blue-collar backgrounds. This was a world anchored by the nuclear family where the male breadwinner was paid a family wage to support a dependent female homemaker and his children.

Much of the prosperity generated in this period also depended on a political settlement between the state, employers and workers. In the aftermath of the Second World War the state emerged with a new mandate to create greater economic security and opportunity through a commitment to economic growth, where all would see their slice of the cake increase even if some were getting more than others. This commitment to 'economic nationalism' within the confines of walled national economies, led the state to effect a treaty between the traditional warring parties of capital and labour. For close on three decades it succeeded in managing the industrial peace necessary to foster prosperity for all. For many Americans and Europeans the standardized, hierarchical and male-dominated nature of society seemed to be a price worth paying as endemic problems of injustice and insecurity were suppressed under a tide of rising prosperity. Indeed, for a brief moment in the twentieth century it looked as if unemployment and poverty would be eliminated through the instruments of government policy. But this proved to be a brief, if not exceptional, period of western social history.

2

The first oil shock in the early 1970s was a decisive moment which marked the end of economic nationalism. Companies found it difficult to maintain their profit margins as the fourfold increase in fuel prices was accompanied by an intensification of economic competition spearheaded by Japan. Western economies have had to come to terms with the new rules of global competition which involve a shift away from

mid-century walled economies towards a highly integrated global mar-
ket-place. This has exposed domestic economies to a much greater level
of foreign competition and undermined the viability of building
national prosperity on the mass production of standardized goods and
services. Enterprises that can deliver a living wage to workers now
depend on the quality as much as the price of goods and services, and
on finding new sources of productivity, innovation and investment. In
such companies improvements in productivity depend upon the
organic integration of applied knowledge, technological innovation,
free-flow information networks and high-trust relations between management and multi-skilled workers. Such 'value added' is most likely to
be found in companies offering customized goods and services in areas
including motor vehicles, electronics, telecommunications, biotechnology, financial services, consultancy, advertising, marketing and the
media. Moreover, national champions such as General Motors and
IBM in America, ICI in Britain and Mercedes-Benz in Germany have
tried to break loose of their national roots, no longer willing (or able)
to guarantee the lion share of jobs to 'home-based' workers, or to pay
high wages to those with low skills.

In response to these new rules, all western nations in their domestic
economies and foreign affairs are having to look to their own social
institutions and human resources to meet the global challenge they
confront. With the election of New Right governments in the late
1970s under the leadership of Ronald Reagan in America and Margaret
Thatcher in Britain, the state was identified as an impediment to economic growth and prosperity. It was blamed for inhibiting personal
initiative and enterprise. This has led to a return to 'primitive' capitalism
based on the deregulation of markets and a demand for acquisitive
behaviour in all areas of social life. The shift to the Right in American
politics is amply demonstrated by Bill Clinton's signing of the Welfare
Act in August 1996, effectively marking the end of Franklin Roosevelt's
New Deal. In Britain, while the rhetoric of New Labour is progressive,
many aspects of its reform programme have conformed to the principles
of market individualism.

The settlement between the state, employers and trade unions also
lies in tatters as western governments have sought to restrict the powers
of trade unions to defend the conditions of workers. A corollary of
market deregulation was a massive programme of corporate restructuring which has seen the 'hollowing out' of the manufacturing base,
as American and British companies transferred large numbers of blue-
collar jobs to countries where wage bills were substantially below those

found in the West. Companies also 'downsized' to increase profit margins by taking advantage of the economies of scale made possible through recent advances in information technologies. The major beneficiaries of these changes have been corporate executives and the global traders who have amassed such personal wealth that even David Rockerfeller was moved to consider 'whether there isn't something unbalanced in the way our financial system is working'.[3]

Such gross disparities in income are the tip of the proverbial iceberg which is freezing out those who are not able to compete in the global labour market. In Robert Reich's *The Work of Nations*, for example, it is argued that income inequalities reflect the ability of workers to sell their knowledge, skills and insights in the global market. As a result, what he calls the symbolic analysts – the design engineers, research scientists, bio-technologists, public relations executives, investment brokers, international lawyers, management consultants – are no longer seen as dependent upon the society in which they live for their economic livelihoods. Their futures do not depend upon sharing a collective sense of purpose with their fellow citizens. The fate of unemployed youth in the inner-city slums which may be little more than a couple of miles down the freeway is quite literally seen as none of their business. Reich suggests that the symbolic analysts and their families are 'quietly seceding from the large and diverse publics of America into homogeneous enclaves, within which their earnings need not be redistributed to people less fortunate than themselves'.[4] They congregate in ghettos of affluence, with private schools, hospitals, roads and security guards. For the rest of the population locked into domestic labour markets the future looks pretty grim, as the symbolic analysts launch tax revolts under the banner of 'user pays' and their obligations to fellow citizens are translated into questions of financial contribution and just deserts.

The accuracy of this account will be scrutinised in this book, but there is no denying that the scale of such changes have made it difficult to envisage a new relationship between the individual and society that offers the potential for a fairer and more cohesive society. This problem has been compounded by the demise of Marxism as a viable alternative to market capitalism. This has led some to ask whether the centre-left can achieve anything tangible through national politics in the wake of global capitalism. The political programmes pursued by the 'Modernisers' like the *new* Democrats in America and *new* Labour in Britain do currently offer some encouragement, but they lack the vision on which progressive social and economic change will depend. In part, this is because they have too readily accepted the New Right view of the global economy that asserts that nation states are no longer able to guarantee the welfare and economic livelihood of citizens.[5] These, it is assumed, are best delivered through individual market competition.

The Western obsession with market individualism has a pedigree which extends back over two hundred years and found expression in Adam Smith's *The Wealth of Nations* (1776). Socialist thinkers of various kinds have attempted to challenge its dominance and during the 'golden era' many of its most undesirable effects were mitigated by the policies of economic nationalism. But if social justice and prosperity are to be reunited, new ways of thinking about ourselves and our relationship to society will need to emerge to meet the radically different social and economic conditions we now confront. In this book we will argue that in the early decades of the twenty-first century the roots of the decent society will only flourish if we can enact a shift from the spirit of competition which has shaped contemporary America and Britain, to a new spirit of co-operation made possible by the seismic changes which have led to the transformation of established patterns of family life, education, employment, income distribution, sexual relations and cultural identities.

Yet at precisely the time when America and Britain have the unique opportunity to 'think the unthinkable', to advance the creation of a decent society with the prospect of a better quality of life for all, we find that this challenge seems to be beyond both the left and right on Capital Hill or in Westminster. They are unable to remove the cultural blinkers of market individualism which is now ingrained in the political culture. It is beyond the realms of reason to suppose that there is any other way of organizing the competition for education, jobs and wealth in a global age. Of course, at times of rapid change and uncertainty it is not unusual for political leaders to reassert the basic principles which are believed to have secured prosperity in the past. In America and Britain the mantra of market competition tells us that the problem of distribution and reward in a capitalist economy can be solved through paid work; that competition is better than co-operation; that the size of one's wallet is a measure of one's social worth; and that there is a limited pool of talent that must be given the incentive to rise to the top.

The question of how rewards are to be distributed in capitalist societies – these rewards being unequal and often allocated unfairly – is fundamental to the question of social progress. The key assumption of market individualism is that people are 'nobody' unless they can make their way in the world through paid employment. That is one of the reasons why the solution to the problem of unemployment is seen to be that of herding single parents into poverty-wage employment. In doing so it denies the Feminist argument for the importance of the unpaid work of child raising and, as we shall show, the realities of the post-industrial world.

The assumption that the competition for education and work is based on individual merit is undermined by the retreat from fair levels of progressive income tax and the increasing privatization and expense of education. The polarization of income is seen as justifiable even by the Modernisers who believe that it reflects the value of individual skills, knowledge and contribution in the global labour market. As to the economy, which in the United States and Britain is distinguished by low skills for many and high insecurity for all, it is either celebrated by the New Right as it has greatly enriched shareholders and corporate executives, or its reform is seen by the Modernizers as too big a job to be taken on by the state. And with the financial crisis in East Asia at the end of the 1990s, the triumphalism of Wall Street (at least until the next meltdown on western markets) has made it more difficult for an alternative centre-left agenda to get a hearing.

While there are important ideological differences between the New Right and the Modernizers, the centre ground of party politics has decisively shifted towards neo-liberalism. Almost every government policy is now made with reference to the 'realities' of the global economy. Education policy is geared to enhancing competitiveness; welfare budgets have to be reduced because money that should be used for investment in the economy is being siphoned to support the unproductive; the taxes of the rich and corporations have to be low because high taxes reduce the incentives to the rich to produce jobs for the masses and act as a disincentive to corporate investors. At the same time, the exercise of state power in the pursuit of economic development is seen as anathema because the development of global competition, it is argued, has taken us a step closer to the holy grail of economic orthodoxy – perfect competition. So current global competition is linked to the virtues of the market and the vices of state intervention. These shibboleths limit the power of the nation state and increase the power of those great barons of the late twentieth century, the multinational corporations. But the current state of affairs is not inevitable. There is no inherent logic to global capitalism which is neutralising the nation state and polarising populations. There remains much that the nation state can do to link prosperity and progress while enhancing economic competitiveness, although in the medium term new ways will need to be found to limit the power of global financial markets.[6]

3

If we are to break the shackles of market individualism, we will need to re-think the relationship of the individual to society within the context of the changes we can anticipate over the next twenty years or so. The basic insight into why market individualism is no longer functional to the modern age has been captured by Alan Ryan when he noted that, 'the rugged individualism that celebrates the qualities that help man across the desert with a message hidden in his boots, are not those of the age of the fax machine'.[7] In an information-rich, knowledge-based society it is brains not brawn which will prove decisive in improving productivity and individual well being. Hence the alternative to market individualism is *collective intelligence*.[8]

Collective Intelligence involves a transformation in the way we think about human capability. It suggests that all are capable rather than a few; that intelligence is multiple rather than a matter of solving puzzles with only one right answer; and that our human qualities for imagination and emotional engagement are as important as our ability to become technical experts. It suggests that our ability to imagine alternative futures and to solve open-ended problems, and our interpersonal skills, should all be included in our definition of intelligence in the future. But collective intelligence involves more than an attempt to change the way people think about intelligence. It also involves more than getting us to recognize that intelligence is a social triumph, which reveals our debt to earlier generations, other cultures, teachers, professors, parents and the TV set. Collective intelligence involves a major change in the way we think about the relationship between the individual and society, and consequently the way we organize our schools, companies, neighbourhoods, and government. This is because the *pooling of intelligence*, through the creation of social structures which enhance the capacity for intelligent action, offers the best prospect of prosperity, democracy and social harmony in the context of post-industrial development. Therefore, if the twentieth century has been dominated by the spirit of competition, the twenty-first century must begin in an attempt to create a spirit of co-operation.

Three observations underlie the importance of collective intelligence for the twenty-first century. First, the wealth of nations will not depend on natural resources, the allocation of capital to productive uses, or labour intensive activity, but on improvements in productivity and innovation through the application of applied knowledge. The inception of what Manuel Castells calls the 'informational' economy and the demands of global competition, have meant that new forms of work organization need to be developed for economies to be both innovative and flexible. Under the old 'factory' model of the Golden era, it has been estimated that workers on the shop floor employed more skill driving to work than in doing their jobs, but if a high skills economy is to be created it will be both brains and the freedom to exercise them that will be required. Equally, 'value added' organizations also depend on the emotional intelligence of their employees, consultants and subcontractors. It depends on them sharing the goal of making a quality product or delivering good service, even if they do not share a commitment to every detail of the organization's mission statement. Quality work performance also depends on being able to work in project teams, often of an interdisciplinary nature, which need people to have good interpersonal skills, to be team players and to be willing to take initiative.

The second observation is that life outside paid employment requires new forms of intelligence and understanding if people are to live fulfilling lives. For example, personal relationships with family, friends and work colleagues and our public relationships with doctors, teachers and social workers tend to be *negotiated* rather than conducted according to prescribed roles where we already know the script. Other changes, including the breakdown of established patterns of family life, work, and leisure; demographic changes in childbirth, marriage, divorce, employment and mortality rates; changes in the relationships between ethnic groups as old colonial mentalities are being consigned to the dustbin of history; growing scepticism about scientific knowledge and the ability of 'experts' to solve social, economic and ecological problems; and greater freedom about how we construct our personal identities, have all placed greater demands on us to be more 'reflexive' about our lives as little can be taken for granted.[9] Much of what was part of our everyday routines now requires a greater level of conscious decision-making. Our conversations with others have therefore become more important, both as a way of making life more congenial and as a tool for mutual understanding. There is an urgent need to develop the 'skills and arts of "conversation" between persons and their worlds',[10] based on a spirit of co-operation because the future of democracy demands that we confront and find solutions to common problems in a rapidly changing global world, where it is difficult to maintain a sense of control over one's life let alone the future of society or the planet.

The third observation is that the distinction between paid work which is assumed to be productive and unpaid work which is not is an anachronism. In recent decades this distinction remained plausible so long as only a few needed to exercise 'intelligence' and that most formal learning could be completed before the age of eighteen. However, now that it is the intelligence of all that is required if people are to live fulfilling and productive lives, the creation of intelligence as well as its exploitation at work plays a major role in wealth creation. Under these changed circumstances the distinction between what is remunerated in the market and what is not is blurred because the more economic performance depends on the quality of human endeavour the more learning, in informal as well as formal settings, contributes to the bottom line. The development of collective intelligence will therefore become the ultimate source of economic security in a global economy, but the pooling of intelligence is impossible to achieve in societies characterized by market individualism, by low trust and by social polarization. These are not the conditions which foster learning. Unless people have a stake in society and feel economically secure and believe they have a future, the capacity for exercising collective intelligence is compromised.

4

In a society based on collective intelligence we can expect a fundamental change in the nature of the state's role. The state must become de facto 'developmental' in a global economy; this involves more than the current Anglo-American practice of offering 'sweeteners' to transnationals in the hope that if the sum is large enough they will locate, say, in America or Britain rather than in France or Brazil. Although it goes against the grain of economic policy in both countries, the state must have a role in promoting 'the competitiveness of the nation seen as one actor in a cut-throat world economy'.[11] The issue is not whether nations compete in the global economy but on what terms. Nations that leave this question to the 'market' will fail to create high-skill, high-wage jobs for more than a small minority of workers despite the political promise of a high-skill, knowledge-driven economy. High-skill economies are created by states that foster their development. We will also argue that a commitment to narrowing inequalities is a condition for societal wealth creation, because a society characterized by extremes of wealth and poverty inhibits the potential for individual and collective growth. A key role of the state must become one of strategic skill formation, working in partnership with key stakeholders to shape (rather than attempting to govern) markets in the development of human capability, trust and economic opportunity. This will require new forms of corporate governance; more emphasis on medium and long-term investment;

experimentation with various forms of corporate and business stake-holding; and a re-negotiated role for the trade unions to enhance productivity and innovation.

Traditional distinctions between economic, social and political spheres also collapse in a society based on collective intelligence. The alleviation of poverty will require that at times of unemployment or periods of care-giving to children or the elderly, people have public support for the material and social conditions conducive to learning. It is through these periods of learning, currently considered unproductive, that people will become more productive. This is one way the state can create a more inclusive society rather than attaching stigma and blame on those who are not in waged work but who may well be making a contribution to the development of collective intelligence through child care or voluntary work. But to overcome these problems new rules will need to be devised by which status and reward are determined. Similarly, the success or failure of national governments will also be judged on the extent to which they facilitate the conditions for the development of collective intelligence through participatory democracy. It is by enabling participation in the key decisions which affect individual's lives that they can exercise the kind of intelligence needed to solve public problems in the twenty-first century. As far as possible this form of participatory democracy should be based on the principles of subsidiarity which Charles Handy translates to mean that 'stealing people's responsibilities is wrong'.[12]

Such a society would certainly be radical but would it be feasible? We are not advocating a return to old-style collectivism, nor the abolition of the capitalist economy, but a quite different way of addressing the problem of how to achieve social progress. Many of the ideas for the implementation of such a society are already in the public arena as are many of the progressive trends on which such a society could be built. The technology and ways of organizing production to enable the majority to have stimulating jobs exist, but their full potential needs to be released. More than ever before, individuals have the possibility for greater choice about the kind of person they want to be and the life projects they wish to pursue. There is a new openness and tolerance to the way people live their lives, although this must inevitably carry obligations as well as freedoms. To date, millions of Americans and Europeans are failing to benefit from the post-industrial possibilities for a better life than now exist. This is the result of a cultural, political and economic system that remains locked into a 'factory' era and that serves sectional rather than common interests,

A society capable of taking advantage of these new possibilities, however, cannot be built purely on the power of ideas, although an appeal to ethic principles is, as R. H. Tawney reminds us, necessary for any significant reconstruction of society because 'social institutions are the visible expression of the scale of moral values which rules the minds of individuals, and it is impossible to alter institutions without altering that valuation'.[13] However, the abstract form of concepts such as freedom, democracy and justice make it unlikely that people will dissent. It is only when grounded in concrete terms, such as when it has implications for taxation or welfare provision, that people become politically engaged. As Karl Mannheim has noted, no reasonable person would disagree that freedom is better than regimentation, self-determination better than dictatorship, and spontaneous culture better than censorship of self-expression, 'but it seems . . . that this is too cheap a victory'.[14] What this book shows is that far from the idea of the global labour market removing the last hope of building a new alliance between social groups, it can create the conditions, along with the increase in social reflexivity, for a new political alliance across class, gender, or racial interests, which has the potential to 'begin to astonish even the gods'.[15]

Part I Economic Nationalism

2
The Secular Trinity

> Peace no less than war, must offer a spirit of comradeship, a
> spirit of achievement, a spirit of unselfishness.
>
> Franklin Roosevelt

1

In August 1941 two old men sat on deck chairs on board a ship off the
coast of Newfoundland. One was wearing a homburg and puffing a
cigar, the other had a blanket over his knees and, as old men often do,
they were putting the world to rights. They were talking of building a
new world order of which the principles of national self determination,
economic advancement and social progress were the cornerstones. This
dream could have been shared by old friends in the local bar but these
two men were different: they were the President of the United States and
the Prime Minister of Great Britain and they were on the battleship
Prince of Wales. Nor were they being quite so idealistic as first appeared
– they were bargaining over the principles on which the future of
Western capitalism would be based after the war with Germany and
Japan was won.

As it turned out the future of Western capitalism closely followed the
principles the two men discussed at that meeting in the aptly named
Placentia Bay in Newfoundland. The next thirty years heralded the most
rapid and comprehensive period of economic progress in the history of
the West. Output in the advanced capitalist countries was 180 per cent
higher in 1973 than it had been twenty-three years earlier. For workers
this boom meant a rise in real wages of some 3.5 per cent a year. If the
population grew at one per cent a year, each generation could expect
to be twice as well off as its parents and four times as well off as its

grandparents.[1] Yet the success of this post-war period could hardly be attributed to these two men and their dreams, however powerful they were. Human beings make their own history but not always as they intend and not in circumstances of their own choosing.[2]

The phenomenal economic success in the thirty years after the end of the Second World War was partly a product of political design: the reconstruction of Europe with American aid and the recreation of an international trading system were politically inspired. But it was also partly a matter of various social forces, ideas and events coming together at the right time to underpin the economic success that Roosevelt and Churchill had talked of in Placentia Bay. If we are to understand better the problems and possibilities of our own times we need to see how these various ideas, forces and events combined so spectacularly. As the Czech novelist Milan Kundera has reminded us, 'The struggle of man against tyranny is the struggle of memory against forgetting'. What is it, then, that we should remember about a past which is so recent and yet already seems so far away?

2

The post-war success of western nations lay in the development of the doctrine of *economic nationalism* in which social progress for workers and their families was advanced through the pursuit of economic growth. It combined, uniquely, three principles which would underwrite life in the third quarter of the twentieth century: *prosperity, security* and *opportunity*. These principles were threaded through the fabric of everyday life in a tightly woven design which linked government policy, business organizations, families and education. Together, these three principles were applied to the resolution of the two fundamental tensions endemic to capitalism: its tendency to distribute rewards unfairly and its chronic instability, thereby delivering simultaneously social justice and economic efficiency, at least in the terms set by the doctrine of economic nationalism.

Economic nationalism arose out of the experience of the great depression of the thirties and the ashes of the Second World War. More than any other war, it had been won in the name of freedom and ordinary people wanted freedom to mean something tangible: the eradication of unemployment with all that it meant in terms of poverty and hopelessness. After all, many of those who had contributed to the war effort knew what it was like to live through the depression. Many also believed that unemployment in Germany had been a major cause of the rise of

Hitler. The popular demand was for an economy which allowed for the equality of sacrifice experienced in war to be matched by a more equal sharing of the fruits of peace.

For economic nationalism to become a reality, ways had to be found to tame the anti-social features inherent in capitalist economies, especially the unequal distribution of wealth. As Karl Polanyi has observed 'To allow the market mechanism to be sole director of the fate of human beings and their natural environment ... would result in the demolition of society'.[3] Equally, through the inheritance of social and cultural capital the successful in a capitalist system can reproduce their privilege from generation to generation unless some method is devised by which the opportunities for success and status are, at least in principle, open to all. The problem created by this tension is not merely about injustice but also economic efficiency. Modern capitalist societies require new ideas and people of ability to create and apply them. An elite based on inheritance will not have a monopoly on ability and an elite that remains in power too long will stagnate in a culture of contentment. The lifeblood of circulating elites bringing new ideas, energy and perspectives is as necessary to capitalism's survival as the balance between risk and security.[4]

As an economic system, capitalism is dependent upon the search for new markets and products. Innovation and risk are the watchwords of survival as tastes change and markets emerge or wither. For individuals the problem of security turns on the fact that capitalism creates few independently wealthy individuals. For the majority, survival is dependent upon wage earning. For them, the problem is that jobs are always at risk because neither companies nor individual skills may survive the collapse of markets or the superior performance of competitors. Periodically, the everyday uncertainties of capitalism are exacerbated by periods of massive slump or fundamental shifts in its organization. Sometimes the two coincide. These earth shattering events threaten the fate of families and communities. As Marx once put it 'everything that is solid melts into air'.[5] Some way has to be found, therefore, of linking the fate of individuals to society in such a way as to satisfy the demands for justice and economic efficiency. The pursuit of economic nationalism in the post-war period was based on the assumption that prosperity, security and opportunity could only be delivered with significant state intervention in the operation of the marketplace. Moreover, it was not only believed that the nation state had the power to deliver economic nationalism but that it had a responsibility to do so.

3

The idea that permanent prosperity could be managed by governments to foster national well-being was novel. It was founded on the idea that the individual would come to recognize that his or her self-interest was inextricably connected to the national interest through the pursuit of economic growth. Within an expanding economy, although the economic pie would continue to the distributed unequally, all would see an increase in their standard of living.

The first attempt to measure national income, as an indicator of national well being, was made by Sir William Petty in his book *Political Arithmetic* in 1676. But is was John Maynard Keynes' *General Theory of Employment, Interest and Money*, published in 1936, which welded together the links between national income as a measure of economic growth and full employment.[6] The key to Keynes' theory lies in his break with traditional, neo-classical, economic thinking which had assumed that capitalist economies were self-correcting, so that economies which had fallen into slump would 'automatically' bounce back to a period of boom and full employment. Keynes rejected this idea arguing that governments could intervene effectively in market economies to solve the problem of slumps, or what one of his contemporaries called the 'gales of creative destruction',[7] so that when demand for goods slackened and workers were threatened with unemployment governments could act to keep the wheels of industry turning. Keynes' theories chimed well with the spirit of the age. Again, the experience of the war years proved vital in the acceptance of Keynes' ideas. War economies were largely government planned and orchestrated, this was even true of the home of the free market, the United States. There, the government bought nearly half of total production giving it enormous power over producers and taxes were also high. In 1944, corporate tax stood at 60 per cent.[8] In post-war Europe the lesson that governments could intervene effectively in the market was extended to national ownership of the economic infrastructure: energy, railways and telecommunications were all bought up by the state.

Keynes argued that a consistent pattern of economic growth could be achieved by manipulating the amount of money people had in their pockets by raising and lowering taxes and hence, what is called the aggregate or national demand for goods and services. At the height of the post-war period President Kennedy explained Keynsian theory by talking about the way tax cuts would increase the money in people's pockets so raising demand and thereby 'creating a rising economic tide which would raise all the boats'. For Kennedy, the tide was the national income and the boats wages. In a recession, cutting taxes gave the millionaire the incentive to buy a new Lincoln Continental and in doing so it raised company profitability giving unions the chance to negotiate a bigger slice of the cake for their workers. In turn, the workers would spend their money on cars of their own and all the consumer goods 'necessary' for maintaining the status and creature comforts of modern living. This raised the profits of other companies and thereby maintained demand and full employment. The government debt created by cutting taxes during the recession would be paid back by raising taxes when the economy recovered.

The record of Western nations in maintaining full employment in the post-war period vindicated the faith in the governments' ability to create economic growth on the basis of full employment and, of course, it vindicated Keynes' theory.[9] Between 1950 and 1973 the average level of growth of the advanced economies was 4.9 per cent, the number of jobs created increased by 29 per cent[10] and the average level of unemployment for America stood at 4.8 per cent and 2.7 per cent for Britain.[11] Unemployment levels were at similarly low levels in most advanced capitalist societies. The achievement of such low levels of unemployment should not be underestimated. Between the First and Second World Wars the average rate of unemployment was 16.5 per cent in the United States and 9.6 per cent in Britain. During the depression unemployment rose to a high of 22.3 per cent and 15.3 per cent respectively.[12] What made the post-war Golden era so remarkable was that it was built on the mass creation of low-skilled, high-waged jobs. In 1950, the average length of schooling for an individual was 8.2 years.[13] At the same time, the weekly wages of manual workers in Britain increased in real terms at a rate similar to that of white-collar and professional workers.[14] This increase was mirrored throughout the western world. In essence, workers in this period could look forward to security in employment and rising wage rates irrespective of their skills.

The basis for a low-skilled, high-waged economy lay in the development of the giant national corporations of the fifties and sixties and the mass markets they created for consumer goods. These corporations became household names: Chrysler and Standard Oil in the United States; Morris and ICI in Britain; Volkswagen and Krupps in Germany; Shell and Philips in Holland, to name but a few. So dominant were they in the workings of their national economies that it was said in the United States that 'what's good for Chrysler is good for America'. The key which unlocked profits for these corporate giants lay in economics of scale. Profit was made on the basis of long runs of products. Innovations in product or production techniques were low because once a production line had been established it was expensive to change. We remember the design of sixties cars like the Mustang or the Mini because they remained largely unchanged for twenty years. In comparison, the Honda Civic fundamentally changed its design three times between 1984 and 1993. Standardization of products and routine in production were the watchwords for the corporate success of the post-war era.

Standardization was achieved, as Emma Rothschild has noted, by reducing jobs which required some human knack or adaptability to their smallest, fastest, least wasteful components, 'dividing and subdividing operations, keeping the work in motion – these [were] the keynotes of production'.[15] For men on the shop floor the work was mind-numbingly boring. Workers were not trusted to think or to make judgements; it was a low trust system of production in which everything was done to eliminate worker initiative and error. The ethos of low trust extended beyond the production line itself. Workers had to ask permission to go to the toilet and in some companies had to hire their knives and forks in the company canteen at lunch time as an insurance against theft. The idea that they would be asked their opinion as to how production should be organized was unimaginable. As one US car worker put it, 'a man checks his brains and his freedom at the door when he goes to work at Ford's'.[16]

The low trust organization of work extended to the corporate bureaucracies which grew exponentially as mass markets and production were extended. The white-collar jobs of the corporation were designed to deliver predictable outcomes. Job roles were carefully delineated within a hierarchy which defined the nature and extent of judgement and discretion each role could exercise. As Robert Reich has noted, 'the war veterans who manned the core American corporations of the 1950s accommodated ... naturally to the military like hierarchies inside them ... As in the military, great emphasis was placed on the maintenance of control – upon a superior's ability to inspire loyalty, discipline and unquestioning obedience'.[17] It was only at the top of the corporate hierarchy, the upper ranks of a corporation's divisions and at head office that the ability to exercise a full range of judgements based on experience and expertise was given rein.

The discipline of work was in direct conflict with the freedom in consumption that the corporate workers of the fifties and sixties enjoyed. As the corporations grew so did the markets for their products. In 1930, one in every five and a half Americans owned a car; by 1960 this proportion had dropped to almost one in every two. Typically, it was housed in a suburban garage. As the corporate bureaucracies expanded so did the suburbs. In America and Britain a move from the inner cities to the suburbs signalled the entry into society of the corporate middle classes and once the economic engine of the post-war period was running hot the exodus to the suburbs became a rush. Between 1950 and 1980 cities like St Louis, Buffalo and Detroit lost between 21 and 27 per cent of the populations. London lost 20 per cent of its inner city population in just ten years between 1961 and 1971, and Liverpool almost 25 per cent of its population between 1946 and 1971.[18] This was not a migration of the kind triggered by the gold rushes of the late nineteenth century. Taking a risk and getting rich quick was the opposite of the suburban ethos. Moving to the suburbs meant the certainty of steady progress: a house, a car, a decent neighbourhood from which to launch the next generation into a better future than that of their parents.

The difference that the consumption boom of the fifties and sixties made to the quality of life is underscored by contrasting the suburban house with all 'mod cons' to the housing of the mid-forties. In America in the mid-1940s, a third of houses had no running water, two-fifths had no flush toilets, three- fifths had no central heating, about half had no refrigerator and roughly one-seventh didn't have a radio. Television and air conditioning were largely unknown.[19] Here, then, was one of the central paradoxes of the age: the quality of private life measured in terms of consumption improved out of all recognition for the majority. But the cost was workers performing best 'when the mind is least consulted' and they were often treated like miscreant children.[20]

There were compensations. A full employment, low-skilled, high-waged economy provided the basis for security and it went a considerable way to solving the problems of the distribution of wealth and social justice under capitalism – at least in the terms set by the doctrine of economic nationalism. The combination of rapid growth and an economy structured for low skills and high wages meant that the benefits of growth in terms of wages were distributed throughout society, albeit unequally. Consequently, there was a clear sense in which even unskilled workers could feel that they were gaining from capitalism and therefore had a stake in it. This led the Canadian economist J.K. Galbraith to observe that 'Increased real incomes provides us with an admirable detour around the rancour anciently associated with efforts to redistribute real wealth'.[21]

4

The security of stable family life was reinforced by the creation of the welfare state and the related idea of the family wage. Both can be seen as a response to the risks and inequalities generated by capitalism. Much is said to justify the high incomes made by entrepreneurs in terms of the risks they take in investing their wealth and energy in new businesses. Little, however, was said about the risks taken by ordinary working people in participating in a capitalist economy. The idea of the family wage was developed as a means of addressing this issue by entering the true costs to workers of participating in a market economy into wage negotiations. In effect a fair day's wage for a fair day's work is substantially higher than that received in the weekly pay packet since it does not take into account health, pensions, and unemployment insurance. In the post-war period the notion of the family wage came into its own. As with many of the ideas which comprise economic nationalism, elements of the idea of the family wage had a long history. For example, in the 1912 presidential campaign Teddy Roosevelt had argued for a 'New Nationalism' in which workmen's compensation was linked to the 'protection of home life against the hazards of sickness, irregular employment and old age through the adoption of a system of social insurance.'[22] In linking social insurance to the obligations of the nation state Roosevelt was following the lead of European socialists.[23] The link, then, between what was considered a national obligation and the family wage was already well established; what gave it a new hue was the idea that governments had an active role to play in managing the economy. In the United States, this had a largely indirect impact on the provision of the family wage. There the fact of full employment, underwritten by the commitment of the state to its maintenance, strengthened the hands of unions which enabled them to include the benefits of the family wage into their negotiations. In Europe, where the state had a more active role in industrial relations, the components of the family wage were provided by the state and used as a bargaining chip in negotiations with workers.

The claims for a family wage were based on an assumed male breadwinner in a typical family of two adults and 2.4 children. In the late 1940s only one in five married women were in paid employment in the United States, in Britain the figure was slightly higher.[24] Accordingly, trade unions on both sides of the Atlantic pressed their case for an adequate family wage and by and large got it. But the victory was of course double-edged as it was assumed that there is only one breadwinner in the family, typically the husband: an argument to be challenged by the Feminist movement in the early seventies, just as it had been by women a century before.[25] But in the post-war period the case for the male breadwinner receiving an income sufficient to support a family was made successfully by unions in part because it was supported by 'enlightened bosses' as it had been by some of the corporate barons of the past. Henry Ford and John D. Rockerfeller were in favour of it because it offered the promise of worker stability and productivity.[26] Built on a consensus between employers and unions, the family wage proved to be the linchpin between the labour market and the foundation of the social structure: the male headed nuclear family. The family was, by contemporary trends, a stable institution which encompassed the vast majority of people. In the United States in the immediate post-war period 94 per cent of the population lived in families. Of those 80 per cent had a husband and wife who were under 65.[27] The stability of the nuclear family in the immediate post-war period is underscored by the number of petitions filed for divorce. Just prior to the war, 1.9 out of every hundred marriages in Britain were terminated. By 1950 the figure had increased to 7.9 and there it remained constant until 1968, when it doubled.[28]

Significant as the family wage was, the role of the welfare state was conceived more widely than simply providing workers with insurance against the vagaries of capitalist work. Capitalism excludes those outside the labour market from participating more widely in society. The notion of citizenship was, therefore, developed in the post-war era to ensure that the entitlements of being a citizen were extended to all members of society. In effect, citizenship was a way of extending some of the rewards of the labour market to all members of a nation regardless of their circumstances. The extent to which this principle was realized differed from one western society to another. It was perhaps most perfectly realised in Sweden where people were automatically entitled to participate in society regardless of circumstance, and least perfectly in the United States where welfare entitlements were less widespread or generous.

Despite these differences in emphasis, the welfare state expanded significantly in all the advanced economies in the post-war period. Between 1952 and 1973 welfare expenditure in the advanced economies grew from 15 to 24 per cent of GDP.[29] This expenditure did not obviate poverty but it reduced its impact. In the United States, the share of the bottom 20 per cent of income earners rose between 1959 and 1969 from 4.9 to 5.6 per cent of total income and this was enough to reduce the numbers in poverty from 22.4 per cent to 12.1 per cent.[30] This brought the incidence of poverty to about the same level as that of France but still well above the 7.5 per cent recorded in Britain and 3 per cent in Germany.[31]

The significance of this reduction, if not elimination of poverty, through the welfare state added a further dimension to risk avoidance for workers in a capitalist society. Previously, it had been assumed that capitalism could only work if workers were threatened with insecurity: unemployment was like a noose, poverty the sprung trapdoor. Without these threats and against the background of work devoid of intellectual content or meaning, it was assumed the strength of workers to push for higher wages was unstoppable. Hence the initial opposition of business leaders both to Keynesian economics and to state attempts to eliminate poverty. As a contemporary of Keynes' put it, 'lasting full employment is not to their [business leaders'] liking'. The workers would 'get out of hand' and the 'captains of industry would be anxious to teach them a lesson'.[32] In the post-war period the captains of industry did not object, at least not vociferously, because full employment and marginal poverty kept up domestic demand which in walled economies dominated by standardised mass production was needed to maintain high levels of profitability.

5

If economic nationalism was founded on a commitment to full employment, increasing living standards and the development of the welfare state, it was kept in motion through what the American sociologist Talcott Parsons called the 'axis of achievement'. No longer should social background, gender, race or ethnicity be permitted to intervene in the competition for a livelihood. All must be given an equal chance to be unequal. The doctrine, whilst recognising inequality to be both an inevitable and necessary feature of western capitalist societies, expressed the view that such inequalities could only be legitimated if they reflected the outcome of a meritocratic competition where IQ Effort Merit.[33] Such a competition would seem to be all the more important in the post-war period as changes in the occupational structure significantly increased the demand for educated white-collar workers. In the United States, between 1949 and 1970 white-collar work increased by 12 per cent, while blue-collar work decreased by 6 per cent and agricultural labour by 7 per cent. Effectively white-collar work comprised 50 per cent of occupations by 1970 of which approximately a half offered the prospect of a career.[34] But whilst there had been an increasing demand for technical, managerial and professional workers there was assumed to be a limited pool of talent with the intelligence required to maintain the pace of economic growth. This pool of talent needed to be selected and promoted through the education system because, as Halsey and Floud noted at the time, 'education is a crucial type of investment for the exploitation of modern technology. This fact underlies recent educational development in all the major industrial societies . . . education attains unprecedented economic importance as a source of technological innovation'.[35]

For the first time education took a central position in the functioning of the advanced capitalist economies because it was seen as a key instrument in the promotion of economic growth *and* as a means of promoting social justice through the notion of equality of opportunity. These roles assigned to the education system were effectively two sides of the same coin. Equality of opportunity was defined in terms of the promotion of the most able through the education system, irrespective of their social background, and it was precisely the most able that needed to be recruited to the top industrial positions.

Consequently, the education systems of the western world expanded to perform their new role of providing the human capital, as it came to be called in the mid-fifties, for the expanded middle-class occupations in industry. In 1930 approximately 7 per cent of American students completed four years of college, by 1960 it had risen to 18 per cent.[36] But despite the expansion in middle class jobs and an increasingly well-educated workforce, the idea that everyone would eventually get a middle-class job allocated on individual merit remained illusive. Working-class jobs did not disappear and the privileged did not witness a reduction in their capacity to pass on social advantage to their children. Universities were still dominated by those from professional and managerial backgrounds and even when intelligence was taken into account social background remained a significant factor in determining individual life chances. In effect, the expanding occupational structure had created more room on the career ladder for those originally from working-class backgrounds, but the forces which reproduced privilege remained. Nevertheless, it could be argued that the expansion of the middle classes and the creation of an institutional route through education into white-collar work and beyond into business and government elites satisfied the necessity in modern capitalist societies for social justice and circulating elites. In Britain, often depicted as the home of class society, over 25 per cent of those in senior business, government or professional occupations in 1972 were recruited from the working class, while only 15 per cent of this group had fathers in elite occupations.[37]

6

Politicians at the time certainly saw economic nationalism as a success. Harold MacMillan, the British Prime Minister, went to the polls in 1959 telling the electorate they had 'never had it so good'. The electorate agreed by returning him to office on the basis of a record that saw the benefits of economic growth distributed throughout the population coupled with workplace security. Equally, if merit did not supersede privilege, enough working class men 'made it' to ensure new blood entered government and business to bring fresh energy and ideas to the capitalist enterprise.

These were the accomplishments of economic nationalism. But from a standpoint outside its doctrines its record can be seen differently. At the heart of economic nationalism lay a contract between men, the state and private enterprise. As women from the late sixties made clear, they had largely been rendered invisible by its workings, shut within the confines of the suburban household. The organization of life outside the home not only reinforced the position of women as invisible, it also acted to exclude or assimilate ethnic minority groups into the dominant white European or American culture. Even for many working-class and middle-class men its success was equivocal; certainly there was prosperity and the opportunity for upward mobility but the workplace allowed little judgement to be exercised and even less trust in individual integrity and competence. Finally, by the late sixties even that most fundamental belief of the era, the imperative for economic growth, was being challenged.

The development of economic nationalism contained the seeds of its demise in the gale of creative destruction which characterized western capitalism for much of the twentieth century. The question of how economic nationalism was able to deliver economic prosperity, security and a degree of opportunity for twenty-five years only then to founder on its own contradictions is vital to an understanding of the possibilities for social progress. The remaining chapters in Part One are dedicated to this purpose.

3
The Engines of Growth

Stabilization of material forces is not sufficient; human relations must be stabilized; stabilization of production is not sufficient; merchandizing must be stabilized. Stabilization of production and merchandizing is not sufficient; general administration must be stabilized Stabilization of an individual enterprise is not sufficient; all enterprises in the industry must be stabilized. Stabilization of one industry is not sufficient; all industries of a nation must be stabilized. Stabilization of national industry alone is not sufficient; international economics must be stabilized. Achievement of any of these ends is a step toward a more balanced and harmonious industrial and social life; each is but a means to another greater end.

Harlow Pearson – Director of the Taylor Society

1

In 1915, enthusiastic crowds at the San Francisco 'Palace of Transportation' rioted in their eagerness to see a working replica of Ford's new Highland Park assembly line.[1] In their excitement at Ford's technological novelty the citizens of San Francisco could hardly have imagined that over the next sixty years Ford's production line was to change the landscape of western civilization. Factories the size of small towns ringed the edges of cities while in their centres the skyscraper bureaucracies which serviced the factories mushroomed.

The prime movers which brought about this remarkable change in economic organisation were the giant national corporations. In 1950 the top 100 American manufacturing corporations owned 39.7 per cent of corporate wealth. By 1971 it had climbed to 48 9 per cent. There was a similar rise in Britain where the top 100 hundred manufacturers raised their share of corporate wealth from 22 per cent to 35 per cent.[2] These corporations accumulated wealth on the scale of small countries and large states. In 1968 General Motors had an income of $22.8 billion, more than three times the revenue of the state of New York, one eighth of the total receipts of the federal government and substantially more than the gross domestic income of a country the size of New Zealand.[3]

Not only did these corporations dominate the industrial landscape in terms of wealth and output but they held the key to full employment. The five largest manufacturing corporations in America employed some two million workers by the close of the 1960s. In Britain, as the corporate giants grew, so did the numbers they employed. Before the war the largest manufacturing employers, ICI and Unilever, each employed 50,000 workers; by the end of the seventies this had risen to 143,000 and 80,000 respectively. Other firms showed an even more impressive rise in jobs created. In the same period GEC's workforce rose from 24,000 to 188,000.[4] These juggernauts lay at the heart of western prosperity for their influence extended far beyond their own wealth. Given their size, they acted like opulent magnates creating work and wealth for others as they generated a rapidly rising demand for raw materials in the production, sales and servicing of their goods. It is little wonder, then, that these corporations came to symbolize national progress through prosperity.

The maturing of the national corporation into the juggernauts of the post-war era was determined by three related features in the history of manufacturing in the twentieth century: the creation and adoption of the Fordist production line, which enabled the mass production of consumer goods; the linking of bureaucracy to the Fordist production line to provide the means to innovate, monitor and control production and sales; and the creation of the multidivisional corporate structure to open new markets and handle the massive expansion in production and sales that followed. This 'factory' model dominated thinking about economic efficiency until the last quarter of the twentieth century.

2

Ford moved to Highland Park to open a new era in the development of capitalism. In the month in which Ford began production of his Model T at Highland Park in January, 1910, *Harpers Weekly* took the view that, 'There is no doubt...that the man who can successfully solve this knotty problem and produce a car that will be entirely sufficient mechanically, and whose price will be within reach of the millions who cannot yet afford automobiles, will not only grow rich but be considered a public benefactor as well'.[5] In Ford, *Harpers* had found their man.

By 1913 Ford was producing 200,000 Model Ts a year. A well-known industrial journalist of the time painted a picture of the sheer magnitude of what was involved in this operation, 'a million lamps; eight hundred thousand wheels and tires, ninety thousand tons of steel; four hundred thousand cowhides; 6 million pounds of hair for seats; and about 2 million square feet of glass went into the year's production. A complete Model T emerged from the factory every forty seconds of the working day. Five trains of forty cars each left the factory daily loaded with finished automobiles. In a span of five years the company had gone from producing about six thousand Model Ts to two hundred thousand and had lowered the costs'.[6] By 1924 the cost of a Ford was $290 or, by the time of the onset of the collapse of the auto-industry in America in the 1970s, the equivalent of $700. The sheer organization of creativity, raw materials and labour which went into the creation of a Model T seems staggering. But this was only the Ford Motor Company in its infancy. In 1917, Ford had company assets of $166 million. By 1948, prior to the boom of the fifties and sixties Ford assets stood at $1,149 million.[7] If the image created by this description of Highland Park is then multiplied eight times to convey the enormity of the Ford enterprise at the edge of the post-war period, and then multiplied many times again to include the great national corporations throughout the economy, the power of these engines of prosperity can begin to be imagined.

3

Ford's dictum that the essence of his production line lay in 'power, accuracy, economy, continuity and speed' made it seem as if he was simply the inventor of a new technology.[8] But these efficiencies of mass production could not be divorced from questions of social power. In order to become the dominant type of production in the twentieth century the Fordist production line had first to take the knowledge which had been the cornerstone of craft production out of the hands of skilled workers. The great theorist of Fordism, Frederick Winslow Taylor, had argued that the basis for productive efficiency lay in science. This meant putting the knowledge of craftsmen onto a systematic and formal basis or, as he put it 'gathering in on the part of those on the management's side all the great mass of traditional knowledge which in the past had been in the heads of workmen and in the physical knack and skill of the workman'.[9] What this meant in practice was that many craft skills were broken down into their simple component parts and so reduced to a series of simple repetitive operations of the order of putting a nut on a screw or, in the case of General Motors' *Vega*, two women jumping onto the assembly line placing a radiator grill behind the headlights and jumping off again – this being one of the more active roles available.

The breaking down of skills entailed a loss of power and autonomy for craftsmen. Not surprisingly the imperialism of the production line was bitterly resisted. Soldiering, industrial sabotage and radical union politics all emerged as part of the struggle against the new forms of industrial production. At Watertown, a US government arsenal, the striking workers had a rare and notable victory. Following an official enquiry Taylorist principles were found to have abused the welfare of workers and were banned on all government-funded work until 1949. But the extinction of prized craft skills was only one way in which Fordism changed the balance of power between workers and their employers. In the late nineteenth century various forms of inside contracting had developed. Such was the status of craftsmen that employers would leave them to hire helpers and determine the nature of their work and their rates of pay. Records from the steel workers of Columbus provide a clear example of a similar kind of practice where teams of workers would contract for each rolling job the Columbus Ironworks undertook. The workers then decided the pay rates for their teams and allocated duties accordingly.[10] Under Fordism, these kinds of worker initiatives and freedoms were lost: efficiency and top down control were inextricably linked.

The breaking of craft knowledge and the loss of worker autonomy made the Fordist production line possible. What made it work was another revolutionary idea: that the production line would determine the pace of work. The inspiration for Ford's continuously moving line came to him while watching butchers in Chicago use an overhead chain to move beef during the dressing process. Describing the principle of the continuously moving line in 1922 Ford wrote,

> Every piece of work in the shop moves; it may move on hooks on overhead chains going to assembly in the exact order in which the parts are required; it may travel on a moving platform, or it may go by gravity, but the point is that there is no lifting or trucking of anything other than the materials... No workman has anything to do with moving or lifting anything.[11]

The men on the line simply stood and waited for the work to come to them. At a stroke the moving line gave management two new weapons in their struggle to impose the techniques and disciplines of mass production on workers. In the past the speed of production had to be negotiated formally or informally with workers. In theory the moving line put an end to that and in doing so it gave management the literally priceless power to determine the pace of production. The key challenge for management now became one of combining materials and humans to produce quality goods at the maximum speed possible. It was this challenge that was met by a combination of power and reason through the techniques of surveillance and scientific management.

Once set in motion the production line demanded iron discipline, because mistakes and breakdowns cost dearly. The discipline imposed on workers was of a kind rarely seen outside a Victorian classroom. It is perhaps a symptom of the 'mind set' which the Fordist production line engendered that Ford himself had his workers spied upon and coerced even outside the factory gates.[12] Surveillance ensured the discipline demanded of high volume production. The speed and efficiency came from the science of 'time and motion'.

From the beginning, the constant monitoring of performance was built into the production line and was supplemented by the knowledge gained by the time and motion expert. In the hands of Frank Gilbreth, one of Taylor's prominent disciples, the obsession with control over the last detail of production was taken to its logical conclusion. His work embodied the credo of the Fordist age, that time costs money, or, as Ford himself put it, that workers, 'must have every second necessary but not a single unnecessary second'.[13] Gilbreth viewed human action as the basic building blocks of production and attempted to break them down into elementary units called *therbligs* – a transposition of his own name. He also added his own technology to the time and motion's experts basic equipment, the stopwatch: a *chronocyclegraph* was a photo of the workplace with the paths of workers' movements superimposed upon it; a *stroboscope* was a picture which showed the changing positions assumed by workers on the production line.

With the aid of this technology he was able to catalogue the various movements of the body as data to determine the time requirements for each job on the assembly line. These *therblig* charts were developed for use by engineers and managers in the construction of production lines. Each motion, as for example, that of grasping, was given a name, a symbol, a colour code, and the time it took to complete in ten-thousandths of a minute.[14] Armed with this information engineers and managers could aim to achieve the maximum 'harmony' between men and machines. At Highland Park, the moving line was subject to constant experiment in an effort to reduce production time: workers' every action was carefully studied to ensure efficient movement, the production line, for example, was raised or lowered in an attempt to provide the most comfortable height for workers to carry out their operations. Despite all this experimentation it didn't satisfy Gilbreth. When he visited Ford he was horrified by what he found. Most of the operations workers performed induced fatigue. The speed of the production line was at the cost of the destruction of the workers.[15] Gilbreth, like his mentor Taylor, genuinely believed in the harmony of men and machines. What Gilbreth saw at Ford's persuaded him that coercion had won out over science.

Whatever the dreams that motivated the likes of Taylor and Gilbreth, the principles of the Fordist production line were now in place, save one: standardization. The production line was expensive to establish. The fewer the parts and the more a single model could be produced the better the economies of scale to the manufacturer. Ford made a virtue of this 'necessity' by initially producing the Model T in one colour. He justified this standardization by reference to consumer taste, saying that if a hundred people were asked how they wanted a particular article to be made 95 per cent would not know. Production, he argued, should be aimed at them. The lesson then was clear,

> If, therefore, you discover what will give this 95 per cent of the people the best all round service and then arrange to manufacture at the very highest quality and sell at the very lowest price, you will be meeting a demand which may be called universal.[16]

By the time Ford had completed his hagiography in 1922 the Fordist production line and its accompanying theory, Scientific Management, had become the blueprint for production in all the industrialized nations.[17] During the fifties and early sixties it seemed as if the dream that drove Frederick Wilmslow Taylor's theory of Scientific Management had come to fruition. In contrast to Ford, who had a cynical view of human nature and social progress, Taylor believed that everyone would benefit from the 'factory' model because it would overcome the traditional class divisions of capitalism. It would do this because the profit generated by Fordist production techniques would be so large that there would be room for ample increases in workers wages and in profits.[18] In this, Taylor's view chimed well with economic nationalism which took exactly the same view and found in Fordism the productive techniques for achieving it. Scientific management was quickly adapted in Britain, France, Germany and even the Soviet Union, where Lenin described Gilbreth's writings as 'an excellent example of technical progress under capitalism towards socialism'.[19]

The principles of the Fordist production line survived until the 1980s as the predominant basis for production in America and Britain with only the elaborations of Alfred Sloan of General Motors who, in the thirties, devised the notion of in-built obsolescence. He extended the capabilities of the production line by making cars out of the same shape and size but with different equipment, engines and accessories, at different prices. Sloan realised that variations of the same model could be made to different specifications and at different prices. To be sure, the techniques for developing Fordist production advanced with computers doing much of the work of time and motion experts, but the key Fordist ideas remained until the final quarter of this century when, unlike the dinosaur, they began the slow road to newly industrializing countries, rather than to extinction.

4

If Fordism was the engine of growth in the post-war era, it needed another key development in the twentieth century to translate its productive capacity into jobs, markets and profits – bureaucracy. Production on the scale generated by Fordism required a massive administration to co-ordinate the process of bringing raw materials to market as finished goods. In the marriage of Fordist production with bureaucratic administration the national corporations of western capitalism were born. As the great national corporations grew in size so the urban landscape changed. Skyscrapers housing the offices of the corporations grew in grandeur leaving no doubt in the minds of the public, as they craned their necks upward, that here were the secular cathedrals of the modern age. The art-deco Chrysler tower, built in New York in 1930, signalled the self-conscious onset of the corporate era. By the high tide of wealth creation in the sixties, self-consciousness had been translated into explicit self aggrandizement. This excerpt from a brochure on the Chase Manhattan Bank building and plaza says it all:

Tall enough at 813 feet to throw the early morning sun back at itself...the Chase Manhattan Bank building represents the fulfilment of an architectural ideal and a high watermark in modern management. It was designed not just to function but to express – its soaring angularities bespeaking an era rather than a transient need...Chase Manhattan Plaza is really many things in one – a product of an age when reaching for the stars is no longer a figure of speech...a benchmark in architectural history a staggering complex of machinery – an art gallery,

and perhaps most significantly an elaborate expression of bureaucratic hierarchy.

The executive suite was invariably on one of the top floors of the corporate tower, placing the CEO and his executive managers close to the boardroom, if not the stars. Below the top management suites were the offices of the managers responsible for one of the key areas of business; below them the middle managers and so on. Each role was tightly specified, each link in the chain of command clearly articulated. Rarely has a form of social organization been so clearly mimicked in its architecture. The effect of this corporate structure was to create an army of white-collar workers between bosses and production workers. An army, was close to what it was in terms of the regimentation of office life, even the functions of white-collar workers, from the top down, were described in military language. Departments within corporations were run by *line* officers and *staff* officers who acted as professional advisors. Marketing divisions had *campaigns*. The watchwords of the corporation, as of the army, were those of obedience, discipline and loyalty. The emphasis on order and control was directly related to the Fordist production line. Just as breakdowns on the production line proved hugely expensive, so mistakes in the administration of the corporation were equally costly.

In the current climate bureaucracy has a bad name. It stands for sluggish insensitivity and much that is wrong and inefficient about the world. Bureaucracy, in the popular imagination is also typically linked to government. But in the period of economic nationalism it was the backbone of the giant corporations – and as we shall see in later chapters it was the foundation of security and career opportunities of a burgeoning middle class. The great historian of the modern corporation, Alfred Chandler, identifies the development of rail in the United States, in the 1850s, as the first instance of the application of large scale bureaucratic techniques to the world of private enterprise.[20] By the turn of the century it was seen as the key to both public and private organizational development. In the United States it was only after the adoption of bureaucracy in the private sector that its techniques were transferred to government. Here it was seen as a means of stamping out the corruption at the local level that had dogged local American politics in the nineteenth century and, largely as a result of the depression of the 1930s, of the co-ordination and regulation of capitalism.[21]

In most of Western Europe, however, it was the state that provided the model for industrial organization. The idea of entry to the civil service in Britain and France, on the basis of merit and examination performance, was well established, as were the values of what could be called the bureaucratic ethos: integrity, a sense of duty, a public spirit and loyalty. As private sector companies grew larger and their production became increasingly dependent on science and technology these values, bred within the state administration, had a clear application in the private sector. The ethos of merit was needed because production was increasingly dependent on scientific and administrative expertise. Loyalty to the corporation became important as these companies were too large to rely, as they had done in the past, on family ties and personal contacts. In essence, bureaucratic values replaced blood ties as the social glue that harnessed the energies of workers to company goals.[22]

Although the early development of bureaucratic governance is part of the story of the organization of the modern corporation, Taylor's theories of scientific management also had a powerful influence. Bureaucracy and Fordism shared many similarities: both were based on minimizing workers' discretion; both sought to achieve this by specifying in precise detail the worker's role, which inevitably involved breaking tasks down to their simplest component parts; both systems were ordered by a hierarchy of command with knowledge and power concentrated at the apex of the organization; both had the same aim to master uncertainty through predictable outcomes; and both systems were characterized by low trust relations.

This 'factory' model which married Fordist production and bureaucratic administration gave rise to a new class of professional managers. In America a large number of managers were trained as professional engineers. As David Noble has shown many of the key managers of the early Fordist era, such as Alfred Sloan of General Motors, were trained as engineers and brought their 'engineering perspective' to the problems of managing production.[23] Harlow Pearson, the President of the Taylor society, observed in the 1920s that 'the first coherent public expression of concern with management problems came from engineers... the management movement arose out of the impact of a group of highly trained engineering minds on an industrial situation of engineering complexity'.[24] The spirit they brought to this complex industrial situation was one which saw society and the social problems of production very much in mechanistic terms.

The vision of society as a machine was much in the air at that time and perhaps found its clearest cultural expression in Cubism. As an art form it traded off the geometry of the machine. But while Cubists plied this 'geometry' as a metaphor for life, the engineer–managers of the factory era took it more seriously. As one commentator wrote at the time:

> When we engage the services of the human machine, we always have certain duties laid out which the newcomer is expected to undertake, and we try to get the best man for the place...Now when we purchase a machine tool and find it slightly unfitted for requirements we can usually make a change in construction which will correct the difficulty in it...If the human machine could be controlled by the set rules that govern machine tool operation, the world would be a much different place.[25]

Such wistful sentiment was not shared by all at the time. Henry Ford in typical epigrammatic style expressed it differently, 'Machinery wears out and needs to be restored', whilst, 'Men grow uppish, lazy, or careless'.[26]

In the context of mass produced standardized goods and services, the contradictions inherent in trying to get vast armies of blue-collar and white-collar workers to behave like cogs in a machine, were contained through the offer of higher wage, career ladders and job security. This in turn depended on the national champions being able to expand their existing markets to remain profitable.

5

The founding national champions in the early twentieth century, called the 'first movers' by Alfred Chandler, saw market stability as the way to manage capitalism, given its unpredictable and capricious nature.[27] The key to stability was to increase market share through what in the technical jargon is called vertical integration. By dominating the market for specific goods or services, a few corporations are able to control prices to maintain market stability. Once established, these corporations could make their profits either out of economies of scale; the more they produced the cheaper each unit produced became, or economies of scope by using the same productive process to make a range of products.[28] The figure below sets out the administrative structure of a typical corporation in the early 1920s.

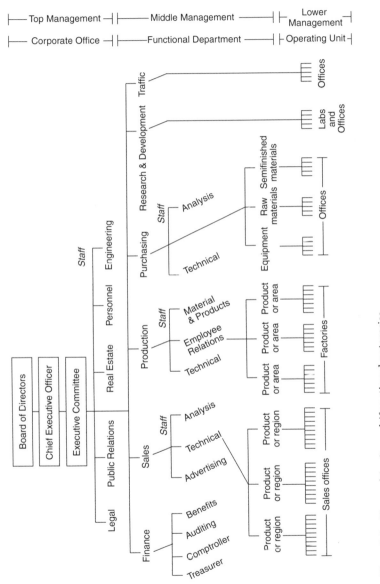

Figure 3.1 The multiunit, multifunctional enterprise
Source: Alfred D. Chandler, *Scale and Scope: The Dynamics of Industrial Capitalism*, Cambridge, Mass.: Harvard University Press, 1990, p. 16.

Here the way in which the diverse talents within a corporation can be harnessed through bureaucracy are depicted. Lawyers, scientists, personnel managers, salesmen and frontline production workers, all fit into the command structure of the corporation. At its apex, bringing the corporation together as an entity, is the top management team who determine strategy and control the many units of the corporation. The key to determining performance and control were detailed blueprints which were developed as early as 1908 by Du Pont: proposals for capital expenditure had to include cost data, market studies and most importantly a breakdown of the expected rate of return.[29] These blueprints were reviewed by the Du Pont executive committee every Monday in the 'Chart Room'. It contained, large metal framed charts displaying the overall return on investment and the contribution of each element of the productive process to it for every division within the corporation. 'A system of tracks and switches allowed any one of the 350 charts to be moved to the centre position. There the committee seated in a semicircle could view and discuss trends'.[30]

This attempt to control the market by creating stability through vertical integration – economies of scale and scope and tight executive control on the return on investment – enabled the first movers to establish a national presence. But there were limits to this form of organization and they were most starkly exposed during the depression of the thirties. Then firms that had diversified into a range of products and across geographical boundaries survived because they had spread their risks in a way in which firms making a single product or a range of allied products did not. The firms that had diversified had effectively created a new conception of how to survive in volatile markets, and a new form of corporate organization to match. Where the engineers, with their emphasis on production, had dominated the first quarter of the twentieth century, it was the sales and marketing experts who began to exert an increasing influence. This is because the fundamental problem of market instability was approached as a problem of sales growth to be solved through an expansion of existing markets and the creation of new ones at home and overseas. It was this new conception of how to respond to the capricious nature of capitalist markets which unleashed the full potential of the 'national corporations' of the post-war era.

By the end of the Second World War there was a massive shortage of consumer goods, but disposable income had risen in the United States from $33 billion in 1940 to $90 billion in 1947. Market research and advertising spearheaded the attack on new markets. *Fortune* magazine estimated that by 1947 $50 million was being spent annually on market research, up from less than $10 million before the war. Advertising expenditures also grew from $3.2 billion in 1946 to $5.6 billion in 1956.[31] This emphasis on marketing and advertising gave rise to new concerns, voiced most clearly in Vance Packard's *Hidden Persuaders*, that consumers were being sold goods they neither needed nor necessarily wanted by sophisticated and increasingly invidious advertising techniques. As the importance of marketing and sales divisions grew, so did their power bases. In corporate politics a clear indicator of the position of power held by the various units in the corporation is the extent to which they report directly to top management. By the early 1950s in the United States, over 78 per cent sales and marketing departments reported directly to top management.[32]

To take advantage of new market opportunities the national champions adopted a multi-divisional structure, where each division of the company is responsible for a particular product line or geographical area. Considerable power of decision-making was devolved to each division in terms of product creation and establishment of market share, with central or 'head office' control being exercised only on the bottom line: the return on investment. This gave the large corporations greater ability to move into new markets and respond to customer tastes and market trends, which were to become even more important in the 1980s and 1990s. Over eighty per cent of the *Fortune* 500 top companies in the United States by the late sixties, had adopted this multi-divisional model. In Europe the development of this type of structure was slower but in Britain, France, Germany and Italy the trend in the third quarter of the twentieth century was to follow the American example.[33] By and large it led to superior performance when compared with companies which were vertically integrated and had a single product line.[34]

As these national champions entered new markets each division, if it was product based, was encouraged to 'take over' the opposition, to increase market share, and gain access to expertise, networks and technology. The effect was to increase further the size and power of these corporations who were expanding into overseas markets as a logical extension of the multidivisional model. This concentration of industrial production extended across the range of consumer items from what was eaten at breakfast to the car that was driven to work. By 1973, 90 per cent of all breakfast cereal foods were manufactured by four companies and 93 per cent of all domestic motor vehicle sales in America were secured by four US companies.[35] As these corporations expanded, a new impetus was also given to bureaucratisation. In effect each division within a corporation required its own bureaucratic structure. As a result the ratio of white-collar to blue-collar workers increased dramatically.[36]

7

Max Weber believed that bureaucracy was the key to understanding twentieth-century capitalism precisely because it was the most powerful technology for social control invented. It was, he said, 'a power instrument of the first order'. When bureaucracy was driven by the knowledge created by the scientific management movement it provided the key to economic growth in the third quarter of the twentieth century. Scientific management bestowed the crown of entrepreneur on engineers and later business administrators and it saw the demise of the myth of rags to riches entrepreneur.[37] Had Weber lived to witness the rise of the modern corporation at mid-century, and the way it coincided with the spread of Fordist production techniques, he would have felt fully vindicated in making the prediction before his death in 1920 that industrial societies were being ensnared in an 'iron cage' of bureaucracy. But human being rarely submit themselves freely to such a fate. Whilst there is no doubt that the 'factory' model – the organization of blue-collar work on Fordist lines and white-collar work on the principles of bureaucracy – has shaped the organization of work for much of the twentieth century, even in the post-war Golden era companies were acutely aware of the problem of how to get workers to stick with it when jobs offered little scope for creative expression or job enrichment.

This contradiction at the heart of the factory model was temporarily resolved through a Faustian bargain between the corporation and the individual. The corporation bought the compliance of the employee in exchange for higher wages and the bonus of improved career prospects for white-collar workers. The way this bargain was experienced by employees and their families is the subject of the next chapter.

4
The Adversities of Good Times

The job. Something more than Orwellian acceptance, something less than Luddite sabotage. Often the two impulses are fused in the same person...It is about a search too, for daily meaning as well as daily bread, for recognition as well as cash, for astonishment rather than torpor; in short, for a sort of life rather than a Monday through Friday sort of dying.

Studs Terkl

Meyersville...contained a large number of identical small houses, each with its own refrigerator and stove and washing machine and fenced yard...Along the main streets of towns like these...sprang up shops selling garden furniture and equipment, used car lots, discount furniture houses, television and appliance stores, carpet outlets. Almost all the people who moved there were young couples with small children...who needed the yard and the washing machine.

Marilyn French

1

Gaylord Freeman retired from being chairman of the board of the First National Bank of Chicago in the mid-1970s. In describing what a career meant for his life he explained how he had worked for the bank all his working life. He tried to be in the office by 6.45 a.m. each day until five-thirty or six. He explained:

'I haven't played bridge in thirty years, I haven't played golf in twenty years...I don't feel I've sacrificed anything. As a younger man, I sacrificed closeness with my children. But in our mature life, it isn't a sacrifice ... This January, I sat down in the afternoon and read a novel. That's the first one I've read since I got out of school in 1934. I never felt I could waste a minute'. Now in retirement he does not feel as mentally sharp or the same sense of duty as when he 'was a more efficient machine'.[1]

Gaylord Freeman's profile as chairman of the board was in some ways typical of his generation. In the 1950s the majority of the top 900 executives in the United States started work in large companies and over a third, like Freeman, never worked for any other company than the one they eventually headed. Most worked for no more than two companies in their entire career and only a fifth worked for three or more.[2] In other respects Freeman was untypical. He entered the First National Bank straight from school and worked his way up, whereas only 24 per cent of the top 900 entered work as clerks or labourers. Indeed, they were likely to have had a college education and come from the upper social classes. As C. Wright Mills put it at the time, 'The typical executives to-day, as in the past, were born with a big advantage, they managed to have fathers on at least upper middle class levels of occupation and income, they are Protestant, white and American born'. In fact, over 60 per cent of American executives came from business and professional families and only 10 to 12 per cent were recruited from blue-collar or clerical white-collar families. British managers had a similar profile.[3]

The initial advantages of social class background were substantially increased by the rewards for becoming a 'machine' and reaching the top of the corporate ladder. In 1950, the top 900 executives averaged $70,000 per year. But salary was only part of the story. Most chief executives were also given bonus payments such as stock holdings. In 1952 Crawford Greenwalt, President of Du Pont earned a salary of $150,000 and stock of $350,000 in bonuses.[4]

The world of Gaylord Freeman was also a man's world. This went beyond the fact that women were excluded from the life of the board-room – except as secretaries, caterers or cleaners. Promotion within the corporation was largely internal, reflecting the organization's side of the 'loyalty bargain'. Those that were smart conformists and worked hard for the company were rewarded. But promotion within the company was also based on a system of male patronage and sponsorship. A British study showed how younger men at that time were promoted by finding a suitable 'father figure' who would identify the junior manager as being promising material.[5] Managers describing their upward ascent talked about their progress being dependent upon a male lineage and of a passage to manhood mediated by a father figure. To be promising material required a certain flexibility if not pliability. For young men this required putting themselves back into a dependency role akin to the one they had just grown out of. It also required frequent and substantial upheaval in their private lives as companies forced them through a rite of passage by transferring them to different divisions as part of their journey through the ranks. Failure to move from one location to another almost certainly meant an end to promotion prospects. A wife was therefore expected to submit to the demands of the corporation in the interest of her husband's career.

Robert K. Merton observed that 'the bureaucrat's official life is planned for him in terms of a graded career, through the organizational devices of promotion by seniority, pensions, incremental salaries, etc., all of which are designed to provide incentives for disciplined action and conformity to the official regulation'.[6] This kind of career planning enabled the corporation to be seen to be upholding its part of the loyalty bargain, whilst at the same time giving the organization a trusted way of promoting people who would conform to the rigours of bureaucratic routine. This was a much safer bet than recruiting from outside of the organization where there were few guarantees that the new recruit would conform to the demands of the corporation.

For those who aspired to career progression, therefore, the trick was to show initiative while remaining subservient to their father figures – initiative kept on a leash. Junior executives often saw this as 'playing the game' until they got to the top. For these men entertaining their superiors and colleagues was all part of that 'game'. As one ambitious assistant plant manager saw it, 'You take the business of entertaining ... You have to go through all that stuff for ten years or so, but then you can chuck it. It's like running for the President of the United States; during the campaign you have to do a lot of things you might not like, but when you get to be President that's all over with'.[7] Playing the game meant cultivating a bureaucratic personality, as it was the demonstration of one's loyalty, commitment and reliability that was as important as technical expertise. But not all executives relied solely on their personal judgement in making promotion decisions as many, particularly in America, drew on the science of psychology to aid them. At companies like Sears, the chairman of the board consulted personality tests that all aspirant executives had to take.[8] In sorting through the entrails of these personality tests what the chairman of Sears was looking for was loyalty, predictability, and a certain kind of engaged conformity.[9]

2

In society at large access to white-collar jobs, especially for men, not only derived more status than blue-collar jobs because they were better paid and usually offered better prospects, but also because they were seen to offer more scope for self-fulfilment than work on a production line. As Harold Wilensky has suggested, the career for white-collar workers has given

> continuity to the personal experience of the most able and skilled segments of the population – men who otherwise would produce a level of rebellion or withdrawal which would threaten the maintenance of the system. By holding out the prospect of continuous, predictable rewards, careers foster a willingness to train and achieve, to adopt a long view and defer immediate gratification for the later pay-off.[10]

This is one side of what Max Weber called the Janus face of bureaucracy. The bureaucratic career offered men stability and the prospect of material progress, and it provided an incentive for those hovering at the bottom of the career escalator to step on. Once on, the other face of bureaucracy became apparent. Most middle managers and white-collar clerical workers did not see the finished product of their work. As C. Wright Mills noted:

> In the case of the white-collar man, the alienation of the wage-worker from the products of his work is carried one step nearer to its Kafka-like completion. The salaried employee does not make anything, although he may handle much that he greatly desires but cannot have. No product of craftsmanship can be his to contemplate with pleasure as it is being created and after it is made. Being alienated from any product of his labour, and going year after year through the same paper routine, he turns his leisure all the more frenziedly to the ersatz diversion that is sold him, and partakes of the synthetic excitement that neither eases or releases. He is bored at work and restless at play, and this terrible alienation wears him out.[11]

Despite the poetic licence which Mills allows himself in this description, it certainly had resonance for Fred Roman, a twenty-five year old auditor with a large public accounting firm, who talked about his job in precisely the terms used by Mills:

> The company I work for doesn't make a product. We provide a service... Is my job important? It's a question I ask myself. It's important to people who use financial statements, who buy stocks ... Whether its important to society... No, not too important. Its necessary in this economy based on big business... I have a couple of friends... We get together and talk once in a while. At first you're afraid to say anything cause you think the guy really loves it [work]. You don't want to say, 'I hate it'. But then you hear the guy say, 'Boy! If it weren't for the money I'd quit right now'.'[12]

Fred Roman wanted to quit and go back to College, get a masters or Ph.D. and become a college teacher but he didn't think he had 'the smarts for it'. That lack of confidence in his academic ability would certainly have helped to lock Fred into his job. What kept him going was that the firm had a career ladder, or more precisely an escalator, which he had to ride ever upwards or get off. So long as he performed, the house in the suburbs, the consumer goods and the 'ersatz diversions' were his. But as he says, 'it's not a very exciting business... You tell people you're an accountant... They don't know quite what to say. What can they say? Maybe I look at it wrong. *There isn't much to talk about'*.

Another negative feature associated with bureaucratic work was that it offered little room for individuality. The roles played by individuals were prescribed according to their function within the bureaucracy, and the successful execution of these roles were judged by clear criteria which left little room for personal discretion. In these circumstances white-collar workers were aware that it was not only production workers whose behaviour was under constant surveillance, as Richard Sennett has noted white-collar workers 'create a psychological shield for themselves against the rather naked light in which they appear to work. The shield is created by splitting the self into an 'I' and a 'me'. The 'I' is the active self which, is the father, the good neighbour or the friend at work. The 'me' is the passive self of the worker subject to a narrowly defined role, explicit rules and the imposed authority of a hierarchy. In a language which is still with us it is the 'me' which is rewarded as in, 'they have given *me*, a raise or a promotion', rarely do people say 'I have earned a promotion'.[13]

Even those close to the top of the corporate pyramid were expected to exhibit smart conformity rather than individual creativity. Recall Gaylord Freeman's description of himself as 'a machine'. Those at the top of the corporate command structure needed to be both politicians as a well as entrepreneurs. But even this freedom to wheel and deal was in some senses illusory for they also found that the iron cage of bureaucracy had entered their souls; they lived for the company and had to act in a way which was strangely depersonalised. As one executive of the time noted, 'The further up you go, the less you can afford to stick out in any one place'. Or, as a typically tough minded company President put it, the ideal 'is to be an individualist privately and a conformist publicly'.[14]

3

The world at the top of the corporate tower was quite different to that on the production line. Routine conformity may have been the watchword in both contexts but at least white-collar workers got to use their brains the more they rose up the corporate ladder. Such an opportunity was not available to men and women on the shop floor. Here work was regulated by the clock and the machine. It was a world in which silence would reign on the factory bus on a Monday morning as workers contemplated, the 'Monday through Friday sort of dying' they would have to endure. A Ford worker of the early seventies saw it this way:

> You don't achieve anything here. A robot could do it. The line here is made for morons. It doesn't need any thought. They tell you that. 'We don't pay you for thinking' they say. Everyone comes to realize they're not doing a worthwhile job. They're just on the line. For the money. Nobody likes to think they're a failure. It's bad when you *know* that you're just a little cog. You just look at your pay packet – you look at what it does for your wife and kids. That's the only answer.[15]

Enduring the production line was a matter of constant mental struggle, of devising strategies to cope with the constant presence of a factory system which denied individuals their intellect, dignity and hope. The challenge of keeping the mind alive is that while the work is repetitive it also requires attention. Some achieved the knack of thinking of other things while doing the job, 'I bring books and crossword puzzles to work. This gives me something to think about when I'm doing the job. You walk out of here in a dream', another Ford worker said. But it is a hard won way of keeping the mind in play. The same Ford workers told of a man on a car assembly line near Liverpool who was six foot two, a bit dozy and not too agile. He was put on the night shift fitting electric wires through the dashboard. He ended up several stations down the line, getting in the way of his mates, falling over and getting cursed. Tall dozy men, they concluded, don't belong on an assembly line.

The men at this Ford plant knew that in some ways they were wasting their lives, all wanted to do other things in which they could use their brains and contribute to society in a more direct and tangible way. In their dreams they wanted to become journalists and teachers, but with children and mortgages, and without education and the confidence to take the risk of studying for qualifications, they were trapped. The reason they felt their work was meaningless was that the production line didn't allow them to see the outcome of their labours. In this, the production line workers were at one with their white-collar counterparts. Asked about his aspirations one worker touched on the emptiness arising from never seeing the completed fruits of his labour:

> I'd like to be a teacher, I think. Something like that anyway. I think I've been through the mill. I think I'd really like to work with young people. I think that like what you [the interviewer] are doing must give you a lot of satisfaction. You're fortunate because you can see your work. It's something tangible which you can get to grips with... come back to... think about. You must feel you are doing something. With us you do something and its gone. Part of your life on the back of a car.

In some jobs the repetitive nature of the work is compensated for by having a laugh with workmates but even this is difficult on the production line. As a worker who places the car off the hoist explained:

> I've been doing that for three years now. With the line you've got to adapt yourself to the speed. Some rush and get a break. I used to try and do that but the job used to get out of hand. I just amble along now... Some jobs you're on you can't talk or you'll lose concentration. When I came here first I couldn't talk at all. Now I can manage a few words with the man opposite me.

The atomisation of work on the production line was a direct product of the low trust ethos that pervades Fordism. In breaking work down into its simplest component parts, the semi-skilled and unskilled line workers had no need to see or understand the bigger picture of factory organization and policy, let alone feel a sense of 'ownership' of the completed product. Work was strictly devised on a need to know basis and the knowledge needed by the average worker was extremely limited. The insights and understanding they might have had were not sought because, as we have shown, the production line was organized according to the gospel of scientific management and its acolytes – the time and motion experts. The production line represented the low trust organization of work with a vengeance.

Of course blue-collar workers did not respond passively to these conditions and various strategies were devised to assert their humanity: practical jokes, Luddism and strikes were all part of factory life. One of the reasons why the Fordist form of work organization began to die a slow death in post-industrial economies was precisely because the industrial disruption, which gathered momentum in the late sixties, threatened its viability. In this sense there was a fundamental difference between the blue- and white-collar workers. The inducement of a career brought loyalty from white-collar workers which was never designed for manual workers: 'I'm like a lot of people here. They're all working here but they're just really hanging around, waiting for something to turn up . . . It's different for them in the office. They're part of *Ford's*. We're not, we're just working here, we're numbers'. What kept them in their jobs was that as unskilled or semi-skilled labourers they received a relatively high wage and there was job stability – the job was there as long as they could stick it out. And they needed to stick it out because the majority of men had the responsibility of earning the family wage. But there was little prospect of blue-collar workers being treated as individuals rather than as part of an amorphous mass of interchangeable components at the beck and call of management. The most poignant symbol of this was the fact that any improvement in the working conditions or pay for blue-collar workers depended on the outcome of collective bargaining rather than individual merit.

4

If the factory model was based on stable employment, the nuclear family was based on enduring divisions of labour between women and men. So long as men could bring home enough money to maintain the family, the roles of men and women remained clear cut. The division between domestic and paid work and the gender roles assigned to each were generated by nineteenth-century industrialism. Prior to that the roles of nurturing and socializing the young, and the economic role of making ends meet, were kept within the family. The British historian E. P. Thompson described the pre-industrial economic role of the family by reference to the way entire families were involved in the business of weaving, 'The young children winding bobbins, older children watching for faults, picking over the cloth, or helping to throw the shuttle in the broad loom; adolescents working a second or third loom; the wife taking a turn at weaving in and among her domestic employment. The family was together'.[16] With the onset of the factory system a separation developed between the economic function of the family and the child-rearing and socializing functions. By the mid-twentieth century it was largely men that went out to work to bring home a family wage, and the role of the family had been reduced to one of child rearing and sustaining the personal and material needs of the breadwinner. Within the division of labour between domestic and paid work the basic roles common to all married women became those of domestic servant and the guardian angel of the family's emotional well being.

The distinction between the public (and objective) world of paid work and the private (subjective) world of the family was reinforced by the rise of bureaucratic work and the prosperity it generated. The factory model emphasized the 'impersonal' and the 'objective' based on the strictures of science. The family was a refuge from this coldly efficient work machine. But it was also the recipient of the machine's products. The consumer boom in the Golden era led to an explosion of products and gadgets for the home and the family: the car, the radio, television, vacuum cleaner, washing machine, were all aimed at enhancing the domestic world. A by-product of this process was that even the measure of family well-being was taken out of the hands of women. For it might be imagined that within the roles defined for men and women, the latter would be judged on their ability to maintain a well-adjusted family in the face of the challenges posed by bureaucratic work. In fact family success was all too often measured by its ability to buy the latest gadgets 'to keep up with the Jones' – and the capacity to do that lay with the husband's earning power.[17]

That women's achievements in the home should be judged more by the husbands' accomplishments than their own efforts may have been bitterly ironic but it was unsurprising, given the rhythms of the working day and the primacy accorded to paid work. In many ways the ordering of family life was determined by and, in fact, mimicked bureaucratic organization. Just as bureaucracies were hierarchically structured so men retained formal power within the family. As breadwinners they had power over the family budget. In Whyte's account of domestic finances, what he called 'budgetism' became symbolic of the way the corporate shadow permeated the middle-class household. Financial obligations were homogenized by the automatic monthly payment in a 'smooth hypnotic rhythm' and even 'impulse buying' he suggested, was deliberately planned.[18]

Within the home roles were as carefully defined as at the corporate desk. Here is a British manager of the sixties, Mr Newington, talking about the gender divisions within the home:

> I do the garden and the car but very little in the house. I don't cook; I do dry up most weekends and evenings under protest but I don't do any housework unless the place is particularly untidy, when I might take out the Hoover. I kept very clear of the kids when they were young. I told my wife they were hers till they were a year old. I didn't feed them, or amuse them or anything. I did things like putting up shelves, and so forth. I feel its a natural and normal sort of division; I don't do anything that's really a woman's province, though I do light the fires which my mother always does in my own home.[19]

This specification of domestic roles by Mr Newington was common on both sides of the Atlantic and across classes. Perhaps the most common and poignant indicator of the rigid nature of these roles was the fact that for nearly thirty years after the Second World War men rarely attended the birth of their children: as Mr Newington says, infants belonged to the wives. In the bringing up of children there were clear differences between classes but the role played by the father was similar in that it was common for him to disappear early in the morning and re-appear at bedtime. Mothers reported the wrongdoings of the day if they were sufficiently heinous and children awaited their judgement with trepidation. As managers were remote figures to production workers, fathers were remote figures of authority to whom mothers reported.

It was within these structures that women's fate was organised. But the corporate influence went beyond structuring domestic life to expecting the wife to play a particular kind of role as a corporate wife. The ideal of the corporate wife was that she was 'highly adaptable, highly gregarious, and realised her husband belonged to the corporation...A good wife is good by *not* doing things – by *not* complaining when her husband works late; by *not* fussing when a transfer is coming up; by *not* engaging in any controversial activity'.[20] In Britain the expectations on corporate wives was not as great as that in America. Nevertheless a role was still demanded. Two sociologists, Jan and Ray Pahl, tell an apocryphal story of this role which is worth repeating:

> A manager's wife had looked forward to the firm's annual dinner with great pleasure. She bought herself a new dress, had an expensive session at the hairdresser and took great pains to have all the right accessories, scent and so on. On the day itself the children got to bed in good time, her mother arrived to baby sit and she had every expectation of a marvellous evening. The final touch came when she found she was sitting next to one of the most senior men in the company, a man who could do much to further her husband's career. She felt confident and pretty and chattered away gaily and intelligently. It was in the midst of a particularly witty piece of conversation that she suddenly realized that she had just leant across and cut her companion's dinner up into small pieces.[21]

Middle-class women were then, in many ways, as much subject to the discipline and demands for loyalty to the corporation as their husbands. The bottom line for this compliance was security. Men found security in their work, women in their families and marriage. The security this gave to women was frequently gained at great personal cost. The economic power given to men in their role as providers could lead to a morally degenerate view of the domestic relationship. As the wife of one manager explained:

> Oh, hell! I thought marriage would give me more happiness than it has, and it's not really given me any happiness, not the marriage itself. I have a nice house, I can afford things, and I have a nice daughter, and my husband has a nice position, but deep down I have not had the happiness I expected...It always goes back to this thing of my husband seeing me as one of his other possessions.[22]

The consequence of being a possession or adjunct to the male provider was spelt out by Meredith Tax:

> When I am by myself, I am nothing. I only know that I exist because I am needed by someone who is real, my husband, and by my children.

My husband goes out into the real world...I stay in the imaginary world in this house, doing jobs that I largely invent, and that no one cares about but myself...I seem to be involved in some mysterious process.[23]

For working class wives the terms on which security was gained were essentially the same: man as provider and woman as homemaker giving emotional and material support. Richard Sennett, in his classic *The Hidden Injuries of Class* written with Jonathan Cobb, describes this bargain through the eyes of William O'Malley, a factory foreman. O'Malley was brought up in the depression. His parents, unskilled labourers, both had full-time jobs and his father also worked two to three nights a week. He recalls that when he came home from school neither of his parents were there and he was able to run wild. He entered work from school and married, in part to create the family life he never had. O'Malley worked hard so that his wife could stay at home to raise their children in a way that his mother never could. But in his mind, there was an implicit contract between himself and his family. He had sacrificed himself to them and in return he expected his family to do his bidding. It was an unequal contract because his wife and children had no say in it. If there is a 'sweetener' underlying this relationship it was the promise of ever better material living conditions for the family and the hope that the O'Malley's children would 'do better' than their parents.

O'Malley's family background and the history of the economic depression which gave rise to it is important for understanding the nature of the unequal contract between husband and wife. The rise of industrial capitalism may have separated home from work, domestic labour from paid labour, but the way individuals understand and interpret the roles they have been allocated will crucially be determined by their own life history. As Sennett and Cobb note, 'O'Malley believed he has rights over his wife because of his sacrifices for her but what he was really doing was sacrificing her to the wounds of his past'.[24]

While the essence of the contract between men and women was the same, the day-to-day life experiences of working class women would have been quite different to that of their middle-class counterparts. The life of middle class women was constantly disrupted by having to move where the corporation sent them. It meant the re-creation of friendship patterns and support networks. In the community they tended to put down many but shallow roots, 'they pick up and drop friends the way they buy and trade cars and homes – speeding up the obsolescence of both'.[25] In settled working-class communities, supporting kinship patterns and networks were well established. In the early fifties in London's Bethnal Green, 45 couples had between them 1,700 relatives living in the borough. People living in the same street were spoken of as 'one big family' and the social universe for children was large because their geographical universe was so small.[26] What these tight knit communities had was a collective resource in raising their children: a system of 'looking out' for each others children, and communal expectations of how they should behave.[27] Men may have been on the periphery of this world but women were not isolated in the raising of children. In his eulogy to traditional working-class life, Richard Hoggart talked of its 'gripping wholeness' – an inclusiveness which eschewed the middle-class worries of loneliness and angst.[28] It is, of course, easy to romanticize such communities and play down the hardship these women endured. As it was, by the mid-sixties the entire character of Bethnal Green and related areas had changed as many of the white working-class families were moved to new towns outside London to be replaced by immigrants attracted by the promise of employment and prosperity.

5

The rigid demarcation of roles within the home, built on inequalities of power, rendered the relationships between men and women mechanical and ritualized. Individuals had to express their identities within the roles to which they had been born: in a phrase, they became one-dimensional.[29] One of the shrewdest insights into the impact of the factory model on the family came from the Italian Marxist Antonio Gramsci who on learning of the introduction of Fordist production techniques in America observed that, 'a new type of man demanded by the rationalization of production and work cannot be developed until the sexual instinct has been suitably regulated and until it too had been rationalized'.[30] According to Gramsci the iron discipline demanded by Fordism required the disciplining of sexual instincts: monogamy, twice a week sex, the 2.4 family were all part and parcel of the servicing of the worker.[31] How could it be different when a man's working life was so governed by the machine and the clock? In retrospect, the combination of rising affluence alongside meaningless work in the factory, routine work in the office, and the strict division of activities in the home, proved to be a heady cocktail. On the surface, the fifties and sixties presented a smooth veneer of stability but beneath the surface the first symptoms of change were appearing which would have a profound impact on the political, economic and social life of the last decades of the twentieth century.

For the post-war period gave rise to a search for authenticity and to the question of how an authentic identity could be constructed. The most systematic intellectual response came from the Existential movement who talked of the creation of authenticity through the realisation of life projects. Individuals, they argued, could be the authors of their own identities. The popular response was different. In his celebrated work of the fifties, *The Lonely Crowd*, David Riesman wrote about the significance of the idea of sincerity to that age. He discussed the role that 'sincerity' played in the way people related to stars like Dinah Shore and Frank Sinatra. Riesman noted that the popular judgement made about these singers was that they convey sincerity and it is for this reason that they were popular. 'I like Dinah Shore because she's so sincere' or 'You can just feel he [Frank Sinatra] is sincere', were frequently given reasons by people who liked them. Having made this observation Riesman goes on to put his finger on the fundamental shift in the way people perceived themselves and others:

> their yearning for sincerity is a grim reminder of how little they can trust themselves or others in daily life, it is less clear what they find 'sincere' in a singer or other performer. One element may be the apparent freedom of the entertainer to express emotions that others cannot or dare not express... The performer puts himself at the mercy of both his audience and his emotions... [he] has left himself wide open and extended the glad hand of friendliness.[32]

The upshot is that judging the quality of the performance is no longer a matter of applying aesthetic criteria as to the quality of the song and the craft of the singer, it is the attitude of the singer to the audience, the degree he or she 'gives' of themselves to the audience which is important.

What Riesman has put his finger on is the popular answer to the threat to personal identity posed by the factory model of Fordist and bureaucratic work. For authenticity, the real self, is to be found in the subjective, in the private emotional life of the individual. Just as 'sincere' singers open themselves up to reveal their emotions so now friendship is judged by the degree to which individuals reveal their innermost thoughts and feelings to one another. The way we use language reveals much about us and the shift in language that occurred between the fifties and now is significant. We no longer 'talk to people' as if we were talking to a particular role or public performance in which the character of the individual is incidental to the role, as indeed it was in the mechanically-formed relationships in the past, we now 'talk with' people in which the talking is part of a sharing of oneself with another. We no longer 'think' something is good or bad, nowadays we 'feel' it is, as in, 'I feel this is a bad idea'. When Riesman was writing, this 'solution' to the one dimensional features of mid-century life was only beginning to emerge, hence his observation that singers could express emotions that others could not or dared not express. By the 1990s, the reverse was true, failure to reveal oneself was to remain an outsider, destined to a relationship with a professional counsellor rather than with friends.

That the life of the emotions should become the locus of authenticity – the source of personal identity – is not surprising. After all, the home and family life was the place of refuge from the impersonal forces at work. And within it the expectations of middle-class husbands and wives were changing. The corporation had understood the significance of wives to their husbands careers and had sought to draw them into their social orbit. Dinner parties, barbecues, and other forms of joint entertaining became *de rigeur* forms of entertainment for corporate man and his wife. Through these pleasures husbands and wives became *couples* who entertained together, and in sharing these leisure activities were also expected to be good friends. This was a new development. Previously the division of gender roles had meant that husbands and wives had their own circle of same-sex friends. Friendships involving both the wife and husband would have been a happy accident rather than an expectation.[33] Even so, the new expectation of friendship between married couples often remained unfulfilled so long as women were isolated in the home and financially powerless.

But the role of women was also undergoing change. In one sense the emotional and personal life of the family was their business, but for middle-class women at least, it was given a particular twist in the fifties. The symptom of this change was the publication of Dr Benjamin Spock's treatise on how to raise children, *The Common Sense Book of Baby and Child Care*. The book begins with a section entitled 'Trust Yourself', but that was not the way the book was understood or rewritten in the popular imagination. Spock's work subsequently became demonized as a manifesto for the permissive raising of children. But this demonization by conservatives missed the point as Spock's work was a symptom of underlying changes in the lives of women.

With the publication of Spock's book, science and the expert stepped into family life and came to dominate views about the raising of children just as it had bureaucratic work. Spock's treatise was the first of many incursions by expert's into the intimate field of family relations and human development. What it represented was a distrust in the traditional rules of thumb and practical remedies that had been handed down from mothers to daughters. Social mobility, particularly for middle-class women, had broken the social bond between them and their mothers. Nor was the future of their children, in terms of the class, gender and the occupational roles they could be expected to play be taken for granted – increased geographic and social mobility and the intervening role of education in both saw to that. Under these circumstances the socialization of the young could not rely on traditional prescriptions. But if 'experts' entered to fill the vacuum left by the inadequacies of tradition, raising children turned out to be less of a science than an art. The guidance that scientific theories offered was often conflicting and the raising of children became a matter of judgement and debate between parents, a source of conflict as much as satisfaction. But this conflict was also uneven for in an important sense women's knowledge and authority in the home was usurped by what were all too often male experts, adding to the crisis concerning the legitimate source of women's identity.

If the fifties saw the beginnings of a change in the source of male identities in the direction of the personal and subjective, in the sixties women began to travel in the opposite direction. The sense that women had of being the possessions of men and having no separate identity from them, meant that the source of their identity needed to be found elsewhere. The search crystallized in the feminist movement and in the slogan: the personal is political. These changes were initially confined to the middle classes. Working-class women stayed with traditional patterns of child socialization because they tended to live in more settled communities, and besides, they had little time to reflect upon their condition. The daily grind of making ends meet still had to be negotiated, even if there was a gradual improvement in their circumstances. Whereas the etiquette of middle-class life dictated that partners would spend some of their leisure time together, the roles of working-class men and women remained separate.[34] It was only with the rise in women's paid work and the advent of mass unemployment, especially for young black men in the seventies and eighties that sources of working-class identity were challenged and changed.

While the shackles of pre-assigned roles were loosened in the fifties it was the younger generation that sought to break free of them in the middle and late sixties. The unleavened romance of Sinatra became the protest of Dylan and the critical interrogations of the Beatles. The sexual revolution of the sixties, which Gramsci would surely have seen as a symptom of deep structural change, was followed by the student and worker protests of 1968. The rate of divorce rose and as western economic prosperity declined in the seventies so did the family wage and women found themselves having to enter the workforce. The stability and security generated by the factory model was under threat. But before we begin our examination of how the Golden era came to an end, we need to consider the nature of 'opportunity' for education and occupational advancement.

5

The Manufacture of Intelligence

He...gave us not that capability and godlike reason to fust in us unused.

William Shakespeare

In the progress of the division of labour...the man whose whole life is spent in performing a few simple operations... generally becomes as stupid and ignorant as it is possible for a human creature to become.

Adam Smith

1

In 1867 Horatio Alger published his first book *Ragged Dick*, which was aimed at teaching the virtues of enterprise, responsibility, patience, hard work, honesty and ambition to juveniles who would shape the American nation. The main characters in Alger's books, and there were many, all achieve success through the victory of character over social circumstances. In *Ragged Dick*, the wealthy benefactor Mr Whitney tells the dishevelled Dick 'I hope, my lad, you will prosper and rise in the world. You know in this free country poverty in early life is no bar to a man's advancement...Remember that your future position depends mainly on yourself and that it will be as high or low as you choose to make it.'[1] Less sanguine observers of American life such as Alex de Tocqueville also reported that America, as the 'first new nation', lacked the rigid class barriers that he had observed throughout Europe. Personified in the experience of American presidents such as Abraham Lincoln's social sojourn from a Kentucky log cabin and Benjamin Franklin's elevation from an apprentice printer and tenth son of a Boston candle-maker, equal opportunities for all had become 'America's promise'. As Lloyd Warner and his colleagues observed in the 1940s, 'It was on the lips of every humble fireside. Every business man, industrialist, and politician proclaimed it and believed it.'[2] In Britain, in the aftermath of the devastating destruction of war, there was also common agreement that the reconstruction of society must include new opportunities for all in a 'land fit for heroes'.

The renewed sense of optimism which gripped the Anglophone countries encouraged the belief that social justice could be secured through the breakdown of social barriers to opportunity. These new opportunities would in turn lead to a blurring of social, cultural and racial differences as people were assimilated into what amounted to the white, male, middle-class ideals which dominated these societies. It was also to serve as a tool of assimilation by giving different class and ethnic groups common prizes to aspire to and achieve in industrial society. This would allow people to forget their roots in the making of 'all Americans' as everyone would have a chance to prosper. But it was the economic argument that advanced western societies could no longer afford to waste the limited pool of talent evident among working-class and ethnic minorities which was to have the most significant impact on the shaping of opportunities at mid-century. In a technological age the idea of log cabin to President had become implausible without access to education. As Talcott Parsons noted at the time:

> The legend of the 'self-made man' has an element of nostalgic romanticism and is destined to become increasingly mythical, if by it is meant not just mobility from humble origins to high status, which does indeed continue to occur, but that the high status was attained through the 'school of hard knocks' without the aid of formal education.[3]

This emphasis on opportunity through education had considerable political appeal because it did not involve taking from the 'haves' to improve things for the 'have nots'. This enabled Western governments to preserve a core cultural assumption that people could be fairly rewarded on the basis of their individual efforts, knowledge and abilities without a significant redistribution of wealth and income. What Michael Young had famously coined 'meritocratic' competition had therefore come to offer a way of selecting individuals for education and jobs on the basis of abilities and efforts rather than social class background, race or gender.[4]

2

This emphasis on meritocratic competition was to transform the role of education from that of the nineteenth century when the education system was seen primarily as a means of maintaining social distance between the elites and the masses. Education for the privileged few provided entry into a select, culturally superior world. It was a badge, distributed according to an accident of birth, which represented and reaffirmed the privileges of the wealthy and powerful. In Britain, H. G. Wells referred to the 1870 Forster Education Act as one designed to 'educate the lower classes for employment on lower class lines, and with specially trained, inferior teachers'.[5] Education was also designed to reinforce the social chasm between the sexes. This existed in all areas of social life as gender inequalities went largely unrecognized, because they were seen as part of the normal order of things. The education of the male was of primary importance given the patriarchal structure of society, and there was a commonly-held assumption at the time that women were biologically inferior to men, both in physique and intellect. In the words of Alexander Walker, 'It is evident that the man, possessing reasoning faculties, muscular power, and courage to employ it, is qualified for being a protector: the woman, begin little capable of reasoning, feeble, and timid, requires protection. Under such circumstances, the man naturally governs: the woman as naturally obeys'.[6] Therefore, education in the nineteenth century was largely geared to leaving no doubt about one's predestined place in community, work place and home.

With the spread of industrial capitalism it was becoming more difficult to recruit sufficient numbers of white-collar workers from within the ranks of the privileged. The demand for the complex and varied skills required by industrial societies could not be satisfied by restricting education to middle-class men. The rapid social, technological and economic changes which confronted all Western industrial societies following the Second World War accentuated these earlier problems and were to have a powerful impact on the direction of educational change. This was because the need to provide a suitably trained and motivated labour force has proved a powerful argument for removing education barriers to working-class mobility, alongside the demand for greater social justice.

In the post-war era education took a central position in the functioning of the advanced industrial societies. It was both an investment in the promotion of economic growth as well as a means of promoting social justice. This was premised on two widely-held assumptions about the nature of education in advanced industrial societies. First, economic efficiency had come to depend on getting the most talented people into the most important and technically demanding jobs, regardless of their social circumstances. If individuals had the ability to succeed, the old barriers of social class were no more than gossamer threads to be brushed aside in the climb up the social ladder. The key to this ascent lay in the notion of intelligence. It was assumed that in society there was a limited pool of individuals with the intelligence required to run the engines of industrial growth. This pool of talent needed to be tapped through the education system because, as Clark Kerr and his colleagues noted, industrialization is characterized by high rates of social mobility which meant that inequalities in the competition for a livelihood are inconsistent with the assignment of occupational roles: 'Industrialization calls for flexibility and competition; it is against tradition and status based upon family, class, religion, race or caste'.[7] It was also predicted at the time that the vast majority of jobs would become increasingly skilled, requiring extensive periods of formal education. Between 1950 and 1960, for example, the U.S. labour force increased by 8 per cent, but the number of professional, technical and managerial workers grew by 69 per cent.[8] Such evidence encouraged the view that everyone would eventually become middle-class, as semi-skilled and unskilled jobs were replaced by machines and workers became technicians, managers, or were appointed to the expanding professions.[9]

Education was also seen as contributing to the foundations of democracy. The link between education and democracy is well established in Western thought, and was given particular impetus in the twentieth century by the work of John Dewey in the United States and in Britain by R.H. Tawney, as well as during the 1950s and 1960s through the writings of Anthony Crosland, A. H. Halsey, and others. The focus on the link between education and democracy turned on a fundamental insight of Dewey's that a democracy is more than a form of government; it is primarily a mode of open association and communication between individuals and groups.[10] The type of school which, it was argued, best contributed to this form of 'associated living' was the common or comprehensive high school. Here students from all types of social background, ethnicity, gender and ability could mix and develop tolerance and mutual respect for each others' point of view – dispositions considered essential in democracy.

The common school ideal embodied much of the spirit of the age. It was designed to provide greater equality of opportunity by deferring the selection of students into 'academic' and 'vocational' streams until later in their careers giving them the chance to manifest their academic potential. It also assumed that male and female students and those from different cultural backgrounds all learnt in much the same way: that they would all benefit from greater equality of treatment. And it assumed that from this common treatment and experience the essential foundations of democratic life could be taught.

For these conditions to be met, greater access for disadvantaged children was extended through 'meritocratic competition'.[11] The common school could be seen as a triumph for a more democratic 'contest' system of social mobility. It enabled the selection of students heading for higher education to be delayed until high school had been completed.[12] Underlying the contest system of mobility in the 1960s was the view that intelligence was randomly distributed among the population regardless of class, race or gender. It follows that if this system is working fairly the spread of achievement should mirror the class, race and gender make up of society. This view was clearly radical in that it challenged the widely held view among white conservatives that blacks are innately less intelligent than whites, although very few conservatives maintained the nineteenth century view that women were innately inferior to men.

Another feature of this commitment to meritocratic competition was that it involved seeing education as something more than a commodity to be bought and sold. It demanded 'irrational' behaviour on the part of middle-class parents who were not permitted to 'buy' an advantage for their child, given that this would be unfair on children from poorer backgrounds who could not afford a private education. As Michael Young noted, in the centuries-old conflict between the principles of selection by family and the principles of selection by merit, in the post-war period the ability of wealthy parents to buy an educational advantage for their children was downplayed despite the continuation of the elite private schools in England such as Eton and Harrow, and the private Ivy League universities in America. These elite schools and universities served as a reminder that self-selection by powerful families remained a preferred option. Despite this it was common to hear politicians, journalists, and policy-makers extol the virtue of 'keeping politics out of education', giving all-party support for the expansion of education and its reorganisation along 'comprehensive' lines as a way of achieving the dual objectives of economic efficiency and social justice.

A commitment to meritocratic competition viewed as equality of outcome was evident in Lyndon B. Johnson's foreword to the 1965 issue of Daedalus devoted to *The Negro American*: 'You do not take a person who for years has been hobbled by chains and liberate him, bring him up to the starting line of a race, and say, "You are free to compete with all the others", and still justly believe that you have been completely fair'. Johnson realized that it was never enough simply to open the gates of opportunity as you need to give people the ability to walk through, and it is this which he saw as the next stage in the battle for civil rights: 'the task is to give 20 million Negroes the same choice as every other American to learn and work and share in Society, to develop their abilities – physical, mental and spiritual – and to pursue their individual happiness'.

Various reforms such as the Supreme Court's 1954 desegregation decision in *Brown* v. *The School Board* and *Topeka* which paved the way to bussing people of colour to more prosperous neighbourhoods and the Head Start pre-school initiative which tried to get children from poorer backgrounds 'up to speed' by the time they began school, were aimed at equalizing educational opportunities in America. In Britain, a programme of compensatory education was introduced along the lines of the Head Start programme, but the major reform in England and Wales was the shift from a selective to a comprehensive system of secondary education in the mid-1960s. This was partly motivated by research which had shown significant class differences in test scores at age eleven, even amongst those with the same IQ scores.

The political consensus about the role of education in the Golden era led to expansion on an impressive scale. In the United States about 15 per cent of 14–17 year olds were in secondary education in 1910, by 1957 the figure had increased to about 90 per cent, of these 62 per cent of 17 year olds were gaining high school diplomas.[13] In the case of higher education about 15 per cent of 18 to 21 year olds were in college in 1940. By 1954 this had risen to 30 per cent and continued to expand to almost 38 per cent by 1960. By the time of the first oil shock in the early 1970s college enrolment accounted for more than half of the college age group.[14] In Britain the expansion was also impressive, but it began from a lower base. Before the Second World War the English system of higher education was dominated by Oxbridge colleges and civic universities, attended by only 3 per cent of the age group and most of these were men. This figure increased to 7.2 per cent by 1962 and then to 12.7 per cent in all kinds of higher education by the end of the 1970s.[15]

This can be seen as a major advance in breaking down the barriers to class, gender and ethnicity. However, despite the expansion in middle-class jobs and an increasingly educated workforce, the guiding idea that everyone would eventually get a middle-class job and that occupation and status would be determined according to merit were myths. The myths were understandable, given the accelerated expansion in middle-class jobs and educational opportunities; but working-class jobs remained, as did the privileges enjoyed by higher socio-economic groups. Universities were still dominated by those from professional and managerial backgrounds; and even when IQ scores were taken into account, social background remained a significant factor in shaping life chances. In effect, the expanding occupational structure had created more room at the top and in the middle of the occupation hierarchy for those originally from working-class backgrounds, but the middle classes were able to use meritocratic competition as a way of passing on their social status to siblings.

3

In Matthew Arnold's well-known statement on culture and the role of education in its development, he notes that culture knows 'that the sweetness and light of the few must be imperfect until the raw and unkindled masses of humanity, are touched with sweetness and light'.[16] But in the cold light of day 'what is taught to whom' always reflects the perceived 'needs' of the age. Education in the Golden era reflected the general trend toward the rationalization of daily activities in all spheres of contemporary life. With an ever more complex division of roles there were intensive efforts to find an efficient system of 'identifying and developing the talent within the population'.[17]

The mid-century development of education was therefore premised on a set of rules, procedures and practices which conformed to the principles of 'factory' organization. Weber viewed the factory model (bureaucracy) as a reaction against the personal subjugation, nepotism, cruelty and subjective judgement which passed for managerial practices in the early days of the Industrial Revolution.[18] He also argued that 'if these principles of bureaucracy are followed it is possible to attain a high degree of efficiency and an organisational structure which is superior to any other form in its precision, stability and reliability'. As well as providing a social technology which could create a set of predictable outcomes, the factory model was intimately related to the idea of a 'meritocracy' because it treated individuals 'objectively' on the basis of achievement criteria. In education this meant that individuals were, in principle, treated according to ability rather than on the basis of ascribed characteristics such as social class, gender, or race. This inevitably led to a rational linkage between intelligence, curriculum, qualifications and suitability for different kinds of work.

The organization of formal educational systems according to these criteria provided a rational means of social selection for expanding public administrations and for private corporations. School and college credentials provided a useful screening device for employers who were concerned that future employees should be inculcated into the appropriate forms of rule-following behaviour, as well as having the knowledge and skills required for their place in the techno-structure. But, given the demand for large numbers of low-skilled workers with little room for individual autonomy, the educational system confronted the problem of espousing greater equality of opportunity whilst limiting the aspirations and ambitions of the majority by defining them as academic failures. This contradiction at the heart of educational opportunity – of seeking to promote a 'talented' few while attempting to 'cool out' the majority – made it difficult for the education system to improve the job prospects of working-class, black or female students.

It is worth considering the tensions confronting the factory model of education in a little more detail because they provide some important clues about the failings of the education system today. There are three areas which are most germane to our argument, these are: the view of intelligence as unchangeable, as measurable and as a scarce resource; the use of academic qualifications as a screening device for prospective employers; and finally the structure and consequences of the factory model of education.

4

The idea that individual intelligence is relatively fixed and unchangeable shackles our understanding of human abilities to the demands of industrial societies. Such ideas have been used throughout the twentieth century in both capitalist and state socialist societies to support the early selection of educational talent, which has consistently operated to the advantage of the socially privileged. In the factory model of education a way needed to be found of identifying and grading its inputs; IQ tests provided just such a mechanism – a single score which summarized the potential range of an individual's achievements. Such a test was quick to administer and offered a simple way of communicating the results.

It is significant that the original IQ test developed by Binet was never intended to 'fix' individuals' intelligence in this way. Indeed he saw the test as a means of establishing a benchmark for future progress. In other words, the IQ test was rather like having a physical fitness exam before being given a conditioning programme. However when Binet's concept of the IQ test was translated into English it came to be interpreted quite differently. It was assumed that the test could be used as a way of *predicting* an individual's intellectual capability and subsequent occupational level.[19]

In 1923 the American psychologist Lewis Terman asserted that there was indeed a good match between the spread of job opportunities and the pool of talent. It was argued that these tests not only had the power to predict future intellectual potential but also served as a measure of an individual's suitability to succeed in different sorts of jobs:

> preliminary investigations indicate that an IQ below 70 rarely permits anything better than unskilled labor: that the range from 70 to 80 is pre-eminently that of semi-skilled labor, from that of 80 to 100 that of the skilled or ordinary clerical labor, from 100 to 110 or 115 that of the semi-professional pursuits; and that above all these are the grades of intelligence which *permit* one to enter the professions or the larger fields of business... This information will be of great value in planning the education of a particular child and also in planning the differentiated curriculum here recommended.[20]

A similar view was taken by the English psychologist Cyril Burt in his 1943 paper 'Ability and income', in which he argued that measured ability could be used to predict subsequent income. Terman and Burt and the psychometric tradition they represent have been largely discredited and their work revealed as little more than an apology for the interests of the middle classes in the societies from which they came.[21] But the fact that Herrnstein & Murray's *The Bell Curve* can command massive sales in the 1990s suggests that genetic explanations for racial and social inequalities have not lost their appeal in America.[22] Yet while these earlier works had the effect of maintaining the position of the already prosperous and powerful, its potency also stemmed from its use as a 'rational' basis for social selection into a rigid hierarchy of jobs. In other words these ideas about intelligence have been used to justify turning the education system into an 'enormous complicated machine for sorting and ticketing and routing children through life'.[23] The task of education was to sift out those with the best brains and raw talent in order for them to receive an extended period of education while others with less potential could be ejected from the education conveyor belt into the lower reaches of the labour market. In essence, it was administratively convenient to argue that the school's sorting process reflected the distribution of talent and the limits of nature, rather than the limitations of the factory model of work.

Recourse to claims about human nature in this way is not without historical precedent. In Plato's *Republic*, Glaucon tells Socrates of the need for 'just one royal lie' in order to preserve the Republic. Citizens are to be told that

> you are brothers, yet God has framed you differently. Some of you have the power of command, and in the composition of these he has mingled gold, wherefore also they have the greatest honour; others he has made of silver, to be auxiliaries; others again who are to be husbandmen and craftsmen he has composed of brass and iron; and the species will generally be preserved in the children. But as all are of the same original stock, a golden parent will sometimes have a silver son, or a silver parent a golden son.[24]

Once Glaucon had finished his tale he asks Socrates 'is there any possibility of making our citizens believe in it?' Socrates was not hopeful but felt that future generations could be convinced. Some sections of modern day psychology have clearly made a concerted effort to turn this 'royal lie' into a 'scientific truth', and with considerable success. Despite the lack of scientific credibility of this view of intelligence, its legacy has been to create a deeply embedded cultural myth which continues to shape our views about human capabilities in the twenty first century. This is a problem we will address at some length in chapter thirteen.

The view of intelligence advanced by Terman and Burt was not limited to judgements about when studies should be terminated for different ability groups, but it also offered a powerful justification for the segregation of students and curriculum within the classroom. 'Intelligent' people, it was believed, should be encouraged to follow a different curriculum from the masses who were thought incapable of benefiting from an academic education. It was assumed that brighter students would take subjects such as physical science, mathematics and foreign languages which were deemed more difficult and demanding. Less 'intelligent' people would take the less demanding subjects such as home economics, office practice or woodwork. It was further assumed that proficiency in the 'difficult' subjects reflected a more general ability to engage successfully in professional and managerial work so that restricting entry to the prestigious and highly paid jobs to those with high credentials was a rational process.[25] We can depict this model as shown in figure 5.1

High IQ	→	Academic subjects	→	High credentials	→	Professional/ managerial jobs
Low IQ	→	Practical subjects	→	Low credentials	→	Semi/unskilled jobs/ unemployment

Figure 5.1   Factory model of education

With all the elegant simplicity of the factory model, it was argued that modern intelligence tests made it possible to identify different kinds of mind which would need to be nourished with different kinds of activities leading to different examination routes and positions in the market for jobs. Or, as the report which shaped the 1944 Education Act in England and Wales expressed it, 'In a wise economy of secondary education pupils of a particular type of mind would receive the training best suited for them and that training would lead them to an occupation where their capacities would be suitably used'.[26] This social fit between innate ability, education and jobs offered a way of justifying social inequalities and rationalizing the failure of the majority of students.[27]

5

If IQ tests came to determine the way individuals were to be 'processed' as inputs into the education system, credentials have come to symbolize the quality of the output. These academic 'badges of ability' are the counterpart to the IQ score in the job market. They provide a simple summary score of an extraordinarily complex set of cognitive and social processes. Like the IQ score, the gaining of a credential is often based on the outcome of a single examination performance, hence it is relatively quick to administer and straightforward for employers to understand. As private companies and public services expanded on the factory model of efficiency, they also rationalized their recruitment practices in the hope that they were recruiting those with the necessary knowledge, skills and personal characteristics for the efficient fulfilment of job requirements. This led employers to place a greater emphasis on academic performance because it was seen to offer an objective measure of an individual's abilities and motivation to succeed, although the latter was not always something which employers had high on their shopping list in the recruitment hall. The problem was that those with the best academic records typically came from advantaged backgrounds – the wealthy and the professional middle classes.

Inequalities of educational opportunity were exacerbated by what Ronald Dore diagnosed as the 'diploma disease'.[28] For while education was being expanded and reorganized to give more students access to the same paper qualification, these qualifications were being used by employers and professional groups including doctors, lawyers and chartered engineers as a way of restricting access. As the supply of educated labour increased, so employers demanded higher levels of credentials. This led Randell Collins to argue that although a significant proportion of jobs in the U.S. were upgraded in terms of their entry requirements, this was often the result of inflationary pressures rather than a reflection of changes in the demand for technical knowledge.[29] This over-supply of qualified candidates inevitably led to what Fred Hirsch observed as an 'intensification of job screening that has the effect of lengthening the obstacle course of education and favouring those best able to sustain a longer or more costly race. These are the well off and the well connected'.[30] Hirsch could have added gender and race to the important factors that influence who wins and who loses. Sexism or racism have led women and students of colour to lose out in the competition for high school grades in many subject areas and in the selection for jobs.

There has also been some doubt cast on the value of credentials to employers. It has been persuasively argued that in the 1950s and 1960s there was little connection between the diplomas held by new recruits and their contribution to the organization in terms of productivity. In Ivar Berg's *The Great Training Robbery* it was shown that there was no necessary connection between engaging in a complex cognitive job such as that done by air traffic controllers and their level of formal education. And even more damaging was Berg's finding, which he and others have subsequently confirmed, that there was considerable under-utilization of educated labour in the workplace based on the factory model of efficiency.[31]

For most middle-class parents however, the intrinsic qualities of work were secondary to the task of arming their offspring with the appropriate badges of ability to be exchanged in the market for jobs. As the middle class expanded fewer families could maintain their social standing through direct inheritance; they therefore became dependent on education as a way of transmitting 'cultural capital' to their children in the hope that they would succeed at school. Academic qualifications had become an insurance policy against downward social mobility, but the widespread use of meritocratic rules of entry meant that there was no cast iron guarantee that children from white-collar backgrounds would get white-collar jobs. Equally, as credentials became an important currency of exchange in the labour market, the 'certificate' was seen by a large number of students and their parents as more important than what was taught or learnt. This proved to be self-defeating because as more people started to playing the same game it led to a decline in the exchange value of qualifications.

So far we have argued that the factory model of education produced a standard 'product' that was ranked in terms of academic grades. In both the case of the IQ test score and the credential, judgements were made about individuals which were apparently impersonal – the bureaucratic hallmark of the treatment of individuals. By what processes were IQ test scores converted into credentials? It is time to look at the structure and some of the consequences of schooling in the Golden era.

6

Max Weber argued that the administrative power of bureaucracy has at least two sources. The first concerns the role of technical knowledge which has been alluded to in earlier chapters, the second source of power stems from learning the disciplined behaviour that conforms to the rules of bureaucratic routine.[32] When we look at the conduct of education in the third quarter of the twentieth century we see that these two principles continued to exert a powerful influence. We also see that learning the appropriate forms of disciplined behaviour as well as acquiring textbook knowledge was part and parcel of grabbing one's opportunities. Academic qualifications, for instance, convey information about the individual's ability and motivation to jump through the appropriate examination hoops, to follow a course of study and to regurgitate the key points under examination conditions, to recognize and defer to the authority of teachers and professors.[33] Knowledge was acquired in pre-packaged chunks called 'subjects' and delivered in pre-arranged slots called 'lessons'. In this way knowledge and discipline were fused into an indivisible set of rules, rituals, and procedures governed by that masterplan – the timetable. This in turn was subordinated to the demands of the examiner's syllabus.

Students were often willing with various degrees of enthusiasm to undergo this induction process partly because it was compulsory, but mainly due to the exchange of student compliance for knowledge which could be converted into credentials to be traded in the market for jobs. It was no easy task to obtain student compliance when the system was designed to confer success on a minority. However, despite resistance to school, especially by those defined as failures, the system avoided serious conflagration. The most celebrated study of male working-class resistance to education was conducted by Paul Willis in a disadvantaged industrial city in England. What is striking about Willis' study is that there was little evidence that 'the lads' posed much of a threat to society although they were a major pain in the neck for those responsible for teaching them. The main response to school was that much of it was seen as a waste of time and irrelevant to their future job prospects. As Joey, a leading figure in the study put it when asked about the possibility of returning to education when he had quickly discovered the realities of unskilled work: 'I don't know, the only thing I'm interested in is fucking as many women as I can if you really wanna know'.[34]

Education maintains its power over the minds, if not the hearts, of students through a series of myths, routines and inducements. The myths about intelligence and ideologies of professional competence create an appropriate climate of awe and mystification. The book that has most clearly captured the subjective impact of these myths of meritocratic competition in the United States is again *The Hidden Injuries of Class*. Sennett and Cobb argue that the key notion legitimizing inequalities in Western societies is the idea of individual ability. They suggest that because qualifications are commonly seen to reflect individual ability, they represent a badge of individual worth which, in turn, creates an image of an elitist society in which a few individuals stand out from the masses. Due to the fact that successful academic performance is the passport to upward social mobility, it provides a personal sense of dignity and self-worth which is reinforced by teachers in an attempt to maintain pupil compliance. The political and moral effect of this ideology is that it perpetuates the inequalities of the world of nineteenth-century capitalism on new terrain for 'just as the material penalties of the old capitalism fell hardest on the workers, despite the fact that both rich and poor might be alienated by the work, so now the moral burdens and the emotional hardships of class are the thorniest and most concentrated among manual labourers'.[35]

They illustrated this claim through a series of interviews with working-class men. The complex way in which the interviewees responded to their exclusion from the club of badge-holders offers an insight into the way compliance was gained and inequalities were legitimated. They described Frank Rissarro's (one of their interviewees) attitudes to the educated in the following terms:

Educated men can control themselves and stand out from the mass of people ruled by passions at the bottom of society; the badge of ability earns the educated dignity in Rissarro's eyes. Yet the content of their power – their ability considered in essence rather than in relation to his personal background and memories – this he finds a sham, and repugnant. Still, the power of the educated to judge him, and more generally, to rule, this he does not dispute. He accepts as legitimate what he believes is undignified in itself, and in accepting the power of educated people *he* feels more inadequate, vulnerable and undignified.[36]

The failure generated by the factory model of education involved more than individual costs in accepting the 'middle class measuring rod' of achievement and then failing to achieve enough badges of ability to maintain a sense of personal dignity. The way meritocratic competition was organized gave education a deeper cultural significance. Achievement demanded cultural assimilation into a white, male, middle-class world view which ignored diversity, pluralism and the rich historical traditions which characterized the multiculturalism of America. In learning to be American or British, ethnic minorities were assessed in terms of how successfully they had managed to rid themselves of the linguistic, cultural, religious and dress codes which their parents or grandparents had brought with them to the United States or Britain. The fight for a voice and dignity among African Americans in recent times is a response to the problem of 'invisibility' and 'namelessness' which resulted from colonization, and is reinforced by these assimilationist policies in the factory era. Although equality of opportunity in the shape of meritocratic competition was supposed to release the talents of disadvantaged students, the demands imposed upon education to perform the role of socializing and selecting students for their future adult roles made the squandering of talent inevitable.

And what of those who were successful: to what extent did they come to appreciate that meritocratic competition inevitably involved a majority losing in order for them to win? There is little doubt that the expansion of educational opportunities did represent a general consensus that all should have a chance to take part in the competition for a livelihood. But the emphasis on individual abilities and efforts encouraged the winners to point to their own innate qualities and moral strengths rather than to their debt to the society which gave them the chance to excel. This was no less true for working-class students 'made good' or for successful African Americans as it was for the sons (and increasingly daughters) of the established white middle class. As Brian Jackson and Dennis Marsden pointed out in their classic 1950s study of working-class students in a northern industrial city in England who gained a middle-class education:

> There is something infinitely pathetic in these former working-class children who lost their roots young, and who now with their rigid middle-class accent preserve 'the stability of all our institutions, temporal and spiritual' by avariciously reading the lives of Top People, or covet the public schools and glancing back at the society from which they came see no more there than 'the dim', or the 'specimens'.[37]

7

Education is always a slice of social history and it clearly shows us how much society had changed in the third quarter of the twentieth century. The prosperity and economic security that parents had fought for was now taken for granted by the children of the new middle class. What is more, the baby boom generation in the 1960s were coming to question the efforts they were being expected to make in order to progress beyond the achievements of their parents. The prospects of a 9 'til 5 white-collar career was seen to be at the price of forgoing the development of one's talents, creativity and individual freedom.

For expanding opportunities involved not only a demonstration of 'ability' but also a willingness to make an effort. After all in Michael Young's formulation it was ability *Plus* effort which equalled merit. This competition placed increasing pressure on middle-class youth to 'defer gratification' in order to win the necessary badges of ability. As Barbara Ehrenreich has noted:

> In the sixties, the pressures on youthful aspirants to the middle class were rising. Graduate degrees were replacing mere college degrees as the ticket to white-collar professional employment. Even the elite colleges were coming to regard themselves less as playgrounds for the children of the rich and more as serious training grounds for future professionals.[38]

Yet at precisely the time the disciplined application of effort was being imposed as a requirement for academic success there was an incipient counter-cultural response among the ranks of the young affluent middle class. Ideas including affluence, consumerism, respectable careers, and bureaucratic discipline which were *de rigueur* to their parents' generation, were now seen to inhibit the qualities of human creativity, freedom and love. In the language of the counter-cultural genre of the time, Jerry Rubin wrote,

> Dad looked at his house and car and manicured lawn, and he was proud. All of his material possessions justified his life.
> He tried to teach his kids: he told us not to do anything that would lead us from the path of Success.
> work don't play
> study don't loaf
> obey don't ask questions
> fit in don't stand out
> be sober don't take drugs
> make money don't make waves
> We are conditioned in self-denial:
> We were taught that fucking was bad because it was
>   immoral . . . We were warned that masturbation caused
>   insanity and pimples.
> And we were confused. We didn't dig why we needed to
>   work toward owning bigger houses? bigger cars? bigger
>   manicured lawns?
> We went crazy. We couldn't hold it back anymore.[39]

The culmination of middle-class resistance to parental values and lifestyles came in the form of student unrest on American campuses in 1968. Although this did not provoke the same sort of threat to the social order as was the case in France, it signalled alarm bells within the professional middle classes. Barbara Ehrenreich once again observes:

> when students challenge the authority of their professors, when they question the validity and relevance of the knowledge from which that authority was said to be derived, they struck at the fundamental assumption of their class. Judged in the context of that class and its interests, they were guilty of treason. They had exposed, in however inarticulate a fashion, the conceit on which middle-class privilege rests: we know more, and are therefore entitled to positions of privilege and authority.[40]

In the same year the assassination of Martin Luther King, Jr. was a stark reminder both of the scale of racial inequalities which remained in America and the crumbling consensus about how to deliver racial justice. The white backlash against what was seen as unfair discrimination in favour of blacks marked the bottom line of 'opportunity'. It also marked the beginning of the end of the Keynesian settlement on which economic nationalism was built.

6
The End of Consensus

Keynes had a solution without a revolution. Our pleasant world could remain; the unemployment and suffering would go. It seemed a miracle.

J. K. Galbraith

1

In previous chapters we have looked at the foundations of economic nationalism. Now we need to see how the state was able to build on these foundations to produce the so called 'golden era'. To do so we need to go back to the close of the Second World War. For it was the lessons learned during the war the enabled consensus about the future direction of the economy and society to be established. At the same time, the way that consensus was built was itself flawed and so carried with it the ultimate destruction of economic nationalism.

In the aftermath of the Second World War scenes of devastation and dislocation were common throughout Europe and Japan. Even worse was the prospect of de-mobbed armies entering the ranks of the unemployed. In the United States alone 10 million service men were ready to be thrown into the labour market without any immediate chance of work. Many feared that further social and economic breakdown was inevitable and that it would be followed by a totalitarianism of the left or right. The communist and fascist regimes had, at least, been able to achieve full employment during the worst depression of the twentieth century. Writing at the War's close George Orwell put his finger on the challenge confronting western democracies. 'Capitalism leads to dole queues, the scramble for markets and war. Collectivism leads to concentration camps, leader worship and war. There is no way out of this unless a planned economy can be somehow combined with the freedom of the intellect'.[1] This view was echoed by a leading economist of the time in the introduction to one of the classic collections of economic papers, 'The authors agree', he wrote, 'well nigh unanimously, that if private enterprise does not provide a high level of employment and a reasonably high standard of living ... Capitalism is doomed'.[2] The most eminent contributor to that collection, Joseph Schumpeter, thought it was doomed. 'The all but general opinion', he declared, 'seems to be that capitalist methods will be unequal to the task of reconstruction'.[3]

The issues confronting the western democracies were as clear as they were dire; produce societies based on full employment and prosperity or face an inevitable slide into barbarism. In facing this challenge western nations had to find, as Orwell had observed, a third way between free market capitalism and totalitarianism. The search for this third way was not without signposts of both a theoretical and practical kind largely due to the experience of the war. *The Economist*, that bellwether of economic fashion, had signalled the direction to be taken a month after the end of hostilities in Europe. With typical *sang froid*, it set out the elements required to meet the objectives of full employment and prosperity:

> It is a matter of the most obvious common sense that in this day and age, the best form of economic organization for a complex industrial country lies somewhere between the extremes of *laisser faire* and bureaucracy, of full control and no control ... There are ... two vital principles of economic action, the adventuring power of the individual and the organising power of the state and if a democratic community is successfully to confront the complex problems of this puzzling age, it will need the maximum assistance that both principles can give.[4]

Keynes, once said that, 'the ideas of economists and political philosophers, both when they are right and when they are wrong, are more powerful than is commonly understood'.[5] He could well have been talking about his own ideas which in one way or another dominated economic thinking about the post-war management of economies. We have shown how Keynes' ideas came to the fore in Britain as a result of the depression of the thirties and by the early fifties had become orthodoxy in most western economies.[6] Throughout the twenties and early thirties Keynes was preoccupied with the problem of economic stability. It was a period of great unrest with a general strike in Britain and increasing violence on the streets in Germany. The United States was plagued by exploitation and a struggle for workers' rights. For Keynes injustice was created by uncertainty and the root of uncertainty was the endemic fluctuations in the business cycles of capitalist economies.[7] These fluctuations created arbitrary shifts in wealth, income and employment. A few lucky individuals gained rewards which may have been unrelated to their talents or efforts while others, through no fault of their own, faced the catastrophe of unemployment. The basis of a just society, for Keynes, was therefore, the certainty that could be achieved by full employment and that, in turn, meant addressing the fundamental problem of the business cycle.[8] The importance of the connection Keynes drew between justice and certainty cannot be exaggerated. In the present climate of uncertainty over jobs, the social and psychological impact of unemployment is often stressed but the idea that certainty in employment is related to social justice is rarely, if ever, recognised. However, the link made by Keynes between the two concepts proved the foundation for the legitimacy of the post-war social order.

The key to Keynes' theory, as we have noted, lies in his break with traditional neo-classical economic thinking, which had assumed that capitalist economies were self-correcting, so that economies which had fallen into slump would 'automatically' bounce back to a period of boom and full employment. Keynes rejected this idea arguing that no such automatic mechanism existed and that economies could remain in a prolonged slump unless governments intervened.

In 1924 Keynes delivered a lecture at Oxford in which he attacked the fundamental assumption that governments had no active role in the life of the economy. 'Let us clear from the ground', he said,

> the metaphysical or general principles upon which from time to time, *laissez-faire* has been founded. It is *not* true that individuals possess a prescriptive 'natural' liberty in their economic activities. There is *no* 'compact' conferring perpetual rights on those who Have or on those who Acquire. The world is *not* so governed from above that private and social interest always coincide...It is not a correct deduction from the Principles of Economics that enlightened self-interest always operates in the public interest. Nor is it true that self-interest generally *is* enlightened.[9]

Keynes believed that his repudiation of *laissez-faire* would prove the death knell of neo-classical economics, thereby opening the way for his own views.

In chapter 2 we explained the ideas at the heart of Keynes' view of state regulation of the economy that governments could profitably intervene to smooth out the boom-bust episodes of the business cycle by manipulating the amount of money people had in their pockets. Taxation was the key instrument for this purpose. By lowering taxes in times of slump, demand for goods and service could be maintained and so, therefore, could full employment. During times of boom, when employers and employees could afford it, the money lost to governments by cutting taxes could be regained by raising taxes. Hence, what is called the aggregate or national demand for goods and services could be manipulated to iron out the business cycle and ensure full employment. Cutting taxes created a multiplier effect throughout the economy in which workers would have more money to buy goods and services providing a twist to a virtuous spiral, in which increased demand sustained employment.

But this multiplier effect only worked because of the unique economic conditions of the time. National economies were isolated by the 'walls' erected around them. These walls were managed exchange rates, trade barriers and other controls on international competition. Managed exchange rates meant that trade in and out of the country could be controlled by governments, as could capital movements. Similarly, trade barriers could protect industries and jobs which were vulnerable to external competition. These 'walls' ensured that when governments raised the overall level of demand, the extra money pumped into the system did not 'leak' out of the country. When taxes were cut governments could be confident that businesses would invest in the national economy and that the money in workers' pockets would largely go into buying home made products. These walls were vital to economic nationalism, especially the controls on capital movements, although just how vital went unrecognized until the French socialist government, in 1981, attempted to apply Keynesian techniques to their economic problems with disastrous consequences; they had failed to recognize that the walls, which had stood for thirty years, had crumbled and that Keynesian fine tuning of the economy no longer worked.

2

Despite the obvious advantages to both citizen and state of full employment 'good ideas do not always win'.[10] The Keynesian revolution was successful because its ideas were consistent with the guiding assumptions of the age and were politically acceptable to both sides of the great divide created by capitalism: employers and workers. If ever there was a theory whose time had come it was Keynes'. His view of the state's role in regulating the economy chimed nicely with the dominant political tune of the time; for capitalists and workers he created a 'win win' scenario. Set against the expectation, held by many at the end of the war, that the coupling of democracy and capitalism had had its day, Keynes threw both a lifeline and earned the reputation of being the mechanic who kept capitalism on the road.

As the mechanic of capitalism, he had found the tools and techniques for turning the right of full employment into a reality. The instrument for applying his theory was the state and its servants, economic experts. The idea of state intervention was well accepted, as *The Economist* leader showed. And, the idea of the economic expert piloting the ship of state exploited the popular faith in science. Just as the belief in science had dominated the organisation of work through the ideas of Frederick Taylor so now the faith was invested in governments and the economic experts who guided them.

The combination of the promise of full employment and the expertise to deliver it, gave the state the potential for maintaining in peace time much of the power that it had accrued during the war. In essence the legitimacy of the state rested on the promise of full employment. This promise transformed the relationship between the citizen and the nation. In the past, being a citizen of a state was rather like being bought a lotto ticket at birth: it entitled the holder, typically a man, to have the opportunity to win a job or in a few cases to hit the jackpot and become wealthy. Keynes took the risk element out of gaining a job. In doing so he enabled the extension of citizens' rights to the right to work. To Keynes this was a matter of social justice as it was to the working classes who were most at risk of unemployment. But it was also a key principle of social integration. As an eminent contemporary sociologist of Keynes, T. H. Marshall, put it, 'A man who has lost his job has lost his passport to society'.[11] Marshall's insight, now well established, came from interviews with unemployed workers during the depression. It was clear from these interviews that unemployment dissolved the partnership between the citizen and the nation-state, and substituted the law of the jungle. As an unemployed electrician turned burglar put it

> When I look back over the last five years I feel I am in some way justified in hitting back at society...I feel I belong to a race apart and wonder what the end is going to be...I have plenty of good food, clothing and shelter, and strange though it seems I feel I am *some-*

body, and I certainly never felt that during my two years of honest idleness.[12]

The fact that virtually all those who wanted work could gain it during the Golden era meant that men as workers and as family wage earners were all passport holders. In turn this created the basis of goodwill for the further extension of rights to free health, education and welfare, at least in Britain.

The redefinition of citizenship under economic nationalism was based on the consensus achieved between the state, capitalists and workers, and it is in the compromise between them that the 'miracle' of Keynesian economics, as J. K. Galbraith put it, lay. The cornerstone of consensus was the ability of demand management to deliver full employment while leaving capitalists to pursue the freedom to make profit and trade unionists to wrest as much of the profit for workers' wages as they could.

Trade unions on both sides of the Atlantic, having gained considerable power during the War, saw full employment as a way of maintaining their power without compromising their freedom. Their reasoning here is not quite as obvious as it seems. Until the advent of Keynesianism it was thought that the only way of sustaining full employment was through a process of state control of the allocation of labour; the primary vehicle for this was the nationalization of industry. At the end of the War, this remained a principal aim of the Labour party in Britain, although it threatened the power of unions to engage in free collective bargaining with employers. After all, in the Soviet Union, where all industries were effectively nationalized, trade unions were little more than puppets of the state. Keynsian policies delivered the best of all worlds to western trade unions. For it was not merely that Keynesian policies maintained the traditional freedoms of the trade unions, or established full employment, as a right, it was also instrumental in delivering high wages to unskilled workers. The walls that economic nationalism erected meant that workers in Detroit or Dagenham were insulated from competition from low wage economies. Unskilled workers' wages were determined, therefore, solely by the balance of industrial power and the interests of national corporations, trade unions and the state. In the 1950s the threat that corporations would locate overseas where labour was cheaper unless the trade unions fell into line was almost unimaginable. As a result unions thrived, growing in power throughout the post-war period. In the United States, 10 per cent of American labour was unionised in the inter-war period, between 1945 and 1960 it rose to 27 per cent. In Britain the corresponding figures were 29 and 44 per cent.[13] It was a power nurtured and sustained by the semi-skilled and unskilled manufacturing workforce. At the height of economic nationalism, 37 per cent of British workers were employed in manufacturing compared with 24 per cent of Americans:[14] figures which bore a close relationship to those for trade union membership. Fordist production techniques brought labour with common work experiences together, in large numbers, under one roof. Not surprisingly, it facilitated union organization and muscle.

For capitalists the situation, initially, appeared different because they feared that the absence of their traditional weapon in the struggle to discipline labour – the threat of unemployment – would fatally weaken their bargaining power. However, they were soon to see that full employment was well suited to Fordist production and market structures. Indeed, it can be argued that without the Fordist mode of production it is unlikely that the Keynesian consensus could have worked.

Within the confines of a walled economy, profit was generated by the economies of scale created through mass production for domestic markets. But mass markets could only be sustained if people had the purchasing power to buy the products churned out by the great leviathans – the national corporations. Under economic nationalism purchasing power always remained high through the commitment to full employment. But there were other reasons why the compromise created by the state suited big business. The Fordist production line needed a docile and predictable labour force since breakdowns or disruption to the line were costly. The certainty of work and ever increasing pay packets provided the conditions for the reliability capital was seeking from its labour force.

If Fordism created the foundation for the compromise between capital and labour it also created the means of delivering and maintaining the consensus. The structure of markets under Fordism was one in which a few companies dominated an industry. Employers could, therefore, agree on a bargaining structure and strategy for the industry. Similarly union bosses, whose own organization came to ape the bureaucracies of the national corporations, could also deliver on agreements struck for the industry and applicable nation-wide. This national, centralized form of wage fixing enabled Keynesian planning because it provided accurate information and a climate of predictability facilitating the fine judgements required for Keynesian regulation. However, the Fordist compromise soon extended beyond the confines of industrial relations. Once the state had thrown its hat into the ring of economic regulation, expectations were raised that it could also deliver on workers' social rights.

3

The pressure for the extension of workers' social rights had begun well before the end of the Second World War. In France a Resistance plan declared grandly that there should in the post-war era be 'a complete plan of social security, designed to secure the means of existence for all French men and women wherever they are incapable of providing such means for themselves by working'.[15] A similar sentiment was expressed about the Beveridge Report, published in 1942, which laid the post-war foundations for the British welfare state:

> the Beveridge Report was the inauguration of a new relation within the state to man, and of man to the state, not only in this country but, throughout the world. The ethic of the universal brotherhood of man was here enshrined in a plan to be carried out by every individual member of the community on his own behalf and on behalf of his fellows.[16]

In the United States, ambitions for a comprehensive welfare state were also entertained. Franklin Roosevelt's National Resource Planning Board submitted a blue print for a comprehensive welfare state, *Security, Work and Relief Policies*, three days before the bombing of Pearl Harbour. The idea of a welfare state which supported individuals, in times of need, from the cradle to the grave, was much in the air. The application of these ideas clearly has to do with the experience of war. The war, as we have seen, strengthened the hand of labour movements and the left. In Britain, the trade union movement achieved a parity of respect with employers in the eyes of government,[17] while in Europe, the lead taken by Communist and Socialist resistance movements, meant that the fate of workers was at least one step removed from the caprice of a market economy. In America, a labour movement, strengthened by the War, entered a tripartite agreement on union membership and wage controls with employers and the government which appeared to offer it a position of potential power similar to that of its counterparts in Britain. Labour became a partner, in a formal institutional sense, in the governance of nations for the first time. This gave it the credibility as well as the industrial muscle to support proposals for the development of the peacetime welfare state.

The increasing influence of labour movements on the governance of nations explains the power which forced open the door to greater welfare expenditure but it doesn't explain how the idea of a welfare state was translated into popular sentiment. For this we need to turn to the ideas of of the celebrated social welfare theorist Richard Titmuss. Taking his lead from Weber's dictum that, 'the discipline of the army gives birth to all discipline', he argued that the burdens of modern warfare, which affected civilians and the military alike, imposed a discipline on society which was only tolerable if there were no great inequalities. The more civilians were involved in the war effort, he suggested, the greater the equalizing effects achieved.[18] The relationships between equality, discipline and social cohesion were vital to the success of the post-war period just as they have been to the success of the Asian Tiger economies today. The disciplines imposed by bureaucracy and Fordist work structures, of high marginal rates of progressive taxation and the acknowledgement of government as the legitimate and primary source of power provided the springboard for the social cohesion expressed in the welfare state.

The initial impetus of war was carried through in peacetime on the back of full employment. Once the commitment to full employment had been established unions could trade-off the guarantee of industrial peace against greater state delivery of social rights. As the wealth of nations grew so did expectations of what constituted a fair social wage. Hence state expenditure on housing, health, education, pensions and various forms of unemployment and social benefits all increased in western societies. In Britain total social expenditure rose between 1950 and 1974 from approximately 14.5 per cent to 25 per cent of GDP. Roughly half of the additional purchasing power of the nation went on public services. In the United States public expenditure on social welfare more than doubled from approximately 8 per cent of GDP in 1950 to 18.7 per cent in 1975.[19]

While social expenditure rose spectacularly during this period the rationale for the development of social welfare, the methods used for its delivery and the level of public expenditure differed markedly within different western societies. What forged the shape of the different types of welfare states to emerge in the post-war period were national responses to two problems: how to determine who the deserving and undeserving among potential recipients of welfare were; and how to handle the problem of a burgeoning middle class. The resolution of these problems was, of course, a matter of political struggle and compromise. In this sense the determination of need is always filtered through the lens of political struggle. Political struggle presupposes political actors. Who those actors are and how they are chosen is itself significant in deciding what constitutes need. In the case of the post-war welfare it was clear that men grouped in trade unions and political parties were the key actors. Women, it was assumed, would largely be recipients of welfare expenditure by proxy.[20] The cornerstone of full employment policies was the male breadwinner, therefore it was inevitable that welfare provision should be shaped around men as the source of family income. Beveridge clearly took the view that a woman's place was in the home and that the role of mothers was, as he put it, was 'to ensure the adequate continuation of the British race and British ideals in the world'.[21] Not surprisingly the centre-piece of his welfare state was a social insurance policy which was to be paid for by men on the basis of regular employment.

Who constituted the deserving rather than the undeserving recipients of welfare also differed according to national political traditions. Theda Skocpol makes the point that Americans draw a sharp distinction between welfare and social security. Those on welfare, the unemployed for example, are, effectively, the undeserving poor while those drawing social security – old age pensioners – are the deserving poor. She traces this distinction back to the failure of the New Deal to develop a comprehensive basis for a welfare state. It was a tradition that even the Second World War could not surmount and she noted how the ambitious *Security, Work and Relief Policies* report amounted in practice to little more than minor changes in social policy. The most significant outcome of the war years for social policy in America proved to be a continuation of the distinction between the deserving and the undeserving. In this case it was the veterans who constituted the deserving and they received a comprehensive set of benefits in the GI Bill.[22]

In contrast, Beveridge made less of a distinction between the deserving and undeserving poor. The welfare state in Britain in the post-war period was based on the idea of universal benefits. Education and health were to be free and available to all. Pensions, sickness and unemployment benefits were covered by a system of social insurance to be paid for by contributions from employees, employers and the state. Social insurance was set at a flat rate for all and at a relatively low level of benefit. For those that fell through this net there were means tested National Assistance benefits. The key question in the British context is why universal benefits were available, especially in the areas covered by social insurance. It seems reasonable to suppose that benefits should vary according to an individual's ability to pay. Why, for example, should a lawyer receive the same social insurance benefit as a garbage collector? The answer turns on the crucial political role played by the middle class in the development of the welfare state.

The dilemma posed by the middle class for the architects of a comprehensive welfare state was this: if the aim was to provide support for the most needy how was the money to be raised from an increasingly affluent middle class? And how was their loyalty to the ideals of the welfare state to be maintained when, in theory, they would pay disproportionately more for benefits than they were likely to call on during their working lives? Trade unions could put the welfare state on the agenda and the sentiments carried over from war could take it so far but in the end the same question recurs – what's in it for the middle class?

There were (and remain) four possible responses to this question. The first is to make benefits universal thereby providing the same value of benefits to all citizens irrespective of their income and financial position. This has the merit of inclusiveness, it treats everyone equally because they are citizens and it effectively forges an alliance between the middle and working class because, with universal benefits, both have an interest in well provisioned welfare services. This solution does however mean that income inequalities remain. The second solution is to provide different kinds of welfare benefits to the middle and working class, in accordance with their status and expectations. This keeps both wedded to the idea of a welfare state but again maintains inequalities between the classes. The third solution is to provide some minimal benefit to all but allow the middle class to top up their provision through private schemes. The final solution is to provide targeted benefits to those in dire need and allow the rest to opt for private benefit cover. Clearly the level at which benefits are set is a significant factor in these 'solutions'. Universal benefits designed to be inclusive of all citizens have to be of Scandinavian proportions to be generous enough to ensure the middle class do not seek to opt out of the state system or 'top up' their benefits through private schemes.[23]

Yet, even a welfare state with low benefit levels such as that devised by Beverage could advantage the middle classes. Peter Baldwin notes that it was calculated that the middle class were expected to pay in contributions twice what they collected in social insurance benefits in the first year of its operation and subsidize unemployment and industrial disability coverage. In reality, the middle class received back in benefits approximately half as much again as they paid in premiums, within the first year.[24]

The link between middle-class interest and welfare-state expenditure provides part of an explanation for one of the enduring puzzles of the post-war period: why welfare expenditure continued to rise under right wing governments, in theory opposed to the idea of a developed welfare state. In Britain, despite the power of the trade union movement the Tories held office for seventeen of the thirty years between 1945 and 1975. But middle-class interest is only half of the story. America, where Republicans and Democrats were equally implicated in perpetuating the rise of post-war welfare expenditure, throws the other half of the story into sharp relief.

In the United States, labour organizations and the Federal government pushed for various welfare schemes to be delivered privately through deals between employees and corporations rather than by the state. By the 1970s more than a quarter of welfare expenditure was delivered by non-public institutions and continued to rise rapidly throughout the seventies.[25] Politically, this strengthened loyalty to the private sector and especially to the national corporations which dominated it. But of course, private welfare was crucially dependent on the idea of a job for life. In the fifties and sixties this was a realistic assumption to make but, as we shall see, it becomes far more problematic from the eighties onward as companies downsized and white-collar workers became 'surplus employees'. Politically, the emphasis on private welfare meant that the American middle class of the post-war period had little direct political interest in state delivered welfare. There the link between rises in welfare expenditure and political interest developed out of the governments' realisation that once they held the levers of macroeconomic policy it quickly became apparent that they had the power to bribe electorates.

Governments on both sides of the Atlantic soon understood the potency of the 'feel good' factor that reduced taxes or increased benefits could induce. In the United States nearly all improvements in social benefits, from the mid-sixties, coincided with congressional or presidential elections.[26] Richard Nixon doubtless saw political advantage when he declared himself a Keynesian. In Britain, the Conservative government realized even more quickly that if it could engineer a boom to coincide with the election, the chances of re-election would increase significantly. It first massaged a boom in the 1955 Budget and went on to use the technique to win three successive electoral victories through what one commentator has called the exquisite timing of the political business cycle.[27] The net result was that welfare expenditure rose dramatically in both nations, as indeed it did throughout western Europe. In the Organisation of Economic Cooperation and Development (OECD), social expenditure more than doubled relative to GDP between 1965 and 1981. In the United States social expenditure as a proportion of GDP rose from 9.9 per cent in 1960 to 18 per cent in 1980. In Britain, it rose from 15.4 per cent to 25 per cent in the same period.[28]

The increase in social expenditure created greater employment opportunities for middle-class professionals, teachers, social and health workers. In Britain in 1961, 15 per cent of the workforce was employed in public sector employment, by 1981 that had increased to 22 per cent. In the same period the United States also increased the percentage of public sector workers, averaging 16 per cent of the workforce.[29] In so far as these workers owed their employment directly to state social expenditure there was a clear electoral bias toward maintaining if not improving social spending.

In essence the development of welfare states reflected a social order established on the basis of a settlement between the state, big business and workers. The combined logic of democratic politics and the Keynes-inspired management of the economy provided a springboard for the extension of social citizenship rights reinforcing the security and justice delivered through full employment. The welfare state achieved some of the high points in western civilisation. At no time before or since has poverty been reduced to such low levels while at the same time opportunities for upward social mobility were increasingly opened through state-provided education.

But as we have seen this was helped by the discipline imposed by a factory model which created fixed roles and identities for individuals both at work and in the home. The structure was hierarchical and male dominated. The welfare needs of women and their dependants were determined by men and delivered to them through the agency of men. It was, alas, those who earned the family wage who were the cornerstone of this system of welfare. It was they who paid the national insurance contributions in Britain and signed up for the family wage in the United States. The social cohesion built around patriarchal relations also turned a blind eye to ethnic differences. The great engines of prosperity, the national corporations, had sucked in the refugees of slavery in America and colonialism in Europe. Just as the identities and needs of women were mediated and determined by men so white people did the same to ethnic minorities and first peoples.[30] It was assumed that if ethnic minorities and first peoples were assimilated by becoming honorary white folk the problems of ethnicity would be solved by the principles of social justice and progress that economic nationalism delivered. In effect meritocratic competition was expected to deliver equality by treating everyone according to their merits but this inevitably led to unequal outcomes because not all ethnic groups began from the same starting point in terms of work and educational opportunities. The great trick of economic nationalism was that it rendered invisible and so marginalized the needs of those groups not officially recognized as citizens with legitimate needs and demands because of their gender or ethnicity. It was not that they were deserving or undeserving of welfare support, they simply went unrecognized. While the great issues relating to cultural, ethnic and gender identities were to surface in the seventies, the achievements of economic nationalism should not be forgotten. Within its own terms, the social cohesion of the post-war years produced the most egalitarian societies in history. Income differentials between rich and poor narrowed due to the high wages paid to the unskilled and, by today's standards, steeply progressive income tax rates, especially for the rich. In the United States the pre-tax share of income of the bottom 20 per cent in 1947 was 5 per cent while the top 20 per cent took 43 per cent of income. By 1979 when the slide towards greater inequality had just begun the figures were 5.2 and 41.7 per cent. But when redistribution through taxation is taken into account there was an even greater trend toward equality. In 1949, the poorest 20 per cent received 5.8 per cent of income and the richest 39.3 per cent. By 1979 the share for the poorest 20 per cent had increased to 8.7 per cent while that of the richest had decreased to 34 per cent.[31] That the willingness to pay high levels of marginal taxation is a reflection of the political culture of the age rather than a function of innate greed or generosity is illustrated by the case of the highly paid in Britain. In 1961, Sir William Lyons, Managing Director of Jaguar cars paid £83,000 of his £100,000 a year in tax while Sir Paul Chambers, head of ICI paid £39,000 of his salary of £50,000 in tax.[32] Once the structures of reward and redistribution had been set, the key to maintaining an egalitarian policy in income distribution lay in ensuring that the benefits of growth were equally distributed. Between 1947 and 1973 in the United States real income grew for the bottom 20 per cent at a slightly higher level than the top 20 per cent (both saw a rise in income of 25 per cent) while those in the middle found their income growing at a marginally higher rate.[33] In general, these figures gave people a sense of national prosperity and progress. What has been forgotten is that economic nationalism had delivered a third way between the tyrannies of the free-market and totalitarianism. Civilization had won out against barbarism.

4

In Part I of this book we have shown that the Keynesian settlement was based on the ability of the three major players – the state, trade unions and employers – to overcome fundamental weaknesses built into the very fabric of the compromise itself. Michael Kalecki, Keynes' contemporary first put his finger on one aspect of this 'fault line' when he warned that employers would not put up with full employment for long because it gave workers too much power to push up wages and, it could be added, with the establishment of the welfare state, the cost of a family wage. The result would be the erosion of profits and inflation. For manufacturers it would trigger the search for cheaper methods of production, either through further mechanisation or by locating production in areas of cheap labour.

If economic nationalism threatened to undermine capitalism by giving unions too much power, it removed some of the competitive pressures which led manufacturers to increase efficiency. The compromise between employers and workers shielded manufacturers from intense competition by guaranteeing mass markets for their goods, precisely because full employment ensured that workers had money in their pockets to spend. It also afforded manufacturers protection from global competition through the walls erected by tariff barriers and restrictions on the movements of capital. Taken together these factors meant that manufacturers did not conceive it urgent to innovate. Indeed, the entire Fordist and bureaucratic structure of production meant that rapid innovation was well nigh impossible. In this sense the factory model of production fitted economic nationalism like a glove, giving rise to the view that the welfare state was an historical 'necessity' because without it the factory model would have died in its infancy.[34]

The symptoms indicating the fault lines in economic nationalism showed up in two ways. The first, was that from the early sixties onward, each boom increased the ratio of the family wage to the private wage.[35] This could be through an increase in social welfare expenditure and, in America, through rising corporate expenditure on employee benefits.[36] In part, the increase in the family wage was used as a strategy to governments to buy off the inflationary pressures trade unions could exert. So instead of agreeing to higher wages, governments offered better social protection. But, ultimately, it had to be paid for through taxes and this triggered tax revolts. From the mid-sixties the average and marginal tax burdens rose to pay for the increases in the family wage. In the United States, marginal tax for a one earner family with two children rose 13 to 24 per cent.[37]

The threat of inflation and rising budget deficits to pay for increased social costs were given a further twist by the oil shocks of 1973. In that year the oil producing and exporting countries (OPEC) wrested control of the pricing and distribution of oil from American hands. This led to a substantial increase in the price of oil. Since the entire western economic system relied on oil the impact of a rapid rise in oil prices led to an inflationary spiral in western economies which hastened the breakdown of the Keynesian consensus. It would be a mistake, though, to see the oil shock as the key which unlocked the Golden era. The collapse of the settlement also lay in the failure of democracy.

The conventional wisdom of the late seventies and eighties had it that economic nationalism was destroyed by greed of one kind or another. For example, in perhaps the finest paper in this vein, Robert Skidelsky argued that the source of the dissolution of the Keynesian welfare state lay in Keynes's faith in the economic expert and the virtue of politicians. The Keynesian policy advisor would exercise the wisdom of his or her craft in recommending appropriate policy adjustments and the politician would carry them out. The question of whether the disinterested policy advisor could ever exist was never fully tested because the virtue of politicians was rapidly tried and found wanting.[38] Once political parties understood the power they had to jack up the 'feel good' factor by priming the economy in time for elections, the basis for rational Keynesian intervention in the economy was severely compromised. The net effect was that rather than producing counter cyclical policies which evened out the business cycle, governments generated debt as they lowered taxes or refused to raise them in the face of electoral pressure and often found themselves operating short term stop–go policies used to slow down the economy when it was overheating and inflation threatened. Incomes policies were a key weapon in the stop–go strategy but they were less than effective because they relied on short term agreements with trade unions, frequently broken by political expediency, rather than long term economic strategy.

In Skidelsky's right-wing account of the breakdown of economic nationalism, unions rank alongside governments as the greed-driven culprits. But government perfidy and union self-seeking was painted on a much wider canvass of the collapse of moral authority underpinning western capitalist societies or in the terms we have used – prosperity, security and opportunity. Interestingly, conservative and Marxist accounts of the breakdown of the welfare state join forces at this point. For Marx, quoted by Skidelsky, had long prophesied the collapse of capitalism as it undermined the social glue, the authority structure, which held it together. In a world in which we seem to be edging ever closer to a war of everyone against everyone else Marx's words are powerfully resonant:

The bourgeoisie wherever it has got the upper hand, has put an end to all feudal, patriarchal idyllic relations. It has pitilessly torn asunder the motley feudal ties that bound man to his 'natural superiors' and has left remaining no other nexus between man and man than naked self-interest, than callous 'cash payment'. It has drowned the most heavenly ecstasies of religious fervour, of chivalrous enthusiasm, of philistine sentimentalism, in the icy water of egotistical calculation. It has resolved personal worth into exchange value and... has set up that single, unconscionable freedom – free trade.[39]

Skidelsky is right to follow Marx in seeing the market as having the potential to strip away all but the cash nexus as the source of meaning and value, but wrong in tracing the failure of Keynesian solutions to the decline of pre-capitalist mores. The source of the decline of moral authority was rooted in the relationship between democracy, bureaucracy, and the individual under economic nationalism.

Under economic nationalism, political and economic power lay in the hands of the institutions of the state, employer groups and trade unions. The compromise they forged under the aegis of Keynesian economic regulation meant that there was no ideological debate between them. Governments of whatever stripe could come and go and it made little difference to the policies enacted. At the time it was claimed that 'the end of ideology' had arrived because the basic framework for delivering prosperity, security and opportunity had been discovered.[40] But this apparent end to ideological conflict created a paradox. The commitment to full employment and the welfare state had extended political citizenship rights to cover social and economic citizenship. In a sense the rights of citizenship both forged and symbolised the strength of the nation state. Democracy, however, suffered. 'The end of ideology' meant that citizens had little to debate or become intellectually involved in. The great schism between communism and fascism which had threatened the western world and which had created so much political fervour, debate and sacrifice now receded to a distant spectre in the internal politics of nations. Moreover, the problems that economic nationalism did generate were deemed to the provenance of experts.[41]

The social distance between the provision of democracy and people's everyday lives was accentuated by the activities of trade unions and employer groups who, in representing their various constituents' political interests, acted as intermediaries between individuals and the state. These intermediate organizations were hierarchical and distant from members which contributed to the well documented feeling, amongst the electorate, that the political affairs of the nation could well be left to others. In other words, they developed what political scientists at the time termed apathy. The moral authority structure of 'natural superiors' that Marx wrote of was replaced by the hierarchical bureaucratic structures of work and political life, with much the same result. But as the clearly defined roles, rules and rituals or work, leisure and family life became subject to increasing individual choice and negotiation, people were becoming more 'reflexive' about who they were and the kind of society they want to live in. The full potential for reflexive solidarity which would involve a new form of democratic participation is yet to materialise for reasons that will become clear in Part Two.

The nature and distribution of work has played a central role in the politics of capitalism because reward, status and self-identity are intimately related to it. In turn this has generated a sense of political identity which has often been associated with class. For example, the history of class politics has often been read in terms of the erosion of skill created by the factory system. Much of the history of class politics and labour has been understood in this way.[42] At the beginning of this history stands the artisan, representing the aristocracy of labour, and at the end the white-collar worker. It is a history of struggle as artisans attempted to hold onto their craft in the face of the advance of Fordist production techniques. As traditional craft work disappeared to be replaced by the assembly line, and with the growth of bureaucratic work, the relationship between the individual, work and political life changed. The decline of the artisan and the rise of the white-collar worker represented a decline of class politics as the 'hard skills' of the artisan were replaced by issues about the personal qualities of workers. The clearest example of this process is the rise in significance of the educational credential. We have seen how access to jobs and promotion were increasingly determined by educational performance. This gave a modern twist to the cherished Western belief that one's fate in life is determined by individual ability and effort. Once the fate of individuals was seen to be determined by differences in personal attributes rather than by political struggle over the nature of work, individuals came to see their success or failure in terms of their personal make-up rather than due to political and economic forces. The political is reduced to the personal, and class struggle is replaced, as Ralph Dahrendorf has noted, by the personal struggle for upward mobility through education.

In terms of democracy, the reduction of the political to the personal merely added to the perceived 'apathy' of the majority. But once the Keynesian settlement broke down it became something else: the politics of just desert. For if individuals come to believe that their success is entirely of their own making then they will see the misfortune of others as also being of *their* own making, through laziness or stupidity. The politics of just desert easily translates into a distinction between those who are fit to survive and those who are unfit – a Darwinian theory which justifies the greed of the 'fit' at the expense of the 'unfit'.

While economic nationalism remained viable the politics of the 'fit' and 'unfit' was muted because everyone benefited from economic growth. But as it broke down, and the benefits of economic growth were unequally distributed in favour of the rich, a Darwinian politics emerged to dominate the 1980s. In one sense, there is an air of inevitability about this recent passage in western history. The structure of democracy under economic nationalism was such that while it accorded citizenship to individuals it removed the commitment and responsibility of active participation in the affairs of society from them. In turn this was consistent with the decline of class politics and the processes of privatization generated by Fordist and bureaucratic forms of work.

Indeed, it is significant that in America and Britain the post-war settlement was based on economic nationalism rather than a 'social partnership'. Two consequences flow from this distinction. First, as the economic downturn hit Western economies following the first oil shortage in 1973, the compact between the trade unions, employers and government was effectively broken because employers in particular believed that the Keynesian settlement was undermining their ability to compete in new economic circumstances. Economic nationalism was no longer seen as a win win scenario. Secondly, economic nationalism promised rising prosperity to all and participation was largely restricted to that of taking the opportunities derived from meritocratic competition and fulfilling one's role of breadwinner or homemaker. A broader sense of social partnership and social participation in community life was largely absent.

How a system initially built on hierarchy and deference could give way to one which encouraged active political participation in the form of a social partnership is hard to see. Arguably, the spirit of consensus which marked out the Keynesian compromise could only have carried over into the eighties if democracy was redefined in terms of a social partnership, because active democratic participation needs as a precondition, a rough equality between citizens and tolerance of others: it assumes in other words, a commitment to and an engagement with the wider society. But even then, the essential *material* precondition for a democratic participatory politics in the eighties was missing. Prosperity was delivered during the period of economic nationalism through economic growth: as economies grew so the benefits were distributed throughout the population. Income and wealth differentials were certainly reduced but this was a far cry from equality. Therefore, when the West encountered the economic crises of the seventies and early eighties, the polarization of society was almost inevitable because there was no moral basis for consensus. Whether, in the post-war period an equalisation of wealth and income was feasible under capitalism is arguable. What is unequivocal, however, is that since the late 1970s we have witnessed a profound transformation in Western societies which now makes the Golden era appear like an abbreviation in an otherwise Hobbesian condition of endless insecurity where nothing is anyone's for certain in a war of all against all.

Part II   The New Realities

7
The New Global Competition

> The fundamental impulse that sets and keeps the capitalist engine in motion comes from the new consumers' goods, the new methods of production or transportation, the new markets, the new forms of industrial organisation that capitalist enterprise creates... This process of Creative Destruction is the essential fact about capitalism.
>
> Joseph A. Schumpeter

1

The euphoria which followed the dismantling of the Berlin Wall in 1989 led a number of commentators to announce the 'end of history'. Western capitalism had not only assigned communism to the archives of world history, but had also offered a final vindication that a market economy was the only way to deliver prosperity, democracy and social justice.[1] Yet at the very moment Eastern Europe was on the march to capitalism, Western nations were experiencing the full force of Schumpter's 'gale of creative destruction'. For most Americans and Europeans the sudden collapse of the Soviet Union did not confirm a sense of well-being but their anxieties about the basic facts of life. Job insecurity and unemployment were no longer the preserve of low-skilled blue-collar workers, as white-collar managers and professionals found themselves among the ranks of 'surplus employees'. Since the mid-1970s the wages of lower-skilled workers have fallen precipitously behind the rest.[2] The real wages of middle Americans and those below them in the income parade have also fallen over the last twenty years.[3] In the European Community close to 20 million workers are recognised as unemployed and in Britain, the gap between rich and poor is greater than at any time since the late nineteenth century.

A proper understanding of why economic nationalism has declined is needed if we are going to find ways of responding to the challenges we now confront. Is there an inevitable logic to economic globalization which leaves little room to create a fairer and more cohesive society? Has the nation state lost much of its power to intervene in the new global competition? Is Kenichi Ohmae correct in stating that 'The nation-state, which was a powerful engine of wealth creation in its mercantilist phase, has become an equally powerful engine of wealth destruction'?[4] What impact have cultural, social and life-style changes had on the way we live our lives today as opposed to the way these were described in previous chapters? Without having a clear sense of the opportunities and limitations on our ability to improve the quality of life for all, we will continue to be trapped in the paradox of increasing wealth and poverty.

We begin, therefore, with an analysis of the new rules *of eligibility, engagement* and *wealth creation*, which are now defining the global economic game by which individuals, companies and nations must earn a living and make profits in the future. First, there has been a change in the new *rules of eligibility*. This involves the shift to an increasingly borderless economy, where national governments find themselves severely limited in their powers to protect domestic workers and companies from competition from foreign competitors who may be able to make better products, deliver better services or simply to meet consumer demands more cheaply. One way of representing this change is to think about the difference between 'closed' and 'open' competitions run by tennis, golf or athletics clubs. The walled economies of the past were organised like 'closed' events which restricted entry to club members, or in this case to American or British workers. But in the new rules of eligibility large areas of economic activity are 'open' rather that 'closed' to international competition as barriers to trade, foreign exchange and financial services have been lifted. In the region of 70 per cent of everything which is now made in the United States is already subject to competition from foreign-based companies.[5]

This is, of course, not to deny that there was some competition between trading nations and their national champions in what we have called 'walled' economies. Ford and Dupont have had plants in Europe for decades, and companies from around the world have been trying to sell more goods and services than their foreign competitors for the past century. On this issue Peter Drucker makes a helpful distinction between trade in Adam Smith's eighteenth century which was 'complementary': England sold wool to Portugal which it could not produce and Portugal sold wine to England which likewise it could not produce, although this win, win scenario overlooks the impact of colonialism which greatly benefited the colonizers at the expense of the colonized. The entry of the US and Germany into the world economy in the mid nineteenth century brought about a shift to what Drucker calls 'competitive' trade. Both these countries sold chemicals and electrical machinery in competition with one another and bought chemicals and electrical machinery from each other. It was this form of competitive trade which became dominant by 1900 and lasted until the halcyon days of economic nationalism. Drucker then suggests that the emergence of Japan and other non-western trading countries has created what he calls adversarial trade. 'Complementary trade seeks to establish a partnership. Competitive trade aims at creating a customer. Adversarial trade aims at dominating an industry. Complementary trade is a courtship. Competitive trade is fighting a battle. Adversarial trade aims at winning the war by destroying the enemy's army and its capacity to fight'.[6] The idea of the 'open' tournament as a form of adversarial trade makes this all sound too much like macho economics, which is an approach taken by Lester Thurow's in his *Head to Head: The Coming Economic Battle Among Japan, Europe and America*. Others, including the OECD, the International Monetary Fund (IMF) and the International Labour Organisation (ILO), prefer to highlight the mutual benefits of globalisation, but as Richard Freeman suggests, 'losses in pay or employment by those who make products in competition with foreign imports, particularly imported goods from less-developed countries, are the flip side of the much larger benefits that trade brings the nation'.[7]

The creation of a global market for ideas, jobs, goods, services and capital has been made possible both as an outcome of a political project involving free-market protagonists including Ronald Reagan and Margaret Thatcher, which will be examined in the next chapter, and because of the revolution in telecommunications. It is this global wiring which has effectively completed the transformation of national into global capital. City brokers in New York, London, Frankfurt, Tokyo, Singapore and Hong Kong are able to trade in Japanese futures, IBM shares and Euros, twenty-four hours a day, anywhere in the world. The daily flow of foreign exchange stands in the region of 1.5 trillion dollars or some 20 per cent of annual world exports.[8]

The speed of these global transactions has been accompanied by increasing volatility in the markets which are subject to wild fluctuations in the value of currencies, shares and futures. On 'Black Wednesday' in London, the Chancellor of the Exchequer Norman Lamont was to learn all about the power of the financial markets to launch dawn raids on national currencies in the relentless pursuit of profit. By 4 o'clock in the afternoon on the 16 September 1992, the Bank of England had gambled away half its reserves trying to bolster the value of the pound. When they finally gave up the pound had lost nearly 9 per cent of its value and George Soros had made a billion dollars out of the speculation.[9] The events of Black Wednesday pale into insignificance when compared to the market turmoil in Asia towards the end of 1997. Countries including Korea, Thailand, Indonesia and Malaysia all witnessed massive depreciation in the value of their currencies. In Indonesia this not only led to political turmoil, but it was estimated that in early 1998 only 22 of the 282 companies listed on the Jakarta stock exchange were financially viable.[10]

The revolution in information technologies has also led to a massive expansion of global networks and information highways which are capable of communicating everything from sales receipts to research reports and computer pornography. In fact it was estimated that 80 per cent of 'hits' on the Internet were sex-oriented as access to the Internet expanded.[11] But what we are now experiencing is a massive expansion of e-commerce. On-line shopping in America was worth $12 billion dollars in 1999 and is estimated to rise to $41 billion in 2002. Consumers in the America account for about three-quarters of global on-line sales in 1998 but this is expected to decline to a little over half by 2002.[12]

In the early 1990s American researchers were able to send data from California to Massachusetts at a rate of 1,400 pages of text each second. It is now possible for the whole contents of Oxford University's Bodleian library to be transmitted in less than 40 seconds! The launch of Internet 2, which is an umbrella of programmes that will link industry, government and academia, offers even higher-speed services than anything else currently on-line and is now being used by more than 70 universities and research facilities.[13]

The introduction of multimedia which combine sound, text and image is further revolutionizing the way global business is conducted as these digital integrated services are able to operate at high speed and low cost. As Peter Sprague, former chair of National Semiconductor in the US and founder of Wave Systems, which is pioneering metering systems for databases says, 'The internet forces you to be global, you literally don't have a choice'.[14] Technological changes and financial liberalization have also greatly improved the conditions for trade in services, which Pete Richardson from the OECD economics department has found to have grown faster than trade in manufactured goods: 'the overall share of invisibles in world trade has risen from around one-quarter in 1975 to more than one-third in 1993.'[15] What is more, the real cost of international travel dropped by nearly 60 per cent between 1960 and 1988, and during the same period the number of foreigners entering the US on business rose by 2,800 per cent.[16] These trends have led Geoff Mulgan to suggest that:

> Today the world is more like a cacophonous city, connected in a million ways. Continents are criss-crossed with roads and railways, airports and distribution centres. Telephones, computers, faxes, television sets, mobile devices, even electronic tags on consumer goods or clothing, can all be connected together, so that the world sometimes seems like the marketplace of a medieval city, a buzz of messages, letters, newspapers, complaints and requests, small advertisements and bombastic slogans.[17]

The major beneficiaries of financial deregulation and the revolution in information technologies have been the multinational corporations. Since the mid-1970s the multinationals have grown more rapidly than the world economy. In 1975, the fifty largest industrial corporations worldwide had sales of $540 billion and $25 billion in profits. In 1990, sales figures for the top fifty had climbed to $2.1 trillion and their profits had reached $70 billion. In real terms, whereas the US economy was growing at an annual rate of 2.8 per cent (the OECD average was 2.9 per cent), the multinationals annual sales growth was in the region of 3.5 per cent during the period between 1975 and 1990.[18]

The United Nations estimate that there are 37,000 of what they prefer to call Transnational corporations worldwide which operate more than 200,000 foreign affiliates in virtually every country in the world. But one-third of the global stock of foreign direct investment is controlled by the largest 100 corporations.[19] Some of the larger multinationals continue to have sales figures far in excess of the GDP of smaller national economies. But they now wield enormous power in the global economy as the growth of cross-border investment has increased the importance of 'foreign' owned companies to the national economies of all western nations. According to the OECD in the early 1990s foreign-owned companies account for over 30 per cent of manufacturing turnover in Australia, Belgium, Canada and Ireland, 20–30 per cent in Austria,

France, Germany, Portugal and the United Kingdom, and 10–20 per cent in Denmark, Italy, Norway, Sweden, Turkey and the United States. Only Finland and Japan recorded a figure of less than 10 per cent. It was also reported that much of this investment was targeted at the chemical, pharmaceutical, automobile, electronics and computer industries.[20]

The level of Foreign Direct Investment is a useful measure of the extent of the global influence of the multinational. The level of inward investment has been seen in most of the advanced economies as a way of generating new job opportunities. Japanese corporations increased their investment in North America and Europe by 15 per cent a year between 1980 and 1990, which generated employment for half a million workers.[21] In the early 1990s this rate of investment declined, but by 1997 despite domestic economic difficulties FDI in the manufacturing sector reached Y2,282 billion, exceeding its 1989 high of Y2,177 billion.[22]

The United Nations estimate that 73 million people, or 10 per cent of employment in non-agricultural activities, are directly employed by the multinationals worldwide, and at least a further 130 million people have jobs indirectly controlled by these corporations.[23] Foreign direct investment has also been seen as a way of improving national competitiveness through the transfer of technology to local firms and the upgrading of worker skills. Alternatively, the scale of outward investment is seen to represent at least a partial diversion of investment from the domestic economy at the expense of local communities, firms and workers. In 1990 the combined inward stock of the developed countries was over $1,230 billion and the outward stock over $1,602 billion. Australia, Canada, France, Germany, Italy, Japan, the United States and the United Kingdom all have a stock of inward and outward FDI of over $100 billion. But it was the United States and United Kingdom who attracted the largest amount of inward investment with $404 billion and $206 billion, respectively. However, both nations had an even greater flow of outward investment, in the United States this amounted to a deficit of $38 billion and in Britain $19 billion. The scale of influence which the multinationals exert over the developed economies can also be judged by the fact that in 1990 over half the value of America's exports and imports were accountable in terms of the cross-boarder transfers of goods and services within multinationals.[24] In the UK there are more than 3,500 US companies, 1,000 German companies and about 200 firms from Japan.[25]

In our discussion of the global economy it is easy to overlook the fact that virtually all outward FDI flows from OECD countries as members of a privileged economic club.[26] The OECD accounts for 96 per cent of all outward investment. The major change in FDI outflows is that whereas the United States accounted for 53 per cent of this in 1975, this had declined to 31 per cent in 1993. This decline was not due to Japan, which saw an increase from 6.6 to 7.3, but to other major OECD countries – Canada, France, Germany, Italy and the United Kingdom – who saw their share rise from 28 per cent in 1975 to a little over 40 per cent by 1993.[27] In terms of inward flows the proportion going to other OECD countries in the early 1990s was about 63 per cent which is little more than it was in the mid-1970s, but the amount going into East Asia, particularly China, grew from 6 per cent to 26 per cent.[28] Therefore despite the dominance of OECD economies they confront increasing competition from developing countries. The share of the newly industrialised Asian economies in world trade has risen from under 8 per cent in the early 1970s to almost 20 per cent in 1995.[29] And whereas the percentage of world output among OECD countries was 75 per cent between 1988 and 90, it was projected to decline to 58 per cent by the year 2000.[30] The Asia Pacific region was also expected to account for about 25 per cent of the world's GDP by the year 2000, and it is estimated that China will overtake the US as the world's largest economy by the year 2015.[31] These figures clearly over-estimated the pace of economic development in Asia given the fallout from the Asia financial crisis in 1997, but this slowed rather than derailed the economic rise of China, Japan and the Asian Tigers.

Such statistics represent only part of a plausible story which can explain the dramatic changes in the economic livelihoods of millions of Americans and British citizens. Although the changing rules of eligibility have been enthusiastically brokered by neo-classical economists who see the potential for greater wealth creation at least by Western companies and greater consumer power resulting from increased choice and cheaper prices, it is seen by others to intensify fears of economic insecurity and inequality. For most of the past 25 years such fears have seemed to be well founded. Western economies have endured significant spells of economic recession and high rates of unemployment, along with a significant decline in their rates of growth since 1973, even when the late 1990s boom in the American and British economies are taken into account. But the most devastating blow to economic nationalism has been the gulf which has emerged between the work rich and work poor. Whereas a bigger pie led to a bigger slice for all in the Golden era (even if the pieces were unequal), a bigger pie is now having far less impact on the prosperity of large numbers of workers and their

Table 7.1   How households divided the nation's income: 1976–1996 (in 1996–value dollars)

1976 Share of all income (%)	Segment average	Household segments	1996 Segment average	Share of all income (%)
43.4	$85,335	Top 20%	$115,514	49.0
24.8	$48,876	Second 20%	$54,922	23.2
17.1	$33,701	Middle 20%	$35,486	15.1
10.4	$20,496	Fourth 20%	$21,097	9.0
4.4	$8,672	Bottom 20%	$8,596	3.7
100.0	$39,416	All households	$47,123	100.0
16.0	$126,131	Richest 5%	$201,684	21.4

families. This is despite the fact that the amount of money in the hands of American households increased from $2.9 trillion to $4.8 trillion between 1976 and 1996. In *Money: Who Has How Much and Why*, Andrew Hacker shows that the top 20 per cent of households have enjoyed a 35 per cent increase in income, although the richest 5 per cent increased their income by 60 per cent. Those in the middle of the income parade had to settle for a little under a 5 per cent increase, which is an improvement on the bottom fifth of households who took a cut of one per cent. The magnitude of household inequalities in America is shown in Table 7.1.

This reveals that in 1996 the bottom fifth of households had an average income of $8,596 whereas the comparable figure for the richest 5 per cent was $201,684. These figures reflect massive inequalities in the per capita income of racial and ethnic groups. The figure for non-Hispanic whites in the late 1990s was about $23,000 which was close to double the figure for African Americas ($13,000). Hispanics faired even worse with a per capita income a little over $11,000.[32] It is therefore not surprising that Richard Freeman was able to plausibly describe the United States at the dawn of the twenty-first century in terms of 'Rising inequality. Stagnant real wages. A declining middle class. High levels of child poverty. Insecure workers. A waning union movement. Homeless people in every city. Bursting jails and prisons. [And] A fraying social safety net'.[33] In the UK the bottom 10 per cent of earners have until recently seen no growth in their earnings since the late 1970s; whilst those in the middle saw their incomes increase by 35 per cent and those in the top 10 per cent increased their incomes in real terms by over 50 per cent.[34] Another way of expressing the extent of these inequalities is to note that in 1980 the top 10 per cent had an hourly wage two and a half times that of the bottom 10 per cent. By 1990 this had increased to 3.2 times following a century of stable or falling inequality.[35] To understand why these inequalities in wealth have emerged we need to examine the changing *rules of engagement*, which will ultimately be shown to tell us less about the inherent logic of global capitalism than it does about how national governments have responded to these changes.

2

Economic nationalism was based on an agreement between government, employers and trade unions that all should share the fruits of prosperity. This led governments to support trade unions in reasonable demands for pay increases as these were needed for workers to be able to support their families and to preserve domestic consumer demand. Employers could also see the benefit of this arrangement as the buoyant demand for goods and services enabled them to maintain healthy profits. But when these profits began to decline in the early 1970s the rules of engagement at mid-century were torn-up and replaced by a set of new rules based on global market competition. Since the first oil shock in the early 1970s there has been a process of corporate secession, which gathered pace as financial deregulation and new technologies not only give the multinationals the 'power to go abroad' but also the 'power to go global'.[36]

In 1991 the largest corporation in the world made the largest annual loss in corporate history. A staggering $4.5 billion which included a loss of $3,000 on every one of the 3.5 million cars and trucks which were made in the United States by General Motors. The old adage of what is good for General Motors is good for America, has been turned on its head. On announcing record losses GM's Bob Stumpel who was CEO at the time, launched a four-year restructuring programme including the axing of 74,000 jobs – 'We've accepted the need for a smaller base on which to become profitable' and in the future GM was to be run 'in an increasingly lean and responsive manner.'[37] This approach was representative of a more general pattern of restructuring in which the American workforce has been forced to pay a hefty price in the drive for corporate profitability. What was 'good' for the national champions such of GM, was the 'down sizing' of its workforce, lower wage costs and investment in other national economies. It has been estimated that some 700 American companies in the 1980s employed more than 350,000 workers in Singapore, Mexico and Taiwan alone.[38] Equally, 40 per cent of the jobs created by British multinationals are overseas.[39]

The trend towards corporate secession is equally true in Europe. Even Mercedes-Benz cars, which symbolized the success of the post-war German economy and the efficiency of its workforce, was not immune from the forces of the global economy. On announcing a DM1.9 billion swing into the red during the first six months of 1993, Edzard Reuter, the Daimler-Benz's chief executive at the time stated 'There is no room for protected species and taboos if production locations in Germany are to remain competitive', and then announced a 20 per cent reduction in the size of the Daimler-Benz domestic workforce by 1995. At the same time, the corporation has increased its manufacturing capacity in what it saw as low-cost centres in the US, Mexico and Asia.[40] For a company like Daimler-Benz globalisation is not seen as an optional strategy 'it is the only one' and by 1997 the new chief executive Jurgen Schempp believed that 'we have been able to show our unions that for every three jobs we create abroad, we create one in Germany'.[41] Daimler has since merged with the Chrysler corporation in the US. Equally in Japan, Nissan Motors announced a $9 billion restructuring programme in late 1999, leading to a reduction in its global workforce of 21,000 or 14 per cent. But most of the job loses are in Japan where three assembly plants and two engine factories will close, while European plants were spared because they were viewed as more efficient that those in Japan.[42]

These examples reflect a change in the nature of competition which has not only led the corporations to transfer the risks involved in making a profit in volatile market conditions onto their employees who can no longer assume long term job tenure. The globalization of the multinationals also represents an attempt to spread the risks of economic downturn. As Jack Welch of General Electric observed in the late 1990s 'there is excess global capacity in almost every sector. Pricing pressures are dramatic across sector after sector', and one way to meet such pressures, as Peter Martin of the *Financial Times* suggests, 'is to go for the greatest possible scale – spreading costs and revenues across the world'. But to operate effectively on a global scale means re-thinking every aspect of the company's activities 'sourcing, production, brand management, distribution, finance, governance, performance targets, executive development – all must be recast'.[43]

The corporate logos of the national champions such as Ford, GM and IBM may have remained unchanged, along with the bill-boards which extol the global success of 'American' big business, and high-profile corporate executives continue to celebrate their contribution to the American economy, but in virtually all other ways these are not the same as the multinational corporations with a national 'parent' company and foreign subsidiaries. In some cases even the corporate name has been changed to reflect the image of globally integrated corporations. Itochu, a Japanese leading general trading company changed its name from C.Itoh to Itochu Corporation to achieve worldwide uniformity between its English and Japanese language names. At the same time it introduced a new corporate credo, 'Commitment to the Global Good'.[44] The contribution of the multinationals to the global good is a moot point. But their secession from the role of 'national champions' is motivated by a desire to establish a significant presence in the key markets of Europe, Asia and North America; to increase flexibility in production and distribution in response to rapidly changing market conditions; and to increase profit margins by reducing labour costs.

The difficulty of assessing what this all means for the future prosperity of American or British workers is compounded by the fact that the multinationals have been transformed into complex global networks. This reflects the *internal* transformation of corporations into webs of smaller companies, business units, profit centres, partnerships and newstreams of entrepreneurial activities.[45] As Robert Reich has noted:

> the core corporation is no longer a 'big' business, but neither is it merely a collection of smaller ones. Rather, it is an enterprise web. Its center provides strategic insight and binds the threads together. Yet points on the web often have sufficient autonomy to create profitable connections to other webs. There is no 'inside' or 'outside' the corporation, but only different distances from its strategic center.[46]

The creation of global webs or networks has blurred the traditional distinctions between American and 'foreign' companies, goods, and jobs. Japanese, British and French owned banks are some of the leading investors in Silicon Valley. Many of the goods bought in America and Europe are likely to be international 'composites'. This has caused considerable problems for people like Margaret Charrington, director of the Invest in Britain campaign. In respect to the motor industry she declared: 'It is a mess. A salesman will find out whether you want a British, German or Japanese car and sell you that, all the same model. Customers' perceptions about what is a British car are sadly well behind the times.' In the United Kingdom, Ford and Vauxhall are regarded as British companies, despite the fact that they are both American (Vauxhall is a part of General Motors). The Ford Mondeo is effectively half British with 15 per cent of its components made in Europe before it is shipped to Asia to be put together and then back to Belgium for final assembly. The Vauxhall Corsa has only 15 per cent UK content, with an Austrian engine in its popular version, German gearbox and Spanish body. Whereas the French Peugeot 306 has an estimated 65 per cent British content![47]

Some of the routine data processing of Western governments is handled in the Philippines or Barbados via satellite communications, while commercials for American diapers are made in New Zealand. The New York Life Insurance company has some of its claims processed by fifty employees in Ireland. Hans-Peter Martin and Harald Schumann in *The Global Trap* describe how companies such as Hewlett-Packard, Motorola and IBM in the mid-1980s began to use computer programmers from India on lower rates of pay than their American counterparts. Following complaints about the influx of Indian workers to Silicon Valley to do the jobs of American software engineers, firms responded by relocating major parts of their data work to India. Bangalore became an 'electronic city' catering for companies including Siemens, Compaq, Texas Instruments, Toshiba, Microsoft and Lotus. By 1995 there were 120,000 university graduates from Madras, New Delhi and Bombay working in the software industry in the sub-continent. Hannes Krummer of Swiss Air had little problem explaining the attraction of Indians, 'We can hire three Indians for the price of one Swiss'. Martin and Schumann also suggest that this is just the beginning as a further million people skilled in computer applications came onto the global market from Russia and East Europe in the 1990s. A firm in Minsk, for instance, performs labour intensive maintenance work by satellite for IBM Deutchland. And there are some who believe that what is on offer in Minsk is even better than in India. Siemen's India expert, Rene Jotten, reported to them that 'costs are already too high in Bangalore', and 'we're thinking of going somewhere else soon'.[48]

The multinationals have also created external networks of strategic alliances, which include various kinds of collaboration with competitors in order to share the financial costs and commercial risks involved in product development. It is estimated, for instance, that the cost of developing a new family automobile is in the region of $4 billion, while it is $3.2 billion for a new generation mainframe computer, and about $1.2 billion for a new camcorder.[49] In the semiconductor industry responsible for the manufacturing and development of computer chips, virtually all the major corporate players formed some kind of strategic alliance in order to reduce the costs of R&D and to stay competitive given the incredible pace of change in 'chip' technology – Intel joined forces with NMB, Siemens with IBM, SGS-Thomson with OKI, Texas Instruments with Hitachi and Motorola with Toshiba.[50] Motorola has also joined forces with MIT's Media Lab to create the Motorola Digital DNA Laboratory, which will experiment with different kinds of 'smart' products. Carol Levin suggests that some of the concepts include 'a treadmill that automatically checks your pulse and adjusts the incline accordingly, clothing with labels that inform the washer what cycle to use, and doors that open for specific people or pets'.[51]

As the multinationals seek to reduce their fixed costs by off-loading as much of the 'risk' associated with fluctuations in demand for products and services onto suppliers, contractors, and workers, it has led to a greater use of outsourcing, subcontracting, franchising, licensing, and network production. One of the pioneering companies to adopt this approach was Benetton, an Italian clothing producer which had in the region of 5,000 retail outlets worldwide. It used eight factories in Northern Italy which employed close to 2000 people engaged in designing, cutting and final ironing. It also used 200 small subcontractors, employing about 6,000 workers, making semi- finished clothes which supplied the eight main plants. Although Benetton does not own these smaller firms, its strategic decision-making clearly controls the fate of those who work for the subcontractors, although they bear none of the responsibility or costs associated with redundancies or changes in product lines.[52]

The organizational flexibility which this has given the multinationals has entailed significant advantages in negotiations with labour. Although trade unions are able to exert a degree of pressure at the plant or national level, they lack cross-border organization and also find it difficult to co-ordinate actions when they are forced to deal with different companies even if they are 'owned' by the same parent company. This has greatly weakened the power of unions to stand up to the multinationals in support of the interest of workers and local communities.[53] Conversely, the multinationals have the capacity to pick and choose where they will locate production. Their aim is to produce in parts of the world where the costs of production are low in terms of labour costs and taxes, and where the infrastructure supporting their production, in terms of workforce skills, transport, and communications, is most sophisticated.

This has created a *global auction* for jobs, which threatens the living standards and job security of all Western workers.[54] As global capital has become footloose, the mass production of standardized goods and services will be located in countries, regions or communities which offer low wage costs, light legislation, weak trade unions and 'sweeteners' including 'tax holidays' and cheap rents. Such investment has significantly increased in the new industrial countries such as China, Thailand, India and Brazil.

In reality, the global auction operates like a Dutch auction. In a Dutch auction corporate investors are able to play off nations, communities and workers as a way of increasing their profit margins. Bidding spirals downwards which impoverishes local communities and workers by forcing concessions on wage levels, rents and taxes in exchange for investment in local jobs. In order to persuade Mercedes to set up a plant in Alabama, the company received an initial $253 million, with tax breaks over 25 years which have been estimated to be worth an extra $230 million. The Swiss Bank Corporation received some $120 million of incentives over 10 years from Connecticut, for moving its US headquarters from Manhatten to the city of Stamford.[55] The Korean conglomerate LG built a new electronics plant in Newport, South Wales for which they were to receive a £30,000 subsidy for each of the 6,000 jobs which the company promised to create. However, part of the plant remains empty as LG was forced to sell some of its operations to Hyundia as a result of the Asian financial crisis in the late 1990s.

However, the global auction not only operates in respect to new corporate investment. The threat of relocation to another part of the country or overseas is also used by employers to squeeze further tax breaks or other concessions from local communities eager to avoid the consequences of redundancies and long-term unemployment. In order to meet 'profit targets' in increasingly competitive global markets employees and their unions have had to confront real reductions in income, inferior job contracts, new working practices, or risk shutdown and corporate flight to other states, regions or continents.[56] The effects of the global auction are not only being felt in the West. In Third World countries the effects of 'footloose' international capital has been to make real wages more likely to fall rather than rise with productivity gains. Richard Rothstein has noted that 'Many developing nations have deliberately suppressed wages and relaxed child labor rules in recent years, so unit labor costs fall even faster than productivity rises. From 1980 to 1989, Mexico's real manufacturing wages fell by 24 percent while industrial productivity (gross output per employee, including national and export-oriented industries) increased 28 percent. In Bangladesh, productivity grew by 20 percent, but wages did not rise.'[57]

If the silence of closed car factories in Detroit or deserted shipyards in Scotland stands as a poignant symbol of a changed world for workers, it also serves to highlight that in the global auction corporate bosses no longer think of American or Scottish jobs, only American or Scottish workers. In the post-war settlement the question of whether 'a car worker in Detroit is worth more than a car worker in Seoul or the Pearl River Delta in China?' would have been beyond Western comprehension. In the old rules of engagement it was taken for granted that the Detroit worker would be paid substantially more, and had to be if he (or she) were not to live on the breadline. However, in the new *rules of engagement* it is much harder to justify and sustain the higher wage of the Detroit worker, because the labour market for car workers is indifferent to national boundaries. In effect the market price of car workers, or indeed any other worker, is set by the world's cheapest car worker. We have been told by corporate bosses and free-market economists that American or British workers and their families should no longer expect to be paid a living wage just because they live in either of these countries, but only according to the skills and contribution they make to profits in the global economy.

Therefore, in high volume, standardized production, where cost is of overriding importance, many American and British workers have found it difficult to compete with workers in newly industrializing countries, where wage costs and overheads remain lower. The problem this poses is illustrated by the fact that in the late 1990s low-skilled workers in Germany could still earn $32 an hour, against $7.28 paid to 30 per cent of American workers, while children working in China could be paid as little as 17 cents an hour.[58] Likewise, the French Senate Finance Committee found that 47 workers in the Philippines or in Vietnam could be employed for the same cost as a single worker in France.[59] Therefore, in the global auction if American or European workers remain locked into low-skilled work it is assumed that they must either accept 'poverty pay' or see their jobs go to Asia, South America or Eastern Europe.[60]

The new rules of engagement are based on market competition between workers, companies and nations in a 'winner-takes-all' global contest. This appears at first sight to reflect an internal capitalist logic which is forcing big business to sacrifice its commitment to the home base and to paying decent wages to all categories of workers as a way of maintaining their profitability. But in the next chapter it will be argued that the new rules of engagement are best understood as a political response on the part of free-market governments in American and Britain in the 1980s. But before turning to this issue, we need to consider the changing *rules of wealth creation*.

3

The fact that national prosperity can no longer be built on the mass production of goods and services has given rise to new *rules of wealth creation*. In earlier chapters we have shown how standardised mass production has its roots in scientific management perfected at the Ford Motor company in Detroit in the early twentieth century. But it was in the car plants in Japan where its fate was sealed. For if Henry Ford and Frederick Taylor were the architects of standardized mass production, Eiji Toyoda (whose family owned the Toyota Motor Company) and Taiichi Ohno, a production engineer at the Toyota plant at Nagoya, were the architects of lean production. In *The Machine that Changed the World*, Womack, Jones and Roos suggest that lean production has succeeded in combining 'the best features of both craft production and mass production – the ability to reduce costs per unit and dramatically improve quality while, at the same time, providing an even wider range of products and even more challenging work'.[61]

Following the ravages of war, doing more with less was a fact of life in Japan in the 1940s and 1950s. It was in 1950 that Eiji Toyoda who, at the time was a young Japanese engineer, visited the Ford's Rouge plant in Detroit. The purpose of the trip was to acquire the 'know how' in order for Japanese companies to master the latest techniques of mass production. It became apparent to Toyoda and Ohno that Fordist mass production techniques could not be imported wholesale into Japan. A key limitation was cost. There were simply not the resources, for example, to buy large numbers of presses used to mould the many different parts of a car. In the West, it was not uncommon for enormous presses to be dedicated to stamping the same fenders, hoods, or doors for months on end. This not only led to long periods when the presses were not used but to massive stock-piling of parts waiting to be assembled. Toyota could not afford such luxuries. It had to make do with a much smaller number of presses and cope with the problem of far shorter production runs because the market for Japanese cars was relatively small. This meant that the dies on each press had to be changed frequently as they were needed to produce different mouldings every two or three hours rather than months as in Western plants. The problem this posed to Ohno was that each die weighed many tons, any misalignment produced wrinkled parts, and in Detroit it was taking the best part of a day for specialist die fitters to prepare the presses.

Over the space of a decade Ohno succeeded in reducing the time it took to change dies from a day to three minutes in the late 1950s. This was also achieved with greater efficiency because Toyota abandoned the idea of having specialist die fitters, by training production workers to make the changes themselves. The fact that Toyota could not afford to have massive stock-piles of parts waiting for assembly, also led to the creation of the Just In Time (JIT) system of production. Here components were bought from suppliers or made in-house just in time for them to be used in production. The development of JIT was only possible given that Ohno was willing to abandon the specialized division of labour found in Western factories. He also recognized that the JIT system enabled the elimination of faulty parts or assembly at an early stage in the production process, whereas in western plants motor vehicles had to be 're-worked' at the end of production lines, as line workers felt no responsibility for ensuring high quality products and management did not entrust workers with the power to stop the production line when problems occurred.

This flexible use of labour at Toyota was the result of a series of fortuitous events of which the economic depression in Japan and the power of the trade unions given by American dictat in 1946, both assumed significance. As a result of the recession Toyota decided to sack a quarter of its workforce. The workers' response was to occupy the factory in protest. After a bitter struggle it was agreed that a quarter of the workforce would be sacked and that Kiichiro Toyoda, the president of the company would also resign in recognition of the company's failings. Toyota also agreed to guarantee lifetime employment to the remainder of the workforce and to link pay to seniority rather than job performance. In reality this meant that a 45-year-old worker would be paid substantially more than someone in their twenties for doing exactly the same job. In return the unions agreed to abandon strict job demarcation and to initiate improvements rather than leave their brains at the factory gate.

In effect this agreement locked workers into Toyota for life, given that seniority pay, also adopted by other Japanese companies made it virtually impossible for workers to leave Toyota and find another job offering them similar wage rates. In turn if workers are expected to stay with the company for forty years, over which time they will cost the firm more to employ, Taicho Ohno needed workers to continuously enhance their skills and contribution, which is impossible under the conditions of the factory model, given that there is virtually no scope for individual initiative.

The combination of a commitment to quality, flexibility and teamwork associated with Japanese companies such as Toyota, Nissan, Honda, Mazda and Mitsubishi led to the creation of lean production that proved to be vastly superior to the production performance of Western rivals. The hard-won improvements in lean production techniques were especially important after the first oil shock in 1973 which led to a demand for more fuel efficient cars rather than the American 'gas guzzlers' produced by companies including GM, Ford and Chrysler. As consumer tastes changed in favour of smaller vehicles and towards quality 'customized' products, Japanese companies won 30 per cent of the American auto market in the 1980s. In Britain, Rover cars was saved from extinction by an alliance with Honda which gave them the know how to produce cars that people wanted to buy, only to be sold in the early 1990s to the German company BMW, who allegedly sold the company to a former Rover manager for £10. The greater efficiency of Japanese lean production was also evident in 'transplants' based in America and Europe. The General Accounting Office of the US Federal Government showed that whereas a typical US firm needed over 4,000 workers to manufacture 200,000 vehicles a year, a Japanese transplant in America produced the same number of automobiles with less than 2,500 workers.[62] The diffusion of lean production to other Japanese companies give them a competitive advantage in a broad range of product areas in the 1980s including TVs, Hi Fis, Machine tools, cameras, computers, steel and semi-conductors. As a result Western companies found it increasingly difficult to remain profitable in these new competitive conditions.

In response Western companies were transformed. In high performance organizations it is recognized that improvements in productivity depend on the 'organic' integration of applied knowledge, technological innovation, free-flow information networks, and high trust relations between multi-skilled managers, professionals and technicians. In the new rules of wealth creation, economic prosperity depends on nations being able to create large numbers of high-skilled jobs which can no longer be delivered according to Fordist principles. Jobs which can deliver a living wage to workers depend on the production of quality goods and services which meet the precise needs of customers and clients. And the creation of jobs offering a decent wage equally depends on new sources of productivity, investment and innovation. Such jobs are most likely to be found in companies such as those involved in microelectronics, telecommunications, biotechnology, financial services, consultancy, advertising, marketing and the media, which can succeed in creating 'customized' niche markets for their goods and services, because it is more difficult for competitors to mass produce the same goods or to offer customers tailored services.[63]

In the new rules of wealth creation the quality of human resources have been identified as a decisive factor in the ability of nations to win a competitive advantage in the global economy. It is notoriously difficult to measure the contribution of human capital to bottom-line profits, but the inevitably crude attempts which have been made to take such measurements have shown its growing significance. In the US, for instance, the output per production worker has virtually tripled since 1930 from a value of $22,000 to $60,000. Over the same period, the proportion of the workforce directly engaged in production has declined from 27 per cent to 15 per cent. Moreover, for every production worker there are another 21 non-production workers who are employed in sales, marketing, clerical, technical, managerial and professional activities. Most of these non-production workers have received some form of tertiary education.[64] Further evidence of the increasing importance of human capital is provided by Manuel Castells who has calculated that in 1990, 47 per cent of the labour force in the United States, 46 per cent in the United Kingdom, 45 per cent in France and 40 per cent in what was West Germany were engaged in information-processing activities.[65] This will include the work of managers, engineers, designers, consultants, teachers and secretaries.

Other commentators have suggested that human capital has increased in economic significance to the point where it has become as important to contemporary society as land was to feudal society and financial capital to the industrial revolution. Between 1948 and 1973 almost a fifth of the increase in GNP has been attributed to the expansion of the American education system. Subsequently, when productivity growth began to falter in the US, between 1973 and 1981 the contribution of education to productivity rose from 25 per cent to more than 30 per cent.[66] In Britain it has been estimated that in 1867 the returns to skilled labour accounted for between 5 and 25 per cent of national income, whereas by 1967 they amounted to between 46 and 58 per cent of pre-tax household income. Today, that figure will have increased significantly as the wage differentials between educated and unskilled workers have polarized in both America and Britain. In the 1980s the earnings of college-educated males aged 24 to 34 in America increased by 10 per cent. At the same time the earnings of those with only high-school diplomas declined by nine per cent. In addition, the earnings of those who were in jobs but who did not hold a high school diploma experienced a 12 per cent drop in their real income.[67] By 1995 the earning of males in full-time jobs between the ages of 35 to 44 were $32,689 for those with no more than a high school diploma and $57,104 for those with a Bachelor's degree. The respective figures for female workers were $22,257 and $36,901. This represents a gain for those with a Bachelor's degree when compared to those with a high school diploma of almost 16 per cent for men and 22 per cent for women since 1975.[68] Robert Reich, who for a time was President Clinton's Labor Secretary, has also shown that in 1920 more than 85 per cent of the cost of a car went to pay routine labourers and investors, by 1990 these two groups received less than 60 per cent. Similarly, of the cost of a computer chip, 15 per cent is divided between the owners of the raw material, equipment, production facilities and routine labour, the other 85 per cent goes to educated labour including designers, engineers and patent attorneys.[69]

What such statistics have been taken to show is that new sources of wealth creation rely on the manipulation of symbols and ideas rather than on manual labour. This represents a logical extension in the mode of capitalist accumulation from the exploitation of muscle to mental power, given that 'it is knowledge, not cheap labor; symbols, not raw materials, that embody and add value'.[70] Such ideas have led many commentators to interpret the *new rules* to represent little more than the evolutionary progression from a low to high-skill economy. They have also led both left and right mainstream political parties to come to the conclusion that the key to economic prosperity lies in attempts to maximize the value of the productive activities of workers through the upgrading of the skills, knowledge and entrepreneurial energies of the population. The US report *21st Century Skills for 21st Century Jobs*, opens by saying:

> Global competition, the Internet, and widespread use of technology all suggest that the economy of the 21st century will create new challenges for employers and workers. For America to compete in this new global economy, it can either create low-wage, low-skilled jobs or take full advantage of the Nation's labor force and create high performance workplaces. However, if Americans value a high quality of life for all, there is no choice. Economic success will require adopting organizational work systems that allow workers to operate with greater autonomy and accountability.[71]

The new rules of wealth creation are also often presented as a global 'head-to-head' competition aimed at 'out-smarting' economic rivals as knowledge, information and human capability are assumed to be the new raw materials of international commerce. In the ensuing *knowledge wars*, schools, colleges, universities and research laboratories have assumed centre stage in the competition for economic advantage.[72] Recognition of the knowledge wars is reflected in current attempts through organizations such as the International Education Association (IEA) to develop comparative measure of academic performance. At the same time nations have been forced to recognize that as 'standards of organizational performance have gone global',[73] the quality of a nation's human resources are judged on relative rather than absolute criteria. Therefore, it is not only the qualities of individual students which are being assessed, but the quality of national systems of education and training as a whole.[74]

In America, the much publicized report from the National Commission on Excellence in Education in the early 1980s, aptly called *A Nation at Risk*, left Americans in little doubt about where they stood in terms of these new realities and the threat it posed to national prosperity:

> History is not kind to idlers. The time is long past when America's destiny was assured simply by an abundance of natural resources and inexhaustible human enthusiasm, and by our relative isolation from the malignant problems of older civilizations. The world is indeed one global village. We live among determined, well-educated, and strongly motivated competitors. We compete with them for international standing and markets, not only with products but also with the ideas of our laboratories and neighbourhood workshops. America's position in the world may once have been reasonably secure with only a few exceptionally well-trained men and women. It is no longer.[75]

The view that western nations would not be able to remain prosperous unless they can improve the quality of their education systems was equally in vogue on the other side of the Atlantic. An influential report from the National Commission on Education suggested:

> For us, knowledge and skills will be central. In an era of world-wide competition and low-cost global communications, no country like ours will be able to maintain its standard of living, let alone improve it, on the basis of cheap labour and low-tech products and services. There will be too many millions of workers and too many employers in too many countries who will be able and willing to do that kind of work fully as well as we or people in any other developed country could do it – and at a fraction of the cost.[76]

This sense of crisis in education has been fuelled by the steady stream of data about the academic performance of foreign students. In Japan, 94 per cent of students stay in higher secondary education beyond the legal limit. In Korea more than 85 per cent of seventeen and eighteen year olds remain in full-time education, in Taiwan the proportion is over 80 per cent. Comparative scores on international tests reveal that in Maths, Biology, Chemistry and Physics, Japan and the Asian Tigers invariably out-perform students from the United States and Britain. In a review of various outcome measures, Andy Green at the Institute of Education, University of London, found that both the USA and the UK had lower aggregate levels of attainment than countries including Germany, France, Japan and Sweden. What he also found was a greater spread of results among students in America and Britain which suggests that whereas some students may be performing reasonably well, even by international standards, a large proportion are not.[77]

Literacy rates also point to the success of the East Asian nations in their attempt to produce a well-educated workforce. Japan has almost no illiteracy whereas estimates in the United States report functional illiteracy at around 20 per cent. Although such comparisons need to be treated with caution, they leave little doubt that Japan and the Asian Tigers have bridged the skills gap at a time when Western nations require a highly-skilled workforce if they are going to increase their share of high-waged jobs. The prospect of a growing proportion of highly-skilled jobs being created or relocated in the Asian Pacific region, where labour costs will remain appreciably lower in the foreseeable future, raises serious doubt about whether the prosperity of large number of American and European workers can be recovered. The prospect of a high-skilled, but relatively low-waged workforce is not however on the international political agenda. But the question of how to reorganize the educational system has gained increasing political prominence and urgency.

There is considerable political appeal in calls to mobilize the population to 'out smart' economic rivals both in nations such as the USA and Britain hungry to reassert their former economic prowess and in countries including Japan, Korea and Singapore who all see an upgrading of their human resources as a way of both stealing a march on the West in the new information age and as a way of coping with intense competition from neighbouring countries. But it would be a mistake to assume that the future of national prosperity solely depended upon what happens in the nation's classrooms, colleges, universities and training schools. Despite the international consensus concerning the increasing economic importance of human capital, there are significant differences in the way nations have so far responded to the *new rules*.

This should alert us to the fact that changes in the rules of economic competition do not automatically lead to changes in the nature of skills and involvement which are required in order to compete in 'high value' production and enterprise. The interests of employers seeking to maximize profits and workers seeking to enhance wages and working conditions remain an important potential source of cleavage given that it is still possible for companies to 'profit' from low-skill, low-wage operations, even if this means a significant deterioration in pay and working conditions of a large slice of the workforce. Equally, the arrival of the information rich, borderless economy should not be read as an evolutionary process from a low to high-skills economy. Differences in the way nations try to shape the new rules of competition – and they retain more power to influence domestic affairs than is assumed by many commentators – are having profound implications on the ability of nations to provide prosperity, security and opportunities for their people in the first act of the new century. The response of free market governments in America and the UK in the 1980s was to expose workers and their families to the full force of global market competition which has led to social polarization, poverty and social disorder. The failure to consider any other way of responding to the transformation of western economies apart from the blind instinctive reassertion of the market and competitive individualism clearly warrants further consideration.

8
Primitive Capitalism

We meant to change a nation, and instead we changed a world.

Ronald Reagan

It is a spring dawn, it is the wrong century.

Hugh Lauder[1]

1

Michael Milken came from modest family circumstances to gain international fame and fortune. In 1986 he 'earned' $550 million dollars trading 'junk bonds' on the world's financial markets. Along with the likes of other entrepreneurs and corporate raiders such as Donald Trump, Alan Bond, Robert Maxwell, Genshiro Kawamoto, he came to symbolise a new era. In the public imagination the 1980s was the decade of 'big names'. It was the exploits of 'self-made' men and women which were splashed on the front of the business pages and glossy magazines. They were acclaimed not simply because they made mind-boggling salaries, but for a brief moment in the history of the twentieth century, Michael Milken and his ilk became the cultural icons of primitive capitalism.

The lionising of the entrepreneur was the response by Ronald Reagan and Margaret Thatcher to what they perceived as the decline of their once great nations. In America, economic growth had fallen from 3 per cent in the period 1960–1968 to under 2 per cent between 1968 and 1973. A similar trend was found in Britain, while Japan's growth at the close of the sixties was close to 10 per cent. The oil price hikes of the early seventies generated stagflation: stalled economic growth and inflation. Faced with the apparently inexorable rise of Japan and the the

Asian Tigers, Margaret Thatcher reported sleepless nights fearing that the British people had lost their entrepreneurial zest for life, 'I used to have a nightmare for the first six years in office that, when I had got the finances right, when I had got the law right, the deregulation etc., that the British sense of enterprise and initiative would have been killed off by socialism'. But in 1988 she conclude, 'But then it came. The face began to smile, the spirits began to lift, the pride returned'.[2]

Ronald Reagan in America shared the sentiment, 'we are talking about the greatest productive economy in human history, an economy that is historically revitalised not by government but by people free of government interference, needless regulation, crippling inflation, high taxes and unemployment'.[3] Reagan's reference to a mythical history was not accidental. The populism of both leaders rested on nostalgic appeals to a past when both nations were once considered great. For the President it was the frontier days of rugged individualism that he had portrayed for Hollywood. For the Prime Minister it was the Victorian era of British Empire. Both were determined to use the full power of the state to return their nation's to the days of primitive capitalism. This would be done by merging global and national strategies into one great market design. For at root was the intuition that through markets alone individuals could thrive in the image of the entrepreneurs so feted by both administrations. In consequence, Reagan and Thatcher unleashed a political response to the challenges and opportunities confronting nations which they hoped would consign the economic nationalism of the Golden era to a footnote in history.

2

In the 1980s, the development that attracted less attention but now seems of equal significance to the domestic reconstruction of society was the globalization of market competition. This we have noted has led to a new rules of engagement between the multinationals and government, liberating companies from national obligations to exploit the opportunities of the new global economy. In *The Integrated Circus*, Patricia Marchak notes that there appeared to be a 'sudden and spontaneous development, business leaders and politicians around the world began using a whole new vocabulary to explain the recession of the early 1980s and to promote a new agenda. Echoing the sentiments of Reagan and Thatcher they argued that government had undercut healthy entrepreneurship through its interference in the free market'.[4] Marchak's evidence shows that this apparent spontaneity was in fact based on detailed planning, organization and funding. Many of the groups propagating these views were independent think-tanks but with close ties to Government. Prominent amongst these were the Mont Pelerin Society in Geneva whose founding membership in 1947 included Robert Nozick, Friedrich A. Hayek and Milton Friedman; the Institute of Economic Affairs in Britain; the Kiel Economic Institute in Germany; and the Club de L'Horloge in France. In North America the list includes the Heritage Foundation, Thomas Jefferson Center Foundation, American Enterprise Institute, National Conservative Research and Education Foundations and the Fraser Institute. In many ways they acted as an international propaganda arm of the Right giving governments the appearance of independence while justifying policies which brought New Right governments ever closer to the interests of global business.

Alongside these organisations stood perhaps the most influential: the Trilateral Commission, established in 1973 by David Rockerfeller, then chairman of Chase Manhattan Bank. The Commission sought to enhance co-operation between North America, Europe and Japan in recognition of the decline in American global economic and military pre-eminence. The Commission represented the international business elite with members from many of the world's leading corporations including the chairperson of Coca-Cola, Exxon, Hewlett-Packard, Bank of America, Fiat, Shell, Mitsubishi, Sony and the Bank of Tokyo.[5] Its membership also included leading politicians such as Jimmy Carter and George Bush, along with prominent academics.

The Trilateralists produced many reports on the future of democracy, international relations, environmental pollution and the Third World debt crisis. Despite tensions between members of the Commission often resulting from different national interests, their core views on the economy remained unchanged. They advanced 'a general programme for achieving a liberal integrated world economic system, secure from protectionist disruption and domestic upheaval'.[6] For this to happen the Trilateralists argued for a further liberalisation of international financial and trading systems to allow the global economy to operate independently of nation states. They also argued for the restructuring of national economies which would require governments to be strengthened relative to the democratic rights of citizens. Governments, they thought, had become overloaded: 'In the face of the claims of business groups, labour unions, and the beneficiaries of governmental largesse, it becomes difficult if not impossible for democratic governments to curtail spending, increase taxes, and control prices and wages. In this sense, inflation is the economic disease of democracies'.[7] This view was supported by a body of thought know as Public Choice theory for which one of its originator's, James Buchanan, received the Nobel Prize.[8] In effect it legitimized the sentiments of the Right for it suggested that freedom was not to be found in the political processes of democracy but in the consumer sovereignty which reigned in the market. It was a theory which was to have a profound influence on current social and economic policies.

At first sight the views of the Trilateral Commission seem far removed from the protectionist and religious fundamentalist elements of the Right which were influential during the Reagan administration. In fact extremist groups in Reagan's 1980 campaign saw the Trilateral Commission as part of an 'internationalist, one-world, pro-Communist banker's conspiracy'.[9] But what united this diverse range of powerful vested interest groups was a deeply-held belief that Western countries had lost the Enlightenment plot of steady social and economic progress. The source of economic strength and social stability in the post-war period, was now seen to epitomize the symptoms of a disease at the very heart of society – the Keynesian welfare state.[10]

3

The mission of the Right was, therefore, to excise Keynes' legacy and the profound changes it had wrought in the role of government in the mid-decades of the century. As we have already seen, during this period there was a massive expansion in the role and cost of government. The expansion was justified as necessary for sustained economic growth, political stability and social cohesion by all mainstream political parties in America and Europe. But for the Right this settlement was bought at too high a price. Taking their cue from Friedrich A. Hayek they assumed Western societies had run into trouble because of what they saw as unwarranted interference by the state.[11] Inflation, high unemployment, economic recession and urban unrest were all believed to stem from the legacy of Keynesian economics and an ideology which promoted economic redistribution, equality of opportunity and welfare rights for all.

In its place a society would be built where individuals were encouraged to pursue their self-interest and where greed was treated as a virtue in the vain hope that the 'hidden hand' of the market would miraculously benefit all through the 'trickle down' of resources from the winners to the losers. 'What I want to see above all', Ronald Reagan stated, 'is that this remains a country where someone can always get rich'. But Reagan was adamant that this could only be guaranteed by getting the state off the backs of the people, for 'if the reins of government were removed, business would boom, spreading prosperity to all the people'.[12]

Attempts to create an enterprise culture involved a series of attacks on the cherished assumptions of the post-war era. First, it was necessary to increase the scope and incentives for enterprising (money making) activities. This involved what was know as 'changing incentive structures' for individuals and for firms. Behind such bland phrasing lay a programme which would help demolish the idea, first formulated by Simon Kuznets, that as industrial nations grew richer so they would become more equal in income. Security, another foundation of economic nationalism, was also to be torpedoed in the cause of getting the incentives right.

For individuals, changing the incentive structure meant reducing the income of those in poverty and raising the income and wealth of the rich. The crude and paradoxical thinking behind the programme was laid bare by J.K. Galbraith at his most acerbic. In noting that the Right wanted to restore the puritan work ethic, he commented:

> In order to explain that the loss of the Puritan work ethic is at the root of the present crisis, however, you also have to explain that there is a crisis because people work too little... Why do they work too little? In the logic of the Puritan work ethic, the rich work too little because taxes are too high, because they lack incentives, because it is not worth their while to work more, i.e., because they are too poor. The poor work too little because they get too much money from the state, i.e., because they are too rich. So what is the solution? If the rich are too poor and the poor are too rich, the solution is obviously that you take money away from the poor and give it to the rich.[13]

This view was bolstered by some voodoo economics know as the Laffer Curve which purported to show that when income tax rates were too high the rich would avoid tax or simply stop working and hence government revenue would decline. This added economic weight to the assertion that the rates of income tax current at the time were too high.[14] The subsequent cuts in income tax meant that in the United States, the pre-tax incomes of the top 1 per cent of earners rose by 104 per cent between 1977 and 1989 at the same time median income rose less than 7 per cent, and the bottom fifth of income earners experienced a ten per cent fall in incomes. The income tax rates for the rich declined from 91 per cent marginal tax for highest income earners in 1961 to 28 per cent in 1989. In Britain, the richest 20 per cent earned seven times as much as the poorest 20 per cent in 1991 compared with only four times as much in 1977. The poorest tenth of the population were 13 per cent worse off in real terms than they were in 1979 while the richest were 65 per cent better off.[15]

If greed was to be the motor of economic growth it had to be institutionalised by making everyone survive by the pursuit of their self-interest. This was done through the second element of the strategy of getting the 'right' structural incentives for firms and by shrinking the safety net provided by the welfare state. The two are related because, as it was argued at the time, money spent by the state was both likely to be used inefficiently *and* it 'crowded out' the productive private enterprise sector. What this meant was that money siphoned off by the state could better be used in investment to grow the economy.

Getting the incentives right for business involved reducing all the impediments or 'rigidities' to free market behaviour. These included removing barriers to entry to trade, and attacking the power of trade unions. In a global economy, it was assumed, barriers to entry simply protected inefficient businesses while the trade unions kept wages artificially high. Predictably there were high profile showdowns with prominent trade unions, the miners in Britain and the air traffic controllers in the United States. In both cases the state won, giving political and symbolic force to their drive to de-regulate the labour market. Placed in the context of the new global economy the result was de-industrialization. Workers in Detroit and Glasgow rapidly discovered that they were worth no more than the lowest wages of their equivalents in Seoul or south of the Mexican border. At the same time the state itself came in for similar treatment. Working off the premise that whatever the state does must be inefficient because it is not subject to market forces, state assets were sold off which resulted in a massive privatization programme in Britain and subsequently exported to many parts of the world.

In effect, these domestic policies were seen as a way to remove the road blocks to a smoothly functioning *global auction*. But the temporary triumph of these policies tells us more about the realignment of political interests and class conflict that it does about the inherent nature of global capitalism. For the careful balance of power between the state, capital and trade unions was now decisively tipped in favour of capital. There is no doubt that the realignment of political interests was carefully crafted and turned on breaking the alliance between the working and middle class that had been forged through the development of the welfare state. The middle class was now invited to identify with the rich in relation to the burden of taxation and the consumer choices open to them. The result was that any suggestion of tax rises for the rich was interpreted as an equal threat to the disposable income of the middle class. At the same time middle-class families were encouraged to believe that the consumer choices open to them enabled them to take greater control over their lives without government interference. Schools, hospitals, pension plans were all now a matter of personal choice and control. In many cases the promise of choice was and is illusory. Private health care of the American kind is expensive and exclusionary; the attempt to persuade people to cash in occupational pensions and buy personal pensions in Britain has since been acknowledged to have been a disaster, and the idea that all parents can send their children to the school of their choice has proved to be a chimera.[16] But even if the middle classes were unconvinced by the rhetoric of the Right the removal of much of the welfare state safety net gave them little option other than to exert their 'freedom' of choice.

In important ways the break in the alliance between the working and middle classes was also connected to social changes in the 1970s. At the personal level, the response to an impersonal bureaucratic working life and the development of negotiated roles had led to new forms of social interaction based on a critically aware sense of self. This new found subjectivity evoked new forms of understanding and interpersonal skills as an integral part of social interaction, particularly the ability to empathize with others and to negotiate relationships with them. These new skills demanded of the population could have the potential to enrich democratic life because they are precisely the kinds of skills required in a democracy in which everyone feels they should have a say. But economic nationalism had also invoked the reaction that personal fulfilment was to be found in the private spheres of personal consumption and the home. In the absence of a democratic space in which people could participate because big business, big unions and big government had articulated their interests for them, the ground had been well prepared for an ideology of individual consumer choice. It gave the illusion of power over one's life and the gratification to enrich it with domestic objects.

Of course, it still needed the Right to capitalize on the potential for primitive capitalism that these developments presented. In a sense the great trick of the Right was to get people to believe that those with talent and a commitment to the work ethic could thrive in a society based on market individualism. The President's sabre-rattling in the face of the

Soviet threat and the Prime Minister's jingoism over the Falklands' War were symbolic in the redefinition of citizenship on both side of the Atlantic. The message was simply, only the tough and the fit would be included as members of the new market society. In this way, the unemployed, single mothers and others in poverty, for whom a middle class destination was as far away as the moon, could be excluded as 'unfit' to be 'American' or 'British'. Not surprisingly it was people of colour and single mothers who found themselves labelled as pariahs.

4

Nowhere was the full force of the power of the right-wing state felt more than in targeting those who showed themselves to be 'unfit' for life in primitive capitalist society. For although the wealth creators were no longer suffocated by government red tape, and profit was no longer a dirty word, there was still a significant, indeed growing, section of the population who seemed reluctant to take advantage of the new opportunities for self-reliance which had been made available to them. The swelling numbers of those categorized as the 'unfit' or the 'underclass' in the 1980s were not seen to be a product of the increased concentration of wealth in America and Britain during this period, rather having introduced the 'shock treatment' of de-industrialization its victims, the unemployed, were now classed as welfare state dependants.

In Lawrence Mead's account of the 'new politics of dependence' he observed that 'at first, the issues were economic, the fear that excessive spending on income and health programs was overburdening the economy. Cuts were made to promote economic growth . . . More recently, however, the greater concern has been declining social cohesion, as evidenced by rises in crime, single parenthood, and chronic unemployment. The response, in Britain and Sweden as in the US, has been new steps to enforce child support and work effort among the dependent. The shift from the older, redistributive agenda to these new, more behavioural issues ushers in a new political age'.[17] For Mead, 'The West as a whole seems destined for a politics of conduct rather than class'.[18]

The politics of class was about how far the free market should be regulated in the collective interest, the politics of conduct concerned 'government supervision of behaviour'.[19] This distinction was, of course, nonsense because the politics of conduct is underscored by a political economy of the free market. Indeed, its rationale was and is to shift attention from questions of employment security and economic redistribution, to focus attention on the behaviour of the poor within a market system. And to legitimize a more 'hands on' and authoritarian state in its attempt to encourage the poor to shape-up. In the new politics of dependency or conduct, as Lawrence Mead described it, the greatest threat to nations was not structural inequalities, outmoded management techniques, a failure to invest in people or technology, or the inability to generate enough jobs, but the new 'underclass' who sap the energies, spirit and finances of respectable society. The road to recovery was to be found through education, criminal justice and benefit cuts, rather than through redistributive justice. For Mead argued that 'The poverty of today's underclass differs appreciably from poverty in the past: underclass poverty stems less from the absence of opportunity than from the inability or reluctance to take advantage of opportunity'.[20]

This, Mead insists, is because the poor have been de-moralised by welfare. De-moralisation is defined as a lack of incentive(s) to remove themselves from dependency by getting a job; and any sense of obligation to do so, or thankfulness (for the charity) provided by those who are 'working' who pay there welfare cheques through taxation. The most celebrated version of this account is Charles Murray's *Losing Ground*. His argument was that during the 1960s a large number of those who were on welfare viewed it as a temporary and somewhat degrading experience, but within a decade most came to think of it as a 'right', which has not only led to far more people claiming benefits, but staying on them rather than seeking employment.[21] It follows that state involvement in welfare should be limited because it acts as a disincentive to the poor and penalises the productive. To penalize the 'productive' and 'deserving' members of society is morally wrong (unfair) and economically disastrous because it reduces the 'incentive' for the employed to work hard and improve themselves. Equally, increasing state benefits to the poor and unemployed does not help them. They become 'discouraged' from finding work or improving their situation, and become reliant on the state which saps both energy and dignity.[22] Murray states 'We tried to provide more for the poor and produced more poor instead. We tried to remove the barriers to escape from poverty, and inadvertently built a trap'.[23]

Murray's account is interesting because his argument that the state's intervention is positively harmful to the very individuals it is trying to help has a symmetry with Public Choice theory in seeking to render what had been common sense, paradoxical. Democracy was taken to be an unquestionable good, in fact it was instrumental in the decline of the West: welfare was seen as a means to social progress, in fact it contributed to social regress. Yet in a moment of insight Murray was able to say, 'My arguments might seem tailor-made to relieve us of responsibility for persons in need'.[24] He was right because it licensed a reduction in state funding of welfare at the very time when it was most needed. The outcome of these analyses was summed up by Mead, 'The question is no longer what the worst-off members of the community should receive. *Now the question is who should be considered a bona fide member of the community in the first place'.*[25]

The consequences of the new politics of poverty have been stark and far-reaching. It represented the logical extension of the ideology of natural selection and primitive capitalism. It activated a vicious rather than a virtuous circle, which is self-reinforcing and self-defeating. As the government ignored economic inequalities, the rich got richer, and the poor, poorer. The behaviour of the poor has been subject to more intensive supervision as a consequence of worsening conditions and increasing breakdowns in law and order in the inner cities. The economic and social security which was the guarantor of social membership was revoked in a dramatic reversal of Marshall's view of what constituted citizenship rights and Keynes's view of social justice.

5

The Right's attack on mid-century economic nationalism was not limited to the redistribution of wealth to the rich or of helping to undermine the foundations of 'security', but extended to an attack on 'opportunity' based on the principles of meritocratic competition. Nothing captures the changing mood of the times better than almost identical quotations from two American Presidents in Office less than a quarter of a century apart. In the era of economic nationalism Lyndon B. Johnson stated 'the answer for all our national problems comes down to a single word: education'. In a different political era George Bush asked us to 'think about every problem, every challenge we faced today. The solution to each starts with education'. But what underlies their common conviction that education is the key to social harmony and prosperity are competing visions of the decent society and how to achieve it.

When Lyndon Johnson became President following the assassination of John F. Kennedy in November 1963, he not only believed that within a free democratic society everyone, regardless of social circumstances, must be given a fair chance to succeed, but equally, if the idea of a fair and open competition was to amount to something more than political rhetoric, it could only be achieved through a comprehensive programme of social reforms geared to improving equal opportunities. As President (1963–1969), Lyndon Johnson introduced over two hundred pieces of legislation aimed at civil rights for blacks; broader educational opportunities for all young people; a war against poverty; the improvement of health care for the aged; and upgrading the quality of life in American cities.[26] Johnson's programmes for the 'Great Society' were seen at the time as a natural extension of policies being pursued in virtually all of the advanced Western nations, offering the chance for all to make it from log cabin to President via education.[27]

However, by the time George Bush came to power the agenda had changed. Educational standards were to be raised by competition not by attacking child poverty. Pronouncing himself 'Education President' George Bush committed his administration to improving High School graduation rates to 90 per cent, and to making America 'number one' in Science and Mathematics skills by the year 2000. In Britain, the Conservative government made similar, if more realistic claims. The means to achieving these targets was not to tinker with the existing system of public education but to scrap it.[28]

Whereas Jonhson had sought to improve standards through government initiatives the Right tried to distance government from issues of educational selection by proposing the introduction of quasi-markets into state education. Priority was given to the restructuring of education because the perceived decline in educational standards was seen as intimately linked to national decline. To again quote from the influential *Nations at Risk* document, which put it so colourfully, 'If an unfriendly foreign power had attempted to impose on America the mediocre educational performance that exists today, we might well have viewed it as an act of war. As it stands, we have allowed this to happen to ourselves.... We have, in effect been committing an act of unthinking, unilateral educational disarmament'.[29] This was a declaration of America's entry into the 'knowledge wars'!

In America, the arguments for markets in education took a familiar form. Eric Hanushek took a first step by arguing that while the cost of state education had risen standards had declined. Most of the money had gone into rewarding teachers for their experience, academic credentials and in reducing class sizes.[30] None of these things he suggested were directly related to improving educational standards. So, again we see the familiar argument that common sense ideas like smaller classes are beneficial are in fact counter to reality. This, by now, familiar paradoxical twist was also at the heart of Chubb and Moe's celebrated peon to markets in education, *Politics, Markets and America's Schools*, where they argued that it was the democratic governance of education that had led to a decline in educational standards.[31] Not only did it lead to a wastage of state resources but was positively damaging, especially to those who most needed a sound education – the urban blacks and Latinos/as.

Competition was considered the way standards could be raised for individuals and between schools because it was seen as natural to human beings. It was the state protection of education from competition through zoning, for example, which reduced teachers' efforts and incentives to achieve on behalf of their students. Under competitive rules schools which could not attract students would be closed down. So teachers would now have the right spurs (the threat of unemployment) and incentives (continued work) to perform efficiently.

The argument for markets in education were augmented on both sides of the Atlantic by an elitism based on 'natural selection'. The pursuit of social justice through equality of opportunity engineered by the state was assumed to push against the laws of nature because it ignored the fact that there is a limited pool of ability. Consequently, any attempt at equalising opportunities would result in mediocrity. In *The Meaning of Conservatism*, the British philosopher, Roger Scruton regards 'equality of opportunity' as an absurdity, as 'such a thing seems to be neither possible nor desirable. For what opportunity does an unintelligent child have to partake of the advantages conferred by an institution which demands intelligence? His case is no different from that of a plain girl competing with a pretty girl for a position as model'.[32] Similar pronouncement were also not difficult to find in the United States. Murray and Herrnstein, for example, suggested that what really lay behind the SAT-Score decline was the drive for equality of opportunity. The answer is that educational leaders need to become comfortable once again with their duty to 'educate what Jefferson called the "natural aristocracy" to be worthy conservators of the republic'.[33]

The view that education should be organised on the principles of the 'market' extended the idea that everyone should act as an entrepreneur. In a knowledge-based economy it was argued that individuals would be motivated to become capitalists not from the diffusion of the ownership of corporate stock, as folklore would have it but from the acquisition of knowledge and skills that have economic value.[34] Fundamental to this view was the belief that individuals are driven by the rational pursuit of self-interest where the goals are wealth and status.[35] In the modern world a clear route to these ends is through the acquisition of credentials. In addition to bringing entrepreneurial values into education it also created the theoretical space to argue that education is essentially a private good which primarily benefits those who invest in it, and therefore should be paid, in part or wholly, by them. The introduction of markets in education was, therefore, consistent with the precepts of primitive capitalism. Education was not to be considered a humanizing force for social progress, but merely a necessary supply-side factor in the cause of wealth creation.

Predictably this policy agenda in education provoked a strong response. Critics of these changes in education argued that the introduction of choice and competition provided a mechanism by which the middle classes could more securely gain an advantage in the competition for credentials.[36] The reproduction of social inequalities within a market system can be illustrated in terms of a game of 'Monopoly'. In this game everyone begins with the same amount of money and chance to win, depending on a combination of choice, luck and skill. Life chances in capitalist societies do not begin with this kind of substantive equality, but begin close to the end of the game with a few players owning houses and hotels on expensive streets such as Fifth Avenue in New York or Mayfair in London. The rest of the players may own property in less expensive streets but they cannot hope to compete because the logic of this 'free market' game does not lead to the equalisation of resources, but a winner who ends up with a monopoly. Of course Monopoly is not like real life in another sense, because when the game is over you can start again on equal terms. In real life those who own property and the advantages which this accrues are able to pass these advantages on to future family members. Therefore, when education is treated as a commodity the economic power of parents, or lack of it, becomes an increasingly important determinant of educational and life chances.[37] In the market for education there is a conspicuous transfer of material capital into cultural capital. Parents who can afford to will invest increasing amounts of their money in private education as a way of reducing the risk of their children failing in an open system of competitive achievement. As Alfred Marshall (1890) recognised, 'The professional classes especially, while generally eager to save some capital *for* their children, are even more on the alert for opportunities of investing it *in* them'.[38] This does not generate creativity and enterprise but a massive wastage of talent and social closure. The underlying disparities in material and cultural resources between the educationally successful and unsuccessful are likely to ensure that the 'best' schools remain the monopoly of middle-class parents and their off-spring. There will be some degree of competition within the market for education, in that working-class schools will compete against each other as will middle-class schools, but the inherently unequal nature of the competition will ensure that the educational provision for the less privileged members of society will not improve. The return to primitive capitalism induced a shift from the *ideology of meritocracy* to the *ideology of parentocracy* where the education a child receives will conform to the wealth and wishes of parents rather than the abilities and efforts of pupils.[39]

In essence market reforms in education starkly increased the inequalities of opportunity that existed in the Golden era.[40] In the context of the global auction this threatened to leave a large majority of the future working population without the human capital to flourish in the global economy. Here the link between market reforms and low skill economies was barely disguised in countries which were dominated by New Right governments in the 1980s. While the principal objective of economic policy was to improve the competitiveness of workers by increasing labour market deregulation, despite the poor work conditions this would inflict on many employees, market reforms in education ensured the conditions in which highly-paid middle-class professionals and elite groups are able to give their children an 'excellent' education in preparation for their bid to join the ranks of Reich's global professional elite.[41]

A related problem is that market reforms failed to overcome some of the major flaws of 'bureaucratic' education. Despite all their claims to be 'radical', the educational proposals of the Right were profoundly conservative both in there appeal and consequences. They clearly took a very dim view of the abilities and motivations of the average person and shared most of the assumptions which have characterised the development of bureaucratic education, with the notable exception that the state should no longer seek to fulfil the conditions of a meritocracy.[42] Ironically, markets in education have simply relocated much of the bureaucracy from the central or local state to the school. In part this is because schools need to provide standardized 'market signals' by which consumers can judge them, and in part it is because the state feels the need to impose arm's length control through extensive monitoring systems which simply add to teachers' paperwork. There is a real danger that these forms of standardization, based on exam results and surveillance, simply serve to de-skill teachers and lead students to cram for the narrow range of skills that are subject to examination.[43] In these circumstances the education system will simply create the personalities and skills for a low-wage, low-skill economy. Indeed, because schools are judged on the basis of the commodities they produce, namely qualifications which can be traded in the market for higher education or jobs, the overreaching concern of parents, students, and teachers, is about the production of 'smart conformists' able to pass formal examinations rather than to develop individual and collective initiative and creativity.

6

At the start of the 1980s the New Right administrations in America and Britain were faced with a series of fundamental changes in the economic and social fabric. These posed opportunities and challenges. The opportunities coalesced around new technology and new forms of economic production based on knowledge and learning. What they offered was the potential for high-skilled employment which was personally fulfilling. Part of this potential stemmed from the social changes in the way individuals understood themselves and related to one another. These changes were set in train in the late 1960s as a new generation broke the shackles of deference and pre-given roles which enabled, among other things, flexible teamwork based on negotiated roles. But the possibilities that this new found flexibility and social awareness offered could equally have been extended into the realm of democracy. For the ability to be socially reflexive and to work in teams are equally perquisites for a democratic society. At the same time, as we argued in chapter 6, the social and economic cards were stacked against a progressive response to these potentials. And, when confronted by the challenges of stagflation and the oil price hikes that these governments faced, it would have required a quite remarkable political transformation to see issues of democracy, security and social justice at the top of the political agenda.

In the end, the 'raw materials' of progress, the potentials and challenges that societies face will always be shaped by political projects which interpret these potentials in specific ways, defining what is possible and what is not. In essence they determine how reality is to be understood and hence what is feasible and therefore 'common sense'. The Right saw these potentials and challenges of the early 1980s in socially regressive ways. The potential that new forms of individual social awareness and flexibility offered were translated into the straight jacket of consumer choice. The only form of reflection demanded of people concerned the choices laid open on the supermarket shelf: a principle extended throughout society. Governments invited those lucky enough to have the money to enter supermarkets to vent their moral opprobrium on those who could not. But the freedom of consumer sovereignty was bought at the cost of deep social division between the haves and have nots.

At the same time the potential for a high skills economy was rejected in favour of a short-term 'casino' economy which exploited cheap labour rather than the possibilities of new technology. The uncertainties endemic to these economies, and their consequences for workers is the subject of the next two chapters.[44]

9
Downsizing the Corporation

Don't think, just do what we tell you, suppress your individuality and play our game, and you will always have a job'. Then it screwed them. I understand the economics of why they did that, but if you make a social contract, you can't violate it.

Wife of a former IBM senior manager, Dutchess County, USA

1

The monolithic nature of the modern corporation evoked the same feeling that one gets sitting on a jumbo jet waiting for it to take off, it is simply too big to crash. For millions of employees and their families the corporation had become a life support machine. The massive expansion of the middle class in the post-war period was, after all, a product of expanding bureaucracies in both the public and private sectors. But in the 1970s there was a widely held belief that at the heart of western economic problems was a failure of management. The bureaucratic paradigm which shaped the modern corporation, was identified as a competitive liability in rapidly changing markets for 'value added' products and services. Management gurus such as Rosabeth Moss Kanter spoke of the need for managers to apply 'entrepreneurial principles to the traditional corporation, creating a marriage between entrepreneurial creativity and corporate discipline, co-operation, and team-work'.[1] The convergence of information technologies and their integration into the workplace, the need to free-up and speed-up the flow of information and decision-making, the increasing emphasis on team-work and project-work, and the need for flexible work practices; along with a new vocabulary of networks, empowerment, leadership, teamwork, downsizing, rightsizing, re-engineering, and contracting out, all became part of the rhetoric of the *flexible* paradigm. Set against the tarnished image of the 'organisation man' emasculated in red tape, dedicated to stifling enterprise, innovation and individual initiative the attack on bureaucracy has proved to be a soft target. Thomas McCraw has neatly summed up Western attitudes, 'Contempt for bureaucracies runs so deep in the popular consciousness that denouncing them is like shooting fish in a barrel'.[2]

At face value who could argue against new forms of organisation which hold out the promise of greater workplace democracy, justice and scope for human creativity. But as the massive process of corporate restructuring got underway in America and Britain, in both public and private sector organizations, much of the progressive potential of the flexible paradigm was lost. Enormous variations exist in the way organisations have responded to greater competitive pressures, volatile markets and technological change. There has been a reluctance on the part of senior managers to abandon bureaucratic command and control systems, despite adopting the rhetoric of the flexible paradigm.[3] David Harvey among others have shown that new technologies and co-ordinating forms of organisation have permitted the revival of domestic, familial, and paternalistic labour systems given that, 'the same shirt designs can be reproduced by large-scale factories in India, co-operative production in the "Third Italy", sweatshops in New York and London, or family labour systems in Hong Kong'.[4] Equally the restructuring of IBM in the early 1990s demonstrated that there is little contradiction between moving towards a more 'flexible' organisational structure and corporate indifference towards technical, managerial and professional staff.[5] To date much of the restructuring in the US and Britain has involved downsizing as a way of cost cutting. This has been based on neo-classical assumptions about shareholder capitalism which Hayes and Abernathy called 'management by the numbers'.

'Management by the numbers' reveals just how deep rooted the internal disease of scientific management has proved to be. Control based on management by the numbers is what Robert Reich has called the 'bastard child of scientific management'.[6] This is because it involves an even more radical separation between planning and production. In Fordist plants although there was a clear division between those who did the company's thinking and those who did the company's producing, the former often had experience of the industry in question, they were the 'organization men'. But management by the numbers values analytical detachment and 'short-term cost reduction rather than long-term development of technological competitiveness'.[7] Planning takes the form of financial targets within corporations broken down into cost centres. In this context it is hardly surprising that American and British top managers 'driven by bonus schemes and fear of stock-market reaction, set ludicrously short pay-back periods, effectively disqualifying all but short-term schemes for patching and cost-cutting'.[8]

2

As a consequence, American and British companies energetically pursued 'downsizing' policies based on a commitment to shareholder value. These include cutting labour costs through layoffs, 'voluntary' redundancy, hiring freezes and contracting-out various activities to other companies, consultants, contractors or self-employed workers. Based on US Labor Department Statistics, a report in the *New York Times* calculated that between 1979 and 1995 some 43 million people became 'surplus employees'. Most of these people were able to find alternative jobs, but in two-thirds of cases they received lower earnings and worse terms and conditions.[9] In another report it is estimated that between 1985 and 1995 some 22 million jobs were cut from Wilshire 5,000 companies.[10] These figures obviously need to be treated with caution as it is difficult to assess their accuracy, but even if we allow for discrepancies which run into the millions, the scale of job turnover in America has been truly extraordinary. In Britain the overall scale of downsizing is difficult to assess due to the lack of statistical evidence, but a representative study of job insecurity suggests that at the end of 1990s, insecurity was higher than at any point in the previous thirty years. Brendan Burchell and colleagues also found that the biggest 'losers' had been professional workers who went from being the most secure workers in 1986 to the most insecure by 1997.[11]

Evidence at the company level offers more concrete examples of the scale of downsizing activity. Michael Useem shows that of the Fortune 500 largest manufacturing firms between 1980 and 1990, 1 in 3 ceased to exist as independent firms, product sector diversity declined by over one-half, and employment dropped from 15.9 million to 12.4 million.[12] In the automobile industry, General Motors, Ford and Chrysler alone announced further reductions of 110,000 workers in the early 1990s. With a significant knock-on effect on their suppliers. Mishra and Mishra point out that this cut came as little surprise to the $200 billion auto parts industry which in the 1980s lost 90,000 jobs when hundreds of firms went to the wall.[13] General Motors cut its workforce from 800,000 in 1979 to 450,000 in the early 1990s.[14] IBM's workforce was virtually halved from 406,000 in 1986 to 202,000 in 1995, then following a return to full profitability in 1996 it recruited an additional 25,000 people.[15] Between 1987 and 1997 British Pretroleum (BP) reduced its workforce from 129,000 to 53,000.

In the early 1990s IBM executives showed a keen interest in a modest five-story building based in Zurich. It is the headquarters of Asea Brown Boveri Group (ABB) an electrical engineering conglomerate, which employs 220,000 worldwide but only 140 in its head office. A spokesperson for IBM at the time reported 'We have made a close study of the Asea structure and found many aspects of it appealing. What we particularly like is the idea of a very lean head office acting more as a holding company, with a family of more independent and flexible businesses around it'.[16] ABB's approach is illustrated by its takeover of Combustion Engineering Inc in the US. Its head office in Stamford, Connecticut was reduced from 900 to 68 and the workforce was cut in half. Gerhard Schulmeyer, who was responsible for ABB's business in the US and Canada, explained what the company call the 30–30–30 downsizing strategy previously used in Finland, Germany and Switzerland. Thirty per cent of their headquarters' staff were laid off, 30 per cent were deployed in other parts of the company and 30 per cent who were employed in marketing and product promotions were employed in a separate company offering services to ABB and other companies. Only ten per cent of the original work force remained.[17]

ABB have taken the logic of downsizing further than most companies but virtually all the Fortune 1000 companies engaged in downsizing and cost cutting during the 1990s. The consequences of 'bottom line' management has also been felt by public sector workers who were conventionally thought of as a closeted species. This has frequently been linked with the growth of privatization in areas including telecommunications, electricity, gas, water, oil, coal, steel, airlines, airports, ports, railways, road transport and broadcasting. The scale of privatization is such that the multinational accountancy firm Price Waterhouse operates a privatisation service for governments and local authorities which is currently active in more than 35 countries. In the UK the impact of privatization on employment has been dramatic. In the 29 utilities companies comprising British Telecom, British Gas, 10 regional water companies and 17 electricity supply and generating companies it is estimated that since privatization, these companies alone shed nearly 250,000 jobs by the year 2000.[18] Richard Davidson and Markus Rosgen, analysts at Morgan Stanley, estimated that \$250 billion \$300 billion of state assets were sold in the late 1990s as a result of European privatizations which is double the sum raised in the decade to 1995.[19]

It is not only the impact of privatization which is undermining the security of public sector workers, however, but a philosophy of public sector efficiency, which emphasizes market competition. According to David Osborne, a co-author of *Reinventing Government*, endorsed by Bill Clinton, reinvention is about 'replacing large, centralized, command-and-control bureaucracies with a very different model: decentralized, entrepreneurial organizations that are driven by competition and accountable to customers for the results they deliver'.[20] The downsizing implications of introducing market competition into the public sector is recognized by Osborne, 'you can't get people to do their best work if you're treating them like 1950s assembly-line workers. Companies have been getting rid of layers of middle management for years, and now government must too'.[21] In the UK a policy of market competition has been vigorously pursued. Even the Treasury, a bastion of the British civil service informed some of its senior staff that they had become 'surplus employees'. The Treasury's role as the inspector of public spending in all government departments including education, health, transport and defence, has been scaled down with the privatization and contracting out to executive agencies which are not democratically accountable and are frequently filled with government supporters and company bosses. Thirty per cent of senior civil servants were axed, amounting to a reduction in senior staff from 99 in 1994 to 68 in 1998. This added in a symbolic way to a decline of over 250,00 Civil Servants between 1986 and 1996.[22]

3

What downsizing reflects is an assessment that keeping a workforce of large numbers of full-time, long-tenure workers is a luxury which organisations can no longer afford if they are going to stay competitive in volatile domestic and global markets. New technologies have also given senior managers the potential to cut out layers of middle management previously involved in the supervision of armies of front-line workers engaged in routine tasks with less than machine-like efficiency. Such changes have made corporate organizations of the past look decidedly top heavy and cumbersome. In response, a key element of downsizing has been to increase 'numerical' flexibility, where organizations maintain a much smaller 'core' of key workers who are indispensable to meeting the organization's goals.[23] They are usually well qualified, work long hours, and expected to directly contribute to the profits of the company in return for high salaries and 'value added' CVs. There may also be a core of production, clerical or support workers, but what underlies the principle of 'numerical' flexibility is the creation of a peripheral labour force of temporary or part-time workers who can be used during busy periods which enable companies to avoid the costs involved in fluctuations in demand, where large numbers of workers are seen to be paid for doing nothing. It has also been used as a way of reducing labour costs by offering lower wages, and rights to sick pay, holiday entitlements, contributions to pension schemes and medical insurance.

Downsizing for numerical flexibility is also achieved through outsourcing to suppliers, consultants and subcontractors, or establishing alliances with other organisations, often in other countries. Even in the initial stages of downsizing in the 1980s Bennett Harrison and Barry Bluestone pointed to the 'hollowing' of America in which 'firms have been merged and acquired, downsized, deindustrialized, multinationalized, automated, streamlined, and restructured. In the process, the rich have gotten richer, the poor poorer, and life for the middle class more and more precarious'.[24] We have already seen that where companies decide to import components, products and services they tended to export jobs. Thus the mentality of downsizing in effect encourages managers to view all activities that are not defined as the organization's core business as suitable for contracting to outsiders, of which some are likely to be overseas. Work that is contracted out may included professionals who have expertise in areas the organization does not have at hand, such as legal, financial, computer and software experts, as well as a large amount of the more mundane aspects of organisational life, such as data entry, or standardized production. In some cases virtually all of the organization's previous activities are now fulfilled by contractors. In other instances, new enterprises have been created within organizations to develop entrepreneurial activities in the hope of creating or exploiting new markets. Factories are now following the lead of the retail 'concessionary' stores, where different companies sell their goods under one roof. Companies such as Ford operate concessionary factories which 'contract in' other firms to undertake key aspects of production such as the control of the stores for essential equipment and spare parts, routine and specialist maintenance, lubricants, machine cleaning and catering.

Another feature of corporate life that has encouraged the use of downsizing is the enduring popularity of mergers and acquisitions. In 1996 there were more that 10,000 mergers and acquisitions with more than

$660 billion changing hands. This amounts to one per hour, round the clock, all year long. David Whitford observes that 'companies are merging like never before for a surprisingly sensible reason. They have no choice. Thousands of companies today of every shape and size are facing the business climate equivalent of 100–year storm. Deregulation has turned entire industries completely upside down. Media companies, utilities, banks, telephony – they're all frantically trying to adapt to a new reality'.[25] In the aircraft industry Boeing acquired McDonnell Douglas for $14.7 billion; in banking Nationsbank acquired Boatmen's Bancshares for $9.8 billion; Gillette razors acquired Duracell International (alkaline batteries) for $8.5 billion; in insurance AETNA Life and Casualty acquired US Healthcare, a managed care company, for $8.2 billion and Thomson publishing acquired West Publishing for $3.4 billion to control 50 per cent of the legal-information market.[26] The consolidation of the UK cable industry moved a step closer when the Cable and Wireless Communications sold its residential cable assets to NTL the American communications group for about $13 billion.[27] A likely consequence of merge activity in recent years is further rounds of restructuring and downsizing as newly merged companies seek to capitalize on the economies of scale which these new alliances are supposed to achieve.

It would appear that the insecurities to which employees at all levels of the organisation have been forced to adjust in the 1980s and 1990s are set to continue. Manfred Kets de Vries and Katharina Balazs suggest that one of reasons why downsizing is likely to continue is that 'A major contributing factor has been the increasing popularity of global benchmarking. Finding one's overhead costs wanting compared to not only domestic but also international competitors has turned into a convincing argument to take large numbers of employees off the payroll'.[28] Up to now we have got used to large companies hollowing out their home base and operating globally. But it is likely that the next stage will be the downsizing of global operations. Kodak, like other US multinationals, has combined a policy of mass firings in the US with investment into new markets for its products around the world. Such investments are followed by 'melding operations into a more efficient global network, reducing overheads and concentrating production in efficient locations'.[29] In the early stages of this process overseas workers are likely to be protected from the downsizing impulse of American and European multinationals, but if they fail to meet the rate of returns demanded by Wall Street, The City or Frankfurt stock markets, cuts in the workforce are inevitable. At Kodak the many small photofinishing businesses it bought outside the US failed to deliver high short-term profits according to Michael Ellman an analyst at Schroder Wertheim in New York which has led to retrenchments as 'Squeezing out costs by trying to consolidate networks in different countries is now the order of the day'.[30] The financial crisis in Asia also led to retrenchments in the Tiger Economies as companies have tried to maintain healthy profits from all sectors of their global operations.

Global downsizing does offer some respite to American and British workers, but this is likely to be short-term, given that there is little evidence to suggest that corporate bosses have abandoned downsizing as a way of cutting costs to maintain historically high profit margins. Corporate after-tax profits are triple the level of the 1960s.[31] There have, after all, been many examples of companies making record profits and at the same time announcing further cuts in staffing. These retrenchments are now explained in terms of global bench-marking and the application of new technologies. But while it is difficult to see how significant cuts can be made in the manufacturing sector, the globalization of service sector activities such as insurance, banking, legal services, media and telecommunication, presents the prospect of major retrenchments of white collar career jobs. Ulrich Cartellieri at Deutsche Bank sees the banks as 'the steel industry of the nineties'. In a Coopers and Lybrand study of the plans of fifty leading banks around the world, it is reported that half the people involved in banking will lose their jobs in the next ten years.[32] Hans-Peter Martin and Harald Schumann calculate that if global benchmarking is adopted in Banks, Telecommunications, Insurance and the Airline business there would be huge job losses in many leading companies. If Deutsche Bank was as efficient as Citicorp it would need 31,076 fewer employees that it had in 1995 to make the same profits. To match the productivity of the French insurance company Assekuranz, German insurance companies would need to lose 104,294 staff and Britain would need to cut about 100,000 staff.[33] Martin and Schumann conclude that based on a survey of future employment from the World Bank, the OECD and the McKinsey Global Institute as well as numerous trade sector and reports, they predict that 15 million white-collar and blue-collar workers in the European Union are at risk of losing their regular full-time employment.[34]

4

Downsizing destroyed a key aspect of mid-century economic nationalism, where regular workers got regular jobs and regular workers with all education got a career. Economic insecurity has been a fact of life for production workers for decades. In previous recessions it has been they who have been forced to bear the brunt of cut-backs. In the 1981–82 recession, Lester Thurow noted that in America 90 per cent of the firms that laid off blue-collar workers did not lay off a single white-collar worker.[35] By the end of the 1980s this was no longer the case. The flattening of corporate hierarchies has primarily been achieved by removing several tiers of middle management and supervisory staff due to the elimination of large numbers of workers doing mundane tasks, requiring close supervision. The 'lean' and 'mean' corporation of the 1990s democratized insecurity. Virtually all employees, at all levels of the organization, are subject to regular appraisal to demonstrate one's contribution to the bottom line, and even those with long track-records and invaluable knowledge of the company may no longer find themselves part of corporate restructuring plans. On 30th March, 1993 7,700 employees were designated 'surplus employees' at IBM in Mid-Hudson Valley, up-state New York. Many of the layoffs were among the professional and technical ranks of 'knowledge' workers. These joined the 10,000 jobs which had already been eliminated by 'big blue' in the area between 1985 and 1992. They became part of an army of unemployed or under-utilized workers, who were laid off by other hi-tech firms in the North-east including Digital, Grumman, Eastman Kodak, Wang, Pratt & Whitney, among others. John Hoerr has shown how jobless IBMers and their families experienced many of the problems commonly associated with the underclass in the urban ghettos, including domestic violence, drunkenness and the bouts of depression. 'That such carnage could occur at a company... held up as the paradigm of high technology is a warning that the "invisible hand" can write epitaphs anywhere. It makes no distinction between rust belt and high-tech industries, private and government sectors, blue chip corporations and barely solvent entrepreneurs, or blue-collar and white-collar workers'.[36]

In such circumstances the social contract between employers and their white collar employees which included long tenure and career advancement could no longer be underwritten as companies were 'downsized', 'merged', 'restructured' or 'taken over' and public sector organisations were subjected to 'market testing', 'competitive tendering', 'contracting out' or were 'sold off'.[37] Since the early 1990s relying on career advancement through working up the corporate hierarchy has become a high risk strategy as there is less scope for upward mobility in flatter organizations. Such restrictions on career opportunities leads to status frustration as employees reach career 'plateaus' earlier.[38] This has not only affected middle-class career planning, but removed a crucial source of advancement for able working-class employees who may have failed to get an appropriate education during their childhood, but who were able to work their way up the internal career ladder by showing that they have what it takes to get the job done.

The problem of how to reward commitment and high performance in downsized organizations is just one of the issues raised by the demise of the bureaucratic corporation. The loosening of the bond between the corporation and employee has, according to Rosabeth Moss Kanter, forced corporate bosses to pay more attention to the training and developmental needs of the individual given that the employment relationship and commitment must come from ensuring 'employability' both within the company and the external labour market.[39] Companies now talk in terms of enhancing 'employability' rather than commit themselves to long-term job security. Manfred Kets de Vries and Katharina Balazs suggest:

> The organisation of the future is described as taking on a guiding role to help employees towards a self-employment attitude. In order to provide at least a modicum of security, organizations encourage employees to keep their work experience as up-to-date as possible so that they are better able to get a new job if laid off. A new, short-term employment contract is proposed as part of this solution – a contract that gives a limited amount of security for a defined period of time. Fine as these new ideas may sound on paper, however, for many people this new way of organizing goes against their need for connectedness and affiliation and necessitates a great shift in thinking and expertise on the part of both employees and executives.[40]

Although this may prove to be a vain hope in many companies, there has been a massive expansion of 'outplacement' agencies. These are designed to help those who have been made redundant to polish up their job search skills, provide personal counselling services to work through the consequences of job lose and to plan for the future along with more practical support in the form of letter writing facilities. It would however be a mistake to reduce the problem of employability to one of out-moded attitudes in the failure to embrace opportunities for career self-management. Research conducted with final year undergraduate students in Britain clearly shows that the extent to which students were willing to break from established forms of career development depended on an assessment of their labour market power. It was male students from elite universities who were most likely to welcome the chance of regular job moves in an attempt to circumvent the old bureaucratic career ladders because they knew that they had the necessary credentials and networks to get another job if they were made redundant. Whereas female students and people of colour from working class backgrounds, who thought they may experience discrimination in the labour market, were more likely to express a preference for bureaucratic careers because it would give them the time to demonstrate their ability once they had found a decent job.[41]

The problem confronting labour market entrants is that downsizing has led to a declining proportion of jobs offering long-term career opportunities, although this remains an issue in urgent need of further study. In turn, it raises the question of whether the middle class is shrinking? How one answers this question will depend a great deal on how the middle class is defined, for example, on income or occupation. Equally important is the issue of what we assume about the individuals and families who constitute the 'middle class'. At mid-century to be middle class was to have an occupational career rather than simply a job, occupational security, decent housing and health care, access to a good education and career prospects for one's children.

In *Silent Depression*, Wallace Peterson offers two sources of evidence that led him to conclude that the American middle class is shrinking. Wallace's evidence is at best suggestive rather than conclusive. First he suggests that if you take income as a measure of class (which would not please the sociologists who prefer some form of occupational classification), and define the 'middle class' to include all families with an income between $25,000 and $75,000 (in 1990 dollars), the percent of families in this category has declined from 59.7 to 54.5 between 1973 and 1990. The percentage of families with income above $75,000 has increased from 8.6 to 12.3 and those with incomes under $24,999 from 31.8 to 33.3 during the same period. The problems associated with taking income as a measure of class makes this kind of data suspect. Regional variations in the cost of living will mean that the same family income in New York City and in Cleveland will result in significant differences in living standards. Equally, if family income is taken as a measure of 'class', a household where two people are working in modest occupations will have a combined income which will often be significantly above those where one member of the household is employed in a profession such as teaching. Therefore the increase in percentage of families earning over $75,000 is largely a reflection of dual-income families. What this data does suggest however is that the middle family income range has been polarized. During this period, the top 5 per cent of families have increased their share of overall income from 15.5 to 17.4 per cent, while the bottom fifth of families have experienced a decline in their overall proportion of the spoils from 5.5 to 4.6 per cent. Middle-income families witnessed a slight decline in the proportion of family income they received which is explained by the fact that they have lost out to the top twenty per cent of households. This tendency towards income polarization is confirmed by more recent evidence presented in our earlier discussion of the new global competition.

Drawing on data from the Survey Research Center at the University of Michigan, Peterson also suggests that the 'middle class' has not only shrunk but that there has been an increase in downward mobility and a decrease in upward mobility. The Michigan University team have been following the fortunes of over 5,000 families and has collected data on all family members in order to construct a moving picture of how individuals fair in their own right and also relative to other family members. Again drawing on income data, but for individuals rather than families the Michigan study found that the percentage of prime-age men and women moving into high-income status (over $55,000 in 1987 dollars) increased from 6.3 to 7.5 between 1980 and 1987. The bad news, though, was that 'downward mobility out of the upper-income range is much greater than mobility upward. For the twenty years of the Michigan study (1967–87), 29.7 per cent of high-income individuals fell out of the upper income bracket of the Michigan study, while only 6.7 per cent of middle-income individuals climbed into the upper bracket'.[42] What this study also found was that the risk of downward mobility from the middle to lower income category was greatest for black families, those headed by a woman, and for younger families where the key worker was under thirty-five years old.

These figures do not take account of the significant improvement in the American economy in the late 1990s which, for instance, has led to the importing of skilled workers to meet employer demands for trained people in the information technology sector.[43] But there is little doubt that much of what was taken for granted about middle-class work- and life-styles can no longer be assumed even when the economy is buoyant. There seems little doubt that a culture of insecurity has become a fact of life for middle as well as working-class workers and families. Research has shown that the prospect of job loss is not the only thing that triggers feeling of job insecurity. It can also be triggered by the loss or erosion of employment conditions.[44] A feature of downsizing has been 'down-benefiting' where companies use restructuring packages as a way of reducing or limiting the benefits such as healthcare, pensions, and redundancy packages, offered to staff. Brendan Burchell and colleagues found that many workers in the late 1990s not only felt insecure because they could lose their jobs but because of the perceived threat to valued job features, 'they are scared of losing promotion opportunities, of losing control over the pace of work, of losing their ability to complete the entire job, and of losing their customary pay rise'.[45]

Equally, the extent of job insecurity is higher than that recorded in official unemployment figures, given that one of the biggest fears for the middle classes is a 'fear of falling' into less prestigious or less rewarding jobs.[46] Managerial and professional workers prefer to 'resign' rather than be made redundant and to define themselves as consultants, self-employed, 'between jobs' or 'retired' rather than 'unemployed'. Thomas Moonedy who was president of the Chamber of Commerce in Rochester, New York felt this was the reason why the official jobless rate in the area was only 5 per cent despite deep cuts at Eastman Kodak the region's biggest employer. Alongside the fact that many Kodak workers were coaxed into early retirement, 'an awful lot of those people became consultants. Whether or not they have any clients, I don't know. But if they get a call asking if they are working, they many say they're con-sultants, and then they're listed as employed, even if it amounts to little more than the occasional days work'.[47]

Projections of the future demand for managerial and professional workers suggest a mixed picture. Figures published by the Department of Labour in the United States, predict that between 1990 and 2005 there will be a 76.6 per cent increase in the number of 'managerial' jobs. In Britain it is estimated that the number of people in managerial, professional, associate professional and technical will grow by over one million between 1997 and 2007.[48] Such figures have led some commentators to argue that although companies are downsizing, new high-skill, high-wage jobs will be created to replace them. However, such predictions are notoriously unreliable and need to be treated with extreme caution. In the US, for example, employment projections for the same period show a decline in the average annual number of vacancies in jobs requiring a degree, compared with opportunities avail-able in the 1984–1990 period.[49] It is also worth remembering that the two largest private companies in America are Wal-Mart the discount retailer with a total of 670,000 employees and Manpower a temporary help agency which employees 767,000 substitute workers a year (see Table 9.1).[50]

Table 9.1 The ten occupations with the largest job-growth, 1996–2006 (thousands)[51]

Occupation	Employment		Change 1996–2006	
	1996	2006	Number	Per cent
Cashiers	3,146	3,677	530	17
Systems analysts	506	1,025	520	103
General managers and top executives	3,210	3,677	467	15
Registered nurses	1,971	2,382	411	21
Salespersons, retail	4,072	4,481	408	10
Truck drivers light and heavy	2,719	3,123	404	15
Home health aides	495	873	378	76
Teacher aides and educational assistants	981	1,352	370	38
Nursing aides, orderlies, and attendants	1,312	1,645	333	25
Receptionists and information clerks	1,074	1,392	318	30

Source: US Bureau of Labour Statistics

Moreover, an increase in the demand for jobs labelled as managerial and professional does not mean that most of these jobs will offer organisational 'careers' as the underlying assumptions about employment contracts, conditions and relations in the Golden era no longer hold with the demise of bureaucratic work. This suggests that the 'work' and 'market' situations of those who have conventionally been grouped together under the label of the middle class are likely to become increasingly divorced. As John Goldthorpe at Nuffield College, Oxford University, has acknowledged, the basis for the expanding middle class (he prefers to use the term 'service' class)

is an essentially bureaucratic one. Bureaucracies, through their very form, tend to establish 'career lines' for those who are employed within them, and success or failure for the latter is then largely defined in terms of how far along these lines they are able to progress. Thus, failure does not usually mean that the individual is actually relegated from the bureaucracy and forced to take up employment of a quite different class character, but only that he [or she] achieves relatively little advancement within the bureaucracy. A contrast may be drawn here with the consequences of failure in an entrepreneurial role, which would seem far more likely to lead to a decisive change in class position.[52]

As corporations have restructured to enhance their entrepreneurial energy this contrast is less clear today, as many employees who would have previously enjoyed extended career prospects have found themselves part of fringe rather than the strategic core. Hence we can anticipate a widening of the divisions between senior managers and the remainder of the workforce, which will include many workers who maintain the trappings of a middle-class job title but without the security or career prospects with which they have traditionally been assumed to convey.[53] As a result, 'flexible' careers, rather than 'bureaucratic' careers have become prevalent.[54] Whereas bureaucratic careers are associated with a predictable linear progression within corporate hierarchies, flexible careers are invariably contingent and retrospective. They involve frequent job change irrespective of whether each move is voluntary or imposed. For those involved the aim is to gain incremental progression with each move in terms of the employment package, including salary, car, holiday entitlement, and private health insurance.

An inevitable feature of 'flexible' career patterns is that they fail to guarantee a progression in income as well as being inherently insecure. A study in the early 1990s found that of 2,000 or so workers made redundant by RJR Nabisco, 72 per cent found new jobs but at wages which were less that half of their previous pay.[55] Moreover, within many jobs 'Work is not the place where one finds personal fulfilment or fellowship; it is the place where survival of the fittest is the goal and the consequence of being less than the best is likely to be a serious drop in one's standard of living'.[56] This suggest that it is no longer simply a question of gaining access to a superior job, but of maintaining one's 'employability', of keeping fit in both the internal and external market for jobs through the acquisition of externally validated credentials, in-house training programmes, social contacts and networks.

This sense of occupational insecurity has been compounded by the growing popularity of 'hot desking' where all but very senior staff are no longer given an office which increases in size as the employee climbs the corporate ranks. They now 'check in' and are allocated a desk, phone and computer. This has intensified middle-class anxieties. Now you no longer have a desk or office, but turn up for work in the hope that you will be given one. Work loses its physical embodiment and sense of permanence, as 'being part of the furniture' gives way to a constant reminder of one's marginal status within the organization as a whole.[57]

5

'It always hurts to downsize, but that is the cost of improvement and efficiency', said Digital's president, Kenneth Olsen.[58] The indelible hurt felt by millions of workers effected by downsizing is beyond dispute. The idea that such pain and suffering has been necessary in order to get companies and workers fit for the new competition is a different proposition. Investors welcomed Digital's efforts to reduce costs as the company's shares on Wall Street went up by gained $2.75 to reach $69.75 by mid-morning on the day of Olsen's announcement. This reaction from the money markets to restructuring has been typical. In 1993 when IBM announced a 60,000 cut in its workforce the companies shares increased 7.7 per cent; Sears' 50,000 reduction in staff provoked a 3.6 per cent rise; and Xerox's shares climbed 7 per cent when it announced the lose of 10,000 jobs.[59] However, the consultancy firm Mitchell & Company found that stock prices of firms that downsized during the 1980s were below the industrial average at the beginning of the 1990s.[60] Surveying the evidence on the consequences of downsizing, Kim Cameron also concluded that 'most firms do not succeed in their downsizing efforts. Most do not accomplish in the long run what they set out to accomplish'.[61] He supports this conclusion by drawing on a Wyatt survey reported in the *Wall Street Journal* which shows that less than half the companies who had downsized succeeded in reducing expenses, and under a third increased profits. Equally revealing is the fact that less than one-in-five of the companies surveyed reported an increase in their competitive advantage. Much the same is true of mergers and acquisitions which are currently being pursued as a way of achieving global economies of scale. There is no clear evidence that massive savings can be made from recent merges in the financial sector. According to Anthony Watson of AMP Asset Mangement, which manages about £44 billion of funds, 'There is no role model for globalization', and asks 'Where is the company saying "This is how you extract huge synergies from operating in different countries"?'.[62]

This will come as little surprise to many of the 'survivors' of downsizing who still have a job but whose work now incorporates large chunks of work previously undertaken by redundant colleagues. Unit labour costs in American industry have fallen by an average of 6.4 per cent a year between 1985 and 1996. This intensification in work activity is reflected in the increasing number of hours being worked by the 'core' workforce. A survey of Executive Talent for the 21st Century including European and US executives shows that executives in both regions work on average 57 hours a week, which is nine hours more than the US executives wanted to work and about eight hours more than those in Europe.[63] To our knowledge there is not, as yet, in the West any equivalent to the Japanese National Defence Counsel for Victims of Karoshi which means 'death by overwork'. But the increasing number of days lost through stress related illness is a good indication of how things have changed. One estimate suggests that stress-related problems cost industry $20 billion annually in America.[64]

Ford followed the trend of reducing staff numbers and increasing overtime. The ultimate problem this presents to companies was not lost on Ford's ex-CEO Alexander Trotman: 'you don't get real productivity by simply ramping up the line speed... In the beginning everyone enjoyed the extra pay, but we all get tired, pressures build up, people get edgy and tensions break out'. Likewise, General Motors at Buick City turned to overtime and the use of 'temps' as a way of meeting the surge in demand for GM vehicles, but the consequence was that more than 1,000 of the 11,500 worker were on sick leave shortly before the unions were able to mobilise support of a strike which led GM to hire 779 more regular workers.[65]

A Vice President in an East Coast financial services corporation put it this way: 'We're all starting to see some of the costs of unlimited cost-cutting. I guess this is our generation's definition of a sweatshop!'[66] Most firms have not returned to the conditions of England in the mid-nineteenth century, but there is little doubt that the threat of downsizing is being used as a motivational tool. Gary L. Millsap left the corporate world to study what he calls the 'worried survivors' who put in longer hours, don't take holidays, and 'play it safe'. Millsap suggests that there is more posturing going on but this is not the same thing as increasing productivity: 'Today it's often more important to be seen as productive rather than devoting head-down effort to do the job. The worried survivor constantly says, "How am I looking to the boss?" which makes for great stagecraft but poor productivity'.[67]

Kets de Vries' and Balaz' study of executives also shows that they are not immune from the impact of downsizing and job insecurity. This research suggest that it has had an enormous impact on organizational effectiveness:

> many of the surviving executives asked themselves if they would be next in line; the dismissal of long-term employees resulted in the loss of institutional memory; head office staffers with a more overall strategic outlook had been dismissed; specialists on whom one could rely for certain types of decision were no longer there; and executives were likely to resort to a short-term approach toward decision making, which was bound to have serious repercussions for R&D, capital investments, and training and development.[68]

A broader implication of getting fewer workers to do far more work is what Victor Keegan, economics editor at *The Guardian* newspaper has described as a 'huge negative work-share scheme'.[69] Roughly the same levels of output are achieved with a significantly reduced, and in some cases better paid, workforce. But the increase in productivity and profits reported by many US and British companies by the middle of the 1990s was achieved through cost reduction and work intensification rather than through product innovation and R&D. By the late 1990s, however, there were renewed calls for the development of economic growth strategies. Stephen Roach, chief economist at Morgan Stanley who had proselytized the virtues of 'slash and burn' restructuring strategies, has changed his mind and now believes that too much has been sacrificed to short-term gain. There has been a lack of investment in the skills of employees as he recognizes that labour can not be squeezed for ever, as 'tactics of open-ended downsizing and real wage compression are ultimately recipes for industrial extinction'.[70]

Likewise, some corporate bosses have recognized the excesses of 'downsizing'. General Electric's chairperson Jack Welch, who earned the nickname Neutron Jack on his reputation for eliminating people while leaving buildings standing, now believes that 'we cannot afford management styles that suppress and intimidate', and suggests that managers need 'the self-confidence to empower others and behave in a boundaryless fashion'.[71] In the field of electronics and electrical equipment General Electric was listed as Fortune's most admired company for 1997. It is ironic that a company that has laid off more than 100,000 people now sees the key to success as the quality of its human resources and a commitment to core corporate values, in Welch's terms 'Making your numbers but not demonstrating our values is grounds for dismissal'.[72] Some corporate values are clearly difficult to change!

The talk is now of re-engineering, rightsizing and growth strategies rather than downsizing. But whatever label is applied, the tough realities of winning competitive advantage through innovation will have to be confronted. This can only be achieved by making systemic changes in corporate culture and industrial relations.[73] Downsizing has failed to generate the commitment and trust relations which are needed if the full potential of the flexible paradigm is to be achieved. Managers must confront many of their own deep-seated assumptions about their role as well as that of workers. Many enterprises have introduced elements of teamwork, devolved decision-making and the empowerment of front-line workers, and a minority have moved towards the creation of 'learning' organizations. But the logic of primitive capitalism has left many companies locked into a culture of 'management by the numbers' and a need to meet short-term financial objectives. Paul Geroski and Paul Gregg have examined how British firms have responded in periods of economic downturn since the early 1980s. What they found is that rather than reduce dividends to shareholders, firms will put pressure of their suppliers to cut costs, postpone investment in plant and equipment and engage in downsizing behaviour of which redundancy is a favoured option. Geroski and Gregg also point out that downsizing is not restricted to periods of recession, as it also takes place in buoyant economic conditions characterized by Britain and America in the late 1990s.[74] In other words, under primitive capitalism the privileges of the shareholders are sustained through thick and thin, leaving the catastrophe of downsizing hanging above the heads of individuals and their families as a perennial condition of post-industrial life.

This discussion has shown that organisational restructuring over the past two decades has been informed by downsizing and market individualism which sees workers wholly responsible for their own fate. But in creating uncertainty and generating a poverty wage sector through 'flexibility', the ability to create profit on the basis of high value added goods is limited. Knowledge, learning and commitment, which are at the heart of how value is added, cannot exist in a hire and fire culture characterised by insecurity and mistrust. We will turn to these issues in the final part of the book, but in the following chapter we look at the effects of these changes on workers which, when allied to the many other social changes that have occurred in the past two decades, produce a paradox: post-industrial economies have the potential to develop human freedom, skills and talent on an historically unprecedented scale, but are instead creating a huge wastage of talent, a culture of insecurity, and social inequality.

10
The Demise of Industrial Man

Even outside of work, industrial society is a wage labor society through and through in the plan of its life, in its joys and sorrows, in its concept of achievement, in its justification of inequality, in its social welfare laws, in its balance of power and in its politics and culture. If it is facing a systematic transformation of wage labour then it is facing a social transformation.

Ulrich Beck

Welfare has essentially ended for economic failures in America.

Lester Thurow

1

At the beginning of the twenty-first century a return to regular full employment is little more than a pipe dream. Unemployment and non-standard forms of work, including part-time, temporary and contract employment are as much a part of the economic landscape as the rust-belt, silicon valley and the Dow Jones Index. Nevertheless, some commentators in the United States argued that at the beginning of our new century, a combination of fiscal probity, technological innovation and global free markets, have tamed the boom–bust nature of capitalism. Consequently, there was the prospect of permanent growth and a return to full employment. Robert Eisner neatly captured the mood: 'the current technological, informational, and communications revolution is spawning all kinds of economies so that we can produce more with less. Only God knows how fast our economy can actually grow, or how low unemployment can get, if we have the purchasing power for all that we can produce'.[1] In Britain, Gordan Brown, as New Labour's Chancellor of the Exchequer, resolved that 'if those who can work take the responsibility to work, if employers take the responsibility to train and to invest, and if all of us show the same responsibility in pay', then Britain can, he argued, deliver 'a goal now within our reach for the twenty-first century – full employment for our country'.[2] A commitment to full employment is politically seductive because it is seen to be a way of resolving the distributional question of 'who gets what', as we will show in the following chapter. But these echoes of the Golden era clearly underestimate the scale of economic and social change.

The meaning of 'employment' has fundamentally changed. Whereas it used to refer to full-time regular employment, it now includes part-time work, temporary employment, and a growing proportion of self-employment. In the late 1990s a little over 7 per cent of employees were in 'contingent' jobs in the UK, including those on fixed-term contracts, agency temping or doing casual work. Over a ten-year period this represented a 71 per cent increase in temporary jobs for men, whilst male permanent employment fell by 5 per cent. The number of temporary jobs for women increased by 21 per cent, and the number of 'permanent' jobs increased by 12 per cent.[3] In the United States in the late 1990s, 4.4 per cent were defined as contingent and 10 per cent of the employed worked for contract firms as independent contractors, were on-call workers, or worked for temporary help agencies.[4]

There has also been a significant increase in the number of workers labelled as self-employed. In Britain, they accounted for 17 per cent of men and 7 per cent of women in employment.[5] The self-employed share of total employment is projected to reach a little over 15 per cent by 2007.[6] In the US the self-employed in non-agricultural employment stood at around 7 per cent in 1996 and no increase was projected to 2006.[7] Self-employment is often celebrated as an expression of the enterprise culture. There are obvious examples of where the image of the self-made man or woman clearly apply. But research evidence has found that the increase in self-employment has contributed to the rising numbers with relatively low incomes. Some of this will reflect the under-reporting of income but 'there is clearly a growing group for whom 'self-employment' involves marginal activities generating little income'.[8]

Moreover, part-time employment in Britain accounted for 29 per cent of employees in 1997 and a modest rise to 31 per cent is projected by

2007.[9] Other projections by the Institute for Employment Research at Warwick University reveal that the number of full-time workers is set to fall at least until 2006 and the only significant growth will be of a part-time nature.[10] In the United States, part-time employment accounted for 18 per cent of the work force in the late 1990s, while the proportion for all non-standard forms of work was 25 per cent.[11]

Although some have experienced an increase in the number of hours worked per week, the vast majority of those defined as employed no longer conform to the 9 'til 5 working day, and the 100,000-hour working life.[12] The changing nature of employment involves widespread 'under-employment'. Charles Handy has argued that the shift away from the factory model means that young people entering the labour market today can anticipate a halving of the number of hours they can expect to spend in waged work during their lifetime to an average 50,000 hours. This will not mean everyone working half as many hours for half as many weeks for half as many years, but people working to a diverse pattern of labour market activity depending upon an individual's qualifications, skills and experience. Handy suggests that this situation will lead the notional retirement age to go in two different directions at the same time. The full-time 'core' workers of professionals, managers, technicians and skilled workers can expect to have shorter but more intense employment biographies. Their 'retirement' age is likely to come down to 50 over the next twenty years, while for the remainder of the workforce the retirement age is likely to go up as they seek to compensate for the shorter hours or low wages they have had to endure. For the latter, the key questions will be 'What shall I do in the missing 50,000 hours, and what shall I live on?'[13] 'They may find themselves working 25 hours a week for 45 weeks of the year (part-time) or 45 hours a week for 25 weeks a year (temporary). In either case they will need to keep on working so long as they can because they will not be able to accumulate the savings via pension schemes or other mechanisms to live on. This will suit organisations who will, in their temporary staff, look for older workers who are experienced and reliable'.[14]

Although Handy presents an up-beat interpretation of these changes offering a liberation from the rigours, routines and rituals of industrial time, he clearly underestimates the divisive and polarizing tendencies which these changes will have on the creation of the work rich and work poor as well as those in good work and poor work. What this de-standardisation of work also signals is the terminal demise of industrial man, typified by the Fordist worker who has become a minor player in the overall pattern of economic life.

2

The overall rate of unemployment in the United States was 4.3 per cent at the beginning of the twenty-first century. The comparable figure for the United Kindom was 6.2 whilst in Germany it was 9.1 per cent and France 11.3 per cent.[15] According to these figures you are more than twice as likely to be unemployed if you live in Germany or France than in the United States. But equally you are three times as likely to be unemployed in the US if you are a younger worker aged 16 to 24.[16] In both the US and UK the unemployment rate for blacks is over twice the rate for whites.[17]

The extent to which unemployment has eroded the foundations of economic security for individuals and their families is obscured because governments may often be accused of being unimaginative in their attempts to create new employment opportunities; but this cannot be levelled at the way they have represented their unemployment figures. Governments invariably under-report the extent of unemployment in various ways for electoral purposes. Unemployment figures are commonly massaged because high unemployment does not help governments win elections. In Britain, for instance, the way of recording unemployment has changed over twenty times since 1979, which underestimates the level of unemployment by at least a million, although the Labour government has recently reincorporated some of these into headline unemployment figures. The official unemployment figures are also typically misleading because they only register those who are defined as actively looking for work. If those who want to work but are not actively looking or ready to start a job are added to the unemployment figures, the joblessness rate doubles.[18] But what we have seen in recent decades is a significant proportion of 'discouraged workers', especially men leaving the labour market altogether well below the official age of retirement. By the early 1990s less than half of men aged 61 or more were in work in Britain, compared to over three-quarters in the mid-1970s.[19] The increased number of discouraged workers is, however, not restricted to those close to retirement. In the United States the proportion of males aged 16–64 who were in jobs or looking for work dropped from almost 80 per cent in 1970 to 75 per cent in 1994.[20] At the same time the female participation rate during this period grew from around 43 to almost 59 per cent. In the European Union over 1.2 million males aged 25–54 disappeared from the labour force in the early 1990s. This led the OECD to conclude that the increasing number of discouraged workers 'may be one of the reasons for the growing numbers of "new poor" who do not participate in the mainstream of social and economic life and who are generally not responsive to economic opportunities'.[21]

The proportion of the population who are economically active can be reduced for other reasons. It is estimated that the US unemployment rate is cut by more than 2 per cent due to the size of the prison population. Harvard University's Richard Freeman has suggested that the lower levels of unemployment found in the US when compared to those commonly found in Europe look far less impressive when it is recognized that 'many low-skilled men who would be on the dole in Europe commit crimes and/or are locked up in the US'.[22] In Texas alone the number of beds in youth correctional institutions rose from 1,484 in 1994 to around 4,800 in 2000.[23] In the mid-1990s more than a quarter of black males aged 18 to 34 years were subject to 'criminal supervision'.[24]

The strategy of increasing investment in law enforcement infrastructure as a way of dealing with the social malaise in 'underclass' neighbourhoods led another OECD report to criticise the Clinton administration in its failure to develop 'more productive investments in members of disadvantaged communities'.[25] The use of the iron fist rather than the velvet glove to deal with the social fallout from unemployment and poverty is, of course, not restricted to the US. In Britain the prisons programme is costing £1.2 billion, which amounts to more than the Government will spend on crime prevention, at current levels, over the next 100 years.[26]

Governments around the world have also sought to defer entry to the labour market by other means, usually through training and education. Work-fare, make-work and various warehousing schemes for young workers have all been tried. One positive feature of the declining proportion of young people entering the labour market has been the expansion of tertiary education. Enrolment in higher education is projected to rise to over 16 million in the US by the year 2008, an increase of 12 per cent from 1996. In Britain the proportion of young people entering higher education has increased from 12 per cent in 1979 to 34 per cent in the late 1990s.[27]

3

The problems unemployment and non-standard forms of work cause individuals and families have been exacerbated by the political tone which implies that the unemployed have no one to blame but themselves. As a consequence, benefits to the unemployed have been seriously eroded on both sides of the Atlantic, sending unemployed households into a spiral of poverty. The real value of the welfare benefit package including cash assistance and food stamps for a family of four with no other source of income fell from $10,133 in 1972 to $8,374 in 1980 and to $7,657 in 1992. This represents a loss of 26 per cent in the spending power of a family of four in this twenty year period (in 1992 dollars).[28] The Current Population Survey found 14 per cent of families to be living in poverty in America. And the impact of making people increasingly dependent on the labour market for their welfare has hit those least able to gain access to employment, such as lone parents whose chances of experiencing poverty were roughly three and a half times greater.[29] It is likely that things are going to get even tougher for those unable to find employment following former President Clinton's decision to end the federal welfare safety net. Welfare has been handed over to the 50 states, where, as Christopher Ogden reports, 'beneficiaries will be required to find work within two years, be limited to five years of benefits during their lifetime and face stringent restrictions aimed at limiting out-of-wedlock births'.[30] This is Lawrence Mead's politics of conduct with a vengeance. Yet, the politicians seem blind to the fact that, as Sara McLanahan has pointed out, 'we have already tried tough love on the mothers: we cut welfare benefits by 26 percent between 1970 and 1990, and it didn't work'.[31]

In Britain during the period between 1979 and 1993 the proportion of families living in poverty increased from 8 per cent to 24 per cent among couples with young children, and from 19 per cent to 58 per cent among lone-parent families.[32] Research in Britain has also shown that the problem of unemployment and poverty has become more acute since there is an increasing polarisation between work-rich and work-poor households. In the period 1975 to 1990 there was about the same number of individuals of working age without employment in Britain, but twice the number of households with no waged income.[33] Gregg and Wadsworth have calculated that between the late 1970s and 1990 the likelihood of workless households having at least one member in employment a year later fell from 60 per cent to around 25 per cent.[34] What these figures demonstrate is the growing tragedy of the wastage of talent for adults and a key source of poverty for children.

It is estimated that around a fifth of American children were living in poverty at the end of the 1990s. Despite a small drop in child poverty the US Census Bureau found that children under six within female households with no husband present experienced a poverty rate five times higher (55 per cent) than for children the same age in married-couple families (10 per cent).[35] In another study in the US it has been calculated that more than half the children born in 1994 will spend some or all of their childhood in a single-parent household, typically the mother. 'If current patterns hold', Sara McLanahan suggests, then 'they will likely experience higher rates of poverty, school failure, and other problems as they grow up'.[36]

4

The social polarization which has fuelled the 'fear of falling' throughout the population is not only a result of job insecurity, contingent work, unemployment and inadequate welfare provision, but to a growth in the working poor. The de-regulation of the labour market has made it harder for many men and women to be the sole breadwinner. Hours of work for husband and wife couples were up by 617 hours per year, amounting to around 15 weeks of full-time work from 1979 to the mid-1990s.[37] Many workers, especially among those who lack tertiary level qualifications, are now in employment which pay less that twenty years ago, although there are national differences. This has challenged the very foundations of *security* found in the Golden era, based on the provision of a family wage paid to the male 'breadwinner'. The OECD report that the male wages for the entire bottom half of the male earnings distribution declined between 1985 and 1995 in America, with the lowest earners experiencing a 10 per cent drop while for those at the median the decline was a little over 6 per cent.[38] For Britain the OECD report an increase in the real wages for all male workers. These range from roughly 10 per cent for low earners to 28 per cent for those in the top 10 per cent. However, Gosling, Machin and Meghir's findings based on 27 years of data from the Family Expenditure Surveys in Britain found that since the late 1970s the real wages of those at the bottom of the income distribution displayed 'zero growth'. [39]

Underlying these changes in men's median income were fundamental shifts in employment patterns. Blue-collar jobs traditionally held by male workers in America have declined from 37 per cent of all jobs in 1960 to 28 per cent in 1987, but the white-collar jobs which have replaced them offer average salaries that are only 68 per cent of the wage paid to smokestack labour. A study of jobs growth from 1989 to 1995 by Randy Llg, found a 20 per cent drop in the proportion of new jobs in manufacturing against an increase of 83 per cent in services. However, whereas the median weekly earnings (in 1993 dollars) was

$452 for manufacturing jobs it was $371 for the newly created jobs in the service sector.[40]

Alongside these shifts in the structure of traditional male waged labour has been a decline in the muscle power of the trade unions, which no doubt has contributed to a decline in men's wages and working conditions. The decline in blue-collar occupations has eroded the traditional foundations of trade union membership. In the United States union membership declined between 1980 and the late 1990s from 23 per cent to 15 per cent of the workforce while in Britian the decline was from 50 per cent to below 30 per cent.[41] At the beginning of the twenty-first century the 'protective' function of the trade union remains strong among members, not only because of fear of job loss but also because of work intensification.[42]

It is difficult to predict how male wages are likely to change over time, but two trends are going to have consequences for the economic security of individuals and families. The first is the decline in the wages of male youth, and the second is, increasing income disparities based on education. In America, males under 25 years of age in full-time employment in 1994 earned 31 per cent less per week than if they had of been in the same job in 1973.[43] Equally, in the late 1960s young workers in full-time employment received nearly 75 per cent of that earned by older workers, but by 1994, Andrew Sum and colleagues report that their relative weekly earnings had dropped to only half the earnings of older workers. This change is putting a heavy burden on young families who are finding it increasingly difficult to meet the cost of raising children.[44]

Sum, Fogg and Taggart also suggest that young workers will not make up any deficit in life-time earnings as they get older. Using the Census Bureau's Current Population Survey they write: 'we can project that the expected lifetime earnings of an employed male in 1973 would have been $1,482 million. By 1993 an employed male's expected lifetime earnings had declined to $1,312 million, a drop of 11 per cent, despite the fact that the pool of employed males is now better educated'.[45] In Britain between 1966 and 1992 the median wage gap between 23 and 40-year-old men increased from 38 per cent to 65 per cent. This decline in earnings relative to older workers conforms to a common picture in many OECD countries including Canada, Australia, France, Germany, Japan and Italy.[46]

Going to college or university makes a substantial difference to earnings. In America the average high school graduate earned 42 per cent more than the average person with less than a high school education,

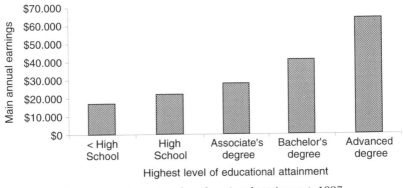

Figure 10.1 Mean annual earnings by educational attainment, 1997
Source: US Department of Commerce, Bureau of the Census.

the average college graduate earned 77 per cent more than the typical high school graduate, and those with advanced degrees made on average over 50 per cent more than those with a bachelor's degree in the late 1990s (see Figure 10.1).[47]

Over the last twenty years there has been a tightening bond between qualification and earnings for both men and women. In concrete terms the problems this has caused for male high school drop-outs is graphically illustrated in the fact that their average real wages fell 27 per cent from $11.85 to $8.64 per hour during the 1973–1993 period (in 1993 dollars).[48] But what distinguishes the experiences of young males in America from those from other countries is that increasing income inequalities reflect their relative ability to gain credentials as a way of stopping their incomes falling! As Sum, Fogg and Taggart explain: 'In 1993 a young male high school graduate earned in real terms only what a comparably aged high school *dropout* was earning in 1973. And a four-year-college graduate in 1993 earned only slightly more than a high school graduate earned 20 years earlier'.[49] This situation is having a serious impact on the earning power of low-and middle-income households despite improvements in the average levels of education for both husband and wife, as Lester Thurow has concluded: 'high school degrees have more than doubled and college degrees have risen by a factor of almost four. Being better educated, these families should be earning more, but they aren't'.[50]

In Britain, a college wage premium is also in evidence but the unqualified have not experienced a decline in their real wages.[51] OECD data only give figures for men which show that the higher educated earned about four-fifths more in the early 1970s. This then declined in the late 1970s only to rise to over twice the earnings of those with no or few formal qualifications.[52] The same pattern emerges for both male and female employees, although the disparities may be even more pronounced for females in Britain. In comparison to upper secondary graduates, those women with few if any qualifications earned about 30 per cent less and those with a university education earned over twice as much in the early 1990s.[53] Clearly, disadvantaged groups including young workers, those with few formal qualifications or skills and lone parents have all fared worse in recent times, the exception in both America and Britain being the senior populations, who showed 'the highest rates of income growth and the most dramatic shift out of the lower ranks of the income distribution and into the middle'.[54]

While economic insecurity has been democratised throughout society, it is those with low or no educational qualifications who are most vulnerable to unemployment, poverty or being locked into poor work. For instance, the minimum wage in America declined from almost half the value of the average wage in 1970 to 38.2 per cent in 1994.[55] In Britain a minimum wage was introduced in the late 1990s but it was set at a relatively low level. Despite an increase in the minimum wage in the US in the late 1990s the growth of the working poor has come to mean that the demand for decent jobs has intensified and it is through education that the poor must compete. Equally, those at the bottom of the social ladder also have to confront the problem of the 'declining middle class' when class is defined in terms of income. A study of employment growth by Randy Llg covering the period 1989 to 1995, found that whereas there was a increase in the number of jobs offering high wages and low wages, due to a decline in various jobs in manufacturing, employment in the middle-earner group fell by 1.1 million.[56] The Bureau of Labor Stastics' projections to 2006 confirm this trend towards a polarisation of the labour market between good and poor work.[57]

5

Industrial man is also having to come to terms with post- industrial woman. The 'security' offered by the family wage at mid-century was not only based on a set of assumptions about the nature of the labour market, but equally about family life. The family wage, as Carole Pateman has argued, was a deal struck by men, for men. It served to reinforce women's dependence. She has also shown how paid employment became the key to individual freedom and citizenship throughout the twentieth century, and therefore beyond the reach of female home-makers.[58] The family wage ensured that women would remain 'social exiles' as a lack of access to employment denied them a legitimate place in public life. Even their relationship to the welfare state was mediated through the male breadwinner. However, Pateman argues that 'In the 1980s the large changes in women's social position, technological and structural transformations within capitalism, and mass unemployment mean that much of the basis for the breadwinner/dependent dichotomy and for the employment society itself is being eroded (although both are still widely seen as social ideals)'.[59]

One of the most significant changes for women has been the way dependency on the male wage has been transformed into a complex interdependency as women have steadily entered the labour market. Part of the opportunity for women to enter the paid workforce has been prompted by the movement from blue-collar to white-collar jobs and from manufacturing to service sector industries. In America the share of the workforce in manufacturing declined from a little over a third in 1970 to 14 per cent in 1996 and is likely to fall to just 12 per cent by 2006. Similarly, in Britain there were 31 per cent of workers in manufacturing in 1971, by 1997 this had fallen to 16.5 per cent and is expected to further decline to 14 per cent in 2006.[60]

Changes in employment opportunities for women mirror the decline in the family wage which has led women to enter the labour market out of economic necessity. This is despite an enduring belief that woman's contribution to the household income is pin-money to pay for the 'extras'. As Marilyn French has noted, by the 1980s in America, many married women had entered employment to raise the family income, but by the end of decade, two salaries brought in only 6 per cent more than one in 1973.[61] In Britain the Joseph Rowntree Foundation inquiry into income and wealth, found that 'For couples aged 24–55, in 1979 male earnings were 75 per cent of gross family income; by 1991 this was just under 60 per cent, while the average female share rose to a fifth. Women working full-time in 1991 brought in an average of 42 per cent of family income'.[62] The combined effect of these changes, along with shifting social attitudes and expectation has been to increase the participation rates of women in employment to its highest rate this century in most industrial societies. Women's share of the labour force in the US is expected to increase from 46 to 47 per cent between 1996 to 2006.[63] The figures for Britain are virtually the same: the share of female employment stood at 46 per cent in 1997 and is expected to reach 48 per cent by 2007.[64] Hilary Land has also shown that even by the early 1980s women were on average spending less than seven years out of employment because of childcare responsibilities. This, she added, was less than half the time spent out of paid employment by their mothers.[65]

Generational changes are also challenging male claims to economic superiority. Wage inequalities between the sexes have continued to narrow, although this is particularly true of young workers. In America, we have already noted that young women and men both experienced a decline in income between 1973 and 1994; this represented a drop of 14 per cent for women against 31 per cent for young men. The smaller drop in wages has meant that a young woman working full-time in 1994 typically earned 95 per cent of the income earned by her male equivalent; this figure increased from 75 per cent in 1973. But, as Andrew Sum and his colleagues have reminded us, 'Near equality of earnings between the sexes, sadly, has also been attained only as part of a broader decline in the earnings of all young adults'.[66] A narrowing of the wage gap between the sexes has also been found among women in all ages in full-time employment. In Britain in the mid-1970s, women's average hourly earnings were roughly 55 per cent of men's in the late 1960s, rising to 65 per cent by the late 1970s, following the introduction of equal pay legislation, and reaching about 70 per cent by 1993, where it has remained.[67]

In addition, significantly more women are also gaining professional qualifications in medicine, accountancy, and law. But even as they are finding their way into professional and managerial jobs, and despite their levels of motivation, commitment and efficiency, few women have yet succeeded in smashing through the 'glass ceiling' which has halted their assault on senior and executive posts. Women still experience sexual discrimination in the work place.[68] While some have entered the best paying professions, others have found themselves trapped in a limited range of low-paid clerical, 'caring' and 'support' occupations. In the late 1990s over three-quarters of those in clerical and secretarial jobs in Britain were women and this was not predicted to change much in the near future.[69]

More women than men work part time which often means low wages, and fewer if any entitlements to holiday, sickness, or maternity payments. In America a little over a quarter of women work part time and there has been little change since 1973. There is a greater share of women in the United Kingdom working part time, which increased from 39 per cent in 1973 to 44 per cent in the mid-1990s. Far fewer males in either country work part time, but it had risen to 11 per cent in America and to around 8 per cent in the UK. The respective figures for men in 1973 were 8.6 and 2.3 per cent.[70] Hence, despite a narrowing in the gender gap between women and men in paid employment, women's opportunities remain restricted. This is undoubtedly because they often take on dual roles of primary carer and wage earner. In these cases women often have to work part time because of inadequate childcare provision (or in some cases alternative care for elderly relatives). Arnlaug Leira describes this as the creation of the 'dual income, single carer' family.[71]

If the prosperity of many families has come to depend on female participation in paid work, then women are themselves becoming more directly part of the class structure. This has served to increase inequalities between women. As Kathleen Gerson has suggested, the impact of social change will vary between social groups for:

> Not only are the alternatives that women and men face structured differently, but within each gender group, the alternatives vary significantly. A growing group of women, for example, have gained access to highly rewarded professional and managerial careers, but most women remain segregated in relatively ill-rewarded, female-dominated occupations. Similarly, the stagnation of real wages has eroded many men's ability to support wives and children on their paycheck alone, but most men still enjoy significant economic advantages.[72]

Nevertheless, for all social groups the security offered by the mid-century nuclear family is dead. Changes in the labour market which are transforming the sexual division of labour, have been accompanied by far-reaching changes in family structure, gender relations and personal identities.

6

The backdrop to Marilyn French's novel *A Woman's Room* was the suburban family which comprised the obligatory 2.4 children, a breadwinning husband and a wife isolated at home in a technological emporium of mod cons, manufacturing R & R for the husband and creating a socially appropriate learning environment for their children. On average, the majority of couples stuck it out together until old age. The experiences of their children have been quite different. In a repeat survey, almost half of women in the early 1960s agreed that 'when there are children in the family, parents should stay together even if they don't get along'; by the 1980s only a fifth of American women held this view.[73] Divorce rates more than doubled in most western countries between 1960 and 1990 and in some they increased fourfold.[74]

In Britain there was nearly seven times the number of divorces in 1993 compared with 1961. Over the same period the share of one-person households virtually doubled from 14 to 27 per cent, as the proportion of families where couples were either married or cohabiting with dependent children declined to roughly a quarter of all families (27 per cent). Meanwhile the proportion of dependent children living in one-parent families tripled since 1972 to 20 per cent by 1995.[75] In the US between 1973 and 1993 the share of families including a married couple with children declined from 55 to 42 per cent.[76] By the end of the 1990s a quarter of all US households were accounted for by individuals living alone.[77] In America even by the mid-1980s only 7 per cent of households conformed to the male breadwinner, female homemaker stereotype, with one to four children under the age of eighteen. Judith Stacey, in her stories of domestic upheaval in the late twentieth century, writes 'Americans today have crafted a multiplicity of family and household arrangements that we inhabit uneasily and reconstitute frequently in response to changing personal and occupational circumstances'.[78] This complex array of family structures is evocatively portrayed in Delia Ephron's novel *Funny Sauce*:

> The extended family is in our lives again. This should make all the people happy who were complaining back in the sixties and seventies that the reason family life was so hard, especially for mothers, was that the nuclear family had replaced the extended family...Your basic extended family today includes your ex-husband or -wife, your ex's new mate, your new mate, possibly your new mate's ex, and any new mate that your new mate's ex has acquired. It consists entirely of people who are not related by blood, many of whom can't stand each other.[79]

Feminist ideas have decisively changed the way women think about themselves by defining the 'personal as political'. This has placed the family and the sexual division of labour at the centre of the political struggle to raise women's awareness of the inequalities between the sexes. The fundamental changes in men and women's paid and unpaid working lives has also been part and parcel of a secular shift from an emphasis on role performance to self-development. The essence of self-development is that roles are negotiated so that they conform, as much as possible, to individual's life projects. The juggling involved in attempting to reconcile life projects with role obligations has inevitably heightened family insecurity for all concerned. But the evidence clearly shows that when it comes to adjusting self-development to family responsibilties it is men who are more likely to choose their own self development over that of their families. Judith Stacey asks whose family bonds are fraying? Her answer is that 'Women have amply demonstrated a continuing commitment to sustaining kin ties. If there is a family crisis, it is a male's crisis'.[80] This answer is supported by reports of a drastic decline in the average number of years that men live in households with young children.[81] The increase in lone parents who are usually women would also support this conclusion, but what it also reflects is an increased emphasis on self-fulfilment rather than role performance, which has made both sexes less willing to tolerate unsatisfactory relationships, whether sexual, emotional or financial. Even if there has not been a decline in the commitment of mothers to their children, there has been a decline in their commitment to a husband who does not live up to their expectations.

A dual consequence of the insecurity in modern relationships is neatly captured in Kathleen Gerson's study of how women are responding to the conflict between family and employment. On the one hand, women who maintain the role of full- time homemakers have become increasingly aware of their dependence on their husbands, as they are aware that marriage is often not 'til death us do part'. An ex-clerk and mother of a young daughter complained to Gerson:

> Having a child has made me more dependent on my husband. I think he was attracted to me because I was very independent, and now I'm very dependent. I don't know what I would do if things didn't work out between us and we had to separate and I had to go to work to support my child. I think I'd be going bananas. It's scary to me'.[82]

Gerson's study also highlights the converse situation where women may be less likely to resolve the classic dilemma of homemaker versus career in favour of a life of domesticity, or indeed the decision to have children, as a childless divorced female executive told the interviewer:

> Having children probably would set back my career... irretrievably. The real thing that fits in here is my doubts about men and marriage, because if I had real faith that the marriage would go on, and that this would be a family unit and be providing for these children, being set back in my career wouldn't be that big a deal. But I have a

tremendous skepticism about the permanency of relationships, which makes me want to say, 'Don't give anything up, because you're going to lose something that you're going to need later on, because [the man] won't be there'.[83]

7

What these statements reflect is a society in which the security of individuals remains largely based on a now redundant male bread-winner model. The consequence is that increasing numbers of women and children are having to negotiate multiple financial relationships and fluctuating financial fortunes depending on their family circumstances. Some divorced women clearly enjoy the return to financial independence which the departure of their husband may bring, but for many women and children they are left in a state close to the old poor houses. Where they have to rely on the state they pay an enormous price financially and morally. To see lone mothers pilloried while governments cut their benefits was one of the more bizarre and frightening spectacles of the late twentieth century. The male breadwinner model may have broken down but the source of status and worth in our society remains based on paid work. It seems extraordinary that women with small children should be forced into the paid labour market, but that seems to be the only solution at which policy makers can arrive.

While lone mothers have been blamed for the moral degeneration of society, policy makers have given no thought to the consequences of their actions for children. The situation for children who grow up with only one of the biological parents, which is nearly always the mother, are reported to be bleak. In the US they are twice as likely to drop out of high school as children who grow up with both parents. Given the commonly-espoused concerns about the high number of black children living in lone parent families, it is also worth noting that family disruption was found by Sara McLanahan, based on national statistics covering over 25,000 children, to be most harmful among Hispanics and least among blacks. The risk of school drop-out as a result of family disruption increased by 24 per cent among Hispanics, 17 per cent among whites and 13 per cent among blacks. In terms of school performance, she concludes that 'for the average white child, family disruption appears to eliminate much of the advantage associated with being white'.[84] But a more important conclusion from McLanahan's analysis is that family disruption is not the principal cause of high school failure but poverty, and delinquency: 'If all children lived in two-parent families, teen motherhood and idleness would be less common, but the bulk of these problems would remain'.[85] Low income was the single most important reason for lower academic achievement among children living in lone parent families.

While there is an urgent need to rethink the relationship between welfare, work and social responsibility to handle these new realities, the changing identities of men as well as women need to be taken into account. As men confront a decline both in established ways of expressing their masculinity in the form of manual labour, and in the role of breadwinner, they also confront an increased demand from their partners for greater commitment to childcare. As a result some are withdrawing from family commitment altogether, while others are becoming more involved fathers. Judith Stacey found that the muted family voices of men in her study 'whisper of a masculine crisis among blue-collar men. As working-class men's access to breadwinner status recedes, so too does confidence in their masculinity'.[86]

There is no innate masculine essence that drives a man to work for someone else for the best part of his life, doing often boring work, compensated by a sense of male pride in grim toil simply to earn enough to support a wife and children. This may give a man a sense of power but in a situation in which he lacks the emotional intelligence to participate fully in the lives of those he loves. In Bob Connell's account of masculinities in recent world history he concludes:

> The distinctive feature of the present moment in gender relations in first-world countries is the fact of open challenges to men's power, in the form of feminism, and to institutionalized heterosexuality, in the form of lesbian and gay men's movements... Whatever the limits to their gains, and the success of the conservative backlash, the historic fact that these movements are here on the scene structures the whole politics of gender and sexuality in new ways.[87]

What this chapter reveals is that the relationships between family and paid work has become far more complex than in the period of economic nationalism. The experiences of both men and women have become more fragmented as a result. Yet the social and policy infrastructure necessary to address the problems that have emerged as a consquence of these changes is absent. Moreover, the traditional forces that could exert pressure for more progressive social policies have been swept away in the process of fragmentation. Trade unions linked to parliamentary party representation used to be a positive force for change. But union solidarity was based on a relatively homogenous, mainly blue-collar male workforce which no longer exists. The political attack on trade unions in the 1980s and the decline of blue-collar work has served to weaken the power base of the unions. In any case, old style unionism was deeply implicated in the perpetuation of the male breadwinner system. The sources of solidarity needed to support progressive social change can no longer rely solely on the revitalization of the Trade Union movement, although it clearly has an important role to play.

The stakes involved in reducing insecurity and in seeking to narrow social inequalities should not be underestimated. Every child and family that lives in poverty, every individual who is unemployed represents a wastage of potential which is detrimental to both the individual and society. The same can be said of those who live in fear for their jobs. In post-industrial societies the range of human abilities demanded of us at home, work and in our leisure time is increasing. The sheer complexity of social and economic life we have described in these chapters testifies to that. People who cannot function cognitively and emotionally to the sophisticated levels necessary today will be severly handicapped. These increased demands on the individuals' capabilities open up the possibility for a greatly enriched individual and collective social life. Yet many of the trends we have described so far have served to stunt these capabilities. The question is whether the current political agenda of the Modernizers can address the social causes which are inhibiting the full development of these capabilities.

11
A False Start

People are born with talent and everywhere it is in chains. Fail to develop the talents of any one person, we fail Britain. Talent is 21st-century wealth.

Tony Blair

The pre-eminent mission of our new Government is to give all Americans an opportunity – not a guarantee – to build better lives.

Bill Clinton

1

The road to primitive capitalism is the road to Barbarism. Its naked market logic exaggerates social differences, insecurities and human greed. Primitive capitalism feeds off the fears of personal and national economic catastrophe which at the same time serves to protect the very forces that perpetuate this danger. But what of the opponents of primitive capitalism? What of those who glimpse a more humane, equal and less divided society? Have they been able to develop a political project that can harness the forces of change in the service of social progress? In short, have they been able to create a new vision of capitalism that can secure national economic prosperity for all in a global economy, whilst laying the foundations for individual freedom and social solidarity?

Over the last decade the Modernisers have been trying to navigate a 'third way' between free markets and state planning.[1] They reject much that was previously taken for granted amongst their socialist predecessors, contending that the transformation of capitalism at the end of the twentieth century has changed significantly the strategies that the Left

175

needed to adopt in its pursuit of social justice *and* economic efficiency. This involves extolling the virtues rather than the vices of competition, profit and the market, 'our enemy is not markets but monopoly, not competition but cartels, not profit but privilege and greed'.[2] Future global competitiveness has become their number one priority as there will be no return to the Keynesian welfare state. As Bill Clinton declared, 'the era of big government is over', and the Modernizers in Britain agreed, 'the present Government will not resort to the interventionist policies of the past. In the industrial policy making of the 1960s and 1970s, to be modern meant believing in planning. Now, meeting the requirements of the knowledge driven economy means making markets work better'.[3]

In a knowledge-driven economy when the talent, skills and know-how of the workforce are seen to determine global competitiveness, the Modernizers have rested their political credibility on creating a high-skills, high-wage economy. Underlying this commitment is a vision of a society permeated by a culture of learning for it is the knowledge, skills and insights of the population that are the key to future prosperity. An examination of the Modernizers is important because they have succeeded in presenting a political vision of social progress that is capable of winning sustained electoral support on both sides of the Atlantic. The New Democrats came to power in 1992 following Bill Clinton's election victory with the campaign slogan, 'It's the economy, stupid'. His emphasis on investment in education and training to create a high-skilled, high-waged economy clearly won support among the middle classes. In Britain, New Labour scored a massive electoral victory in 1997 adopting a similar policy agenda. The performance of the Democrats and New Labour in Office reveals how difficult it is to make a discernible difference to the shape of the economy and the quality of peoples' lives, but our argument is that despite a number of positive features there are serious flaws in the Modernizers' argument.

2

The Modernizers' account of how to rebuild economic nationalism can be summarized in the following way. It begins with the idea that managed national economies have been weakened by economic globalization. This has seriously diminished the power of the nation state to control the rules of economic competition, including their power to protect uncompetitive indigenous companies and workers. Moreover, the shift to a global economy is associated with a change in the rules of economic competition described in an earlier chapter. The mass production of standardised goods and services can no longer provide the foundations for economic prosperity in advanced western societies because companies can no longer afford to pay high wages to low skilled workers. Indeed, the multinationals are increasingly using cheap labour in the newly industrializing countries to undertake low-skilled operations. The only way western nations can successfully respond to the global economy is by generating business and enterprise which cannot be easily duplicated or mass produced – these are goods and services that are customized; meet the needs of niche markets; or are at the forefront of technological innovation. At the same time, corporate 'ownership' is seen to be far less important than the quality of employment opportunities. The importance the Modernizers attach to the quality of human resources also stems from a belief that increasing wage inequalities in America and Britain over the last decade reflect the returns to skill in a global auction for jobs and wages. The essence of this idea was captured by Bill Clinton in a major address on education:

> The key to our economic strength in America today is productivity growth . . . In the 1990s and beyond, the universal spread of education, computers and high speed communications means that what we earn will depend on what we can learn and how well we can apply what we learn to the workplaces of America. That's why, as we know, a college graduate this year will earn 70 per cent more than a high school graduate in the first year of work. That's why the earnings of younger workers who dropped out of high school, or who finished but received no further education or training, dropped by more than 20 per cent over the last ten years alone[4]

This view was echoed by Tony Blair, the British Prime Minister in his electoral rallying cry of 'education, education, education'. Hence, for all western societies the route to prosperity is through the creation of a 'magnet' economy capable of attracting high-skilled, high-waged employment within an increasingly global labour market. Education and training opportunities are therefore pivotal to this vision of a competitive and just society. For not only can education deliver a high value-added 'magnet' economy but it can also solve the problem of unemployment. In addition it is a mistake for nation states to 'guarantee' employment because this harbours the same kind of vestigial thinking that led to previous attempts to protect uncompetitive firms from international competition; they simply become even less competitive.

The only way forward is to invest in education and training to enable workers to become fully employable. In this account, social justice inheres in providing all individuals with the opportunity to gain access to an education that qualifies them for a job.

The Modernizers believe that a flexible labour market of the kind advocated by the Right should largely remain intact because the realities of the global auction are such that multinationals will not invest in countries like America and Britain unless the 'obstructions' that trade unions and extensive worker rights represent are removed. In addition, they also take the view that as technology and tastes change so the labour force needs to be flexible in order to respond to consumer demand. In advocating this view they claim the success of flexible labour markets by pointing to the lower official levels of unemployment in America and Britain compared to continental European economies.

The Modernizers are, however, aware that there are problems with an economic policy which is so dependent on the willingness of individual workers to upgrade their educational qualifications and skills. They know, for example, that this policy will be compromised unless it is accompanied by a minimum wage. Unless there is a reasonable floor beneath which wages cannot fall employers will prefer to make profits from cheap labour rather than from introducing sophisticated technology which requires highly-skilled labour. So in both America and Britain the Modernizers support a minimum wage, albeit at a low level of remuneration.

In addition, the Modernizers believe that there is a large group of unemployed people who have either lost the will or, in the case of single mothers, do not have the opportunity to work. Here they have taken over the Right's rhetoric of dependency arguing that many claiming benefits ought to be contributing to society through paid work. For once in the labour market individuals will have the incentives to climb the ladder of opportunity by investing in education and training. This is why there has been an emphasis on welfare to work programmes designed to get people into jobs. Where the Modernizers differ from the New Right is in the belief that some groups have not had the opportunities for work and that the state should create those opportunities by, for example, providing single mothers with child care facilities. In return for a commitment to provide these facilities single mothers are expected to take advantage of their new found opportunities.

This policy programme to 'earn' a living is now presented by New Labour in Britain as a 'third way' between primitive capitalism and the high social costs of the corporatist tradition in mainland Europe. At a time when America and Britain are at the top of the economic cycle and have relatively low official unemployment, there are clear attractions in this 'third way'. Not least because of its political appeal. It is a programme that is largely inoffensive to everyone. It is not seeking a massive redistribution of income, the rich are left well alone; it assumes that nations can only *respond* to the global auction by servicing the needs of the multinationals and the money markets, while it appears to address the concerns of workers through the mimimum wage and through opportunities to develop their human capital. At the same time, middle-class anxieties about the taxes they pay for others dependence are also allayed through welfare to work programmes. As a political formula for a new settlement its appeal is obvious.

The problem is that it addresses few of the fundamental problems now confronting capitalist societies and will prove inadequate when the economic cycle turns down and the fundamental tensions underlying post-industrial societies resurface. Our purpose in exposing the flaws in the Modernizers' account is to set the scene for a more radical and thoroughgoing debate about social justice, economic efficiency and social cohesion in the early decades of the twenty-first century. Our criticisms cluster around a series of related problems which suggest that the Modernizers can at best offer a palliative unless they can embrace the historical opportunity that now exists to create a decent society for all.

3

The Modernizers' view that the future wealth of nations will depend on the exploitation of leading-edge technologies, corporate innovation and the upgrading of the quality of human resources can hardly be quarrelled with. Nations will clearly need to have a competitive advantage in at least some of the major industrial sectors, such as biotechnology, telecommunications, electronics, pharmaceuticals, chemicals and automobiles.[5] There is also little doubt that this will create a significant number of jobs requiring highly skilled workers but this is not the same as assuming, as in the case presented by the Modernizers, that jobs of this kind will be available to all those who have the appropriate education and training. The plausibility of the Modernizers' account hangs on the idea that the global auction for jobs offers the potential for western nations to create 'magnet' economies, attracting highly-skilled and well-paid jobs. This is an idea which has obvious appeal to a broad political constituency. It serves to replenish the spirits of those who were fearful of the US following Britain in a spiral of economic decline after a period of global dominance. We are presented with the comforting picture of a global economy which, although no longer likely to be dominated exclusivily by American and European companies, is characterized by prosperous Western workers making good incomes through the use of their skills, knowledge and insights. In reality, however, this characterization represents an imperialist throw-back to the idea that innovative ideas remain the preserve of the advanced Western nations with the possible exception of Japan. They assume that as low-skilled work moves into the NICs and Third World economies, America, Japan and the EC countries will be left to fight amongst themselves for the high value-added jobs.

The problem with this view is that it misunderstands the nature of the economic strategies pursued by the Asian Tigers for at least a decade. They have been actively developing strategies which will take them from low to high-skilled economies and already have human capital infrastructures which are comparable to many western countries.[6] This is reflected in the international convergence in the expansion of higher education. Therefore, whilst we should not rule out the possibility that multinational companies, when making inward and outward investment decisions, will judge the quality of human resources to be superior in particular countries, it is extremely unlikely that a small number of nations will become 'magnets' for high-skilled, high-waged work. The Modernizers have overestimated the extent to which even the most successful modern economies depend on the mass employment of highly skilled workers. Indeed, an unintended consequence of the massive expansion of tertiary education may be to create a substantial wastage of talent amongst college and university graduates unable to find a demand for their skills, knowledge and insights. In effect these graduates will become a reserve army of educated labour which will serve to bid down the wages for high-skill work, thereby creating the spectre of a high-skill, low-wage economy.

This is especially likely in the American and British economies which are not characterized by a high-skills or low-skills, but a bi-skills route. Here we find high-skilled work being created in certain sectors of the economy, such as in Silicon valley in the US or around Cambridge in Britain. But this is underpinned by a vast army of low-skilled service sector workers.

This problem is reflected in economic growth rates and productive performances. The underlying trend data in the United States and Britain points to the fact that with each economic cycle since the 1970s economic growth has declined. Against this backdrop the recent spurts in economic growth in both countries does little to change this overall trend. There are those who believe that the United States, in particular, has reached the nirvana of a 'new paradigm' in which the business cycle has been abolished and the spurt of high levels of growth that we have witnessed in the last years of the twentieth century and at the beginning of the present century will go on for the foreseeable future.[7] However, there are some laws of capitalist development that are extremely difficult to buck. Wall Street remains perilously over-valued by historical standards and ultimately unsustainable. While inflated market valuations have led to new capital investment it is premised on short-term gain over long-term investment and commitment. This means that while the demand for skilled labour has risen it has not been uniform throughout the economy. In effect we have economies divided by skill demands. While a certain percentage of workers have high-skilled, relatively secure work the majority have low-skilled, often insecure work. In the United States, Lester Thurow warned in *Head to Head* of the dangers of continuing to pursue the orthodoxies that have led to primitive capitalism, while in the UK Will Hutton's *The State We're In* performed a similar service. Both authors show how an economy based on market individualism will fail to deliver high-skills economies in the twenty-first century.[8]

The key point both Hutton and Thurow make is that primitive capitalism is short term in its orientations, being fundamentally concerned with dividends to shareholders and not with productivity or market share. This makes little economic sense in the long run because those companies that take the long-term view will win out in the competition for market share. Hence, Hutton argues that we need a stakeholder economy in which the interests of employees, shareholders and managers are balanced. Not only does this make for sustained competitive advantage but also provides security for employees. The institutional source of short termism, as we have shown, lies with a financial system that demands high returns on investment over short time periods. Companies considering new investment expect to make a 20 per cent return on the investment with a pay back period of two to three years.

Under these conditions it might be expected that rather than engage in investment to improve productivity, through the introduction of new technologies, or the development of new products and services, managers will seek to make profits by other means such as hostile takeovers, leveraged buy outs and asset stripping – all ways in which rapid profits can be made without increasing productivity. Not surprisingly, under these financial conditions the United States and Britain come out lowest in measures which link investment in capital used for production, to worker output, when compared to Germany and Japan.[9] A concrete example of what is at stake here, is that in the early 1990s the Japanese had somewhere between 175,000 and 275,000 robots on production lines while America had 37,000, but the latter has twice as many production workers. The proportions remain very much the same now for Japan and the United States, while Britain is almost bottom of the advanced economies when it comes to the use of industrial robots.[10]

The Modernizers have failed to embark on a radical restructuring of investment funding, or shift towards the kind of 'stakeholder' model which would see the creation of a new settlement between workers, employers and the government.[11] This is a prerequisite for any significant improvement in productivity which would lead companies to engage in a genuine effort to lift the skills of their employees. An additional problem with the Modernizers' assertion that they can generate a high-skilled, high-waged economy is that the market flexibility which they judge to be essential in a high-tech, global economy is unlikely to generate the economic conditions on which the push for high skills depends.

4

Current orthodoxy has it that we are placed on the horns of a dilemma. Either we have a floor set to give workers a living wage, in which case a significant number of workers will price themselves out of work causing historically high unemployment, or cheap labour is permitted, thereby reducing unemployment but at the cost of poverty wages. Most European Union nations have placed themselves on the first horn while the United States and Britain have opted for the second by creating flexible labour markets. A segment of the labour force hired on a casual basis can be fired in times of economic downturn and rehired when demand rises, thereby reducing the risks and costs to corporations during downturns. There is an element of economic imperialism attached to this proposed 'solution' to the dilemma. Advanced economies which don't follow this model are described as sclerotic in much the way that the Right assumed that all national economies would have to follow its recipes.[12]

The commitment to flexible labour markets, however, is likely to sabotage the pursuit of a high-skills route because those in part-time work or on short-term contracts are unlikely to receive the training they need to 'rise up the ladder of opportunity'.[13] The research evidence 'shows that there is a trade-off between expanding the more marginal forms of employment and expanding the proportion of the workforce getting work-related training'.[14] An interesting outcome of this research is that the presence of unions in a workplace raises the likelihood of training, despite the fact that unions are often considered part of the problem not part of the solution.[15] The upshot is that there is a contradiction between the idea of flexibility as it is embodied in casualized forms of labour and the capacity of the workforce to adapt to new kinds of skill. Rather than having an increasingly highly skilled labour force, those that advocate labour market flexibility exacerbate one of the key fault lines in Anglo-saxon economies, namely: the division between those with few skills and marginally employed and those with greater skills whose employment is more secure.

Unfortunately, the negative impact of labour market flexibility as introduced in America and Britain extends beyond the 'skills trap' in which those in casualized work find themselves. One of America's leading labour market economists, Michael Piore, has argued that where labour market regulation is weak, as it will remain with a low minimum wage, there is no incentive for employers to invest and use new technology in a way which raises value added or the quality of work.[16] Rather, weak labour market regulation leads to a vicious circle whereby profit is extracted through long working hours and low wages. In effect, what regulated labour markets do is to create an incentive for entrepreneurs to invest in capital-intensive forms of production in order to generate the high value added to pay for higher wage levels.[17] If Piore is correct then we would expect the patterns of future work to develop along different trajectories depending on the degree to which domestic labour markets are regulated.

Projections of labour supply and occupational change need to be viewed with some scepticism, but an OECD report on this subject certainly supports Piore's position when the United States is compared with Holland.[18] On all indices of social protection and labour market regulation Holland provides an example of far greater social protection for workers, yet the vast majority of new jobs being created could be classified as 'skilled'. In the United States approximately half the jobs being created were in service occupations requiring little formal training. The lesson here is that, the route to a high-skilled economy must involve an analysis of factors affecting the demand for educated labour. The implicit assumption, harboured by the Modernizers, that through investing in the employability of workers, employers will automatically recognize this potential and invest in up-grading the quality of their human resources, is clearly naive.[19] The historical record in both America and Britain shows that while there are firms that recognize investment in people to be vital to the medium term success of their companies, there are many others who equally recognize that fat profits can still be made off the backs of poorly-trained, low-waged workers. Equally, the idea that Western nations can compensate for the failings of local employers by attracting inward investment from blue-chip multinationals is clearly not going to be sufficient to move from a low-skill to a high-skill economy. Therefore, there seems little doubt that although in some important respects the Modernizers will succeed in producing some improvement in the quality of employment opportunities, they will not achieve the goals of high-skill development because in a flexible labour market investment in education and training, as the focal point of their policy, does little to increase the demand for highly-educated workers.

5

The Modernizers' strategy also relies on the labour market to resolve the question of who gets what? The immediate problem with this approach is that it assumes a return to something close to full employment. Here the Modernizers are able to point to the relatively low levels of unemployment in the United States and Britain compared to Germany or France. In the previous chapter it was shown how unreliable official unemployment statistics have become as they have been massaged on numerous occasions to give artificially low figures. We have noted, for example, how unemployment figures exclude millions of people who have retired early, those on sickness benefits, people in prison, or in tertiary education. We cited the work of Richard Freedman who has calculated that the unemployment in America would increase by two per cent if young black men in prison were added to the unemployment count. In Britain the numbers registering for sickness benefit have climbed rapidly. In 1987 some 800,000 men claimed invalidity and incapacity benefits, ten years later the figure had doubled to 1.6 million. For women the figures are even higher at just over a million rising to just under three million. It is estimated that a significant proportion of these are people who no longer seek work thereby taking thousands off the unemployment register.

But what presents the biggest challenge to the Modernizers' conviction that we can return to the days of full employment is the large numbers of households where no members of working age are in paid employment. In Britain approximately 16 per cent of households are in this situation, which is one of the highest figures in Europe. In the United States the problem of unemployed households is being addressed by forcing family members of working age into various kinds of low-skilled or make-work schemes as a condition of receiving benefits. The fact that people in the United States and Britain now work for poverty wages is recognised by both governments as they allow tax credits for people in poor work. This amounts to a subsidy to employers of cheap labour which discriminates against employers who offer decent wages. Therefore although the implementation of flexible labour market policies in both countries has led to a genuine reduction in unemployment, the way this has been achieved makes little sense in terms of a high-skilled, high-waged economy. It is better understood as a cheap form of social policy in which some of the unemployed are driven into the rear end of the labour market as a way of removing them from the streets and the unemployment statistics. Hence full employment now means something quite different to what it did in the 1950s and 1960s. Many of those defined as employed are no longer in regular full time employment, but in irregular, insecure work on low wages.

The problem for the Modernizers is that at the same time that they have encouraged the creation of large numbers of casual, part-time, low-skilled and low-waged jobs as a way of reducing unemployment, the same 'flexible' labour market approach can be applied by employers to other groups of workers including those in technical, managerial and professional occupations. This suggests that any economic downturn will lead companies to reduce their workforce according to their immediate human resource needs. When the instability caused by the logic of deregulated markets is coupled to the economic cycle of peaks and troughs it is easy to see how fragile the policy of welfare to work is. It only takes a bout of restructuring coupled with a downturn in the economic cycle and welfare to work policies will be put under serious strain. At this point the true colours of the Modernizers will be revealed. If they do nothing to address unemployment in such circumstances we will know that there is little difference between them and the advocates of primitive capitalism.

There are further threats of unemployment posed by jobless growth. In Spain the economy grew by 93 per cent between 1970 and the early 1990s and lost 2 per cent of its jobs.[20] But crucially the problem of jobless growth is exacerbated by the global auction. We know that the relocation of blue collar jobs from America and Britain has had a significant impact on employment. One estimate is that up to 1990, changes in trade with East Asia had reduced the demand for unskilled relative to skilled labour in the advanced economies of the West by approximately 20 per cent;[21] although as wages have declined in America and Britain some of those jobs are being repatriated, but for cheaper wages. Until the financial crisis in Korea, for instance, low-skilled manufacturing wages in Wales were 30 per cent cheaper than in Seoul.[22]

But there are two other features of the global economy which make the return to full employment as understood during the Golden era a remote possibility in any of the advanced post-industrial economies. First, the current economic orthodoxy asserts that interest rates will rise with economic growth as a way of controlling inflation, thereby choking off the level of investment in new jobs required to have a significant impact on unemployment.[23] It is argued that within nations interest rates have become the key instrument for the control of inflation. If economies experience rapid growth there is a tendency for prices to rise which fuels inflation, therefore before national economies have a chance to 'overheat' interest rates are raised by central banks to throttle back demand. This use of interest rates to control inflation is claimed to be successful in a way in which other measures tried in the seventies and eighties – incomes policies and control of money supply – were not. The new global economy has a key role to play in understanding why the control of inflation has become a crucial element in any successful national competitive strategy. If inflation in any one country rises to appreciably higher levels than in competitor countries, its goods are likely to be priced out of the market. However, the cost of using interest rates to this end is that economies are permanently run under capacity.[24] The rise in interest rates simply chokes off demand before reaching near full employment.

Secondly, it has been argued that rising unemployment since 1973 has been caused by lower economic growth among the OECD countries during the same period.[25] The problem for the Modernizers, however, is that even if there was a return to the growth rates achieved between 1960 and 1973, they are unlikely to have the same impact on unemployment today. This is because in a global economy the prosperity which derives from economic growth may be spent on imported rather than home-produced goods and services. Whereas, in the post-war 'walled' economies a rise in demand would percolate through the economy, thereby creating jobs, a similar rise in demand today may simply create jobs in some other part of the world. This may be especially so in countries where increases in incomes are accruing to the wealthy, who spend their money on luxury goods from overseas.

When placed against this background, the Modernizers' aim of full employment based on the twin policies of 'education, education and education' and 'welfare to work' seem weak indeed. There is clearly more that the Modernizers could do if they had the political will to take on the vested interests of Wall Street and the City. For one of the ways in which job creation can be engineered is through long-term, low-cost investment. But this nevertheless leaves a range of factors affecting employment growth which are indeed outside the control of individual states. It seems extremely unlikely that the problem of unemployment can be solved by any of the conventional remedies and to pretend otherwise merely holds out false promise to a generation of unemployed. Therefore, the most important conclusion to be drawn from this discussion is that the Modernizers lack an adequate account of how all will share in future prosperity. The *distributional* question of how to reward fairly the wide varieties of paid and unpaid work in a capitalist society, which was temporarily solved in the post-war period through full employment and the even spread of the fruits of growth across the occupational structure, can no longer be resolved through the job market.

7

If unemployment and underemployment cannot be solved by making people more 'employable', the question remains as to whether we can explain the polarization of incomes in terms of the demand for higher skills. At stake is whether incomes are being allocated fairly and efficiently according to skill, or whether the polarization of incomes reflects inequalities of power created by the logic of primitive capitalism: in which case the equation 'high wages   high skills' is a rationalisation which masks an inefficient allocation of human resources. The Modernizers' argument that the polarization of income reflects an increased demand for educated labour and a decrease in the demand for the unskilled lies at the heart of their programmes. The dramatic increase in income inequalities in both America and Britain since the late 1970s is taken to reflect the relative abilities of workers to trade their knowledge, skills and insights on the global labour market. According to the Modernizers, as low-skilled jobs have been lost to developing economies with cheaper labour, the wages of less skilled workers in the West have declined. By the same token, in the new competitive conditions described above, those workers who have the skills, knowledge and insights that can contribute to 'value added' research, production, consultancy or service delivery in the global labour market have witnessed an increase in income. Hence analysis and remedy are closely related in the Modernizers' account: if the reason so many workers are in low paying jobs, or worse, unemployed is that they lack skills, the solution is to give them the skills. It's an appealing analysis but at best it is based on a partial truth.

Is increasing income polarization a genuine reflection of the market value of different skills? If wage inequalities are a reflection of the shift to a global labour market we should find the same trend in all the advanced economies. But the evidence suggests that the increasing polarization in income is far more pronounced in America, Britain and New Zealand than in any other OECD country. In Germany there has actually been a decline in income differentials![26]

The best interpretation of the causes of income polarization is that there has been a rise in demand for skilled labour but this has been uneven across the advanced economies.[27] Over and above this, there are a range of political and institutional factors involved. When we compare the extremes of polarization in nations like America, Britain and New Zealand, the explanation for this race to inequality is to be found not in the neutral operation of the global labour market, but in the way these countries have *responded* to global economic conditions. This response, like the global economy itself, has as we know from our earlier discussion been shaped by the New Right political projects of Reagan and Thatcher. What income inequalities reveal in America and Britain is the way in which the 'casino' economies of these countries in the 1980s enabled company executives and senior managers, along with those who worked in the financial markets to engage in 'wealth extraction' rather than the development of sustainable forms of 'wealth creation'.[28] This largely explains why a study reported by Bound and Johnson found that in America a large part of the increase in the returns to a university degree was due to an increased premium put to use in the business and legal fields. The wages of computer specialists and engineers actually *fell* relative to high school graduates.[29]

Equally, if an increased dispersion of income was a result of the changing cognitive and skill demands of work, then nations with the highest levels of technology and investment in research and development would lead the table of income inequalities. Yet, the evidence suggests that both America and Britain lag behind in the use of technology. Our illustration of the use of robots is but one example. In a broader survey of the use of technology, Wood shows that, 'Japan and Sweden are leaders in applying new technology, while the USA and UK are laggards'.[30] This would suggest that rising incomes at the top do not reflect the growth of a high-skill economy but, in part, the peculiarities of casino economies which allow wealth creation through 'paper entrepreneurialism'.[31]

This is not the whole story. For alongside the institutional structures which have enabled money to be made out of wealth extraction are changes in domestic as well as global labour markets. Robert Frank and Philip Cook argue much of the explanation for mega-dollar salary packages can be found in what they call winner-take-all markets. These have long been known in the sporting and entertainment industries but have now been extended to corporate management, medicine, financial and legal services and even universities. They are characterized by the disproportionate earnings of a new class of 'superstars', key players who they argue, 'spell the difference between corporate success and failure. Because their performance is crucial and because modern information technology has helped build consensus about who they are, rival organizations must compete furiously to hire and retain them'.[32]

But these winner-take-all markets have unfortunate consequences. They attract large numbers of individuals to compete for these 'glittering prizes' when the majority will fail to attain them. This causes a massive wastage of money, time and effort as students struggle through professional postgraduate studies in business, law or medicine in order to enter this high stakes competition. At the same time, professions which don't have such conspicuous winner-take-all labour markets, such as engineering, may experience a shortage of skilled labour, as the most talented students pursue the chimera of fame and fortune.

In short, winner-take-all markets misallocate labour. They also distort the competition for credentials. As the numbers going into higher education increase so the elite institutions raise their entry requirements and tuition fees. Equally, the role of the elite schools as the gatekeepers to society's most prized jobs is thrown into even sharper relief by winner-take-all markets, because only students from the most prestigious schools and universities are recruited to them. Frank and Cook tell the story of an applicant to Harvard's graduate programme in economics from a small Florida college with a straight-A transcript, who like many others from similar colleges was rejected in favour of straight-A students from Stanford, Princeton and MIT. The student from Florida may have been as good or better than those from these prestigious universities but clearly, selecting those from the likes of MIT is going to be a 'safer bet'. Once students could compete for entry to the top jobs by going to their local state universities but no more. The threat to the principle of meritocracy is clear, not all those of equal talent are likely to get equal opportunities under such a system. This is a point to which we shall return.

If the rising incomes of the work rich is explicable in terms of the wealth extraction and winner-take-all markets, can the decline in the wages of the unskilled be explained in terms of the neutral operation of the global economy? In addressing this question there is the problem of measuring the extent to which semi-skilled and unskilled work have been transplanted to the developing nations. Clearly there has been a sizeable effect. However, it is not only that industrial blue-collar jobs were lost, but that the perennial threat of companies relocating to developing world countries has led to a relative decline in the wages of those unskilled jobs which have remained. It is, of course hard to measure the degree to which this threat has been material in keeping down wages. Nevertheless, it is worth noting that there is little correlation between manufacturing competitiveness and low wages. In the most successful industrial economies – Germany and Japan – manufacturing wages are higher than anywhere else. However, we have described how New Right governments in America and Britain helped to drive down wages by labour market deregulation in the 1980s. Estimates for the United States and Britain calculate that the decline in unionization on the 1980s accounts for 20 per cent of the increase in wage inequality.[33] It could be suggested that the decline in unions was inevitable once low-wage competition from East Asia was established. But not all advanced economies have seen union strength diminish as it has in America and Britain. Given our previous argument, attacking unions is a recipe for a low-skill, low-wage economy.

The upshot is that the Modernizers assumed that income polarization has been caused by a change in the relative demand for skilled workers, rather than as a response to the global auction based on the principles of primitive capitalism. This then relieves them of the problem of creating the framework for a high skills economy and saves them from the difficult question of tackling the vested interests that extract wealth rather than rewarding those who producing it. The Modernizers seem unwilling to tackle the short termism of which wealth extraction is a symptom, or winner-take-all markets, and are only prepared to place a low floor on low incomes. In effect, the invisible hand of the market has now been extended to the invisible hand of the global economy which, it is falsely assumed, will deliver prosperity to all, through extending opportunities for individuals to invest in their human capital.

Even if there was a simple link between skills and income the Modern-izers are left with one further problem: how are people living in poverty going to acquire the appropriate education to get high-skilled, high-waged jobs, when research has demonstrated that social deprivation has a profoundly negative impact on academic performance?

8

In responding to this issue the Modernizers have come up with two 'solutions'. The first is to claim that schools can improve students' performance despite their social and ethnic background. To claim other-wise is to commit heresy in the present climate. Of course this is con-venient for politicians who are reluctant to attack the problem of poverty through the redistrubution of income. And it also feeds the myth that education can solve the fundamental problems of society. But it has as much bearing on reality as Canute's efforts to turn back the waves. The facts are that the best single predictor of educational success is social background. The room schools have for adding to children's educational performance, once their backgrounds have been taken into account, is relatively small.[34] As one of the world's leading educational researchers, Basil Bernstein argued in the early seventies: schools cannot compensate for society. The research since then has simply confirmed his original prognosis.

This is not just a matter of the deficits that children from poor back-grounds often enter school with, but of the active political intervention by middle class interests to sustain the advantage their children already have. The pressure on the professional middle class to sustain this advantage has increased as job insecurity has become endemic. With the decline of a lifelong corporate careers the educational credential has assumed greater importance in securing an individual's job prospects.[35] Access to elite schools, colleges and universities has therefore become even more important to professional middle-class parents. As a con-sequence the commitment to a unified system of schooling within which students are educated according to ability, effort and equality of resources has been abandoned in favour of consumer sovereignty based on parental 'choice' and a system of education based on market princi-ples. A consequence of this change in the organization of educational selection from that based on 'merit' to the 'market' is that it serves to encourage the creation of under-funded sink schools for the poor and havens of 'excellence' for the rich. Therefore, the school systems in both America and Britain no longer reflect a commitment to open competition but gross inequalities in educational provision, opportunities and life chances.

Faced with these developments the Modernizers' response has been to turn away from the questions of social justice by redefining equality of opportunity as equity. Equity to the Modernizers means no more than everyone having the right to a sound basic education. To them the old national competition for a livelihood, based on the principles of meritocratic competition, is of far less importance than that of how to upgrade the quality of the education system as a whole. Again we find the idea of a 'magnet' economy being used to extract the political sting from questions of social and educational inequalities.

Although equality of opportunity has been traditionally recognized as a condition of economic efficiency, the Modernizers have effectively avoided perhaps the most important question to confront the centre-left at the beginning of the twenty-first century, that is: how to organize the competition for a livelihood in such a way that a genuinely equal opportunity is available to all? Avoiding this problem by appeals to the need to raise educational standards for all in the global market offers little insight into how the question of social justice is to be addressed. The consequence is that without a clear sense of social justice and in the absence of an adequate foundation for material and social security, people constantly watch their backs putting their child first in the educational and labour market jungle. In such circumstances, the culture of market individualism becomes translated into the Hobbesian condition of 'all against all'. Therefore, the state must intervene to regulate this competition in a way which reduces the inequalities confronting those trapped in poverty and the discrimination confronting people of colour, not only as a matter of economic efficiency but also for reasons of social justice.

The fact that at least a fifth of children in both America and Britain live in poverty is inevitably going to have a detrimental impact on the ability of these children to respond to educational opportunities and to recognize the relevance of formal study when living in neighbourhoods with high unemployment, crime and deprivation. Indeed, the importance of equity to the question of social learning is graphically illustrated in Julius Wilson's study of the urban underclass in America. He suggests that '... a perceptive ghetto youngster in a neighbourhood that includes a good number of working and professional families may observe increasing joblessness and idleness but he may also witness many individuals going to and from work; he may sense an increase in school dropouts but he can also see a connection between education and meaningful employment'.[36] He goes on to argue that the exodus of 'respectable' middle- and working-class families from the inner city neighbourhoods in the 1970s and 1980s removed an important 'social buffer' that could deflect the full impact of prolonged and increasing joblessness, given that the basic institutions in the area (churches, schools, stores, recreational facilities, etc.) are viable so long as more economically stable and secure families remained. Hence, the more social groups become isolated from one another the less opportunities exist for the kind of social learning which even in the deprived neighbourhoods of American and British cities could offer role models to children other than those associated with a 'political economy of crack'.[37]

9

We have called this chapter 'A False Start' for reasons that will now be evident. The Modernizers entered government faced with low trend growth, high-skilled, high-waged jobs for a small minority, polarised incomes, and child poverty.[38] The 'third way' represents an important advance, but it has failed to break free of market individualism where the fundamental question of capitalist societies of 'who gets what and why?' is left to the 'market' to decide. But crucial problems of unemployment, underemployment, poverty, job insecurity, justice and social cohesion will not be addressed within the confines of the assumptions that guide centre-left politics in the US and Britain today.

Part III The Future of Society

12
The Problem Restated

For at least another hundred years we must pretend to ourselves and to every one that fair is foul and foul is fair; for foul is useful and fair is not. Avarice and usury and precaution must be our gods for a little longer still. For only they can lead us out of the tunnel of economic necessity into daylight.

John Maynard Keynes

1

In John Maynard Keynes' essay on the 'Economic possibilities for our grandchildren', he suggested that from the early eighteenth century, greed, self-interest and market individualism have been necessary evils to advance the material prosperity of modern societies. In the post-war period this form of social deception appeared to be paying dividends, but by the end of the twentieth century millions of people remain condemned to unemployment, insecurity and/or poverty wages. We seem no nearer Keynes' vision of a society 'beyond scarcity'. Yet he believed this vision would become reality in the early decades of the twenty-first century, where the love of money as a possession would be exposed as a 'somewhat disgusting morbidity, one of those semi-criminal, semi-pathological propensities which one hands over with a shudder to the specialists in mental disease' and where society would honour 'those who can teach us how to pluck the hour and the day virtuously and well, the delightful people who are capable of taking direct enjoyment in things'.[1]

A key reason for our failure to fulfill Keynes' hopes for his grand-children is that we have forgotten that the pursuit of economic prosper-ity is a means to improving the quality of life and not the sole purpose of

197

human endeavour. We have created one-dimensional societies where the whole of human activity is reduced to a series of economic calculations and measurements, bereft of moral principles on which to judge when 'enough is enough'. When 'fair is foul and foul is fair' and when greed and envy are systematically cultivated the inevitable result is a situation where 'we can count but we are rapidly forgetting how to say what is worth counting and why'.[2]

Underlying this failure to improve the quality of life for all is a failure of moral purpose. Social change since the 1970s has led to a petrifaction of political vision, blind to the post-industrial possibilities which now exist for redefining the relationship between the individual and society. As Fred Block has observed, 'we may no longer know what kind of society this is, but *we do know* that it is a market economy, and the best way to make a market economy work is through a minimum of governmental interference'.[3] We have seen how dominant political interests coalesce around the doctrine of market individualism which Keynes thought a necessary but temporary evil. At best we must hope that narrow self-interest will miraculously serve the common good.

This doctrine has exaggerated competition, insecurity and suspicion at the expense of co-operation and trust – the lifeblood of a decent society. We have described how this has led to intense class and racial conflict as individuals and social groups try to cling on to those economic boats which remain afloat as others list or sink around them. In the walled economies of the past, competition was stressed within a set of assumptions about full employment, economic security and meritocratic competition. Economic security was largely taken for granted because alongside full employment, the state provided support for those who could not survive in the labour market. The only issue was how to allocate people to the job market in a fair manner. But in an era of primitive capitalism Alfred Marshall's 'strongest motive' of private interest has been elevated to the status of a wonder drug able to cure all social and economic ills. We now live in what Richard Wilkinson has called a cash and keys society, 'Whenever we leave our homes', he says, 'we face the world with two perfect symbols of the nature of social relations on the street. Cash equips us to take part in transactions mediated by the market, while keys protect our private gains from each other's envy and greed'.[4]

This highlights a failure to remove the political and mental shackles of self-interest, envy and greed. But 'cash and keys' do not control the commanding heights of human nature, assumed by Adam Smith in his famous statement: 'It is not from the benevolence of the butcher, the brewer, or the baker, that we expect our dinner, but from their regard to their self-interest. We address ourselves, not to their humanity but to their self-love, and never talk to them of our necessities but of their advantages'.[5] Rather, these human traits can be encouraged or discouraged depending upon social, cultural, economic and historical circumstances. Market individualism enslaves people within its systemic logic which make it difficult for people to express other human qualities such as co-operation, empathy, self-sacrifice and love for others. It breeds and feeds on insecurity, leading people to behave in excessively acquisitive ways when they feel insecure about their jobs, income, status and opportunities. In order to enhance individual freedom to live more fulfilling lives in the future, a major question is how to maintain some of the benefits of market competition at the same time as building the foundations for learning, co-operation, justice and social cohesion.

2

Globalization, we are told, has made the kind of society Keynes hoped for his grandchildren ever more remote as it is not only the battle against scarcity, but the fight for economic competitiveness, which demands that we keep up our guard against anyone who dare call a 'foul a foul'. The threat of a ruthless global capitalism which will seek out any inefficiency – corporate fat; over-staffing; inflated wages; inferior skills; mental timidity; generous social spending; or state interference in the operation of the market – has become a ghost that lurks in the shadows and makes us fearful of talk of liberation from the 'dull compulsion of economic life'.

Yet the failure to emerge from the tunnel of economic necessity into daylight has *not* been derailed by the new global economy, although it has led to large obstacles being placed on the track. The most significant is the view, shared by many on the centre-left, that the nation state is virtually powerless to do anything other than organize society on the principles of market individualism. As Tony Blair told the *Financial Times*, 'The determining context of economic policy is the new global market. That imposes huge limitations of a practical nature...on macro economic policies'.[6] This highlights a key problem for the Modernisers as they extol the virtues of co-operation, opportunity and social cohesion whilst advancing policies based on market individualism. But Will Hutton has correctly noted that 'the most insidious doctrine of our age is that we have no choices. We are predestined to continue as we are. The only efficiency we can consider is the allocative efficiency of the market'.[7] The view that nation states now have little choice but to reduce the social costs incurred by business and get people fit to win in the global auction is based on an, at best, partial account of global capitalism.

The collapse of the Soviet Union reinforced the view that the nation state is in decline, given that if the repressive hands-on controls of the Soviet authorities proved to be powerless when confronted by the will of the people, then it suggests that all nation states must be weak. A sign of this weakness is the way that the major western nations have established free-trade agreements aimed at increasing economic co-operation and trade with neighbouring countries. These include the North American Free Trade Agreement (NAFTA) incorporating the US, Canada and Mexico, creating a block of 360 million consumers with an economic output of $6,000 billion, and in Europe, the single market embracing 15 member countries forms part of a European Economic Area of 360 million consumers across 19 nations. Such agreements are taken to signal the declining power of individual nation states to control the economic forces which determine their growth rates, unemployment figures and whether incumbent governments are likely to get re-elected.

The decline of the nation state is a theme that chimes well with the conservative renaissance of the final decades of the twentieth century, with its rhetorical slogan of 'getting the government off the people's back'. The fact that it could interpret changes in global capitalism as a decisive victory for markets over states, added political weight to their assertions.[8] Commentators on the Left have also announced the demise of the nation state with some relish, because it is held responsible for many of the worlds problems. As Anthony Smith has observed, nationalism is often blamed for 'many of the conflicts which infest our planet', and its critics tend to assume that a world without nations will be free of the attendant ills of racism, fascism and xenophobia. A world without nations, they claim, will be a more stable and peaceful, as well as a more just and free world – a dream that is in fact common to liberals and socialists for whom the nation was at best a necessary stage in the evolution of humanity and at worst a violent threat and distraction'.[9]

There is no doubt that national governments have lost some of their executive powers in the context of the new global economy. They cannot control market forces in areas such as exchange rates, but even the most cursory examination of differences in the organization of European states and the factors that contributed to the economic success of leading East Asian economies, suggests that national governments maintain more clout than is often supposed. Japan and the Asian Tigers are still characterized by significant state intervention in economic planning. Indeed, even in Singapore, which has the highest proportion of any workforce in the world working for foreign multi-national companies, there is a major government involvement in economic planning as we will show in the penultimate chapter.

It is vitally important that we do not conflate issues concerning the deregulation of world markets with those of how nations are responding to these changing rules of international competition. In effect, market individualism is a political rather than an inevitable response to the deregulation of global markets. The deregulation of national markets is part of a political project extolling the sovereignty of the market both at home and overseas. The nation state is not powerless, but rather the linkage between the 'nation' and the 'state' should not be taken for granted. Within the walled economies of the past it was assumed that 'by definition' the state acted as the protagonist of a nation's citizens. Some got more out of this arrangement than others, but nevertheless the hidden hand of the market was helped by the visible hand of the state. Whereas in the context of the global economy, the state in both America and Britain have not worked in the national interest but in the interest of an elite of wealthy and powerful people. The *laissez faire* response to the global auction has led to polarization and social conflict.

Contrary to proclamations of the end of the nation state, the economic competitiveness that benefits the many rather than the few will depend on the way national governments respond to global competitive pressures. Globalization has made it more important to have a democratic political voice which serves the 'national' interest. What is more, there is no other institution apart from the nation state which has the power and moral authority to balance the interests of individuals and social groups. This is reflected in the fact that at least half the spending of modern states is concerned with income redistribution in forms including taxation, universal education and health care. Such internal income transfers are as much as 50 times larger than international ones in the form of economic, technological, or other aid programmes.[10]

There may, therefore, be nothing intrinsically worthy in nation states as such, they are for the most part a recent historical creation and they have their dark side – jingoism and imperialism. But the fact remains that it is the national framework of social, cultural, legal and economic institutions which will determine the well-being of workers, families and communities. Again as Anthony Smith has argued, 'nationalism's core doctrine which includes the idea of national autonomy, unity and identity, is little more than a basic framework for social and political order in the world, to be filled out by other idea-systems and by the particular circumstances of each community's situation at the time'.[11]

But there is a real danger that global economic competition will increase nationalist sentiments when political leaders present the issue of future prosperity as a zero-sum game between nations, where the aim is to conquer other countries in the battle for regional or global economic dominance. Much of this rhetoric fails to acknowledge that economic integration is an inherent feature of globalization. Any serious downturn in an OECD economy is likely to have knock-on effects for other countries. Equally the attempt by leading global economies to support the Yen in the late 1990s to reverse Japan's slide into recession, reflected fears that a serious recession in Japan would have sparked a global recession. What this suggests is that competition must take place within the limits of economic co-operation.

The need for co-operation is also recognized in the increasing importance of supra-national organizations such as the World Trade Organisation (WTO), the Organisation for Economic Cooperation and Development (OECD), the International Monetary Fund (IMF) or the European Union (EU). Currently these international agencies are being driven by a model of shareholder capitalism led by the United States. As a consequence it has allowed the multinational corporations to pursue profit maximization often with scant regard for the economic and social aspirations of developing nations. Naomi Klein makes the point that Nike paid Michael Jordan $20 million for endorsing its trainers in 1992, more than it paid its entire 30,000 workforce in Indonesia.[12] There is also little doubt that a more integrated global economy will require international agencies to deal with such problems as environmental pollution, exchange rates and fair competition. But there is no reason why nation states cannot flourish in a world where laws are made in conjunction with other nations, where international laws are externally imposed on nations who break internationally agreed principles of human rights, or where nations have externally controlled currencies under a system such as Bretton Woods.[13] Whatever happens nations will be forced to develop much greater co-operation in an attempt to mitigate the worst features of global financial markets and environmental degradation.

Equally, there is no reason why nation states cannot flourish at the same time as greater powers are given to local communities and regional assembles to manage their own affairs and to fulfill the growing demand for greater recognition of regional, ethnic and religious identities. The nation state is the key instrument for decentring power in much the same way as Ronald Reagan and Margaret Thatcher understood that in order to introduce market reforms they needed to be both 'in and against' the state. This, of course, is to stand accused of adopting a parochial or nationalistic view from an affluent, Western standpoint. Susan Strange rightly poses the question, 'how much does it matter to the system, to the people living in and by it, that half of Africa and certain parts of Latin America and Asia remain sunk in political chaos, economic stagnation, recurrent famine, endemic disease, and internecine warfare?' and goes on to say, 'I do not know the answer, but it does seem that social scientists shirk the responsibilities that go with their privileges if they fail to think about that question'.[14] Strange is obviously correct to raise this question, but without the transformation in social outlook argued for in this book, there seems little hope that Western nations will restrain from the market individualism that has led to the creation of first- and third-world conditions within the United States and Britain, let alone one which recognizes our common global humanity. There is also little chance of narrowing the extremes of wealth and poverty between countries if it is assumed that these reflect the outcome of global market forces which affluent nations are powerless to change.

3

At the beginning of this century, as at the last, questions of material inequality and barriers to opportunity remain critical to the future of social democracy. At the beginning of the twentieth century the French social theorist Emile Durkheim was preoccupied with the problem of how social integration could be maintained in a rapidly industrializing world. *The Division of Labour in Society* added to the weight of Western intellectual history in coming to see waged labour as the foundation for social justice. Durkheim described this work on the division of labour as having 'its origins in the question of the relations of the individual to social solidarity'.[15] Although he was interested in the causes and conditions on which the division of labour depended, it is the functions served by the division of labour which has received paramount attention, for as George Simpson pointed out in his 1933 English translation of this work, Durkheim 'saw economic life much as Adam Smith did, a spontaneous working out of harmony'.[16] Durkheim saw the move to an increasingly complex society as posing a problem of social order because in the pre-modern condition is was largely achieved through established routines of daily life which were rarely subject to question. Durkheim defined this form of solidarity as 'mechanical', given that it was an integral feature of life which required little political justification; it was simply the way things were. As societies became more complex, he assumed that a new 'organic' form of solidarity would emerge through the organization of occupational groups or corporations which would not only regulate the behaviour of their members, but also lead to a recognition of the contribution made by other occupational groups in the pursuit of social progress. In other words, as everyone makes an economic contribution (or at least the male breadwinner), so they deserve to share the benefits accruing to members of that society, regardless of their socio-economic status.

Durkheim was aware of the dangers of what he called the 'forced' division of labour, where people are allocated to tasks on grounds of social class, race or religion rather than on individual aptitude or abilities, because the division of labour can only be a source of social cohesion 'if society is constituted in such a way that social inequalities exactly express natural inequalities'.[17] The main problem envisaged by Durkheim was class or caste wars resulting from the privileged seeking to reserve the most powerful positions and best jobs for themselves and their offspring, while the lower classes or castes try to improve on their lot. Durkheim argued that if social harmony is to be based on the division of labour there needs to be 'absolute equality in the external conditions of the conflict'.[18] In other words, there needs to be equality of opportunity for all regardless of social circumstances. Yet decades of sociological studies have shown this has never been achieved, and for much of the last three decades inequalities of opportunity have been increasing rather than narrowing. What is also significance today is that the organization of work is clearly not a 'spontaneous working out of harmony', but a source of conflict, cleavage, insecurity and desperation. By operating welfare on the male breadwinner model there has been a massive waste of talent as millions of children have, through no fault of their own, been forced to grow up in poverty. The great paradox is that the more both the political Left and Right seek to make people even more dependent on a job for their economic and social welfare, the less chance there is to create the foundations for social justice. While we continue to define work and individual worth in terms of paid employment we will continue to experience political impotence rather than empowerment.

The extent of our obsession with waged work is evident when single mothers are forced to leave their children with a child-minder, while they look after someone else's children for a wage, in order to demonstrate their contribution to society. Equally, this obsession with waged work is robbing millions of people of the opportunity to make a contribution to society, as they are trapped in unemployment or meaningless jobs. Many of the long-term unemployed are condemned to living in neighbourhoods that are in desperate need of regeneration, requiring skills that some of the unemployed will possess. There is, as Charles Handy reminds us, no shortage of work to be done, only a shortage of waged work. The problem is that the Modernizers have found it politically expedient to leave the distributional question of 'who gets what' to be decided by the market value of one's labour. This has done little to alleviate the massive inequalities in income that they lament, but it has also failed to encourage and reward the 'regenerative' work in the form of childcare, voluntary work, community improvement, the welfare of the elderly, etc., which is not regarded as making a contribution to society because the market place has no way of rewarding these essential activities. Another key question raised by our analysis is that in post-industrial societies, waged work cannot be the only way of deciding who gets what. The contribution of individuals to society often involves far more that the market value of their labour. If the development of human talents is the foundation for wealth creation then the work of those who are not employed in the formal economy will need to be given greater recognition. A reduction of social inequalities will involve rewarding those who further the growth potential of others, whether in the home, community, school, or workplace.

4

Social progress depends on narrowing inequalities and removing barriers to opportunities in education, employment and entrepreneurial activities. This has been the traditional clarion call of the centre-left, and there is nothing in these pages that questions its significance. However, the reinvention of society in the twenty-first century involves more than a narrowing in inequality, as it challenges the very essence of capitalism. Marx suggested that in the womb of the old there is the germination of something new, but at this moment in history it is not the overthrow of capitalism, but the potential for a new form of post-industrial co-operation which reflects the growing importance of human collaboration, knowledge, skills and talents in raising economic productivity, enhancing democracy and improving the quality of life.

In the new economic competition, areas of social and economic life that were the subject of political conflict and struggle will need to be reconfigured in ways which emphasize a 'community of fate'.[19] Especially as the capacity for a nation to compete for high skilled employment depends upon the quality of human resources, social cohesion, investment generating new value added businesses, and the wealth to create a learning dividend through taxation to pay for lifelong learning for all. Equally, if standards of education and training have 'gone global', as part of the assessment criteria used by multinational companies to decide on where to invest in labour, plant and technology, it is in everyone's interest to upgrade the quality of the nation's human resources. Equally, if American or British companies go out of business it can no longer be assumed that an indigenous company will emerge to meet market demand. It is far more likely that consumer demand will be met by importing from foreign businesses, which means that local jobs are permanently lost. Workers, managers, and frequently employers share a common interest in keeping businesses productive and innovative. Managers, professionals, technicians, secretaries and shopfloor workers share a vested interest in increasing their bargaining power *vis-à-vis* employers through new forms of stakeholding given the power of employers to relocate or sell-out or to be subject to a hostile take-over. Hence in a global economy the emphasis on market individualism is profoundly destructive in terms of the ability of nations to economically compete, because excessive competition in a market context leads to polarisation and economic weakness. It prevents the appropriate forms of investment and cooperation between workers, companies and government. It fails to utilize the full potential of new production techniques and the flexible paradigm of organizational efficiency, which depend upon high trust, co-operation and teamwork. And perhaps most critical of all it leads to under-investment in the knowledge, skills and insights of the workforce.

In a global, knowledge-based economy, we will need some other way of thinking about the wealth of nations other than in terms of the stock of individual skill, knowledge and know-how. Seeing humans as expensive machines, as Adam Smith did, misses the essence of a high quality workforce. As Fred Block has observed, 'It is not actual human beings who are an input into the production process, but one of their characteristics – their capacity to do work. But this is an inherently paradoxical strategy since the individual's capacity to do work is not innate; it is socially constructed and sustained'.[20] And in an economy where a premium is placed on teamwork, project work, flexibility and personal and social skills, in order to tap the productive potential of new technologies and to raise the quality of work that people do, ways have to be found to both empower people to benefit from lifetime learning opportunities and to engender a sense of common purpose.

It is no coincidence that many writers have recently returned to the idea of 'trust' and 'social capital' as significant ingredients for economic success. The limitations on human collaboration evident in low-trust Fordist relations have been judged to be increasingly counter-productive. Alan Fox has observed that for the last two centuries the costs of such limitations were 'outweighed by the benefits of the extreme division of labour from which the limitations sprang.' So long as the elite groups 'could rely on holding a supervisory, planning, and managerial superstructure within a high-trust fraternity or shared values, status, and kindred expectations, they could see the system as viable'.[21] However, evidence suggests that productivity is higher in countries or companies when people pull together, work co-operatively, trust each other and have a common commitment to social justice. There is, therefore, a need for Western countries to rediscover the social character of life obscured by the obsession with market individualism. This need not be based on an anti-competitive ethic. On the contrary, competition is an indispensable feature of everyday life, but what is needed is a proper balance between competition and co-operation, which recognizes our mutual dependence on society. In devaluing human co-operation Western societies have 'shot the bird that caused the wind to blow, and now had to go about its business with an albatross round its neck'.[22]

But the irony is that over the past thirty years the potential for much richer human interactions has also developed. As we saw in earlier chapters, the collapse of the 'linear life course' has led to a greater awareness of our individuality, indentity and life projects. As Anthony Giddens suggests, social reflexivity involves decisions that

> have to be taken on the basis of a more or less continuous reflection on the conditions of one's action. 'Reflexivity' here refers to the use of information about the conditions of activity as a means of regularly reordering and redefining what that activity is. It concerns a universe of action where social observers are themselves socially observed; and it is today truly global in scope.[23]

Social reflexivity and the negotiated life-syles and patterns of interaction that it engenders have the potential to create a richer democratic life based on John Dewey's definition of democracy as a form of association. This is a key issue which will be discussed in the next chapter. But the problem that will need to be overcome if this potential is to be achieved, is how to transform market individualism, which has channelled our reflexivity into the argot of the sophisticated consumer. We need to reconstruct society in a way which taps into the potential for *reflexive solidarity*, without it being reduced to the idea of a nation of shoppers!

The question of how to 'reinvent' society based on the principles of learning, justice, efficiency and solidarity in post-industrial, knowledge-driven societies is the biggest challenge confronting all the advanced economies. In the final part of this book it is argued that social progress must be built on the individual and collective talents of citizens; that the market value of one's labour is singularly inadequate as a way of allocating rewards, status and entitlements; that the nation state has a central role to play in the reconstruction of society; and that society must be based on high trust.

Equally, post-industrial lives will increasingly require us to think reflexively about our changing circumstances in order to learn from them. This is as true of our lives in paid work as it is in the home. Learning has become the basic principle for the organization of society. Economic prosperity and social justice require individuals who can exercise cognitive and emotional intelligence, but they can only achieve this by working co-operatively. It is through the development and pooling of intelligence that social progress will be achieved. Engaging in a struggle for *collective intelligence* offers the best prospect of creating such a society.

13
Collective Intelligence

> It is often social hierarchy and the world views associated with
> it that restrict the unfolding of human capacity, and not the
> limitations of natural endowment.
>
> Charles F. Sabel

> Every expansive era in the history of mankind has coincided
> with the operation of factors which have tended to eliminate
> distance between peoples and classes previously hemmed off
> from one another.
>
> John Dewey

1

In a survey of the moral and spiritual worlds of 'middle' Americans,
Robert Bellah and his colleagues concluded that if there was a selfish
'me generation' in America they did not find it. But what they did
find was that the language of individualism, as the primary language
of self-understanding, limited the ways in which people think.[1] In
another celebrated work, *Small is Beautiful*, E.F. Schumacher tells us
that we can not free ourselves from the bondage of the existing system
without the development of a vocabulary which is capable of mounting
a challenge to the logic of market individualism. To reassert conventional ways of thinking about the relationship between the individual
and society, therefore, is to effectively rule out new ways of understanding ourselves and the world in which we live. In this chapter
we examine the idea of 'collective intelligence' and argue that it is
integral to the reinvention of society. In presenting collective intelligence as an alternative to market individualism it can be shown that it is

capable of improving economic performance and the quality of life for all.

2

The first step in the move towards a definition of collective intelligence is to reclaim 'intelligence' from the grip of the eugenics movement and from its impoverished representation in the form of IQ tests. Axiomatic to the idea of collective intelligence is an understanding of human intelligence limited by social hierarchy and cultural learning which has led to feelings of inferiority, stupidity and incapability among the majority, at the same time that a minority have staked their superiority on membership of nature's aristocracy of talent.[2] This premature excommunication of many people from their natural capabilities is not congenital but a cultural and institutional problem within society's power to correct, as each period in history can be characterized by both its mode of economic organization and its model of human nature.

In the twentieth century Western culture has harboured a dim view of intelligence among the majority.[3] Despite a culture that has celebrated the victory of human endeavour over nature, it has remained sacrosanct to Western thought that there is a limited pool of talent. This faith in the few who have been blessed by nature, or managed to rise above it, are the people whose faces fill the biography and business shelves of bookshops and TV chat shows. This is the 'great man' and 'token woman' view of history. It is a celebration of individualism which recognizes social progress to result from the extraordinary efforts and insights of a few.

In many respects this dim view of intelligence was analogous to Plato's 'royal lie', given that in the Golden era only a few were required to develop their intellectual potential fully, while the recourse to a gift of nature served to legitimize to the many why they were not among the elite. Nevertheless, the social distribution of intelligence has remained an active battleground for debates about equality of opportunity and social justice. On the one hand, the concept of intelligence has been embodied in the notion of IQ. The gist of this tradition is, as we have seen, based on the view that intelligence is measurable; that it is largely decided by nature rather than the social environment; that it is largely immutable or fixed, which means that it can be predicted at an early age; and that high intelligence is in limited supply as suggested by the metaphor of the bell curve. Unsurprisingly, this view of intelligence has been consistently used to explain the exclusion of various social groups in society and, as Stephen Jay Gould has noted, to justify the privileges of those in whose service the notion of IQ has been pressed.[4]

A celebrated attempt to explain the obdurate existence of the underprivileged and underrepresented is *The Bell Curve* (1994) by Richard Herrnstein and Charles Murray. The book is subtitled *Intelligence and Class Structure in American Life*, and purports to explain why African–Americans are at the bottom of the social pile and why the rest of society should not do much to help them because it reflects the blueprint of nature. For Herrnstein and Murray some 'races' are simply more intelligent than others and this is what explains their relative positions in the class structure. Accordingly, it is asserted that we are now confronted with a genetically-determined meritocracy in which those at the top are the most able and those at the bottom the least able for whom there can be little expectation of self-improvement, even with state support. This attempt to shackle the opportunities of the poor and powerless is connected to Murray's account of the urban underclass, which claims that it is largely the product of a culture of dependency resulting from overgenerous state handouts. Murray obviously had a Malthusian solution in mind given that the poor should not receive state support because of its cultural consequences, but there is also no way of improving their lot because they are too stupid!

On the centre-left of the political spectrum there have been those who have developed counter-arguments about the nature of IQ and intelligence. They point out that intelligence as measured by IQ tests has been steadily rising in the United States and elsewhere since the 1930s, which suggests that these gains in intelligence cannot be genetically based.[5] It has also been shown that people from disadvantaged groups consistently underachieved in terms of school performance or in the job market, even when their IQs were found to be equal to those from privileged backgrounds. What these researchers have argued is that rather than there being a limited pool of ability in the population at large, there is a massive wastage of talent among those from lower socioeconomic backgrounds, from minority ethnic groups and among women.[6] In Britain in the 1960s, for instance, Floud and Halsey were able to show that a selective system of education, in which children were sorted according to various tests (including IQ tests), into different kinds of school at the age of 11, meant that many able working class students were prevented from following an academic syllabus which was a requirement for entry to University. Research by Bowles and Gintis in the United States was also able to demonstrate the significance of social class background on educational achievement and subsequent job destination, even when IQ scores were taken into account.[7] More recent research by Lauder and Hughes replicated Bowles and Gintis' studies in New Zealand – considered one of the most egalitarian of nations until recently – and arrived at similar results.[8]

This research into the social influence on achievement is conveniently ignored by the likes of Herrnstein and Murray. But others who have reanalysed their data have shown that Herrnstein and Murray have exaggerated the impact of IQ on performance.[9] This re-analysis has demonstrated that if everyone had the same IQ scores but came from different social backgrounds, the impact of equalizing IQ is a 10 per cent reduction in income inequality. If everyone had the same social background but different IQ scores, Fisher and his colleagues claim that inequality in income would be reduced by 37 per cent.[10]

This tradition of centre-left research has been important for refuting what has been at best a narrowly mechanistic and naive approach to questions of intelligence. It has drawn attention to the all-important influence of environmental factors – especially the influence of social inequalities – in determining educational achievement and in exploring the legitimizing myths used to explain that achievement. While inequalities of race, gender and class are always intertwined, we should bear in mind that the racial targets in Herrnstein and Murray's study are part and parcel of a resurgence in the politics of racism in the United States, whereas in Britain it has been used, primarily, to support class inequalities.[11] And in both countries the IQist tradition has been an instrument in the maintenance of patriarchy as Murray and Herrnstein's analysis of unwed African–American mothers testifies. Had they looked at the utterances of their precursors they may not have leaped so confidently into their geneticist claims about single mothers. After all, it was only a little over a century ago that Broca was claiming that it was well known that women, on average, were less intelligent than men on account of their smaller brains, and that his colleague Gustav Le Bon was warning that to give women higher education would be to unleash a social revolution.[12]

Although much of this research has targeted genetic accounts of IQ in showing that it varies significantly according to social circumstances, what is implicit in much of this work is the fact that intelligence is a social achievement. The idea of meritocracy offers an instructive example of the social nature of intelligence. In meritocratic competition the winners are encouraged to exhibit little sense of obligation to the losers because the competition was judged to be fair and based on individual qualities. Intelligence is usually seen as an attribute of individuals.

IQ tests, for example, are given to individuals rather than groups. Student examination results are taken as a mark of individual ability rather than as a reflection on the quality of teaching, course material or the quality of a culture. In Christopher Lasch's description of *The Revolt of the Elites*, he notes that although hereditary advantages play an important part in the attainment of professional and managerial status the new elite, he suggests, has 'to maintain the fiction that its power rests on intelligence alone. Hence it has little sense of ancestral gratitude or of an obligation to live up to responsibilities inherited from the past. It thinks of itself as a self-made elite owing its privileges exclusively to its own efforts'.[13]

This is a view which holds considerable sway among the population at large. Becoming an eminent professor is seen to result from extraordinary individual ability rather than as the product of a massive collective adventure involving family, teachers, colleagues and the authors of all the books, articles, television programmes, etc., that have informed the work for which the individual has received personal acclaim. But it is not only eminent professors who stand on the shoulders of their ancestors and who rely on others. We all do. As John Dewey suggests, 'The conception of mind as a purely isolated possession of the self is at the very antipodes of the truth. The self *achieves* mind in the degree in which knowledge of things is incarnate in the life about him; the self is not a separate mind building up knowledge anew on its own account'.[14] As individuals, we possess only the potential for intelligence, in the sense of an ability to acquire and interpret information; to solve problems; to think critically and systematically about the social and natural world; to communicate ideas to others; and to apply new skills and techniques. It is developments in the social world that stimulates the mind's potential for new forms of feeling, reasoning and understanding.

3

If 'intelligence' is to be reclaimed for more progressive purposes it is also important to show that what counts as intelligence is historically variable. The idea of intelligence in the Golden era, for instance, is redundant in the world in which we now live. The way work and family life are organized; the way we interact with one another; and the tools we use to create wealth and communicate have changed dramatically. Intelligence is not, therefore, a fixed capacity as is so frequently asserted; rather the capacities and potentials of what we consider intelligence and intelligent action change in relation to new demands and practices of any given age. It follows from this view that new forms of intelligence will be invoked as the institutions and practices of society change.[15]

We have shown that the dominant conception of intelligence in the Golden era was represented by the IQ test. That this should be the case was not surprising since it chimed well with the way the world of paid work, education and everyday lifestyles were arranged. We have seen how economic activity was organized on the basis of giant corporate hierarchies and Fordist assembly lines. This involved a clear division of labour, usually with an elite at the apex making policy decisions, a large number of white-collar workers overseeing a reluctant army of blue-collar workers whose tasks could be performed best when 'their minds were least consulted'. This division of activity was mirrored in the education system where it was only the managerial and professional elite that received an extended period of formal education beyond the age of eighteen. Hence, the normal curve depicting the distribution of IQ mapped quite well on to this distribution of corporate decision-making power. But equally important was the view that intelligence was in the main cognitive. It involved the learning of pre-existing bodies of knowledge in the sciences and the humanities which were neatly subdivided into 'subjects' and offered according to the perceived future destination of the student. Technical and craft knowledge were assumed to require less intelligence to master than the academic. And the acquisition of tacit knowledge, especially by people of colour, women or the working class, stood beyond the conventional definition of intelligence dominated by the precepts of scientific reason. As Western societies have moved into a more technologically advanced and knowledge intensive world, the limitations of this understanding of intelligence have become more obvious with the decline in bureaucratic work structures, and more flexible labour markets.[16]

Howard Gardner's *Frames of Mind* is indicative of a sea change in our understanding of what constitutes intelligence in a post-industrial world. In this book he argues against the unitary idea of intelligence as represented by the IQist tradition and instead outlines a theory of multiple intelligence, numbering among them linguistic, musical, logical and mathematical, spatial, bodily–kinesthetic and personal intelligence. Our concern here is not with the way Gardner has de-limited different forms of intelligence but to note how the changing social world has made a theory of multiple intelligence relevant, if not inevitable.[17] Of particular interest is his theory of personal intelligence. For Gardner, personal intelligence involves access to one's own feelings and an ability to notice and make distinctions between the moods, temperaments, motivations and feelings of others.

In the factory model roles were carefully de-limited both at home and at work. Knowledge of oneself and of others in the exercise of work roles was discouraged as unprofessional or irrelevant, beyond an evaluation of the individual's job title, authority or certified expertise. Pre-existing roles prescribed the way individuals should act and it was only from the late 1960s that these were subjected to serious challenge. Now, knowledge of oneself and of others is necessary to function adequately. Where once roles were prescribed, now they are more likely to be negotiated. Under such conditions the interpersonal skills which come from such knowledge are at a premium. In the corporate world hierarchies of roles have been replaced by team work in which the 'person' is as important as the technical skills they may possess; indeed the two have become inseparable.[18]

Of course, it is not just changes in the world of work that have brought personal intelligence to the forefront. For some time feminists have been pointing out that personal intelligence has been the prerogative of women precisely because as 'homemakers' they have been the keepers of subjectivity and the emotions. But with the increasing flexibility of gender roles within the home and at work feminists have also pointed out the stunted nature of the male psyche because of the absence of personal intelligence. The emergence of personal intelligence as a necessary quality for *all* individuals can, therefore, be seen partly as a consequence of the breakdown in the division of labour between women and men. The net results of these changes in the division of labour and in our modes of interaction has been that our ideal of the intelligent person has changed, especially for men. A well-rounded personality is one in which emotional or personal intelligence is as important an attribute as logical and mathematical intelligence. Since the Enlightenment, emotions including fear, anger, sadness, love and happiness have been bracketed off as expressive, and therefore seen as irrational in an age of scientific rationality. The labelling of the emotions as 'feminine' has been used by male elites as a convenient way of demonstrating the inferiority of women in a scientific world. This mind numbing-interpretation of intelligence is far removed from Aristotle's philosophical enquiry into character, virtue and the good life. Here the issue is not cast in terms of how to eliminate emotions from everyday interactions and activities, but rather one of how to manage our emotions with intelligence. And this, as Daniel Goleman's account of *Emotional Intelligence* suggests, will include self-control, zeal, persistence, and the ability to motivate oneself.[19]

It follows from this account that what we consider as intelligence needs to extend well beyond the boundaries of book learning to include among other things the artistic, communication and emotional dimensions of human capability. Intelligence in post-industrial societies must include the ability to solve problems, to think critically and systematically about the social and material worlds, to apply new skills and techniques, to empathize and to have the personal skills needed to communicate and live alongside others. Above all, in a society characterized by risk and insecurity, it means being able to imagine and assess alternative futures. In turn, this means being able to go beyond established paradigms of thought. As Colin Lacey has suggested, 'Intelligence has to do with . . . making judgements about when it is appropriate to create new courses of action or avenues of thought' and 'it involves the development of a morality that is capable of guiding action'.[20]

This definition of intelligence is consistent with the ethical, emotional and cognitive processes, feelings and ideas that constitute collective intelligence. Indeed, collective intelligence depends on the development of the capacities for problem solving given that in a context of rapid personal, social and technological change this is the basis for personal empowerment, whether it involves dealing with the emotions of love or hate for an estranged lover; negotiating bedtime with young children; working through a restructuring package with work colleagues, or managing a successful career strategy. John Dewey, the American educationalist and philosopher, centred his whole intellectual enterprise around the concept of a 'problem'. This approach is well summarised by Alan Ryan in his biography of Dewey:

Individuals and societies alike are stirred into life by problems; an unproblematic world would be a world not so much at rest as unconscious. Such a world is unimaginable. Life is problematic; even when we are not thinking about our situation, our bodies are continuously solving endless problems of their own sustained existence. Problem solving is the condition of organic life. Societies, like individuals, solve problems and, like individuals, must do so by acting on the environment that causes the problem in the first place. Interaction with the environment alters the society or the individual that acts on the environment, with the result that new problems arise and demand new solutions. To the degree that this process gives the organism more control over itself and its environment, more ability to rethink its problems, and the potentiality for fruitful changes along the same lines, we may talk of progress. Dewey's preferred expression was always 'growth'.[21]

If the development of these capacities and skills is an indisputable feature of collective intelligence, then we must rid ourselves of the dim view of human intelligence which infects self-confidence and our view of others. The fact is that all rather than a few have growth potential in terms of practical and intellectual achievement, of creative thought and insights, and of taking responsibility for making informed judgements and choices. We need to jack-up the 'normal curve' of ability so beloved by conservatives eager to explain social inequalities as a product of genetics.[22] Critics will argue that we are utopian. That we are ignoring the fact that there are differences in innate make-up. There is no need to deny this argument because it is irrelevant. None of what we are suggesting gainsays the existence of innate differences in the potential for intelligence (although it clearly depends on what is taken as a measure). What we are arguing, on the basis of research evidence, is that the vast wealth of talent has not been harnessed by current systems of education and training; in the jobs available to the vast majority; or in patriarchal family structures. It is simply nonsense to suggest that current levels of academic performance or economic productivity are an accurate reflection of individual and collective capability.

This view is supported by comparative evidence which shows significant differences in the proportion of students participating in higher education. These reflect societal differences in terms of culture, economy and politics. We do not, for instance, subscribe to the view that American or British students are innately less intelligent than the Japanese or Koreans![23] Here, evidence of the impact of culture on educational achievement is conclusive. Lawrence Steinberg has shown that at every level of measured ability migrant Asian students outperform their American counterparts, but this is not the case for second-generation Asian students. In other words, Steinberg is able to demonstrate a strong cultural component to educational performance even when measured ability is taken into account.[24]

We are also struck by the ever increasing numbers of 'mature' students who previously had few, if any, formal qualifications. Given a clear reason for undertaking college or university study (and the opportunity), they generally prove themselves to be able students. Education and work must be organised in order to nurture this wealth of talent. It will require the redirection of attention away from the attributes of individual students or workers as the source of low ability systems of education or poor levels of productivity, to focus on the cultural and institutional context in which the learning or work process takes place.

This will also involve abandoning another cherished cultural myth that there are a few born to lead while the masses are born to follow. All must be armed with the power tools to make individual and collective judgements. This is not an argument for mass indoctrination, but involves a celebration of the iconoclast, the critic and the diverse ethnic cultures and religious faiths which characterize post-industrial nations. Erich Fromm correctly reminds us that 'The right to express our thoughts means something only if we are able to have thoughts of our own'.[25] The failure to recognize this rich diversity and to learn the lessons of the past in the attempt to confront short-term concerns is to fail in the pursuit of collective intelligence. The denial by nation states of full and accessible information to their citizens about the key issues of the day – for instance, the causes and consequences of environmental pollution or the risks and causes of HIV and AIDS – or failure to offer political education as part of the school curriculum, is symptomatic of a failure to develop a nation's collective intelligence.

4

The redefinition of intelligence is a key part of the struggle for collective intelligence. But it is inadequate because of its limited focus on individuals. There are many private troubles felt by people that require public solutions, such as raising productivity, knowledge production, reducing poverty and crime, or improving education or the quality of employment opportunities, which cannot be resolved without collaboration with family, friends, neighbours, co-workers or fellow citizens.[26] In post-industrial societies it is the collective intelligence of families, communities, companies and society at large, which will determine the quality of life as well as economic competitiveness. Despite the obsession of some who still believe that we can find ways of controlling human beings – if not by turning them into machines, which was popular for much of the twentieth century, then by rendering them redundant through the development of artificial intelligence – for the first time in human history we confront the task of developing and pooling the intelligence of *all* of the population of post-industrial societies.

Collective intelligence can be defined as empowerment through the *development and pooling of intelligence* to attain common goals or resolve common problems.[27] It is inspired by a spirit of co-operation rather a Darwinian survival of the fittest. In a society that eulogizes the virtues of competition, self-interest and acquisitiveness, rather than co-operation, common interest and the quality of life, it is difficult to maximise human potential or to co-ordinate opportunities for intelligent action in an efficient matter. The struggle for collective intelligence therefore involves more than a democratization of intelligence, it involves making a virtue of our mutual dependence and sociability which we will need to make a dominant feature of post-industrial society based on information, knowledge and lifelong learning.[28]

To develop our understanding of the social foundations of collective intelligence at any given historical moment, a distinction can be made between the *capacity for intelligence* and *relations of trust*. The capacity for intelligence describes the raw materials on which the development of intelligence depends. It refers to the state of knowledge, scientific discovery, technology and learning techniques, on which societies can draw. It includes the knowledge and technological resources amassed in society in the form of books, journals, databases, computers and computer programmes, universities, research institutes, museums, laboratories, and super-highways to name but a few. In many respects the capacity for intelligence has become global in scope as new ideas, fashions, technologies and sources of productivity traverse the global in real time through the media, Internet and MNCs. The Human Genome Program launched by the US Department of Energy and the National Institutes of Health in 1990 is an example. One of its major aims was to identify all of the approximate 100,000 genes in human DNA and combined universities and research centres in the US, the UK, Australia, Canada, Germany, France, Japan, Denmark, Israel and Italy. At a societal level the capacity for intelligence would also include the scale of investment in the knowledge, learning and research infrastructure in the form of schools, colleges, universities, libraries, museums, training centres, research institutes and information superhighways.

Conventional economic approaches have limited our horizons to trying to measure certain facets of the capacity for intelligence, such as attempts to measure the national stock of human capital. Obvious problems with this approach are the crude measures, such as years of formal education, which are used to calculate the quality of a nation's human resources, and the way that human intelligence and learning are reduced to a question of earning a living. If these are serious problems, the death knell of human capital models is the failure to acknowledge intelligence as a social gift. How intelligence is defined; whether it.

cultivation is restricted to a few or extended to all; the extent of 'our' knowledge, including scientific discoveries, art, literature and music; whether we have the opportunity to use our brains at work; and the quality of the culture which furnishes the definition of intelligence and human nature, are shaped by individuals as members of society. We make our own history but in co-operation with others, and not always in way that we choose or intend. The nature and distribution of intelligence will be shaped by the social groups to which an individual belongs and the cultural, economic and political fabric of society more generally. In low trust societies, for instance, education, knowledge and learning are treated as part of a zero-sum game, where extending opportunities to less privileged groups and the pooling of intelligence is seen as a threat to the positional advantage of social elites.[29] Therefore, the development and pooling of intelligence is severely restricted for less-advantaged social groups and hence for society as a whole.

As human capital ideas have come to dominate government policies there has been a considerable emphasis on increasing post-compulsory access to tertiary education, adult training and wiring-up schools to the Internet. This kind of capacity building is important but inadequate as such policies fail to take account of how the raw materials of post-industrial economies are weaved into the social fabric. The inter-relationship between *capacities* and *relations* is vital because it addresses the extent to which people are institutionally encouraged to pool their intelligence.

To aid our understanding of relations of 'trust' we need to distinguish it from its everyday meaning of whether we think someone is honest. Trust is used here to refer to whether the development and pooling of intelligence is reflected in the relationships between individuals, groups, and social classes that are embedded in classrooms, offices, shopfloors, households, neighbourhoods, welfare policies and taxation systems. This emphasis on institutionally embedded trust does not ignore the importance of national cultures or political ideologies. Confucianism as exhibited in some Asian countries is, for example, usually seen to encourage social harmony, whereas the tenets of Western individualism as applied in the last twenty years or so, has made it virtually impossible for people (even within the same family) to think in terms of co-operation and mutual dependence. The cultural context will clearly have a powerful impact on social values and attitudes: as, R.H. Tawney reminded us in our introductory chapter, it is impossible to achieve significant social change without changing the 'scale of moral values which rules the minds of individuals', because it is these values which have shaped social history.[30] But we have to do more than look at the principles which guide how people treat each other. Allan Fox correctly highlights the need to focus on the way social relationships are embedded 'in the institutions, patterns, and processes themselves which are operated by people who are capable of choosing differently'.[31]

At a societal level, the taxation paid by different income groups, the generosity of welfare provision for those who do not have access to waged work, or the provision of lifelong learning to all sections of society whether rich or poor, act as important signals which are easily decoded by people into 'this is a society which is pulling together in the interests of all' or 'this a society based on looking after number one'. The more inclusive the society the more people from all walks of life are likely to feel that they have a stake in the system as Richard Wilkinson has demonstrated in his international study of *Unhealthy Societies*, mentioned above. He found that the social polarization in the 1980s led to a growth in the number of poor people dying prematurely, committing suicide, getting divorced, and whose children were underachieving at school. He is able to show that these social pathologies were less a direct consequence of material deprivation, than a symptom of a collapse in trust as those in poverty saw fellow Americans or Britons as indifferent to their suffering and felt that they were no longer bona fide members of society.

This research not only shows that poverty leads to low trust relations between the haves and have nots but that it undermines the capacity of disadvantaged neighbourhoods for informal 'social learning' because of their social exclusion. Social learning is central to building social capital at the grass-roots. James Coleman, thought that social capital inheres in the relationships between individuals in a community which is characterized by high trust relations and shared responsibilities.[32] An example would be a network of the mothers of kindergarten and primary school children, who share the duties of ferrying kids to and from school, and who share the responsibility of looking after other children when the need arises. The reason why this leads to the creation of social capital is that these activities also involve communicating to children a shared set of expectations about appropriate standards of behaviour, the value of education, and the benefits of sharing resources including cars and time. This form of informal learning may not be overt or even oral, but is achieved by prompting such as 'have you got homework today?', or by parental interest in what the children did at school that day. It is the messages of the community in sum that is significant in the creation of social capital. The relative wealth of communities in this respect is reflected in the performance of their children in school as Coleman and Hoffer have demonstrated.[33]

The impact of inequality on the development of informal learning is not difficult to understand, although it often operates in subtle and complex ways. Communities or networks which are rich in social capital, for instance, take time, energy and resources to build. They also depend on a high degree of stability in the family and neighbour context. This is highlighted in Coleman and Hoffer's research as they found that the most significant impact on educational failure was the amount of times a child moves school. But this kind of instability is most frequently found in poor school districts.[34] This is not the only malign effect of poverty in the creation of social capital. The impact of the ghettoization of American inner cities on the decline in social capital is graphically portrayed in the work of William Julius Wilson which was noted earlier and is worth reiterating here.[35] Wilson shows how a perceptive ghetto youngster in a neighbourhood where some people have been able to keep good jobs, even in a context of increasing joblessness and idleness, can continue to see a meaningful connection between education and employment. The problem is that these neighbourhoods show signs of becoming even more polarized when those who are able to find decent jobs leave. As a consequence, the more social groups become isolated from one another the fewer opportunities exist for the kind of informal learning which contributes to collective intelligence.

Building high trust relations is at the heart of the struggle for collective intelligence, in that it is a way of moving towards a form of associated living which involves making experience more communicable by removing the social distance which makes individuals impervious to the interests of others.[36] This conforms to John Dewey's notion of democracy which is more than a system of government as it defines the way people live together and pool their intelligence.[37] Collective intelligence is exercized through the development of the art of conversation and by giving an authentic voice to all constituencies of society. This in turn depends upon the breakdown of social divisions which inhibit the free communication and interaction between people and groups. This applies equally at the level of society where social barriers are constructed around class, race or religion, as it does to the workplace or home, when sharp distinctions are imposed between management and workers or breadwinners and home-makers. Such barriers serve to undermine the potential for collective intelligence. But it is not only the powerless who lose out in these circumstances, its consequences for social elites may be less material and less obvious, but remain insidious as, 'their culture tends to be sterile, to be turned back to feed on itself; their art becomes a showy display and artificial; their wealth luxurious; their knowledge over-specialized; their manners fastidious rather than humane'.[38]

In such a society the development of intelligence is severely constrained by inequality, poverty and cultural elitism. As a result all social groups lack the trust upon which conversation is possible. It denies a society of novel and challenging ideas which frequently stem from diversity in situations and social and cultural experiences. Collective intelligence involves a 'widening of the circle of shared concerns and the liberation of a greater diversity of personal capacity'.[39] A trivial instance was given recently by a friend whose favourite radio programme was *Desert Island Discs*, produced by the British Broadcasting Corporation. The programme involves someone, usually a celebrity or prominent public figure, talking about their life and selecting pieces of music which they would take with them to listen to on their deserted island. Our friend commented that two of the recent castaways were people she had disliked on the basis of their media image. On both occasions she observed how listening to their life stories, anxieties and concerns, had led her to cast these individuals in a more positive light (of course, greater understanding can also lead to the opposite response) because she had had the, albeit brief, opportunity to recognize common points of contact and concern. To share what amounts to a common humanity. In a pluralistic society of different life styles, patterns of behaviour, language and customs, it is basic to the establishment of collective intelligence to recognize aspects of common humanity and for these to be institutionally encouraged.

The development of high trust relations therefore offers the best chance of making a positive feature of cultural pluralism and of meeting post-modern calls for a politics of difference. What is recognized in the struggle for collective intelligence is that different voices which reflect the rich diversity of cultural identity and social experience are the lifeblood which fuels the collective effort to resolve common problems in an attempt to improve the quality of life for all. Equally, this involves recognizing that there are different ways to live a life. But in polarized and divided societies people come to feel isolated and fearsome of groups with which they share little in common and with whom they rarely come into contact. This situation fuels the ideology and practice of self-interest which neutralize ethical decisions, and despite the fact that the struggle for money, power and status leaves most people unfulfilled, it robs people of the opportunity to engage in 'conversations' about the nature of society, working life and personal relationships

Relations of trust also have profound implications for the organization of economic life in the early decades of the twenty-first century. This is because they shape the nature of co-operation between economic actors, whether as employers, employees, trade union representatives, government policy-makers or consumers. The nature of this co-operation has been historically transformed. Co-operation in pre-industrial societies involved acting for purposes of economic production or distribution on established routines and 'mechanical' solidarity.[40] Co-operation involved little scope for human freedom, as Marx suggested, 'the individual has as little torn himself free from the umbilical cord of his tribe or community as a bee has from his hive'.[41] Marx noted that there were few examples in ancient times of co-operation on a large scale and where this did occur is was founded on slavery. With the rise of industrial capitalism new forms of economic co-operation developed based on the 'free' wage-labourer who sells his or her labour-power to employers and the development of the factory model of production. The factory system involved a fundamental change, in that workers had to be disciplined to co-ordinate their working day and work activities, which greatly increased productivity, as Marx observed, 'the socially productive power of labour develops as a free gift to capital' whenever workers are organized in this way.[42]

Marx saw this form of social co-operation as a valuable source of capital (although he did not use the term social capital). He also believed it to be exploitative as the owner and controllers of production appropriated the fruits of this collective activity, but as workers came to understand the injustice of capitalism production he believed that they would seek to overthrow the system as they had 'nothing to lose but their chains'. History has proved Marx wrong. The development of mass production in the twentieth century not only enhanced corporate efficiency and profitability, but it also gave workers the chance to collectively mobilize to claim an increasing share of the fruits of productive co-operation as we have described in this book.[43] However, the low-trust relations inherent in the factory model inhibited the patterns of commitment and communication which made it difficult to compete with Japan and the Asian Tiger economies in the 1970s and 1980s.

Low-trust relations led to worker resistance, minimum levels of commitment, high rates of absenteeism, and wild cat strikes. These responses have traditionally been interpreted by management as a manifestation of the feckless and irresponsible nature of most workers. Indeed, managers have typically used these responses to justify the introduction of intensive surveillance and the threat of sanctions in the control of the workforce. A more plausible interpretation is that they are a rational response to working conditions where little is expected of workers and little is given in return.[44] Again, we do not subscribe to the view that American and North European workers are innately more lazy, selfish or incapable of assuming responsibility than those in Japan or Singapore. The higher rates of productivity achieved by Japanese manufacturing companies is not simply due to having more robots than their competitors, or having more efficient inventory systems such as JIT, but it also results from having a human relations regime which encourages workers to think rather than leave their brains at the factory gate, to participate in work teams and to feel empowered in the work setting, rather than as a moron who is so distrusted by management that they are forced to pay a deposit if they want to use a knife and fork in order to eat their lunch.[45]

Today the economic imperatives of capitalism in its post-industrial phase represents an historically unprecedented opportunities to redefine co-operation and the foundations of trust relations. The declining significance of mass employment organizations; the decline of the factory model of efficiency and with it the demise of bureaucratic careers and jobs for life, are transforming the model worker–citizen. Co-operation in high-performance companies depends on the collective intelligence of economic actors, as intellectual and emotional intelligence have become a key feature of the learning, innovation and productivity chain. In a knowledge-driven economy characterized by rapid change, adequate job performance cannot easily rely on external controls, as people need to be proactive, solve problems and work in teams. It is no longer enough to bring people together to generate the 'socially productive power of labour'; co-operation which is value added depends on the development of collective intelligence.

There is a growing body of literature which suggests that in circumstances where employees are given room for individual discretion and see some point in what they are doing, they will show a strong tendency towards co-operation and competence rather than resistance and resentment. The reason? It conforms to a basic human trait – the desire for individual and collective growth. Daniel Goleman has noted that the single most important element in what he calls group intelligence is not the average IQ in the academic sense but social harmony, 'it is this ability to harmonize that, all other things being equal, will make one group especially talented, productive, and successful, and another – with members whose talent and skills are equal in other regards – do poorly'.[46] Equally, Nahapiet and Ghoshal build on these insights to argue that the development of high trust can improve the productivity of knowledge workers and the organizational capacity for innovation.

This works best when all social actors have a stake in the economy and society; when they have a sense of security; when there are open networks of communication and interaction; when people have a wide degree of discretion and freedom about the way they work and live their lives; and when mistakes and failures are seen to be part of a learning process of experimentation and innovation rather than as negligence or ineptitude. Then people will be institutionally encouraged to pool their intelligence.

5

Collective intelligence, therefore, depends upon a new disposition of mind which rejects the absurd excesses of Western individualism and sensitizes us to what binds people together in co-operative human activities, as well as our interdependence and responsibilities to ourselves and others. A. H. Halsey, who has been a keen observer of the nature of social change in the twentieth century, would no doubt remind us that 'Exhortation alone is futile, whether to altruism or to tolerance or to recognition of the equal claim of others to share in the bounty afforded by society. The problem is to discover, to establish, and to strengthen those social institutions that will encourage and foster the kinds of relations between people that are desired'.[47] The task is one of both re-socializing the mind and of embedding the principles of collective intelligence in the social structure. The difficulties involved in this enterprise should not be underestimated. We can not start from scratch nor can we stand still. We may not, as Giddens depicts contemporary social life, be riding the juggernaut of modernity careering out of control, but there is little doubt that any concerted attempt to build a society based on the struggle for collective intelligence will, as Karl Mannheim recognized, be rather like trying to change a wheel on a train in motion.[48] Despite the enormity of the task, the remaining chapters will show how a society based on the principles of collective intelligence would transform the nation state, economy, education, welfare and the foundations of social justice.

14
The Learning State

We are floundering, both in practice and in analysis, because we no longer know what holds a society together.

Daniel Bell

1

The nineteenth-century German philosopher, Friedrich Hegel, observed that the strengths that build great nations invariably become obsessions which eventually destroy them. In America and Britain we have argued that the dominant response to the transformation of social and economic life has been to return to the first principles of western capitalism based on market individualism. The argument of this book is that such a position is unsustainable given the social and economic challenges of the twenty-first century. The fundamental tasks confronting nations are those of providing the conditions which will enable their citizens to develop the collective intelligence required to meet an economic and social environment which demands ever smarter people.

The development of collective intelligence can only be achieved if we are prepared to re-think radically the way capitalist societies are organized. We need to recognize that the distribution of rewards can no longer be left to the job market in which a large minority have to survive on poverty wages and others are excluded from finding meaningful employment altogether. Equally, whereas the world of paid work provided the cornerstone of family security, it no longer can. In essence, the foundations of social progress, based on prosperity, security, opportunity, and participation in democratic life have to be rebuilt although on a different terrain from that of the post-war Golden era

Ways need to be found to increase real incomes for all, to improve job security on which income depends and to reduce income inequality. These are important because they form the springboard for opportunity and participation. Rising incomes offer people a sense of hope while a measure of income security takes the edge off fear. It is a fear felt throughout the community not only debilitating to those on low incomes, but also to those on higher incomes who will protect what they have by deliberately or inadvertently closing off opportunities to others. Income inequality needs to be reduced because we know that the process of polarizing incomes creates a range of social pathologies that contaminate the lifeblood of healthy societies.[1] Together, a more equitable distribution of rising incomes, along with greater job security, provide the impetus for a more open society in which people can seize opportunities and feel a commitment to their society. But if the principle that people should be rewarded according to market value is inadequate to the challenges ahead, how is the distribution of rewards to be organized?

The first step is to question current policy which draws a sharp distinction between productive and unproductive work. Productive work is assumed to be waged work. The measure of an individual's contribution to society is typically based on how much they earn. Unproductive work includes all activities which do not generate an income. A further distinction is also made between 'unproductive' people who are 'deserving' or 'undeserving'. Political debates over social policy have been dominated by concerns about distinguishing the deserving from the undeserving, so that those deemed worthy of support could be helped from income redistributed through taxation. In recent times the line seems to be drawn in an ever more arbitrary fashion. In the United States pensioners by and large are seen quite rightly as deserving. In Britain, state pensions have declined over the past fifteen years which suggests that they are seen as less deserving. On both sides of the Atlantic between a quarter and a third of children are treated as undeserving as a consequence of the economic status of their parents. Lone parents are being forced into low-waged jobs by welfare to work programmes because to care for their own child and not being paid for it is seen as an 'unproductive' activity.

There is a further complication. If a rich man decides to lead a life of leisure there is no onus on him to get a job or to retrain. For a poor single mother there is no such option. Rights are assigned differentially according to wealth. Part of the reason why these crude and now dysfunctional categories endure is because neo-classical economics, which has been so influential in policy formulation, assumes that all individuals are motivated to trade off work for leisure. As we are principally calculating pleasure machines, according to neo-classical economists, it follows that we will seek as much leisure as we can afford.[2] But consideration of the role of caregivers such as lone mothers makes a nonsense of this distinction as eminent feminist economists like Marilyn Waring have pointed out.[3]

During the post-war period the distinction between 'productive' and 'unproductive' did not lead to the scale of regulation we have today. For a start, the concept of the family wage enabled the material necessities of life at that time to be covered for the majority of workers. In the 1970s, families on middle incomes in America averaged around $32,000; by 1995 they had seen an increase of $2,000; but the increase was bought at the cost of declining wages for men and more women doing paid work for longer hours. At the same time, both houses and cars were relatively cheaper than they are now for a young couple building for a family. In 1970 a new home cost a young couple twice their annual income; by 1994 the price had risen to four times their annual income. During the same period, a car for a young couple rose from 38 per cent to 50 per cent of their income.[4] However, as the family wage has declined and women have had to go out to work, the rising cost of childcare has led many couples to consider whether it is cost-effective for both parents to be in full-time employment.

Equally, in terms of collective intelligence it is important to note that in the Golden era something close to half of the employed population required very little education since they were destined for semi-skilled and unskilled work. What was required of parents, particularly mothers, was that they socialise their children to be law abiding and imbued with the work ethic.[5] Arguably, little economic value was attached to the primary socialisation of children which may go some way to explain why the work of mothers was accorded little value. Now, instilling children with the basic norms of society is not enough. In post-industrial societies, the educative role of parents has become far more important as the early years of a child's life set the platform for subsequent learning. This role clearly produces a major return to the society and it should be recognized as doing so.

In a society based on collective intelligence, reward and status need to be extended to include not only those who are directly involved in the production of goods and services, but also those who contribute to the growth potential, productivity and quality of life of others, for instance, through the pre-school, home-based education of children or, at the other end of the age spectrum, the care of the elderly. However, even this extension does not go far enough to address the needs of such a society for it fails to take into account the unemployed.

It has been assumed by the Modernizers, like the New Right before them, that unemployment is a sign of fecklessness, that it is an expression of the desire for leisure over income supported by taxpayers' money. Hence in America, George Gilder could claim that the poor need nothing more than the spur of their own poverty to propel them out of their condition, while in Britain a luminary of the Thatcher administration claimed that all the unemployed had to do was 'get on their bikes' to find employment.[6] These arguments lead to the view that the unemployed should not qualify for financial support from the community because they are 'undeserving'. A further twist to this argument is the claim that by living on benefits these people are likely to grow dependent and lose the will to work. Hence, the idea of the dependency culture has grown as unemployment has become entrenched in post-industrial societies. The vocabulary of dependency, as we have seen, is as much a part of the Modernizers' rhetoric as it was that of the Right. In both cases it represents a Canute-like response to the realities of the age.

Being made redundant is one of the most traumatic events in people's lives. In America, Britain and Europe the story is the same. Those who are unemployed are far more likely to be unhappy than those in employment. This is true of the higher as well as the lower educated, and the unemployed are more likely to display symptoms of mental distress than those in jobs. Moreover, some studies indicate that unemployed people are up to ten times more likely to attempt suicide than those in employment.[7] The view that the higher the level of benefit the more likely individuals will trade off income for leisure is false. The levels of unemployment benefit appear to have little impact on the numbers unemployed. For example, Sweden provides the unemployed with 80 per cent of their previous income and during the 1990s some 4.4 per cent were unemployed. New Zealand provides people with about 30 per cent of their income and has double the unemployment of Sweden. The USA had approximately 6.2 per cent unemployment during the early 1990s and provided approximately 50 per cent of an employed person's income, albeit for a limited period. The Netherlands has had 7 per cent unemployment while compensating individuals to the tune of 70 per cent of their previous income.[8] The conclusion to be drawn from this comparative evidence is that the majority of people want to engage in paid work, if they are not caregivers and if the alternative is unemployment. The only impact that lower levels of benefit have is to make life even more difficult for those who don't have paid work. Given the current rhetoric of dependency this immiseration is compounded by the stigma of being 'dependent'.

This conclusion is not surprising once we discard the naive and damaging assumption that human beings are merely 'pleasure machines' and see that productive and reproductive work is intimately related to a person's sense of identity and well-being. As Ian Gough has put it, 'Cooperative labour, including unpaid care work is a defining feature of all social groups... Participation in universally socially significant activities, including work, is a crucial contributor to autonomy and human welfare'.[9]

That said, it needs to be acknowledged that on some estates and housing projects there are generations of families who have never worked in the official labour market (although they may well have worked in the black economy) and for whom paid work or caregiving has been divorced from their sense of identity. This is a small group of people relative to the majority who are unemployed and yet in the rhetoric of 'dependence' culture they have come to represent all those who are unemployed. This rhetoric and the policies that accompany it have to change. If we take the plausible view that larger numbers of workers will be more frequently unemployed in the forseeable future, even if they are for short spells, the stigma and financial misery that unemployment visits on individuals has to be addressed.

In a society based on collective intelligence unemployment cannot be seen as a problem but as management gurus would have it, an opportunity – *for the society as a whole*. Periods of unemployment should not be seen as down time or wasted time but *necessary* in a high-skills economy in order that individuals have the time to upgrade their skills. Viewed in this way unemployment is not a matter of fecklessness or a reflection on past poor performance. The corollary to this is that unemployed people need a relatively high level of compensation so that they can focus on using the opportunity to retrain rather than be distracted by the question of where the next meal will come from.

These arguments lead us to the inescapable conclusion that a society based on collective intelligence, geared to more efficient high-skills production, must be a society with a very significant element of redistribution of income and wealth. After all, if it is true that productivity is the ultimate source of wealth creation, more people are bound to lose their jobs as companies and the economy become more productive.

Therefore the unemployed are not an impediment to economic prosperity but are paying the ultimate sacrifice to maintain company profits and the income of those who remain in jobs. This needs to be recognized in the way society rewards contribution and defines responsibilities. But how can this be achieved when the entire thrust of government policy in the past thirty years has been to reduce taxation on income and wealth?

2

It should be recalled that taxation was the principal expression of social solidarity in post-war societies. Taxation acknowledges the 'needs of strangers' as fellow citizens who lived together in mutual dependence.[10] In the Golden era, this understanding of mutual dependence was a response to the common sacrifice of war. In the 1980s politicians on both sides of the Atlantic sought to bury the memory of mutual dependence by elevating individual wants, divorced from the common good, in the doctrine of market individualism. The problem this has posed for the centre-left is that in the absence of any alternative vision of society, taxation of income and wealth has appeared to be profligacy if not theft.[11]

The doctrine of market individualism gave political shape to a trend towards private consumption. We have suggested that people have become more reflexive in their social interactions, because roles are more open to negotiation, but that much of the potential for reflexive solidarity has been channel into a matter of consumer choice. The challenge is to reunite the needs and wants of persons with the common good.[12] It is this the Modernizers have singularly failed to do because they have not recognized that old solutions are inadequate in the face of new realities. It is not enough to extol the virtues of social cohesion without it being embedded in our households, schools, companies and political institutions.

The aim must now be to fashion a vision which links the need for the redistribution of income and wealth to social progress while sustaining economic competitiveness. However, this can only be achieved within a framework which gives recognition and expression to individuals' desires to pursue their life projects.

At the heart of this vision stands the learning state which would be designed to foster collective intelligence. The learning state would enable individuals to enhance their own personal growth at the same time as making a positive contribution as worker–citizens to society. It is through the state that the redistribution and security of income would be effected, and it is through the reorganisation of education that opportunity would be created. Far from having a diminishing role in the organisation of society, the state will have the principal function of creating the political settlement between citizens, capital and labour on which policies for the development of collective intelligence can be built. Once it is acknowledged that we can no longer rely on the market to allocate incomes it is inevitable that the state takes on these roles.

Critics from both the Left and the Right will complain that the state is not to be trusted, that it is subject to the pressures of vested interests which undermines its authority to create such a settlement. This is not a criticism to be dismissed lightly.[13] The modern state, as Claus Offe[14] has cogently argued, is caught between supporting the interests of capitalist profit-making and the democratic demands of its citizens. It needs to support profit-making because it is only by sustaining a viable private enterprise sector that profits can be redistributed. But at the same time, in a democracy, governments rely on the popular vote so that there has to be a compromise between the demands of entrepreneurs and the interests of citizens. The problem has been that since the break up of economic nationalism, the political project of the Right has shifted the balance in America and Britain in favour of short-term capitalist interests. Hence the polarization of income, the attack on unions and the mass creation of junk jobs. To redress this balance means strengthening the way democracy is organized. But it must also involve a means of negotiating a sustainable settlement to which the vast majority of people can sign up. To create this new settlement the learning state has to address the questions of income distribution, education and democracy.

3

The argument so far has established that we need new rules for income distribution which take into account the need to support various groups who are in conventional terms considered 'outside' the labour market. We should, however, resist a vocabulary which implies that there is a straightforward distinction to be made between those who are 'inside' and 'outside' the labour market. Rather, a better metaphor would be that of a sports team in which some are in the starting line up and some on the bench, as well as numerous support staff such as coaches, physiotherapists, ground staff, equipment manufacturers, sales personnel. No one considers those who are not on the field of play at a given moment as out of the team, they are all part of the team, although they may be paid different rates. So it is with a society based on collective intelligence, every one is part of the team – some are playing, some are in reserve, some injured and some are the 'back up' behind the scenes. The only proviso for staying on the team is that everyone plays their part as best they can.

On this kind of scenario the questions to be asked are: how can the contributions of all be recognized despite the fact that it is only a small proportion of the team who get most of the recognition for their effort and abilities? How can the profits made by the team through ticket sales; television rights and sponsorship be distributed among all those who have made a contribution? Of course, the analogy of a sports team quickly breaks down in light of how winner-takes-all markets dominate professional sport. But the point is that all those who care or have previously contributed to the production and reproduction of collective intelligence should be entitled to a decent income.

Notice two things about this entitlement. The first is that it carries with it both *rights* and *obligations*. In the past the Left has argued that those outside the market should have the right to some kind of income while the Right have argued that it is through self motivation and effort that those outside the market should re-enter it.[15] Our principle of entitlement brings these two points together. There are no free lunches attached to this entitlement. People who receive an income but don't participate in society do themselves no good for as we have argued self identity and motivation are linked to the great productive tasks that confront humanity. The second is that economic contribution has been redefined to include early childhood education by caregivers; retraining by those who have been made redundant; and non-waged work within the community. This leaves some groups out of the frame including the severely impaired and some of the elderly who are no longer able to make a contribution during their third age. For the elderly we need to look no further for a justification to support these people than the quotation by Friedrich List which heads the next chapter. It is upon their shoulders, in terms of their efforts and knowledge, that we stand: we are in their debt and we should acknowledge it through the pension system. One of the worst legacies of the eighties and nineties has been the loss of a sense of history which has rendered the elderly not merely redundant but a liability. For those who cannot fulfil their obligations as citizens we should argue that a common humanity would assure the extension of the same entitlement to them. In a decent society it goes without saying that suffering through ill health whether mental or physical should be alleviated wherever possible with the material and social support to live as active and fulfilling lives as possible.

In the current political climate we recommend a two-stage progression to the entitlement of a citizen's wage: that is a wage above the level of poverty eligible to all citizens, taking into account the number of dependents. The move to a citizen's wage would mark a decisive step in freeing individuals from the material fear of poverty while ending material exclusion based on race, gender or class. It provides one of the foundations of a society based on collective intelligence and gives expression to the way in which collective intelligence can be seen as a principle of social integration.

The motivation for introducing a two-stage process towards the goal of a citizen's wage is that of achieving what is feasible while providing a vision towards which we can aspire. But there is also a political motivation to this incremental approach. Inevitably, where the steps fall short of a citizen's wage for all, issues of who gains and who loses, of the deserving and the undeserving will arise. Each step would be designed to reduce these problems but in the end it is only if these measures are seen as part of a wider vision that people will accept them. The role of ideology and political vision should not be underestimated. During the Thatcher and Reagan years people were sold an ideology which targeted the 'unfit' including lone mothers, as pariahs in our society with the consequence of creating child poverty on a scale which would have been unimaginable twenty years before. Now the reason this occurred is because the policies and rhetoric of primitive capitalism created a vision which foresaw an end to state dependency if its recipes were followed. Of course this ultimately created more rather than less 'dependency' because the ideology didn't square with reality. But in Britain shortly after the Blair government was elected it followed Thatcherite policies by cutting lone mother benefits assuming that the popular animus against lone parents remained. It didn't. Once it was seen that the Right's recipe had failed, support for an attack on the weakest section of the population withered.

The first step in the progression to a citizen's wage is a *carer's* wage, to be paid to those who contribute to the collective intelligence of society through the education of their children but who are not rewarded through the labour market. This wage will be paid to all carers whose children are in poverty to lift them above the poverty line and tapered to the point where a percentage of the wage will be paid to a significant proportion of families. While a carer's wage set at abolishing child poverty will require far higher levels of redistribution than are currently the case, the principle of child support which benefits a majority of families is already in practice. For example Jane Millar notes that the integrated system of child support, in Australia, benefits 80 per cent of families on a sliding scale based on income and assets.[16] The purpose of this taper is to make the carer's wage as inclusive as possible, thereby increasing economic flexibility and security for a large sector of the middle class as well as political commitment to the idea. To reiterate research findings from Paul Johnson and Howard Reed in Britain, 44 per cent of sons of fathers who were unemployed or in the lowest income jobs in the early 1970s are in the same situation now. As they say, 'It seems safe to conclude that there is a clear intergenerational transmission of poverty through unemployment'.[17] These findings need to be set against the overall lack of income mobility during the past twenty-five years. For example in the United States, of those in the lowest income bracket, 42 per cent found themselves in the same position 17 years later and of those that were upwardly mobile the largest group went no further than the next step up in income. So the picture is one where a large population is trapped at the bottom of the income parade. This will certainly help to generate the kind of culture which will disadvantage many. The consequence is that the intergenerational transmission of poverty involves underachievement at school and discrimination in the labour market.[18] No doubt in some areas like the housing projects of the great American cities and the council estates in Britain, a culture which resists paid employment has developed. But as William Julius Wilson has so eloquently argued the root cause of the development of these cultures are a lack of jobs, which means lack of income *and* lack of meaningful activity.[19] When Wilson's insight is translated into a carer's wage policy it would mean that carers, as part of the condition of receiving the wage, become involved as their children's co-educators. This may mean assisting in the pre-school programmes of their children; that will have many advantages including the participation of parents in the community.

The carer's wage would be given to both partners where there were two caregivers where they were sharing the care but mostly it would be given to the primary caregiver – usually but perhaps for not much longer – the woman. It would also provide an incentive for men to stay within the family. Of course this rather simple statement of policy hides some hideously complex issues. How do we adjust income for family size and how do we determine what the poverty level is?[20] Nevertheless, thinking about these technical issues jumps the gun, what we need to focus on is the vision underlying such a programme and its likely consequences,

There are three immediate criticisms that people often make of such a programme: that it would act as a disincentive to work in the labour market; that it would create a sense of social injustice amongst those above the poverty line who would not recieve a carer's wage; and that it is unaffordable.[21] None of these critcisms tell against a carer's wage. For a start, its introduction would almost certainly increase the wages of the low paid. Some carers would choose not to be in the labour market, thereby creating scarcity for poorly paid labour. Hence low wages would rise. This would have a series of beneficial consequences. Many now in poor work would find that their incomes had increased thereby mitigating the sense of injustice of those who were above the poverty line and did not receive a carer's wage. At the same time the increased wages of those below the poverty line would mean that the state had fewer families to pay the carer's wage. In effect the state would stop subsidizing employers for offering such low wages. Against these advantages, the rise in the income of the low paid would lead to greater costs in some areas, for example, hospitals, security work and the hospitality industry. But pressure on public expenditure may actually decline as a result of the introduction of a carer's wage as crime and ill health are clearly linked to poverty.

There are further 'spin-offs' from a carer's wage which extend the reasons for its attractiveness. It would enable role substitution where there are two caregivers in the family and would address some of the problems of women taking the primary role in caregiving as a wage of this kind would enable men and women to swop roles and increase labour market flexibility. It would also address one of the fundamental problems for the majority of parents which is how to balance paid working and family life. As Arlie Hochschild as so clearly documented in *The Time Bind*, achieving this balance requires the skills of manipulating time and coping with stress in equal measures. Since families with two parents in paid work are likely to be amongst the 'better off', a carer's wage of this kind creates the opportunity for the balance between home and family life to be managed in a way that reduces the level of stress for both partners. Although 'better off', we have seen that the cost of 'big ticket items' like cars and houses have risen as family income has also risen so that effectively two-income families are running to stand still.[22] Women are definitely not working for pin money! At the same time research shows that men with working wives and families are significantly penalized in their careers relative to those without families.[23] Married women are similarly penalized, for never married women earn on a parity with men while married women earn, on

Table 14.1   Redistributing dollars via a maximum income in the USA (with transfers to the poorest 20 per cent of households)

Households that would benefit by income transfers		
Number to benefit	19,798,000	
Average Income Now	$7,764	
Households that would lose by income transfers		
Possible Maximums	$200,000	$100,000
Number to Lose	1,096,000	4,499,000
New Minimum Income	$15,527	$22,219

Taken from Andrew Hacker, 1997, p.56

average less.[24] Put these facts together and they amount to a powerful further argument for middle-class support for a carer's wage. Roles need not be fixed once decided on. For example, a carer's wage may enable carers to retrain and upgrade their skills while looking after their children. This is a strategy that many women have adopted over the past twenty years. Add the reduction in stress in managing a balanced life and it is possible to see why a carer's wage could appeal as much to middle-income families as to anyone else. Overall, the carer's wage could not only solve a series of significant social problems but enhance economic performance since it would create greater job flexibility in the labour market and job sharing opportunities throughout the nation as well as providing a better-educated younger generation.

These advantages probably pall into insignificance when confronted with the question of cost. Is such a programme feasible? Andrew Hacker has made the following calculations for the United States on the basis of creating a ceiling of either $200,000 or $100,000 on what people could earn, if all the money beyond these levels were redistributed to the poorest 20 per cent of households.[25]

We can see from this table that the redistribution of income from the upper maximum earnings would substantially alleviate poverty. Hacker believes that it would be erradicated if the limit were set at $100,000. But is the introduction of a maximum wage politically feasible?

Hacker draws on a Roper-Starch survey conducted in 1995, which found that when people were asked how much money they would need to fulfil all their dreams less than a fifth said they wanted to be really rich and half reckoned an income of $100,000 would do the trick.[26] In the current political climate there is little prospect of this scale of redistribution but what these figures show is that it does not boil down to a question of whether it is affordable but one of political choice. We could significantly reduce poverty if we had the political will to do so. It is because of this lack of political will that we have opted in the first instance for a carer's wage, rather than the introduction of a citizen's wage. But it is important to put the citizen's wage on the agenda because it will become a major issue in the decades to come and it raises two related issues in the development of collective intelligence. First, how to alleviate poverty as a way of improving learning opportunities and building social capital in poor neighbourhoods, and secondly, a citizen's wage is not only a question of giving people financial resources but of generating meaningful forms of social participation and building personal responsibilities in ways that are not directly linked to the formal labour market. As Jeremy Rifkin has argued in *The End of Work*, 'opportunity now exists to create millions of new jobs in the Third Sector – the civil society. Freeing up the labor and talent of men and women no longer needed in the market and government sectors to create social capital in neighbourhoods and communities'.[27] Although Rifkin has exaggerated the decline of waged work in Western societies, redefining opportunities and responsibilities for a large minority of people without jobs in the formal economy is going to become a pressing social issue in our new century.[28]

A *citizen's* wage would be designed to bring all out of poverty, irrespective of whether they were active in the labour market or not.[29] So in addition to families the citizen's wage would apply to all those over the age of eighteen. The only condition of receipt of the citizen's wage is that there is evidence of community or labour market participation, this would include participation in education or training. No one would be allowed to remain idle. Community programmes, the arts and government initiatives to strengthen the industrial and social infrastructure of the country would all be ways in which a contribution could be made.

The net effect of the citizen's wage would be to spring youth from the trap it is caught in by current policies. The current policy dilemma in relation to unemployment is that between exploitation and exclusion.[30] Exploitation is the American solution to unemployment based on cheap labour. Exclusion is the European solution in which the unemployed are recipients of fairly generous benefit payments but are excluded from the labour market. Young people have been especially hit by persistent unemployment and poor work representing an enormous loss of potential. A citizen's wage within the expanded notion of what is socially meaningful work helps to tackle this dilemma.

Despite the clear advantages of a strategy which leads to a citizen's wage, there are criticisms from both Right and Left arguing that the entire programme is misconceived. From the Right the criticisms are to do with the economic havoc that, it is claimed, would be wrought by it. At the micro level it is argued that a citizen's wage would destroy the incentive to paid work. The rich would not continue to work because they were 'taxed' too much, while the poor would not work because they were 'given' too much. This criticism, as we have seen, is derived from the theoretical assumption that human beings are pleasure machines but it has little basis in the real world. Authoritative studies like Robert Lane's *The Market Experience* show quite clearly that there is no correlation between high income and high job satisfaction. To a significant extent people will engage in paid employment from the sense of personal fulfilment and satisfaction they get rather than the money they earn. Part of the reason for this is that our value systems have become far more diverse than in the Golden era. As Ray Pahl has shown in *Beyond Success*, the uniform measure of success of that era, based on a scale of how much money and power an individual held, has given way to pluralistic values, one of which is the desire to achieve a balance between home and paid work. This pluralism is based on an equality of values which presents a two-edged sword. On the one hand, there is a tolerance of those earning astronomical packages because not everyone sees earning that kind of money as desirable – they have better things to do with their lives. On the other hand, the lack of desire to be more than comfortable creates the opportunity in a popular democracy for greater redistribution of income from the very rich.

As to those in poverty, the incentive to paid work will be achieved by the higher incomes those in low-paid jobs will earn. More to the point, a citizen's wage would give them genuine choices rather than stigmatized alternatives as to how they can best take control of their lives. The problem of dependency has been greatly exaggerated as very few people would actually want to subsist on the meagre benefits provided by the state in America or in Britain, as we have seen from the evidence on the effects of unemployment on mental health. Dependency has been created, with some exceptions, by a political class that has been unwilling to think through the radical solutions that are needed to address the economic and social problems that now confront us.

However, the dependency created by primitive capitalism has a paradoxical effect. The more the fiction is stressed that individuals owe nothing to society in their pursuit of economic self interest the more difficult it is to construct a society in which the individual's very real debt to that society is expressed in a commitment to the common good. Yet the motivation of individuals to engage in lifelong learning in the form of retraining, community participation and the labour market, will depend, in the last resort, on a new ethos which emphasizes the importance of the individual's obligation to participate fully through these different avenues of opportunity. This ethos can only emerge as the institutional structures of a society are transformed on the principles of collective intelligence. Within this framework, however, the ability of individuals to think reflexively about their relationship to society becomes an important rational means by which that commitment can be internalized.

The second criticism by the Right would be at the macroeconomic level. Here the argument would be that the redistribution of income would effectively mean that much of private investment in the economy would be taken from the wealthier sections of the community and redistributed to the poor. In this way state expenditure would 'crowd' out the private sector reducing investment and be detrimental to economic performance. This is the tired old canard of the Right in its attempt to justify reductions in state expenditure. In one of the most thorough reviews of the evidence to date Ian Gough argues that there is no direct relationship between state social expenditure and economic competitiveness.[31] Rather we need to look at the ways in which the economy is integrated into other parts of the political and social organization of societies to understand whether the impact of the creation of a citizen's wage would be beneficial to economic competitiveness. Part of the problem with the Right's criticism is that it has underestimated the importance of human resources to future economic competitiveness. As such, criticisms of this kind have viewed the redistrubution of income on the basis of a citizen's wage as essentially a waste because it is unproductive or leads to a culture of dependence. Once, however, a citizen's wage is seen as integral to a thriving economy based on collective intelligence we arrive at the opposite conclusion.

The reservations, if not outright criticism, from some on the Left are of a different kind but they too depend on the assumption that it is only from the labour market that we can derive a sense of worth as social beings. In two cogent critiques of the notion of a citizen's wage Ann Orloff and Andre Gorz argue that the key to greater freedom lies in the labour market because as Gorz puts it, 'access to work in the public sphere is essential to economic citizenship and full participation in society' because work in the public sphere (the labour market) earns the social recognition of usefulness,[32], Ann Orloff acknowledges that a citizen's wage would change the balance of power between men and women in families but questions whether it would raise the value of women's domestic work.

The key response here lies in Carol Pateman's argument for a citizen's wage which she sees as breaking down existing patriarchal meanings of key terms in the current debate like 'independence', 'work' and 'welfare'.[33] In an important sense these changes are already part of a trend, as more women go into the labour market while their male partners are unemployed' it is leading to a re-examination of masculinity, as a range of films including *The Fully Monty* imply.[34] Within the framework of a society based on collective intelligence there should be a recognition of the equal value of the various key ways in which individuals can participate.

Overall, a citizen's wage within the context we have sketched would indeed be a 'giant leap' in removing the material barriers of exclusion by gender, race and class. We have concentrated our discussion on poverty and gender but no one should be left in any doubt that a citizen's wage would tackle the material basis of racism. We know from the work of Andrew Hacker and Martin Carnoy, among others, that poverty and race are intertwined and that the political agenda of market individualism has exacerbated problems of racial discrimination which have left African-American families three times more likely than white families to be on low incomes in the United States.[35] Exclusion is not just a matter of social justice or social integration, but also a massive wastage of individual and collective talent. That said, we have emphasized that the citizen's wage should be seen as a springboard for opportunity and participation. To realise these opportunities we now need to turn to the central role of education.

4

Education systems of the twenty-first century need to prepare students to be active citizens in a democracy; to provide them with the appropriate skills to contribute to the economy; and to organize the competition for credentials according to meritocratic criteria. These are the traditional aims of schooling but in a society based on collective intelligence, they take a different form from current dominant intepretations of how these aims should be achieved. Education should no longer be seen as something which is 'front loaded' during the early years of life, but a lifelong process where learning, work and leisure are inseparable.

Education systems based on collective intelligence confront a number of problems which need to be addressed if they are to meet current challenges. These are: the cultural myth that educational achievement is limited by genetically determined 'intelligence'; the conservative impulse for a curriculum based on a narrow view of individual achievement; a monocultural system of education; choice and competition as the mechanisms for achieving higher standards in education; and the upward spiral in credential inflation. When taken together these problems combine to act as a polarising force in society, while creating skills which are of marginal relevance to the varied forms of work and particiaption that will be required in the future.

Of all these problems, the myth that educational achievement is limited by genetically determined 'intelligence' is the most corrosive. Think about it like this. In the post-war period of bureaucratic education, schools were set up, fundamentally, to process failure. The chief task of the system was to select the elite for higher education and 'cool out' the rest; that is, to get the majority to accept that they had failed. This system was extraordinarily effective in accomplishing this task. One of the major instruments in this success was the myth that if students failed it was because they didn't have the intelligence to succeed. Invariably, it was working-class students who had to 'learn' that they were less intelligent than their middle-class peers. But if collective intelligence is premised on the view that all rather than a small minority are capable of significant achievement, and if universal higher education is to become the norm in high-skilled economies, it is essential to transform an educational system based on the dim view of intelligence discussed in the last chapter. This, however, is not an easy task because a culture of mediocrity is deep rooted in American society while English education remains class divided. Research by Lawrence Steinberg and his colleagues, which we mentioned above, has shown that significant numbers of white American adolescents of all social classes believed they have little control over their learning. More ominously, 'Compared with individuals from other cultures, Americans are far more likely to believe that success in school is dependent on native intelligence, that intelligence is fixed, either by genes or early experience – and that factors in emotional and social realms play only an insignificant role in students' academic success'.[36] The film *Good Will Hunting* is a graphic example of these cultural mores.

The consequences of this view are quite shocking because it means that students will only try hard up to the level of what they believe to be the limits to their ability and they see no motivation for working harder since they will not be able to transcend those limits. The contrast with new Asian immigrants in the United States could not be greater since they are far more likely to believe that their success or failure at school is within their control. For them working hard, not a conception of their intelligence, is the key to success.[37] What is most interesting about this research is that second generation American-Asian students are far more likely to share the fatalistic assumptions of the mainstream culture and this leads them to lower educational performance than that achieved by the first generation. In other words, there is clearly a strong cultural component to educational performance even when measured ability, as in Steinberg's research, is taken into account.

If we are to erase this damaging myth we will need to eschew traditional definitions and measures of intelligence. Students need to know that adult life in the twenty-first century will require multiple forms of intelligence for the reasons we have previously discussed. Interpersonal skills, emotional intelligence and creativity as well as cognitive intelligence will be required to aid self-reflexivity, to work in teams in learning organizations, as well as to deal with rapid personal and social change. Once accepted, the idea of multiple intelligence will have powerful ramifications for the school curriculum.

These multiple forms of intelligence underpin many of the so-called key or core skills that employers now see as vital to competitiveness. They are also necessary for participation in a democracy. Yet education systems have still to catch up with the implications of the changing demands now being made. Education, on both sides of the Atlantic, remains firmly based on the ethic of competitive individualism, and in the past two decades there has been a renewed emphasis on teaching the basics of reading, writing and arithmatic. The poor performance of the United States and Britain in comparative studies of educational achievement, has led to the demand for a back-to-basics curriculum. This is at a time when those nations at the top of the global league table like Singapore, Korea and Japan are trying to reform the curriculum and teaching methods to encourage student initiative and creativity. Clearly, all students need basic literacy, numeracy and to be conversant with information technologies, otherwise they will not be able to participate fully in society. But students' interpersonal, emotional and communicative skills also need to be fostered. There is considerable research on how these key skills can be taught and assessed,[38] but too often they are seen as marginal when compared to the preparation of students for formal tests and examinations.[39] These key skills and the multiple intelligence that underlie them need to be a central part of the curriculum.

Straight away we confront another major problem. The best way in which these skills are learnt and assessed is in terms of group work. Yet, although educational research has demonstrated its benefits and many educators would like to develop these practices, they are prevented by examination systems which only recognize the abilities of individuals in a social vacuum, as if each indvidual was an island unto themselves.[40] Part of the problem is that group work tends to be frowned upon because the whole of education has been based on individual performance. Ability and achievement, like the idea of meritocracy itself, is assumed to be judged on an individual basis. Equally, the development of group forms of assessment, which is an essential part of encouraging teamwork, must break the administrative convenience of the educational establishment where everything is individually evaluated and graded. This aspect of education for collective intelligence must inevitably challenge the credibility attached to academic credentials which remain based on the so-called 'objective' assessment of knowledge epitomized by the unseen timed examination paper. In elite schools, colleges and universities the formal teaching of personal and social skills, along with the development of collective assessment procedures are interpreted as the latest version of 'compensatory' education for those who lack the personal qualities which come 'naturally' to those from more privileged backgrounds.[41] But, if students are to be educated for best practice, whether it be in schools, colleges, universities, communities or within corporations aiming to become learning organisations, policy makers will have to grasp the nettle of how to reform learning and assessment in ways which are consistent with the development of collective intelligence.

5

Students from social groups that underachieve do badly because of their historical circumstances not their genes. Asian migrant students do well but Black and Latino students do not. Maori students in New Zealand, although 'catching up', consistently fail to achieve as well as their white counterparts. In Britain, the picture is more complicated but the general principle holds. Educational performance is linked to past history and the extent to which people have been subjected to policies of cultural assimilation, suffered from social deprivation or economic exclusion.

In order to create a more inclusive education system we need a new settlement between under-performing ethnic groups and society. If there is a unified system of education in a pluralist society it confronts the danger of being assimilationist. The majority of students will continue to go to common or comprehensive schools. However, if particular ethnic groups seek to establish their own schools they should be encouraged to do so. Different ethnic groups should be able to take control of their schooling according to their own cultural predispositions and assumptions. Edward Said once said that it is not what people know but who they are that counts.[42] In our view the two must go hand in hand: *we learn in the secure knowledge of who we are.* Culturally autonomous schooling can create the basic security that some students may need because they will not be subject to the discrimination and invidious comparisons made with more educationally successful ethnic groups. Instead of being challenged by practices and mores that they find strange, they will experience forms of schooling which go with the grain of their culture.[43] There can be no clearer example of a high trust society than for the state to provide equitable funds to groups of parents to organise the education of their children, so long as they meet certain standards in terms of school sizes, staff student ratios, and health and safety, as well as impart core elements of a common curriculum.

In a pluralist society we need to embrace pluralist schooling. This means that the styles of teaching and curriculum will vary in different kinds of schools because they will be consistent with the cultural mores of particular ethnic groups. But all schools must have some aims in common. All schools will be expected to teach students what is required to live in a globally interconnected world making them multicultural but with a secure base in their own ethnic identity. This involves developing the multiple intelligence of all. They will also be expected to teach the principles of tolerance and mutual respect in order that they may become citizens in a democracy based on collective intelligence.

A pluralist education system means that the processes of selection and upward mobility through education are unlikely to conform to a common standard. In the Golden era the way students were selected for the next stage of the educational ladder was seen in terms of either sponsored or contest mobility. Sponsored mobility described an elite educational system in which 'talent' was identified at an early age and selected for the academic factories which churned out smart conformists. Contest mobility assumed a greater pool of talent that could manifest itself later in a person's educational career. Therefore, selection for higher education was delayed until much later in a student's career. The problem with both these forms of mobility was that they were based on the IQist notion of intelligence. The link between cultural identity and educational performance was not considered because the criteria for selection were supposed to be objective and universal – that is, applied in the same way to every individual as a matter of justice. This led to a focus on differences in innate ability despite the fact that the idea of meritocratic competition was based on effort as well as ability. But because it was assumed that everyone shared a desire to achieve, especially in the United States, the motivation to achieve in school was taken for granted. The problem with this approach is that effort and motivation are related to the cultural context of schooling.[44] We know that alongside socio-economic status, cultural background is a significant determinent of educational performance.

The challenge in a pluralist system of education is to juggle the need to pay attention to the particularity of cultural identity and yet create rules of competition which are fair for all groups. The need for fairness across groups is necessary because at the end of the day educational credentials will still be a prime determinant of career opportunities. For this reason we believe a new concept, that of *attested mobility* should be introduced into the discussion. To attest is to affirm or bear witness. In this context it draws attention to the link between a person's cultural identity and educational performance. The entry and socialization of a person within a system of pluralist education will be on the basis of the identification and affirmation of their cultural identity. Since the style of teaching and curriculum will be grounded in a particular context, individual performance will be assessed according to culturally diverse criteria. This may apply at all stages of the education including high school, college, university and the myriad forms of adult and distance learning. The key to the success of organizing education on the basis of attested mobility is whether it achieves what Olive Banks called 'parity of esteem' in terms of the standards achieved by different educational providers. This will require a unified qualification framework within which graduates from different high schools or universities can be awarded the same qualifications. They therefore need to be based on comparable standards not only within the same society but ultimately globally. As the question of educational standards has been globalised, so the same problems of achieving comparability between different systems of education around the world, is similar to the problem of instituting attested mobility within America or Britain writ large. Achieving comparable standards between educational establishments offering culturally diverse forms of education is a key element of equality of opportunity, especially in the labour market, where employers may downgrade the qualifications of students from deprived areas or held by people of colour unless parity of esteem can be achieved.

Equality of opportunity will also involve different groups in society being able to raise the educational standards of their people in culturally appropriate ways, on the basis of access to equitable funding. The fact is that in America there are massive disparities in resources between states and neighbourhoods. For example, Connecticut spends approximately $5,000 per school student and has 25 per cent 'minority' students, while Mississipi spends approximately half that and has over 50 per cent of students from 'minorities'.[45] As Jonathan Kozol has so graphically shown in *Savage Inequalities* these inequalities in resourcing simply add salt into the wounds of disadvantage that people of colour have suffered in America. The learning state should set national guidelines on staff: student ratios; number of senior teachers; quality of buildings; pay budgets; etc. which all schools must adopt. No school should fall beneath this target and no school should be able to reduce the staff:-student ratio, for instance, as a way of giving their students an advantage over others. Therefore it does not matter whether schools are public or private, or in Connecticut or Mississippi, they must be resourced to the same standard as a principle of equity. Given the scale of inequalities that currently exist in America and Britain it will be necessary to extend this notion of equity to allocate resources according to an 'equality of results'. This idea was first articulated by James Coleman and despite deliberate misinterpretation by the Right it remains as relevant today as it did when it was first introduced.[46] Coleman meant by this idea that groups should achieve equally in education in proportion to their numbers in the population. It does not mean that everyone should end up with the same qualifications. Using this measure significant compensatory funds should be provided to build up the achievement of those groups which are under performing.

These policies inevitably raise the issue of parental choice in education. We have already argued a market system of education will exacerbate existing inequalities rather than lead to equal opportunities for all. The development of collective intelligence clearly depends on a learning state which seeks to empower individuals and groups with the maximum freedom to decide how to live their lives. But if society is to be based on the principle of equality of opportunity then the state must intervene in the operation of the market for education to ensure as far as possible that the competition for a livelihood is fair.

However, within the system of education we have sketched here there is an inevitable tension or trade-off between school choice based on attested mobility which gives priority to cultural, religious or gender identity as opposed to school mix which focuses on the composition of school intake according to the social class backgrounds of students. The issue of school mix is important to the question of equality of results because the research evidence suggest that working-class students benefit from attending schools which have a balanced intake including students from higher socio-economic groups.[47] There can be no way of resolving this issue by policy-making 'from above'. The best solution is to create local social partnerships between stakeholders to supervise a system of mediated choice in order to balance the principles of attested mobility with those of school mix with the aim of raising school standards. This system would encourage considerable local experimentation and the process of developing local educational partnerships will itself contribute to the creation of social capital.

Within this system of education there are also likely to be tensions between delivering equality of opportunity to all and the specific cultural norms of religious or ethnic groups. We would argue, for example, that there can be no gender discrimination within such a system. But how discrimination is interpreted in a specific cultural context may itself be contested. Certainly, pluralist schooling of this kind will bring its own problems but it will solve more than it creates. Harold Bloom, a strong defender of the view that cultural assimilation is essential to democracy, would disagree. And there is no doubt that ways must be found to overcome the problem of what Paul Hirst calls the 'Ottomanization' of society where plural and largely self-regulating communities co-exist side by side with different rules and standards. The answer as Hirst suggests is the 'acceptance of a substantial measure of self-regulation, at the price of mutual tolerance', as 'No society has been devised that lets each do exactly as he or she will, contribute what he or she wishes, and yet have the enjoyment of the security and common advantages of a community'.[48] There is no reason why a system of education based on attested mobility would create a Tower of Babel rather than a vibrant democracy. Attested mobility should be seen as an expression of mutual trust and tolerance. Indeed, there is little that is 'revolutionary' about such an system of education. Elements of it have already been established with Black universities in America, Kura Kaupapa Maori schools in New Zealand and Muslim schools in England. Even the proposed funding arrangements has common elements with those in the Netherlands and Sweden.[49] What we are arguing for is a viable way of creating collective intelligence in postcolonial societies.

6

The next task is to address the competition for academic credentials pushed by middle-class insecurities and pulled by winner-takes-all markets. In the Golden era the middle classes were secure in the knowledge that if their children could get a foothold on the corporate ladder they had a career for life. But as 'flexible' patterns of career development have become more common it is essential for people to remain fit in the market for jobs. A key indicator of fitness, is of course, a person's qualifications. The implications of winner-takes-all markets has been discussed in an earlier chapter, where we showed that the astronomical salaries which some of the winners can now command has led to fierce competition for entry into the elite universities through which these markets recruit. This inevitably lead to credential inflation as more and more people try to improve their qualifications to compete for jobs which large numbers of well qualified students have little chance of getting.

The solution to this problem lies in pursuing the general approach we are presenting here. The introduction of a citizen's wage would certainly reduce the level of middle class insecurity. In a pluralist education system we might also expect the hierarchy of universities to change as new universities catering for specific ethnic groups come alongside traditional universities. If these new universities can demonstrate the same standard of educational achievement as the old, there is no reason why the pool of graduates from which employers recruit will not increase, thereby improving opportunities for ethnic groups who are currently under-represented. In the end, if companies are dealing with diverse ethnic markets they will stand or fall on how well they understand these markets and therefore more enlightened employers will become more inclusive in their recruitment practices. The management of diversity is an issue with which global companies are currently having to grapple.

The learning state should not try to dampen down the demand for higher level qualification, because it does place greater pressure on society to improve the quality of job opportunities. But there does need to be a systematic re-education of employers who frequently maintain a Darwinian view of intelligence. In other words, that the most intelligent people in a limited pool of ability are to be found in elite institutions because they are the most difficult to enter. This prejudicial view results in companies ignoring vast numbers of potential recruits who may add much more to the organization that the elite brand of smart conformists who have the right social background and early education to get a place at an elite university. What our understanding of collective intelligence would also suggest is that private and public sector organizations are stuffed full of junior staff such as secretaries, supervisors or front-line operatives who are capable of doing many of the jobs, if they are given the appropriate training, for which the organizations seek an external applicant with higher formal qualifications. There is little doubt that if more companies promoted staff within the organisation it would help to dampen the inflationary pressures involved in printing more paper qualifications.

In sum, an education system for collective intelligence means providing the material and cultural basis which will allow people to thrive. It does not mean an end to competition or meritocracy, but rather their reconstruction in pluralist societies based on attested mobility. It does not mean an end to choice but an end to market competition based on the wealth and wishes of parents. It does mean an end to inequalities in funding which has served to undermine the principles of excellence and social justice in American and British education. Another feature of education for collective intelligence is its extension throughout an individual's life time. Much of what is taught in vocational courses has a built in obsolescence which will necessitate regular periods of retraining. The impact of technological innovation and corporate restructuring to meet changing market conditions will also mean that people will have to regularly change jobs even if they stay in the same company. The extensive period for self-development during an individual's third age will also be a time for active learning and experimentation free from the constraints of childcare and job demands. One way of encouraging people to think in terms of learning as a lifelong process is to establish a 'learning bank' which individuals, parents, employers and the government can pay into to help fund education and training after the period of compulsory education. Some form of bonus scheme could be organized to encourage people to make the most of this resource after the age of thirty. Eventually, individual learning accounts could become an integral feature of the citizen's wage. This would send a clear message to people that learning is at the heart of participation in the twenty-first century. It would also convey the message that the learning state's fundamental role is to promote the development of collective intelligence.[50]

7

Learning is essentially a social practice which will determine the opportunities as to whether and how we learn.[51] It is the role of the state to promote the policies which will generate these social practices conducive to the development of collective intelligence. This will require a holistic approach based on what Zsuzsa Ferge has called societal policy, rather than social policy, in recognition of the need to integrate social, economic and education policies. As Ferge suggests, the concept of societal policy 'encompasses the sphere of social policy (the organization of social services or the redistribution of income), but also includes systematic social intervention at all points of the cycle of the reproduction of social life, with the aim of changing the structure of society'.[52] Societal policy should be based on the assumption that people want to participate constructively in society because it is through such participation that they gain a sense of self-empowerment and common purpose. Providing people with a citizen's wage is, for instance, an expression of trust, confidence and collective fate. By the same token, devolving funds for education to identifiable ethnic groups, trust is expressed through the principle of subsidiarity. In these ways the learning state is *both* inclusive and minimalist. A citizen's wage and a pluralist system of education are both inclusive policies because, for example, women will not be discriminated against by a patriarchal welfare state and students will not be marginalized because they come from a different culture.[53] But these policies also represent minimal interference by the state. Solo parents will not be pried upon to see whether they are truly deserving of state benefits and the disadvantaged will not be told what is in their best interests. Of course, both sets of policies will demand accountability. Participation and performance will be the watchwords guiding accountability not, as they are now, those of shaming and blaming. In this sense the learning state is consistent with the emergence of human beings who are empowered to engage individually and collectively on their life projects, with the proviso that it will not disadvantage others.

The cost in terms of redistribution will be high but the advantages are commensurate to the cost. In essence, as society becomes more complex the capabilities demanded of individuals become equally so. Indeed, as post-industrialist societies demand higher cognitive, emotional and imaginative performances, so the collective cost of developing individuals capability increases. The paradox is that under the principles of market individualism governments have become less willing to make the necessary levels of investment required. Hence there are no guarantees that societies will take the opportunities which are now open to them. At this point capitalist societies can go in two directions: they can either hold to a doctrine of market individualism which led to primitive capitalism, or economic transfers can be made from the rich to the poor, with some help from those in the middle, to create the collective intelligence which offers the prospect of improving the quality of individual and community life. Of course, this potential will depend on the capacity for wealth creation in the context of economic globalization. It is to this issue we now turn.

15

A High-Skills Economy

The present state of the nations is the result of the accumulation of all discoveries, inventions, improvement, perfections and exertions of all generations which have lived before us: they form the intellectual capital of the present human race, and every separate nation is productive only in the proportion in which it has known how to appropriate those attainments of former generations and to increase them by its own acquirements.

Fredrich List

1

Economic prosperity now depends on the capacity of nations to take a high skills route which utilizes the collective intelligence of their people.[1] We need to create a *virtuous circle* of rising skill levels, increasing wages based on gains in productivity, and the obliteration of poverty through an investment in the collective intelligence of society, which will feed the economy with skilled, motivated and able people. There is great potential for small and medium sized companies, as well as the MNCs, to create value added for workers, shareholders and the community, when they can succeed in producing quality products and services for the global market place. Success in these terms depends on the knowledge and commitment of the workforce and the learning capacity of both organizations and the state. As Peter Drucker has concluded:

The productivity of knowledge is increasingly going to be the determining factor in the competitive position of a country, an industry, a company. In respect to knowledge, no country, no industry, no company has any 'natural' advantage or disadvantage. The only advantage it can possess is in respect to how much it obtains from universally available knowledge.[2]

Collective intelligence is the source of productivity in knowledge-driven economies because whereas information is stored in books, on CD roms and in data-banks, knowledge, like intelligence, is embodied in people who have considerable scope in the way they can interpret information, apply existing knowledge or commit themselves to the development of new knowledge.[3] Hence, a high-skills economy will require a transformation in our understandings of the model worker, organizational efficiency and the economic role of the state. This will involve embedding leading-edge practice throughout the economy rather than them being restricted to islands of excellence.

This will, in turn, require a change in what is 'valued' in companies. In the Golden era companies were valued according to their physical assets, brand name, market share, etc. But accountancy practice has been slow to catch up with the increasing importance of the 'human side of enterprise'.[4] Human capability, along with investments in R&D, are very hard to quantify and price. Yet as Thomas Stewart has noted in *Intellectual Capital*, if all Bill Gates' workers quit, *Microsoft* would have little value. There are effectively few quantifiable assets in this company in the traditional sense. Likewise, a simple way of quantifying what counts as a high-skills economy will also remain elusive. This is because the social capacity for learning, innovation and productivity, which are its defining features, are difficult to measure. In turn the definition of a high-skills economy also needs to be extended to include issues of process and trust relations. This will include issues of co-ordination across government departments and 'joined up' policy-making involving education, training, industrial relations and the labour market.

A high skills economy can be characterized as having the following facets:

- an inclusive system of education and training which achieves comparatively high standards for all social groups irrespective of social background, gender, race or ethnicity;
- a systematic process of skills upgrading linked to learning, innovation and productivity;
- a high level of entrepreneurial and risk-taking activities whether in terms of new business ventures or through innovation within existing enterprises linked to new technologies, R&D and the upgrading of skills;

- institutionally embedded relations of 'high' trust which encourages individual discretion, collective commitment and the pooling of intelligence;
- a model of human capability based on an assertion that all have the potential to benefit from skills upgrading and lifelong learning;
- a system of occupational selection which values the diverse range of human talent, knowledge and creativity whether these are based on gender, social background, ethnicity, race or religion;
- a means of co-ordinating the supply and demand of labour. This will include a way of incorporating the increasing numbers of those with tertiary education into high-skilled jobs.

Therefore, while accountants and economists may be having a hard time catching up with the vital role of ideas, knowledge and collaborative effort in business today, unless these become central to economic and management theory, organized around the notion of collective intelligence, the defining feature of high-skills economies of the twenty-first century will fail to be grasped.

2

We have seen that in the space of fifty years the advanced economies have undergone a major transition from the factory model of Henry Ford to the Japanese-inspired model of lean production. Competitive advantage in manufacturing has depended on the introduction of new social technologies of production based on worker commitment in a bid to meet the ultimate target of 'zero defects'. But as Antonio Gramsci observed at the time that Fordism was emerging in America, that once its techniques were copied elsewhere the competitive advantage which a new social technology of production brings is lost.[5] We are now approaching that situation with the establishment of variants of Japanese production systems throughout the world. This means that the search is now on for new forms of economic advantage in which the stakes will be raised again.

The next phase in the search for economic advantage will depend on further innovation. Blue-skies research *and* its conversion into goods and service are both fundamental to the production of wealth. An example is the race to cross-fertilise micro-chip and bio-technology research to produce a 'living' chip exponentially more powerful than anything in operation today. The prizes for the winners are enormous because in future every computer will have to accommodate these new chips. But if companies are to achieve competitive advantage they have to marry 'big bang' innovation with that based on incremental improvement in design, marketing, sales, components or productive processes. Indeed, Randell Colins has suggested that a 'remarkable fact' emerging from his historical analysis of technological innovation, is that the generation of new ideas is not necessarily the difficult bit, 'the initial idea itself is rarely the crucial part of any invention...it is the social conditions for their sustained development that is more central'.[6]

To give an idea of what can be achieved when these different aspects of innovation are combined, think no further than the development of hi-tech industries in Silicon Valley, California. It has about 6,000 companies related to the computer industry which employ about 22 per cent of all US hi-tech jobs. The two million inhabitants have a GDP of approximately sixty-five billion dollars, the same as Chile's fifteen million inhabitants.[7] In the mid-1990s the workers in the Californian computer industry generated $196,300 per worker. Average pay in the computer industry was $60,000 a year, double the amount paid to workers in California's metal industries. The cutting edge of innovation produces great dividends. The question is how organizations based on collective intelligence can best be developed?

One popular vision of the future is that companies will become more like sets of related project teams, much like the teams assembled to make films; expertise is bought in for the duration of the film. Work is then based on a succession of short term contracts. In *Intellectual Capital*, Stewart has precisely this vision, arguing that most roles in an organisation can be performed by outsiders and that careers are made in markets not company hierarchies. Recent trends in the United States and Britain appear to support this description. As we have seen, the number of temporary workers or those on short-term contracts has increased and if management gurus are to be believed these numbers will increase rapidly over the next twenty years. As one expert has put it, to retain jobs all workers will have to develop a 'self-employment mindset'.[8] But the way films are produced is not the way production in general, whether of goods or services, can be reliably sustained. The motion picture industry is high risk: the quality of a film is a matter of putting the right project team together which involves little investment in training, industrial relations or building long-term high-trust relationships. Most companies are not like this, they depend on producing high quality products and services over a long period, even if what is produced or the range of services change. Japanese lean production, for instance, was developed based on lifelong employment as a way of achieving continuous improvement in efficiency and quality. This is because the success of the link between innovation and reliable production requires a stable workforce which has an holistic understanding of the production chain. It is only then that problem solving, teamwork and continuous improvement can become part of the innovative process.

But even in Japan and Korea, lifelong employment means very little unless companies are able to remain profitable. Indeed, access to lifelong employment was always limited to a minority of the workforce in both countries. Equally, it can be argued that not all forms of highly innovative enterprise need stable employment. As an in-depth study of the semi-conductor industry has shown, the American recruitment system based of 'plug-in-and-play' rather than offering an extensive period of initial training, and a policy of 'hire and fire' appears to suit the logic end of the semi-conductor market which is primarily concerned with the development of computer software, while the Japanese system of employment was found to be more suited to the development of memory chips.[9] However, the semi-conductor industry, like the film industry, although important to the economy, differs from most other kinds of business activity, which need to offer job security if they are to provide high quality goods and services.

This is not to suggest that American and British companies should return to the 'jobs for life' mentality of the 1950s. But the preoccupation with downsizing to improve short-term profitability and 'hire and fire' employment policies do not generate the discretionary commitment of employees because if employers are not prepared to offer or honour durable contracts of employment, employees will keep one eye on job opportunities elsewhere. They will also ensure that they stay fit in the external market for jobs. This may limit their willingness to make a significant personal commitment to aspects of their current employment which are not seen to have a pay-off in the external job market. Therefore, the numerical flexiblity that companies have sought over the last twenty years may have served their immediate purposes when there were few alternative jobs available, but when labour markets are tight the tables turn, and it is usually the most marketable staff who are first to leave.

A further consequence of downsizing is that it has wiped out the 'institutional memory', which is a vital source of collective intelligence. Some will argue that this is beneficial because companies have been subject to discontinuous change, where established forms of knowledge and experience are an impediment to innovation and change management. Lester Thurow argues that 'what makes the era ahead different is the extent to which it will be dominated by recently acquired knowledge and skills', consequently 'experience is just less valuable'.[10] He is able to point to the declining 'returns to experience' in America which he takes to reflect the declining productivity of employees who have stayed with the same company for a long time. There are clearly some people who have little interest in developing new skills sets or changing their work routines, but this should not be taken to mean that a revolving door employment policy is preferable to offering employees job security. Institutional memory can be an invaluable foundation for new ideas, especially if it involves an ingrained culture of experimentation, innovation and high trust. Seventy-five per cent of what Siemens sells has been brought to the market place within the last five years, but this innovation is based on a stable workforce at its Munich headquarters. The reason why there has been a decline in the 'returns to experience' in America is because knowledge workers have been able to ratchet up their salaries by playing the market rather than staying with the same company, especially in circumstances where companies are downsizing and in the process destroying opportunities for internal career progression.[11]

Our argument is that the development of collective intelligence within innovative companies, involves combining learning processes which enable workers to problem solve and develop functional flexiblity within a context that encourages relationships of high trust. In most sectors of the economy this is best achieved through signing up to employment contracts that offer job security. This is a matter of enlightened self-interest as it creates a commitment by employees to the company. It enables companies to be flexible in response to changing technologies and market demand because in return for job security, companies can expect their employees to change their skill sets. Here the importance of workplace learning can be reinforced by a system of reward based on contribution and skill acquisition rather than time serving. This will encourage all employees to focus on personal development and their contribution to the organization, rather than putting all their energies into polishing their CVs. Single status deals which seek to reduce disparities in conditions, pay and entitlements can also be used to reduce conflict over status and rewards. This is important because where there is conflict over status within the workforce it is far more difficult to achieve the functional flexibility needed in innovative organizations. Hence, given the demands now made on workers in 'zero defect' production systems or in the delivery of high quality services, the importance of reorganization on the basis of collective intelligence becomes clear as it depends on a high trust bargain between workers, managers and executives. Its linchpin is job security in a highly uncertain world in return for commitment, skill and creative endeavour.

3

Economic activity based on collective intelligence also challenges the power base of managerial authority. In Shoshana Zuboff's celebrated text about new technologies and human intellect, *In the Age of the Smart Machine*, she draws a distinction between *automating* and *informating*. Automating is the process by which human creativity and intellect are replaced by the machine which is used by management as a tool of surveillance. In contrast, informating is where human creativity and technology are harnessed so improvements in production are linked to learning. As one of the workers she interviewed put it, 'If you don't let people grow and develop and make more decisions it's a waste of human life – a waste of human potential...Using the technology to its full potential means using the man [or women] to his [or her] full potential'.[12] In order to capture the potential of informating technologies Zuboff believes that learning has to be at the heart of the enterprise. This involves an expansion of the knowledge base but 'not knowledge for its own sake (as in academic pursuit) but knowledge that comes to reside at the core of what it means to be productive'.[13] Learning, she concludes, is the new form of labour. But whereas in automating organizations power remains in the hands of managers who use new technology as a form of surveillance, in informating organizations, learning amongst employees depends on the democratization of knowledge. It also confers the power that knowledge brings.

One aspect of Zuboff's insight that she doesn't highlight is that more egalitarian relationships in terms of power and reward are likely to overcome *information rigidities*. Arguably, information rigidity needs to be understood as a key problem confronting productive efficiency in the twenty-first century. If information is withheld as a personal source of control or power, it is a loss to the decision making capabilities of an organization. But we should not see workers as merely passive recipients of knowledge. The more they are given the initiative and power which is generated by high trust organizations, the more knowledgable they will become, seeking out leads and developing networks which benefit the organization.

Organizations based on collective intelligence, therefore, need to be boundaryless in the sense that information can flow freely. However, this imperative is in tension if not contradiction with the idea of a flexible labour market in which many workers in an organization are casualized. Insecurity will not breed trust, and as we have argued, it will not facilitate the free flow of information. In markets geared to short term profits this may not be a major problem. Individuals can opt out of companies, start up their own or bid up their own wage by transferring to other companies. But in organizations which are based on long term strategies the experience and knowledge developed over time within an organisation becomes decisive. It enables an organization to learn from its mistakes as well as capitalizing on the knowledge and networks that employees generate.

Information rigidities extend beyond the company. Some of the leading multinational companies have come to realize the co-operation between global businesses, especially in the area of research and development, can reduce the cost of blue-skies research and improve competitive capacity. More importantly, in terms of national economies, some of the most successful economic regions in the world have learnt how to overcome the debilitating consequences of low trust and excessive competition between local businesses. Addressing the problem of information rigidities is especially important in the case of small and medium-size enterprises (SMEs) because they do not have the resources to engage in research, overseas marketing, sales promotions, or specialized staff training. By pooling resources SMEs are able to compete in niche markets with the biggest and best corporations in the world. These clusters of companies are known as industrial districts. To be successful in the new competition they have to do more than resemble a 'collective entrepreneur' involving different firms delivering various parts of a product or service. As Michael Best has noted in his discussion of the Third Italy located in the Emilia-Romagna region, its major strength is the institutional capacity for continuous learning, flexibility and improvement in economic competitiveness. 'An innovative industrial district can be described as a dynamic constellation of mutually adjusting firms. The constellation is dynamic in that the responses to new challenges and opportunities involve the continuous redefinition of the inter-firm networks and external boundaries of the district'.[14]

This capacity for innovation and quality production depends on the high trust relations which are embedded in the local communities which make up the Emilia-Romagna region. They also depend on giving workers greater knowledge and decision-making powers. It may surprise some people that Modena in the heart of the Third Italy has the highest trade union density in the country and they serve as a active force for innovation and skill development. However, one of the biggest challenges confronting industrial districts is the impact of globalization which will require a more international approach and greater global scope in terms of marketing, sales and information gathering. In such circumstances, the ability of these regions to breakdown the information rigidities between workers and companies will become even more important.

4

The potential for this transformation in economic activity depends not only on re-thinking what workers and mangers do, but on making a successful challenge on our deep-seated cultural assumptions about the abilities, motivations and personalities of employees. The flattening of organisational structures require new models of symbolic control in the attempt to overcome the classic problems of converting the potential to work into actual contribution. But it is precisely the existence of the ranks of foremen, supervisors and inspectors which testify to how difficult this has proven to be in the past. They exist because workers in low-trust organisations are not assumed to be capable of initiative or to share the goals of management, they are neither trained to show, nor are they rewarded for initiative.[15] It is never simply a question of providing workers with the skills and assuming that the job will get done. It is the subjective facets of capability which are of vital importance in work organizations based on collective intelligence. It is a battle for the hearts, as well as the minds of workers, which will increasingly determine competitive advantage. In flexible organizations frontline workers are expected to be more self-directed and for social control to come from participation in work-teams rather than through the watchful eye and threat of sanctions from shopfloor supervisors.[16]

If the flexible paradigm is to be used to its full potential it is not only frontline workers but managers who must confront many of their own deep-seated assumptions about their role as well as those of workers. In bureaucratic organizations what Zuboff described as the 'spiritual dimension of power' derived from the impersonal public performance of bureaucratic routine. This was a dominant feature of the bureaucratic personality discussed in Part One of this book. But in flexible organizations, managerial qualities will need to be characterized much more in terms of the 'charismatic' personality. Here emphasis is upon 'can do' rather than 'will do'. The charismatic personality seeks to break from routine actions and rule-following behaviour to create new order in innovative settings.[17] They are able to lead or work collectively through the use of charismatic rather than bureaucratic authority. To base their authority and leadership on their contribution as colleagues rather than through seniority in the command structure.[18] The overriding emphasis is upon being able to see the 'bigger picture' and to avoid a mechanistic mindset which leads to an understanding of the organization in terms of its component parts at the expense of their interactions.[19]

In essence the charismatic personality is the opposite of the bureaucratic in that it is based on personal and inter-personal skills. The ability to get on with others is paramount. Moreover, as the learning of workers increases so managers have to learn from junior staff to understand the nature of the business they are managing. All this means that the personalities that can thrive in an organization built on collective intelligence will be radically different to that required in bureaucratic organizations or in those companies that have a flatter structure but cling onto the trappings of hierarchy. For managers and workers alike it means having to juggle various, often ill-defined roles, whilst working alongside people with different levels of authority, from different departments, with different knowledge specialisms and in project and team-work settings.

But the most important managerial quality is the ability to develop and pool the collective intelligence of colleagues, project teams and organizational networks. The failure of organizations to achieve this are legion. Rush and Bessant found that most manufacturing companies had not benefited from advances in computer-aided design, robotics and flexible manufacturing systems because they fail to achieve the comprehensive integration of the new technologies and the reorganisation of work methods that this requires. Full integration 'entails connecting each computerized stage of the production process, from product design and development to packaging and despatch, into a coherent, communicating whole – computer-integrated manufacturing (CIM)'.[20] To benefit from CIM systems there needs to be a change to the knowledge base and roles of individual workers, the way production is organised and the way different project teams and departments interact.[21] The same potential and problems exist in virtually all areas of employment. The information payoff from secretarial support staff is another clear example of how many organizations in both the public and private sectors are failing to exploit the full potential of new technologies. As Paul Strassman has suggested clerical work should now

Table 15.1   Human ability and motivation

The Factory Model	Collective Intelligence
The average human being has a dislike of work and will trade it for leisure wherever possible.	The expenditure of physical and mental effort in work is as natural as play or rest.
People must be coerced, controlled, directed, to fulfil organisational goals.	People will exercise self-direction and self-control to fulfil aims to which they are committed.
Most people avoid responsibility, have relatively little ambition and above all want security	Under the right conditions most people will both accept and seek responsibility
Intelligence is a scarce resource, but can be 'scientifically' identified among children at an early age	The unfolding of human capacity is limited by social hierarchy and cultural attitudes.
The organisation of education and employment corresponds to the normal distribution of talent.	The capacity to exercise imagination, ingenuity, creativity etc. is widely distributed in the population.

include many of the specialist tasks still performed by professional and technical workers: 'We already have sufficient experience to know that clerical personnel can deliver superb results in such positions, provided that their organizations make the necessary investments to make such work possible.'[22]

These sources of economic inefficiency will continue until we challenge the dim view of intelligence and outdated assumptions about human motivation. The radically different model of human nature on which collective intelligence is based can be highlighted when we compare it to the factory model summarised in Table 15.1.[23]

Here we can see the assumptions about the character, abilities and motivations of workers in organizations based on collective intelligence. Many organisations have recently adopted the discourse of the right-hand column but a large number of these cling onto the old certainties of the left-hand column. Whether they get beyond the art of word games will to some extent depend on a broader cultural change which encourages people to lift their heads to replenish their sense of self-worth in rejecting the dim view of intelligence and human nature which have dominated Western societies during the twentieth century.

One of the consequences of adopting the guiding principles of the right hand column is that organizations would give more attention to developing the capabilities of junior staff. Currently, it is the most educated and senior staff who receive the most employer-provided training. Close to 90 per cent of American employees with at least a bachelor's degree received some form of formal, employer-provided training, compared to 60 per cent of those with a high school education or less.[24] But to make matters worse Laura Liswood, President of the American Society for Training and Development has noted 'corporate investments in education and training, while growing, remain small. Throughout corporate America...firms are spending as much as 10 times per employee on information technologies as they are spending on training'.[25] A consequence of this blind faith in technology is that organizations turn to the external labour market in search of 'talent' rather than develop their existing staff. Again, this has fuelled the growth of winner-takes-all markets, where senior staff are able to add phenomenal 'value' to their CVs by job hopping between competitors. If this represents a classic case of market failure we now need to look at the role of the state in the creation of a high-skills economy.

5

One of the most striking features of the last two decades is the way governments around the world have invested in their education and training systems. Al Gore's statement at the US summit on *21st Century Skills for 21st Century Jobs* conforms to the new rules of wealth creation: 'America's competitiveness and the prosperity of our people in a changing economy depend increasingly on high-skill high-wage jobs. Realizing our potential will require investing in education and learning for all our people throughout their lifetimes'.[26] But for many in America and Britain (as well as neo-classically trained economists), the idea that government has a key strategic role to play in the co-ordination of skills up-grading, through education and training, labour markets, industrial relations, social welfare and economic development agencies, will appear strange if not suspect.

It could be argued that the federal state in America has only actively intervened in a way that continental European and Pacific Rim countries are accustomed to twice in history: during the New Deal and during the Kennedy–Johnston period of the Great Society. As one political economist has said of the United States:

> the philosophical repugnance against government involvement in industrial promotion is such that the government lacks both detailed knowledge of industries and analytical capacity to elect appropriate actions...whether industry becomes more competitive,

moves offshore, or goes out of existence is a matter of government indifference – because the market outcome is assumed to be best.[27]

But in the new competition nations will stand little chance of moving up the value-added skills chain unless part of the fundamental culture shift to collective intelligence involves changes in the nature and actions of government. The shift to a high-skills economy cannot be achieved throught market mechanisms alone.

The main economic role of the learning state, beyond attempting to maintain stable macroeconomic conditions, is to up-grade the skills profile of the workforce through developing collective intelligence within which the social capacity for learning, innovation and productivity is critical. Further investment in supply-side policies such as education and training is not going to be enough. All the advanced and developing economies are increasing their budgets for education and training, therefore, what really matters is how these investments contribute to a virtuous cycle of learning, innovation and productivity. This means that states need to seek actively, to raise employers' demand for skills.

The importance of focusing on the demand side, that is on the jobs people get rather than simply the training they receive, is captured in research undertaken by Melvin Kohn and his associates in the United States over the last thirty years. Their studies found that many of the psychological dispositions which are key ingredients in the functioning of intelligence are determined by job conditions.[28] What is especially interesting is that cognitive complexity and responsibility associated with a job were found to have an impact on the ability to manage change and sense of personal empowerment. The more complex the job, the more workers are likely to be self-directed, to believe that they can act on the world rather than merely have its conditions imposed upon them, and be more flexible in their ideas. They also identified an inter-generational link: if parents think that they can act upon the world and make a difference this is likely to be passed onto their children. Kohn's research sends a powerful message, as mental flexibility, self direction, the belief that we can act on the world are all necessary qualities in a post-industrial society.

The implications of this research are far reaching because it suggests that the way we organize working life is central to the development of collective intelligence. Nations that follow a low-skill route are unlikely to generate the kinds of collective intelligence required to meet the complex cognitive demands of a high-skills economy. This supports the contention that a key role of the learning state is to co-ordinate the supply *and* demand for jobs. This cannot be left to investments in education and training systems, in the hope that in combination with new technological breakthroughs, it will lead the market to soak up the supply of 'knowledge' workers now leaving tertiary education in droves. Ways have to be found to stimulate the demand for high-skilled workers. Equally, attempts need to be made to help employers attract talented students to pursue careers in key areas of the knowledge economy, especially in science and engineering.

This approach rejects the either/or distinction between state knowledge and market knowledge.[29] Saying that the state has a key role to play in the creation of a high-skills economy is not to say that the state should try to monopolize knowledge of new techologies, innovations or market opportunities. Rather it is based on a recognition that markets can be organized in different ways and with different consequences for skills, wages and economic opportunity. We know, for instance, that there remain healthy profits to be made for low-skilled, low-waged work which give employers little market incentive to improve the skills and wages of employees unless there are ethical, legal or material incentives for doing so.

The role of the learning state is not to 'govern' markets. Even if this were desirable, which it isn't, the globalization of markets and advances in information technologies have exponetially increased the amount of market knowledge that governments would need to 'govern'. The mounting list of casualties resulting from global finanicial crises, including much of East Asian, Russia, Brazil and Britain, underlines the limitations on nation states to govern international financial markets. Nevertheless the way work is organised within countries and the extent to which it is dominated by 'low' or 'high' skills and wages is crucially shaped by the quality of government involvement (or the absence of it) in collaboration with key stakeholders.

The role of the learning state is to develop and pool intelligence and knowledge in a strategic alliance with employers, trade unions, educators and communities, in a common commitment to skills up-grading. Indeed, the German model of social partnership offers a good example of how all economic stakeholders can be involved in the development of new skills and product development, integrated into a federal agency for strategic skill formation.[30] However, there is no 'one best way' as each country will need to develop a learning state and stakeholder model depending of specific historical, cultural, regional and economic circumstances.

To understand the importance of a strategy based on collective intelligence, we need look no further than the collapse of the Soviet Union on the one hand, and the de-industrialization caused by Reagan and Thatcher's market revolution on the other.[31] The price of primitive capitalism has been high, as we have documented: unemployment, insecurity, low morale, massive child poverty, and the mass production of low-skilled, low-waged service sector jobs. This was not a gale of creative destruction but of simple destruction. The lesson to be learnt is that national systems need to be put in place so that fundamental change can be managed that builds rather than destroys the foundations for collective intelligence.

This will include identifying key areas of the economy where efforts can be made to create new employment and increase the skill content of jobs, such as in high performance manufacturing and exportable service clusters, including telecommunications, wafer fabrication, bio-technology, precision engineering, international business services, health and education. This will require sophisticated foresight planning, which will include the co-ordination of regional economic development through networks of local stakeholders, national strategists, research institutes, technopoles, and global companies. Equally, global forces make it more important to create 'indigenous capability' which can not be easy transplanted elsewhere, as we were told by the National Science and Technology Board in Singapore: 'when you say indigenous capability, what we mean is that Hewlett Packard, Singapore will not be able to do it elsewhere, the ideas, the decision-making, are all from here'.[32]

In order to attract (or retain) corporations on the basis that they will increase the levels of skill demanded various 'incentives' can be offered including tax-break and joint ventures because these companies are seen as strategic to skill formation. But any capital invested by government should not be seen as venture capital as the aim is not to return a quick profit, but to support the growth of companies to build indigenous capability. Once this is established public money can be reinvested in other businesses. The other consideration here is that the incentives offered to companies to relocate (or to remain) should not be seen as cash hand-outs, but rather as part of an overall strategy to train and upgrade the workforce. They need to be linked to investments in training, which could be undertaken by local colleges, univerisities or training centres to supply well trained employees in advance of a company's arrival. This will obviously work best when there is a cluster of companies in the same industry, and when training incorporates state of the art equipment supplied by firms.

The contrast to the *ad hoc* strategies adopted in many parts of the United States and Britain could not be clearer. Global companies invite an auction for investment, individual states in America or regional development agencies in Britain respond by offering 'incentive' payments or tax holidays to create jobs. There is little sense of any underlying strategy to this courtship or sense of generating synergies between the forward and backward linkages associated with high-skill industries and local education and training centres. In fact, in the United States and Britain the extent of state involvement has simply been to outbid other countries in offering 'sweeteners' for direct inward investment. Consequently, these sweeteners have often funded the creation of low skill jobs 'dumped' from elsewhere.

This problem is exacerbated when it comes to SMEs. Most countries now look to their SMEs to generate much of the dynamic in a modern economy but it is in the nature of this sector that it cannot generate alone the indigenous capability to function effectively. They do not have the resources to engage in information gathering (whether it concerns new technologies, international markets or production techniques); the time to build domestic, let alone international networks; access to cheap investment capital to help them compete in national and international markets; or the resources to provide skills training in anticipation of business expansion. Rosebeth Moss Kanter has observed that 'the independence of entrepreneurs and small businesses is often stressed in popular lore, but the truth is that small businesses gain competitive advantage through collaborative advantage'.[33] The agencies of the learning state in partnership with local business, trade unions and communities can play a key role in breaking down the information rigidities that have already been discussed in relation to successful strategies for industrial districts. It can facilitate the 'infrastructure for collaboration that ensure that small businesses will grow and prosper through business excellence'.[34] Thus the role of the learning state is not to direct but to inform, facilitate and co-ordinate networks of stakeholders for innovation and economic development. Local or regional economies can not rely on inward investment from multinationals to deliver prosperity. Such a strategy must be balanced with policies aimed at growing indigenous small and medium size companies into global players. Only a learning state can have the long term vision, foresight and collaborative power to build the societal capacity for learning, innovation and productivity. This conclusion is underlined when we consider the role of research and development.

6

The learning state will need to provide strategic and financial help in research and development where there is clear evidence of market failure to undertake this work. There has been a tendency to treat R&D as basic research adding to the stock of scientific knowledge that has little immediate relevance to skills, employment or company profits. This view is outdated, as a great deal of activity that goes under the rubric of R&D is dedicated to the application of knowledge to create new products and processes. In Japan, for instance, almost all its R&D resources has a strong emphasis on 'development' and market application.[35]

Britain has a history littered with people making discoveries and inventions that have been capitalized on elsewhere, often in America. But competitive advantage necessitates the building of an integrated model of basic R&D, application and downstream continuous improvement, which can be linked back into R&D activity, and related to stretegic skill formation. In reality, this is another example of the need to breakdown information rigidities and to develop collective intelligence, involving research centres, scientists, production engineers, computer software experts, technicians, marketing and sales personnel and frontline workers in the process of innovation. The development of basic or blue-skies research based on the principles of collective intelligence can become a major source of competitive advantage and a push towards high-skilled work. Lester Thurow points out that the United States' R&D budget is three times the GDP of Israel. He also suggests that smaller countries may do better if they combine their R&D budgets with other countries, in much the same way that companies are doing in areas of blue-skies research which are often expensive and risky, 'Within Western Europe, a lot of money is wasted by countries betting small amounts on different technologies but not betting enough on any one technology to make a difference. If the European Economic Community could pool its research and development spending, there is every reason to believe that the payoffs could be substantially enhanced for everyone'.[36]

Much of the funding for R&D should come from big business and through various forms of venture capital, but the state will need to fund some strategic areas of R&D as private funds will not always be found to take the long-term risk of devoting resources to research which has an uncertain pay-off. This has certainly been the case in the United States and Britain. The key figures here are that 99 per cent of Japanese and 87 per cent of German R&D is financed by industry, while in the USA and

Britain the figures are 67 and 71 per cent repectively.[37] But a state willing to invest in R&D is confronted with a major problem: in a global economy dominated by transnational companies the gains produced by R&D may not be captured by the nation in which public investment in research is made. There are many who now think that state investment in R&D is throwing good money after bad in the mistaken belief that national boundaries still count for something. The research evidence suggests the opposite. Most technology production, reflected in patent applications, remains close to the home base of multinationals. The reasons why this may be are canvassed by one of the leading authorities in the area, Pari Patel, who believes that the inputs of knowledge and information in relation to innovation are essentially embodied in individuals and, with a high degree of uncertainty surrounding successful innovation, frequent and personal communication is desirable.[38]

There is also another reason as much of the knowledge generated in the search for innovations is tacit knowledge. Groups of researchers informally share assumptions and practices that are not made explicit. Even when they are through the publication of papers, the precise ways of achieving results are often omitted. This is common practice in sciencific endeavour and, in part, is clearly designed to keep competitors at bay. So there is a double barrier for multinationals seeking to locate their basic or blue-skies research overseas: the culture as well as the language of a research team has to be translated. It is a recognition of these boundaries which seems to be behind the thinking of agencies such as MITI in Japan when it funds overseas partners to join their R&D projects. These foreign partners may find it hard to penetrate the tacit knowledge underlying the research and even when they do, it is assumed that Japanese firms may have gained vital time to put their products first into the marketplace.[39]

American evidence suggests that one of the major beneficiaries of government funding in research and development, such as through research universities and technical laboritories, is the small business sector. As Rosabeth Moss Kanter has noted, Massachusetts Institute of Technology (MIT) and Stanford University can be considered as the foundation of much of America's technological prowess in the second half of the twentieth century, giving rise to Route 128 and Silicon Valley high-tech regions.[40] She also reports a 1997 BankBoston study that showed that 'MIT graduates have started 4,000 companies, with 1.1 million jobs and $232 billion in 1994 sales worldwide – economic power equal to the 24th largest world economy'.[41]

This suggests that the global economy has not made the role of the state redundant in stimulating R&D where it perceives market failure. In fact its role now may be more important than in the past. For, given the kind of investment needed to fund new ideas, the state (or a number of states in collaboration, such as through the European Community) may be the only source of long term, low cost venture capital especially for SMCs. This raises the question of the limits and possibilities for encouraging long-term investment.

7

There are clearly changes in the global economy which will make it much harder to establish a financial system geared to long term investment. One of the disturbing aspects of the merger between Daimler-Benz and Chrysler in 1998 is that the new company will adopt the investment culture of the New York stock exchange. German companies have been the beneficiaries of long term, low cost loans, but when the Daimler-Benz chief executive, Juergan Schrempp, was asked how the new company would deal with American shareholders his reply was that the new company would pay American-level dividends.[42] As more multinationals become truly global in scope and outlook it is likely that a single investment standard will prevail for these companies which will demand Wall Street–City returns on investment. This is all the more likely now that we have seen how the OECD nations have responded to the Asian crisis. Intense pressure by the American government and international agencies such as the IMF, are effectively forcing the Asian Tigers to fall into line. As Robert Wade has suggested, this appears to be a matter of power politics rather than a misunderstanding of how the very different systems of financing in the Asian economies actually work. The fact is that the Wall Street–City axis stands to gain by the imposition of the IMF 'medicine' that has been forced down the throat of the Tiger economies.[43]

We should bear in mind that the United States and Britain invest approximately half their capital overseas while consistently under-investing in their own economies. This shortfall needs to be made up. The best way of doing this would be to have a series of regional economic development boards with the financial power to pump prime small and medium-size companies. In this respect the Labour government in Britain is opening the door to such a strategy through its emphasis on local democracy and regional development boards. The federal system in America has been based on this model for decades given the role of the states in education, training and economic development. What is required is for economic advantage to be taken of this infrastructure through active strategic planning.

An emphasis on subsidiarity is important because we have learnt that old forms of central state economic policies are likely to be inefficient in a post-industrial economy. The federal state does have a key role to play in co-ordinating industrial foresighting and as a source of low cost finance for strategic research and investment, but the whole point of the exercise is not to make decisions in isolation but to facilitate decision-making at the lowest possible level, involving as many stakeholders as possible. This is, after all, what collective intelligence is all about. Therefore, subsidiarity can reduce the power of the central state to allow regional policy-makers to be held accountable by local communities through the democratic process. In economic terms, subsidiarity is desirable because the knowledge to make sound financial and investment decisions requires a detailed understanding of local companies, labour market conditions and training provision at the ground level. In effect regional economies should aim to integrate both local and transnationals firms in local partnerships subject to democratic forms of accountability, whilst conforming to a national strategy of skills up-grading.

Will Hutton draws attention to another important dimension of our discussion in seeing 'stakeholding' as the antidote to primitive capitalism, through a recognition of the importance of other stakeholders, apart from shareholders in companies. By according importance to workers, suppliers, consumers and local communities, as well as to shareholders, companies would move away from the narrow aims of simply enhancing shareholder value. As we have seen this may become more difficult if multinational companies have to meet Wall Street–City rates of return to shareholders, but it could be made possible through regional economic development boards which provide cheaper long-term funding to companies and link it to worker participation in company policy. Indeed, broadening the base of economic stakeholding to include trade unions, NGOs, community representatives and regional economic agencies, is a way of up-grading local skills and developing high trust.

8

The more complex the economy in its global scope, technologies and demands on human resources, the more the state must be concerned with building the societal capacity for learning, innovation and productivity as an integral feature of collective intelligence rather than just focusing on discrete areas of social, economic or education planning. But one of the dangers of this holistic approach is that everything gets reduced to whatever the 'needs' of the economy, as seen to be at any particular point in time. We have argued that economic activity is a means to improving the quality of life for all. Equally, the more societies are organized on the basis of collective intelligence the better their chances of being able to sustain economic growth. This is why the introduction of a citizen's wage is a key economic as well as social policy. It would help to overcome the negative impact of inequality on economic performance. Will Hutton has summed up why extreme inequalities damage the economy:

> Inequality between classes and regions adversely affects both demand and supply. Demand becomes more volatile and unbalanced while supply is affected by underinvestment and neglect of human capital. Economic cycles are amplified; firms become more like opportunist traders than social organisations committed to production and innovation. As a result, the long-run growth rate tends to fall, unemployment rises and the government's underlying fiscal position deteriorates, and a vicious circle intensifies the volatility of demand and the weakness of supply.[44]

The greater equality provided by the citizen's wage would provide the foundation for a genuinely high-skills workforce which would also be flexible because it would not be afraid of change. Sclerosis through fear would be a thing of the past. In fact, it is only under the conditions of a citizen's wage that a flexible labour market of the kind admired by the Modernisers could possibly work. Recall the dilemma that a flexible labour market creates: on the one hand it does produce flexibility in the use companies make of employees, they can be laid off in times of slump and re-hired in times of boom. The paradox is that this 'flexibility' is bought at the expense of developing a high-skills, high-wage economy because the removal of protection to workers means that they be hired and fired not only easily but also cheaply. Under the conditions of a citizen's wage employers gain the flexibility which is necessary when there are rapid shifts in technology and consumer tastes, but not in cheap labour. They are therefore 'forced' to take the high-skills route of investing in technology and linking it to human ingenuity. However, a flexible labour market under conditions of a citizen's wage would enable people to exercise their wide range of abilities in a context of high trust and risk taking. Of all the risks they can take that of continuous learning which will often challenge their previous understandings is the most important. The learning state is therefore central to a high-skills economy. But while the fate of nations still remain in crucial ways in their own hands, how the global economy is regulated will play an important part in determining whether the strategies we have outlined here can be implemented successfully. The political feasibility of a society based on collective intelligence is the issue discussed in our concluding chapter.

16
Conclusion

> The human race after so long standing in shame at its failed
> possibilities should now move towards a new millennium,
> where overcoming our pettiness and our fears, we might
> begin to astonish even the gods.
>
> Ben Okri

1

We have reached a tantalizing moment in Western history. We live in an
age of extraordinary wealth, of technological revolution, of a global
compression of time and space, of great transformation in our secret
worlds of dreams, aspirations, desires and expectations for self-fulfilment, love and sense of purpose, of new gender relations and ways of
living together in and outside families as parents, children, partners,
lovers and friends, of unimaginable potential for work which is cognitively demanding, emotionally engaging and collectively rewarding, of
opportunity for everyone to have a decent standard of living and to
develop their multiple intelligence, of new ways of living together
which celebrate our cultural diversity and common humanity. This is
the promise.

This promise of life in the twenty-first century can be glimpsed from
time to time in our own lives, in the actions of friends, in the achievements of leading-edge companies, and even through the albeit rare
actions of government. But the general conclusion to be drawn from
our analysis of America and Britain today is one of missed opportunities,
of the spectre of barbarism rather than the hope of social progress. Our
current path has reached a dead end. Society has exhausted its capacity
to manage ignorance and selfishness. Edward Luttwak believes that by

2020 America will be a third-world nation in terms of the extremes of wealth and poverty, along with the bleak life chances of black males in some urban districts.[1] Even George Soros, who has made his fortune from financial speculation on the world's money markets, is worried about the social consequences of market individualism:

> Insofar as there is a dominant belief in our society today, it is a belief in the magic of the marketplace. The doctrine of laissez-faire capitalism holds that the common good is best served by the uninhibited pursuit of self-interest. Unless it is tempered by the recognition of a common interest that ought to take precedence over particular interests, our present system – which, however imperfect, qualifies as an 'open society' – is liable to break down.[2]

The alternative presented in this book is to build a society on the principles of collective intelligence. This is based on two features of our human nature which have been neglected in a culture of market individualism and an age of industrialism. Collective intelligence combines the growth potential of all to develop their multiple intelligence and to pool their capacity for intelligence through sharing, co-operating and building trust. But we have shown that the struggle for collective intelligence involves more than changing the way we think about our own capabilities and our relationship to society; it also includes weaving the principles of collective intelligence into the very fabric of society. Collective intelligence needs to be reflected in our schools, neighbourhoods, companies and government, as well as in our cultural attitudes.

We do not hide the fact that a society based on collective intelligence will have its costs. It is inevitable that wealth will have to be redistributed more fairly. We have argued that the introduction of a carer's wage and ultimately a citizen's wage are essential to tackle poverty and to enhance the freedom of individuals to make meaningful choices about the lives they lead. Issues of redistribution will, of course, be extended in years to come for reasons beyond those we have discussed. The problem of ecological survival will necessitate a transfer of wealth from the most profligate users of natural resources to those who seek a sustainable ecology. The logic of wealthy nations, who consume most of the world's resources, paying developing countries to sustain their rain forests, is compelling. But it is only compelling to those who are willing to acknowledge the social and economic debts that we have to our society and to others.

The logic of collective intelligence will also take us beyond national boundaries in two additional ways. First, although this book has focused on building a new relationship between the individual and society, there is ultimately no reason why our sense of the 'collective' needs to be confined in this way. In an age of instant global communication and economic interdependence, alliances, social movements and networks, can all be developed on the principles of collective intelligence elaborated in this book. Secondly, the costs of a citizen's wage will make it difficult for any one country to 'go it alone' if the rules of the global auction remain in their current anarchic form. The increasing cost of labour and social overheads is likely to lead some SMEs as well as multinational companies to consider moving to countries where costs are lower. Indeed, the great promise of the European Community, for example, is that a citizen's wage across such an economic powerhouse would change the nature of the global auction. Capital will not disinvest where the potential for profit is so great. But this is a partial solution. The broader solution lies in the introduction of new regulations controlling the operation of global financial markets in the interests of democracy, which allows electorates rather than market speculators to determine the kind of society in which people want to live.[3]

2

The 'side effects' of market individualism which contribute to insecurity, inequality and social disorder are not restricted to one social group, but cut across traditional class, gender and racial boundaries. This suggests that there is scope for a new centre-left alliance based on the principles of collective intelligence. It will be a formidable but not impossible task. We have seen how the affluent consensus in the Golden era was broken in the 1970s and 1980s. In the rhetoric of primitive capitalism a new alliance was forged between the middle class and the rich which offered little hope for the 'losers' in America and Britain. But in the 1990s large numbers of middle class voters switched from the Republicans to the Democrats in America and from the Conservatives to Labour in Britain. There was a recognition that 'one cannot have one's cake and eat it', as well as an appreciation that 'there is no such thing as a free lunch'. It is impossible to have tax cuts and provide a decent standard of public schools, social security, health care, municipal facilities, or a society of which one can be proud. But images of the class structure and the political messages which have been drawn from prominent commentators such as J.K. Galbraith and Robert Reich lead to the conclusion that there is little prospect of a new cross-class political alliance on which to mobilise the struggle for collective intelligence. In our view these writers have obscured the common concerns of the middle and working classes and the potential for a new reflexive solidarity. Galbraith suggested that whilst the working class was a spent political force, the middle class exuded a 'culture of contentment' which presented little scope for a new class alliance on which social solidarity could be rebuilt. The 'contented' includes managers and those who staff the middle and higher ranks of large financial and industrial firms; independent business men and women; professional lawyers, doctors, engineers, scientists, accountants, journalists and university professors. There are also some skilled manual workers included among the contented, especially where there are dual paycheques with both partners earning. What gives them political power in the democratic process is not that they are the majority of citizens, but the majority of those who vote in elections. And what unites this socially and occupationally diverse group is a determination to preserve their present comforts even if they recognize the longer term problems involved in opting for 'short-run public inaction' or in getting 'government off the backs of the people' in those areas where it does not affect subsidies and government support to the contented. 'What is important', Galbraith observed:

is that there is no self-doubt in their present situation. The future for the contented majority is thought effectively within their personal command. Their anger is evident ... only when there is a threat or possible threat to present well-being and future prospects – when government and the seemingly less deserving intrude or threaten to intrude their needs or demands. This is especially so if such action suggests high taxes.[4]

Galbraith's analysis is surely correct when he suggests that the problem today is not only one of securing real change in the quality of people lives, but the moral will to attempt it.[5] However, the political shift away from New Right governments in the 1990s represents more than an attempt on the part of the contented to reaffirm their sense of self-satisfaction. We have shown that whilst it may be true that the middle classes appear 'contented' to exert their market muscle in a belief that it is sufficient to maintain middle-class status for themselves and their families, it is motivated by worries about economic insecurity. The middle classes can no longer guarantee their own welfare, at a time when the stakes have increased, because decent quality education, employment, health care, and housing depend upon positional advantage in the labour market. The whittling away of the welfare state has meant that middle-class families have much further to fall! Galbraith also underestimated the divided fortunes of the middle class, between those who have been able to find or maintain 'core' jobs in high value added companies and those who have become part of the flexible workforce. Indeed, Robert Reich has argued that the reason why there is little scope for a political alliance between different socio-economic groups is because of the revolt of the elites who have 'struck out' for a much bigger share of the spoils through reduced taxation and access to superior goods and services including health care, education and legal services.

In Reich's view, the 'two nations' of the contented haves and the hapless have-nots is replaced by the 'two worlds' view of national economic life. Reich's symbolic analysts are no longer seen to be dependent upon the society in which they live for their economic livelihoods. Indeed, they are the new social elite who are paid handsomely for being able to sell their skills, knowledge and insights in the global market place. The symbolic analysts represent a new 'over-class' because they are not locked into the national class structure in any meaningful sense. Their futures do not depend upon sharing a collective sense of purpose with their fellow citizens. We have already noted Reich's view that the plight of the poor is seen as none of their business. 'The symbolic analysts and their families have seceded from public life into ghettos of affluence, within which their earnings need not be redistributed to people less fortunate than themselves'.[6]

This 'two worlds' view exaggerates the disconnection of the professional and managerial middle class from the fate of others. For example, many American symbolic analysts work for American multinationals whose profitability continues to depend in large measure on factors directly related to the 'home base'. Equally, many of those who work for foreign multinationals are dependent upon local, state and national initiatives used to attract inward investment. If they lose their jobs, as many have, they will fall back onto local services for support and may well find a new job with a local company. We have also shown how the salaries of the symbolic analysts have not uniformly increased; some have actually experienced a decline in their income, suggesting that they do not share similar working conditions and hence interests. Moreover, a significant category of managers and professional workers in the public sector have largely been ignored in Reich's account. This obscures the fact that many workers who Reich would categorise as symbolic analysts do not depend on the global economy for their livelihoods but on the public sector and therefore on the taxes the state can raise. Any diminution of the welfare state whilst directly affecting the poorest sections of society, also reduces the range of occupational opportunities for the middle classes in the public sector.

Most importantly, the idea that those who are no longer dependent on a national labour market for their economic livelihood will inevitably abandon the society in which they live is an example of where political dialogue is unable to get beyond the bounds of economic reason. In a society which celebrates market individualism, it is hardly surprising that the 'seriously wealthy' in American have retreated from society. But this is not an inevitable response. Egoism is not 'a moral rule for all times and circumstances'.[7] Indeed, although the appeal to market forces can help to soothe the 'conscience of obligation' among the socially powerful and economically successful, it has at the same time robbed them of the opportunity to express themselves and their moral responsibilities to others. If there are people who have lost any sense of social purpose beyond the accumulation and consumption of wealth and who have no commitment to their neighbours or to the broader society, these are people to be pitied rather than envied. In the context of the twenty-first century they are what Ulrich Beck has called 'ugly citizens' who are playing a zero-sum game at the expense of others, as they monopolise the best of everything that money can buy.

There is, no doubt, a small proportion of Americans and Europeans who are so wealthy that they can, at least to some extent, insulate themselves from the rest of society. This is clearly not the case for the vast majority of middle-class Americans or Europeans. The exclusionary tactics that the middle classes have been forced to adopt, as tax cuts have been bought at the expense of public squalor, is ultimately self-defeating as many are finding to their material and psychological cost. We have shown that people are having to earn more to stand still as 'defensive expenditure' has increased. At the same time, private expenditure on education, health, and housing is either out of the reach of many middle-class families or an uncomfortable drain on household income. These realities have exposed the identification of the middle class with the interests of the rich as a myth.

In John Rawls' *A Theory of Justice*, we are told an 'if so' story of how people are likely to respond to a situation where there is a 'veil of ignorance' about where we are likely to end up in the social pecking order. Rawls suggests that the veil of ignorance would increase concerns about what happens to those at the bottom of society, because we have no guarantee that we will avoid that fate. If people respond rationally to the situation they are likely to opt for a more egalitarian society, as it is better to be at the bottom of such a society than one characterised by extreme inequality. The veil of ignorance is, of course, a fiction. But there is nevertheless a generalized 'veil of uncertainty' which has increased the sense of social risk among all social groups. At the beginning of the twenty-first century there may therefore be more scope for a left-of-centre politics based on the principles of collective intelligence than is commonly assumed.

A further consideration is that the breakdown in 'us and them' class politics has been accompanied by a growth in new social movements such as ecology parties, campaign groups such as Amnesty International and self-help groups which engage in a myriad of social activities from attempts to stop developers build a new shopping mall to support groups for parents who have lost children as a result of cot death. Some of these groups, which often have memberships which cut-across traditional 'party' lines, have the potential to form political alliances especially at the grassroots level which could contribute towards the struggle for collective intelligence. Indeed, there is no doubt that a new political alliance of this kind will be decisively shaped by women.

The days in which women voted according to the political leanings of their husbands are dead. In America the sea-change in male and female voting patterns came in the 1980s after the election of Ronald Reagan. While male voters tended to shift their allegiance to the Republicans, females shifted to the Democrats. This gender gap got wider with the ascendancy of Newt Gingrich. Frank Wilkinson who worked for Emily's List (a campaigning organisation to raise funds for female Democratic candidates), observed at the time that this gender gap existed because 'men seem to believe a lot of what they hear from the likes of Gingrich: this idea that if you just cut off these programmes, everything will be much simpler and take care of itself. Whereas women say, "Wait a minute, what do you mean you're going to cut child welfare, and student loans, and school lunches?"'[8] This response from women is hardly surprising given that poverty has been feminized.[9]

Women have a much better sense of the importance of collective security and also have the most to lose when social life is reduced to a series of market exchanges. Yet the power of women to have a decisive impact on the political process has never been greater. Naomi Wolf has noted that women outnumber men in most of the western democracies: in the USA it is 51 per cent to 49 per cent, in the UK it is 51.2 per cent to

48.8 per cent, and for Europe as a whole it is 51.3 per cent to 48.4 per cent. Although these may not appear to be enormous differences, if voting trends continue the 7 million additional women voters in the USA will increase to 10–12 million.[10] Therefore, if Wolf's claim is true that 'women often have trouble fighting on their own behalf, but are fearless warriors on behalf of children, communities, spouses or the environment', the potential for collective intelligence is a genuine prospect.[11]

3

The political feasibility of a society based on collective intelligence has been couched in terms of the rational self-interested individual. The problem of basing our argument on an appeal to self-interest is fully grasped by David Marquand:

> why should I make sacrifices for others? The answer, 'Because it is in your interest' is unlikely to carry much conviction for long, while the answer, 'Because you are a kindly altruist, who feels compassion for those less fortunate than yourself', dodges the real problem. However emollient the language in which it is put, the answer has to be, 'Because it is your duty; because you are part of a community, which existed before you were born, which will endure after your death, which helped to make you what you are and to the other members of which you have obligations; because you are a member of the human race, and no man is an island unto himself.[12]

Society comprises more than a collection of calculating pleasure machines: it is a moral community. It is because of our common human-ity that our schools, neighbourhoods, government, and economy should be structured in terms of what unites people rather than what divides. It is the values underlying the idea of collective intelligence which stand at the core of a decent society.[13] No matter how much the nature of self-interest can be shown to have changed in post-industrial societies, it is impossible to avoid some basic questions of social justice. As Jeremy Rifkin asks:

> Does every member of society have a right to participate in and benefit from increases in productivity brought on by the information and communication technology revolution? If the answer is yes, then some form of compensation will have to be made to the increasing number of unemployed whose labor will no longer be

needed in the new high-tech automated world of the twenty-first century.[14]

The great ethical hope at the beginning of the twenty-first century lies in the development of social solidarity based on the reflexivity of individuals who recognise that their quality of life depends on co-operation with others rather than relentless competition, and sees our mutual dependence as a strength to be celebrated as the essence of society. In the Golden era the problem of social solidarity was reduced to the 'mechanics' of how to deliver material prosperity to all. The distributional question of how goods and services were to be shared among the population was transformed from a political and moral question about social justice into a technical issue of how to equalize access to the labour market based on an assumption of full employment. This involved the application of 'impersonal' scientific knowledge by professional experts who were empowered to 'social engineer' the conditions for equal opportunities and economic growth, whether it concerned questions about the control of inflation, worker productivity, or child-rearing practices. Even the system of progressive taxation, which registered a commitment to redistributive justice, was organized in such a way that it served to minimize the individual's sense of ownership and personal involvement beyond the 'automatic' payment of money into the public purse. In these circumstances, democracy was reduced to its 'representative' form where votes were cast for someone to represent one's interests in local, state, or national government assemblies, since there was little direct participation in the political process.[15] Where participation did take place it usually took the form of pay disputes where trade unions exerted their collective muscle in the bid to gain a larger slice of corporate profits. Moreover, because political democracy had been reduced to a difference of emphasis rather than substance concerning the role of government, conflict between political parties represented little more than a contest over who could best deliver economic prosperity to all. Despite the efforts of the Modernisers to find new ways of recreating economic nationalism at the start of the twenty-first century, they will inevitably fail for reasons outlined in this book.

If centre-left parties are to fulfil their aim of delivering freedom, justice and opportunity to all in a more cohesive society, they will have to exploit the potential for reflexive solidarity. What makes the reflexivity of modern life a potential source of solidarity is that it disrupts, challenges and forces us to reorder the routines of everyday life.[16]

In unintended but decisive ways, it is creating the opportunity for those on the centre-left to mount a challenge at the very heart of western capitalism – its internal guidance system based on market individualism. We are presented with an unprecedented historical opportunity at the beginning of the twenty-first century to build decent societies for all. This book has argued that this challenge should be based on the struggle for collective intelligence.

Notes

1 Introduction

1 See 'Money income in the United States 1998', Current Population Report, US Census Bureau, Department of Commerce, Washington DC, 1999, p. xiv at http://www.census.gov/hnes/www/income.html.

2 Richard J. Murnane and Frank Levy, 'Why today's high-school-educated-males earn less than their fathers did: the problem and an assessment of responses', *Harvard Educational Review*, vol. 63, 1993, 1–19.

3 Quoted in Kevin Phillips, *The Politics of Rich and Poor*, New York: Harper Collins, 1990, p. 211.

4 Robert Reich, *The Work of Nations*, New York: Simon & Schuster, 1991, p. 268.

5 Although Ross Perot and Pat Buchanan in the United States and James Goldsmith in Europe offered an alternative to this in the call for 'protectionist' measures in order to recreate the conditions of the Golden era, it has been correctly rejected by the Modernisers as offering false hope. New problems require new solutions.

6 See, for instance, Will Hutton, *The State We're In*, London: Jonathan Cape, 1995; Larry Elliott and Dan Atkinson, *The Age of Insecurity*, London: Verso, 1998; Edward Luttwak, *Turbo Capitalism: Winners and Losers in the Global Economy*, New York: Harper Collins, 1998; John Gray, *False Dawn: The Delusion of Global Capitalism*, London: Granta Books, 1999.

7 Alan Ryan, *John Dewey and the High Tide of American Liberalism*, New York: W.W. Norton, 1995, p. 33.

8 The term 'collective intelligence' was first used by Colin Lacey in a paper 'The idea of a socialist education', which appeared in a collection edited by the authors, *Education in Search of a Future*, London: Falmer Press, 1988. The development of the concept began when the authors published 'Education, economy and society: an introduction to a new agenda', in Phil Brown and Hugh Lauder (eds) *Education for Economic Survival: From Fordism to Post-Fordism?*, London: Routledge, 1992. What appears here is the first fully worked out development of the concept.

9 See Ulrich Beck, *Risk Society: Towards a New Modernity*, London: Sage, 1992; Anthony Giddens, *Modernity and Self Identity: Self and Society in the Late Modern Age*, Cambridge: Polity, 1991 and his *Beyond Left and Right: The Future of Radical Politics*, Cambridge: Polity, 1994.

10 Stanley Manfred, *The Technological Conscience: Survival and Dignity in the Age of Expertise*, New York: Free Press, 1978, p. 221.

11 Ronald Dore quoted in David Marquand, *The Unprincipled Society*, London: Jonathan Cape, 1988, p. 103.

12 See Charles Handy, *The Empty Raincoat: Making Sense of the Future*, London: Hutchinson, 1994.

13 R. H. Tawney, *The Acquisitive Society*, Brighton: Wheatsheaf, 1982, p. 10.

14 Karl Mannheim, *Man and Society in the Age of Reconstruction*, London: Kegan Paul, 1940, p. 9.
15 This is part of a quotation by Ben Okri which appears at the beginning of our concluding chapter.

2   Secular Trinity

1 These calculations are taken from Philip Armstrong, Andrew Glyn, and John Harrison, *Capitalism Since 1945*, Oxford: Basil Blackwell, 1991, p. 117.
2 This is a paraphrase of Karl Marx from *The Eighteenth Brumaire of Louis Napolean*, cited in J. Elster, *Karl Marx: A Reader*, New York: Cambridge University Press, 1986, p. 277.
3 Karl Polanyi, *The Great Transformation*, Boston: Beacon Press, 1957, p. 73.
4 Mancur Olson, *The Rise and Decline of Nations: Economic Growth, Stagflation and Social Rigidities*, New Haven: Yale University Press, 1982.
5 Karl Marx and Friedrich Engels, Manifesto of the Communist Party, in L. S. Feuer (ed.) *Marx and Engels: Basic Writings on Politics and Philosophy*, New York: Anchor Books, 1959, p. 52.
6 John Maynard Keynes, *The General Theory of Employment, Interest and Money*, London: Macmillan, 1936.
7 Joseph Schumpeter, *Capitalism, Socialism and Democracy*, New York: Harper, 1947, chap. 7.
8 Philip Armstrong, Andrew Glyn, and John Harrison, *Capitalism Since 1945*, (n. 1 above), pp. 12–3.
9 There is considerable debate now as to whether Keynes' ideas were indeed applied in a way that was consistent with his theory. For the widespread but varied impact that Keynes' ideas had on different nations' economic policies see Peter A. Hall (ed.), *The Political Power of Economic Ideas: Keynesianism Across Nations*, Princeton: Princeton University Press, 1989.
10 Philip Armstrong, Andrew Glyn and John Harrison, *Capitalism Since World War II*, London: Fontana, 1984, pp. 167 and 168.
11 These figures are taken from Angus Maddison, *Phases of Capitalist Development*, Oxford: Oxford University Press, 1982, p. 208.
12 ibid.
13 ibid.
14 This figure is calculated from George Sayer, Robert Bacon and John Pimlott, 'The labour force', in A. H. Halsey (ed.), *Trends in British Society Since 1900*, London: Macmillan, 1972, Tables 4.10 and 4.11, pp. 121 and 122.
15 Emma Rothschild, *Paradise Lost: The Decline of the Auto-Industrial Age*, New York: Vintage Books, 1973, p. 34.
16 Ibid. p. 116.
17 Robert Reich, *The Work of Nations*, London: Simon and Schuster, 1991, p. 51.
18 Krishnan Kumar, *The Rise of Modern Society*, Oxford: Basic Blackwell, 1988, p. 31.
19 Frank Levy, *Dollars and Dreams: The Changing American Income Distribution*, New York: Norton, 1988, p. 25.
20 Adam Ferguson quoted in Adam Smith's *Wealth of Nations*, edited by R. H. Cambell and A. S. Skinner, Oxford: Clarendon Press, 1976, p. 782.

21 John Kenneth Galbraith, *The Affluent Society*, London: Hamish Hamilton, 1963, p. 4.

22 See Gaston Rimlinger, *Welfare Policy and Industrialisation in Europe, America and Russia*, New York: John Wiley and Sons, 1971, for a history of the relationship between nationalism and the idea of social insurance.

23 Ibid., p. 64.

24 The American data is taken from Frank Levy, *Dollars and Dreams* (n. 19 above) p. 15. The British data from George Sayer, Robert Bacon and John Pimlott, 'The labour force', in A. H. Halsey (ed.) *Trends in British Society Since 1900* (n. 14 above) Table 4.7, p. 118.

25 Hilary Land, 'The family wage', *Feminist Review*, vol. 6, 1980, 55–78; Martha May, 'Bread before roses: American workingmen, labour unions and the family wage', in Ruth Milkman (ed.) *Women, Work and Protest: A Century of Women's Labor History*, Boston: Routledge & Kegan Paul, 1985.

26 Martha May, 'Bread before roses', p. 2.

27 Frank Levy, *Dollars and Dreams* (n. 19 above), p. 34.

28 Constance Rollett and Julia Parker, 'Population and family', in A. H. Halsey, (ed.) *Trends in British Society*, (n. 14 above), p. 49. While these statistics tell a story of relative stability the sudden jump in divorces to the still comparatively low figure of approximately 8 per cent may have something to do with the dissatisfaction of women being forced back into a traditional role after the war. In the United States, 35 per cent of women over the age of 14 participated in the labour market.

29 Philip Armstrong, Andrew Glyn, and John Harrison, *Capitalism Since 1945*, (n. 1 above), p. 195.

30 Frank Levy, *Dollars and Dreams*, (n. 19 above) p. 56.

31 Philip Armstrong, Andrew Glyn, and John Harrison, *Capitalism Since 1945*, (n. 1 above), pp. 197–8.

32 Michael Kalecki, 'Political aspects of full employment', *The Political Quarterly*, October/December, 1943. Vol. 14 No. 4 322–331.

33 See Michael Young, *The Rise of the Meritocracy*, Harmondsworth: Penguin, 1961.

34 These figures are calculated from Frank Levy, *Dollars and Dreams*, (n. 19 above) Table 3.2, p. 32, and Jerald Hage and Charles Powers, *Post-Industrial Lives: Roles and Relationships in the 21st Century*, Newbury Park: Sage, 1992, Table 1.3, p. 40.

35 A. H. Halsey and Jean Floud, 'Introduction' in A. H. Halsey, J. Floud and J. Anderson (eds), *Education Economy and Society*, New York: Free Press, 1961, p. 1.

36 Fritz Ringer, *Education and Society in Modern Europe*, Bloomington, Indiana University Press, 1979, p. 252.

37 John Goldthorpe, Catriona Llewellyn, and Clive Payne, *Social Mobility and Class Structure in Modern Britain*, Oxford: Oxford University Press, 1980.

3   Engines of Growth

1 Emma Rothschild, *Paradise Lost: The Decline of the Auto-Industrial Age*, New York: Vintage Books, 1973, p. 34.

2   These figures are taken from Robert Heilbroner, *The Making of Economic Society*, New Jersey: Prentice-Hall, 1989, p. 121; Michael A. Utton, *The Political Economy of Big Business*, Oxford: Martin Robertson, 1982, p. 21; Graham Bannock, *The Juggernauts: The Age of the Big Corporation*, Harmondsworth: Penguin, 1973, p. 39.

3   John Kenneth Galbraith, *The New Industrial State*, London: Andre Deutsch, 1967, p. 76.

4   The America figures are calculated from Galbraith, *The New Industrial State*, p. 75, the British figures are from Leslie Hannah, *The Rise of the Corporate Economy*, London: Methuen, 1983, p. 146. S. J. Prais' *The Evolution of Giant Firms in Britain*, Cambridge: Cambridge University Press, 1976, has an international comparative analysis of employment in large corporations, p. 156.

5   Quoted in David A. Hounshell, *From the American System to Mass Production, 1800–1932*, Baltimore: John Hopkins Press, 1984, p. 217–19.

6   Fred Colvin writing in the American Machinist, May–November, 1913, cited in David, A. Hounshell, *From the American System to Mass Production: 1800–1932*, Baltimore: John Hopkins Press, 1984, p. 228.

7   These figures are taken from Alfred Chandler, *Scale and Scope: The Dynamics of Industrial Capitalism*, Cambridge, Mass.: Harvard University Press, 1990, Appendices A.1 and A.3.

8   There is considerable debate as to the nature of Ford's innovation. Much of the technology of the production line was at hand before Ford's production line. For discussions of this issue see David A. Hounshell, *From the American System to Mass Production, 1800–1932*, (n. 5 above), Judith Merkle, *Management and Ideology: The Legacy of the International Scientific Management Movement*, Berkeley: University of California Press, 1980; David F. Noble, *America By Design: Science Technology and the Rise of Corporate Capitalism*, Oxford: Oxford University Press, 1977.

9   Emma Rothschild, *Paradise Lost: The Decline of the Auto-Industrial Age* (n. 1 above), p. 129.

10 See Dan Clawson, *Bureaucracy and the Labor Process: The Transformation of US Industry, 1860–1920*, New York: Monthly Review Press, 1980, p. 161 for a discussion of the Columbus Iron Works.

11 Henry Ford, *My Life and Work*, New York: Garden City Publishing Co., 1922, p. 85.

12 Judith Merkle, *Management and Ideology: The Legacy of the International Scientific Management Movement* (n. 8 above), p. 97.

13 Henry Ford, *My Life and Work* (n. 11 above), p. 85.

14 Harry Braverman, *Labour and Monopoly Capital: The Degradation of Work in the Twentieth Century*, New York: Monthly Review Press, 1974, pp. 173–4.

15 Judith Merkle, *Management and Ideology: The Legacy of the International Scientific Management Movement*, (n. 8 above), p. 98.

16 Henry Ford, *My Life and Work* (n. 11 above), pp. 47–8.

17 This term is almost certainly justified, see John Kenneth Galbraith, *The Liberal Hour*, Harmondsworth: Penguin, 1960, Chapter 9, 'Was Ford a Fraud?'

18 See Taylor's testimony before the Special House Committee, in Fredrick W. Taylor, *Scientific Management*, New York: Harper and Brothers, 1947 pp. 79–85. The key passage is worth quoting: 'The great revolution that takes place in the mental attitude of the two parties under scientific management is that

> both sides take their eyes off of the division of the surplus as the all important matter, and together turn their attention toward increasing the size of the surplus until this surplus becomes so large . . . that there is ample room for a large increase in wages for the workmen and an equally large increase in profits for the manufacturer'.

19   Judith Merkle, *Management and Ideology: The Legacy of the International Scientific Management Movement*, (n. 8 above), p. 103.

20   Alfred Chandler, 'The railroads: pioneers in modern corporate management', *Business History Review*, 1965, 16–40.

21   For a discussion of the historical relationship between bureaucracy in the private sectors see Marshall W. Meyer, *Limits to Bureaucratic Growth*, Berlin: Walter de Gruyter, 1985; Alfred D. Chandler and L. Galambos, 'The development of large scale economic organisations in Modern America', *Journal of Economic History XXX*, 1970, 201–17.

22   Jurgen Kocka, 'Capitalism and bureaucracy in German industrialisation before 1914', *The Economic History Review*, 33, 453–68.

23   David F. Noble, *America By Design: Science Technology and the Rise of Corporate Capitalism*, Oxford: Oxford University Press, 1977.

24   Harlow S. Pearson, 'Basic principles of administration and management', in Henry Metcalf, *Scientific Foundations of Business Administration*, New York: Williams & Wilkins Co., 1926, p. 201. Quoted in Noble, *America By Design: Science Technology and the Rise of Corporate Capitalism*, p. 263.

25   Quoted in Noble ibid., pp. 262–3.

26   Quoted in Emma Rothschild, *Paradise Lost: The Decline of the Auto-Industrial Age*, (n. 1 above), p. 34.

27   The following discussion on corporate strategies of market control is taken from Neil Fligstein's *The Transformation of Corporate Control*, Cambridge, Mass.: Harvard University Press, 1990.

28   For further discussion of the concepts of scale and scope see Alfred D. Chandler, *Scale and Scope: The Dynamics of Industrial Capitalism*, Cambridge, Mass.: Harvard University Press, 1990.

29   Alfred Chandler, 'Corporate strategy, structure and control methods in the United States during the 20th century' *Industrial and Corporate Change*, 1, 1992, 263–84.

30   Joanne Yates, *Control Through Communication: The Rise of System in American Management*, Baltimore: Johns Hopkins University Press, 1989, 266–7.

31   Business Week, August 30th, 1958, p. 64, cited in Fligstein *The Transformation of Corporate Control*, p. 232.

32   Neil Fligstein, *The Transformation of Corporate Control*, (n. 27 above), p. 231.

33   Bruce R. Scott, 'The industrial state: old myths and new realities', *Harvard Business Review*: March–April, 1973, pp. 133–48, is the source of figures on the development of the multidivisional corporation in the post-war period in the United States and Europe.

34   Ibid., pp. 143–4.

35   These figures are taken from Barry Bluestone and Bennett Harrison, *The Deindustrialisation of America*, New York: Basic Books, 1982, pp. 119–20.

36   Marshall W. Meyer, *Limits to Bureaucratic Growth*, Berlin: Walter de Gruyter, 1985, p. 37.

37 Margali Sarfatti Larson, *The Rise of Professionalism*, Berkeley: University of California Press, 1977.

4 The Adversities of Good Times

1   See Studs Terkl, *American Dreams Lost and Found*, New York: Pantheon Books, 1980, pp. 18–21.
2   C. Wright Mills, *The Power Elite*, New York: Oxford University Press, 1956, p. 132. The situation was similar in Britain. In the early 1950s, 63 per cent of managers in large companies had worked for the same company all their lives and over 90 per cent of managerial jobs were filled by promotions within the company. These figures are taken from the *Management Succession*, London: Acton Trust Society, 1956.
3   C. Wright Mills, *The Power Elite*, pp. 128–9. The background of British executives was similarly elitist. See Gloria Lee, *Who Gets to the Top? A Sociological Study of Business Executives*, Aldershot: Gower, 1981.
4   C. Wright Mills, *The Power Elite*, p. 129.
5   Michael Roper, *Masculinity and the British Organisation since 1945*, Oxford: Oxford University Press, 1994.
6   Robert K. Merton, *Social Theory and Social Structure*, New York: Free Press, 1964, p. 200.
7   Quoted in William H. Whyte, *The Organisation Man*, Harmondsworth: Penguin Books, 1963, p. 147.
8   ibid., p. 163.
9   See Samuel Bowles and Herbert Gintis, *Schooling in Capitalist America*, London: Routledge & Kegan Paul, 1976; Melvin L. Kohn, 'Bureaucratic man: a portrait and an interpretation', *American Sociological Review*, vol. 36, 1971, 461–74, for a discussion of the personal traits required for bureaucratic work.
10 Harold, L. Wilensky, 'Work, careers, and social integration', *International Social Science Journal*, vol. 12, 1960, 543–60, p. 555.
11 C. Wright Mills, *White Collar*, New York, Oxford University Press. pp. xvi–xvii.
12 Quoted in Studs Terkl, *Working People Talk About What They Do All Day and How They Feel About What They Do*, New York: Pantheon Books, 1972, pp. 263–6.
13 Richard Sennett, *The Fall of Public Man*, Cambridge: Cambridge University Press, 1974, p. 331.
14 William H. Whyte, *The Organisation Man*, (n. 7 above), p. 147.
15 Huw Beynon, *Working for Ford*, Wakefield: EP Publishing, p. 118. The following quotations by Ford workers are all taken from Huw Beynon's book.
16 E. P. Thompson, *The Making of the English Working Class*, London: Gollancz, 1963, pp. 306–7. Quoted in Eli Zaretsky, *Capitalism, the Family and Personal Life*, London: Pluto Press, 1976. This brief book provides the classic statement of the impact of the separation of family life from paid work on the creation of subjectivity.
17 There is a debate about the degree to which all classes felt they had to 'keep up with the Jones's'. William H. Whyte, for example, argues that managers had to carefully keep step with the 'Jones's' rather than ahead of them. Nevertheless what is clear is that the advent of the 'consumer' society brought with it new ways of defining status based on consumer products.

18   William H. Whyte, *The Organisation Man* (n. 7 above), p. 297.
19   Jan M. Pahl and Ray E. Pahl, *Managers and their Wives: A Study of Career and Family Relationships in the Middle Class*, London: Allen Lane, 1971, p. 214.
20   ibid., p. 181.
21   ibid., pp. 183–4.
22   ibid., p. 217.
23   Meredith Tax, *Woman and Her Mind: The Story of Daily Life*, Cambridge: Cambridge University Press, 1970.
24   Richard Sennett and Jonathan Cobb, *The Hidden Injuries of Class*, Cambridge: Cambridge University Press, 1977, p. 126.
25   Harold Wilensky 'Work, careers and social integration', *International Social Science Journal*, vol. 12, 1960, 543–60, p. 555.
26   Michael Young and Peter Willmott, *Family and Kinship in East London*, London: Routledge and Kegan Paul, 1957.
27   This resource can be understood as part of the social capital of a neighbourhood. See James Coleman's classic account, 'Social capital in the creation of human capital', *American Journal of Sociology*, supplement to vol. 94, 1988, 95–120.
28   Richard Hoggart, *The Uses of Literacy*, London: Pelican Books, 1957, p. 68.
29   The phrase is taken from Herbert Marcuse, *One Dimensional Man*, Boston, Beacon Press, 1964. This was a seminal critical text of the sixties examining the impact of bureaucratic capitalism on rationality and individual freedom.
30   Antonio Gramsci, *Selections from the Prison Notebooks*, trans. Quentin Hoare and Geoffrey Nowell-Smith, London: Lawrence and Wishart, 1971, p. 296.
31   Antonio Gramsci would have been intrigued by the first major treatise on sexual behaviour by Alfred Kinsey and his associates: it bears all the hallmarks of Fordist modes of thinking in that their massive study is almost entirely taken up by questions of incidence and frequency. Never mind the quality, feel the regularity! See Liz Stanley, *Sex Surveyed 1949–1994: From Mass-Observation's 'Little Kinsey' to the National Survey and the Hite Reports*, London: Taylor and Francis, 1995.
32   David Riesman with Nathan Glazer and Reuel Denney, *The Lonely Crowd*, New Haven: Yale University Press, 1961, p. 194.
33   The historical gendered separation of friendship and the role of male bonding has only recently become a legitimate area of research. See Bob Connell, 'The big picture: masculinities in recent world history', *Theory and Society*, vol. 22, 1993, 597–623.
34   See Mirra Komarovsky, *Blue Collar Marriage*, New York: Vintage Books, 1962, for an American account of working-class relations between husbands and wives at this time. However, relationships within more affluent working class families were obviously beginning to change by the early sixties, see the paper by Lee Rainwater and Gerald Handel, in Arthur B. Shostak and William Gomberg, *Blue Collar World: Studies of the American Worker*, New Jersey: Prentice-Hall, 1964.

5   The Manufacture of Intelligence

1   Horatio Alger, Jr. Quoted in John E. Schwartz and Thomas J. Volgy, *The Forgotten Americans*, New York, W. W. Norton, 1992, p. 8–9.

2 W. Lloyd Warner, Robert J. Havighurst and Martin B. Loeb, *Who Shall be Educated? The Challenge of Unequal Opportinities*, London: Kegan Paul, 1946, p. 45.

3 Talcott Parsons, 'The school class as a social system: some of its functions in American society', Harvard *Education Review*, xxix, 1959, 297–318.

4 Michael Young, *The Rise of the Meritocracy*, Harmondsworth: Penguin, 1961.

5 Quoted in David. G. Glass, 'Education and social change in modern Britain', in A. H. Halsey, Jean, Floud and C. A. Anderson (eds) *Education, Economy and Society*, Glencoe: Free Press, 1961, p. 394.

6 Alexander Walker (1840) quoted in June Purvis 'Towards a history of women's education in nineteen-century Britain: A sociological analysis', in J. Purvis & M. Hales (eds) *Achievement and Inequality in Education*, Milton Keynes: Open University Press. See also June Purvis *A History of Women's Education in England*, Milton Keynes: Open University Press, 1991.

7 Clark Kerr, John T. Dunlop, Frederick Harbison and C. A. Myers, *Industrialism and Industrial Man*, Harmondsworth: Penguin, 1973, p. 53.

8 Martin Trow, 'The second transformation of American secondary education', in J. Karabel and A. H. Halsey (eds) *Power and Ideology in Education*, New York: Oxford University Press, 1977, p. 111.

9 Burton Clark, *Education and the Expert Society*, San Francisco: Chandler, 1962; Clark Kerr, John T. Dunlop, Frederick Harbison and C. A. Myers, *Industrialism and Industrial Man*, Harmondsworth: Penguin, 1973.

10 John Dewey, *Democracy and Education*, New York: Macmillan, 1916, p. 101.

11 Michael Young, *The Rise of the Meritocracy* (n. 4 above).

12 In contrast, 'sponsored' systems of education such as that found in Britain in the 1950s and 1960s were based on the early selection of children for academic and vocational programmes, with a small minority of socially disavantaged students being 'sponsored' by middle class society to join their ranks. See Ralph Turner, *The Social Context of Ambition*, San Francisco: Chandler, 1964.

13 Martin Trow, 'The second transformation of American secondary education', in J. Karabel and A. H. Halsey (eds) *Power and Ideology in Education* (n. 8 above), p. 107.

14 ibid., p. 109–10.

15 A. H. Halsey, *Opening wide the doors of Higher Education*, National Commission on Education Briefing No. 6, London: National Commission on Education, 1992; see also A. H. Halsey, *Decline of Donnish Dominion: The British Academic Professions in the Twentieth Century*, Oxford: Clarendon, 1992.

16 Matthew Arnold, *Culture and Anarchy*, London: Smith and Elder, 1891, p. 30.

17 Aron V. Cicourel and John I. Kitsuse, *The Education Decision-Makers*, New York: Bobbs-Merrill, 1963, p. 139.

18 Warren Bennis, 'The decline of bureaucracy and organisations of the future', in J. M. Shepard (ed.) *Organizational Issues in Industrial Society*, Englewood Cliffs, Prentice-Hall, 1972, p. 107.

19 See James Fallows 'The case against credentialism', *The Atlantic Review*, 1985, December, 49–67.

20 Lewis Terman, *Intelligence Tests and School Reorganisation*, New York: World Book Co, 1923, p. 27–8.

21 See the discussion in Leon J. Kamin, *The Science and Politics of IQ*, Harmondsworth: Penguin, 1977.

294 *Capitalism and Social Progress*

22 Richard Herrnstein and Charles Murray, *The Bell Curve: Intelligence and Class Structure in American Life*, New York: Free Press, 1994. For an informed discussion of this book see Steven Fraser, (ed.) *The Bell Curve Wars*, New York: Basic Books, 1995.
23 W. Lloyd Warner, Robert J. Havighurst and Martin B. Loeb, *Who Shall be Educated? The Challenge of Unequal Opportunities*, London: Kegan Paul, 1946.
24 Plato's *Republic*, vol. 1, book III, London: Heinemann, 1937, p. 125
25 An outstanding example of how this notion of intelligence influenced what children learnt was the introduction of selective secondary education in England and Wales in 1944. Under the influence of Sir Cyril Burt's findings, which reported that it was possible to scientifically measure the potential of a child at the age of eleven, children were examined for selection to three kinds of school: academic (grammar), technical and practical (secondary modern).
26 Committee of the Secondary Schools Examinations Council on Curriculum and Examinations in Secondary Schools, *Norwood Report*, London: HMSO, 1943, p. 4.
27 Several hypotheses have been developed as to why schools have failed large numbers of students from working-class backgrounds and students of colour, including many of those with high IQs. The curriculum, school organization, teacher expectations and methods of selection, have all been advanced as causes of such failure. Over the past thirty years considerable research time and effort has been devoted to testing these hypotheses, yet the evidence clearly shows that despite important changes and improvements, there has not been a *substantial* reduction in the wastage of talent. This is because problems of inequality and wastage cannot be blamed on, or resolved within, the confines of the educational system. Some Western researchers have concluded that schools cannot compensate for the inequalities created by the nature and rewards of work in capitalist societies. More recently the problem of sexual and racial inequalities in education has also received sustained analysis. Much of this work has arrived at a similar conclusion, that although there is decisive room for improving the educational performance of female and ethnic minority students, the success of reforms in schools must be part of a broader campaign to combat sexism and racism which exists within the wider social structure. Some researchers have also found it useful to incorporate theories of capitalist development and class culture to explain why students from working-class backgrounds remain 'disadvantaged' with respect to social destinations relative to their counterparts from professional and managerial backgrounds. For an interesting account of the relationship between social class and race see John V. Ogbu 'Racial stratification and education in the United states: why inequalities persist', *Teachers College Record*, 96, 1994, p. 264–98. See also Martin Carnoy and Henry Levin, *Schooling and Work in the Democratic State*, Stanford: Stanford University Press, 1985.
28 Ronald Dore, *The Diploma Disease*, London: Allen & Unwin, 1976.
29 Randell Collins, *The Credential Society*, New York: Academic Press, 1979.
30 Fred Hirsch, *The Social Limits to Growth*, London: Routledge, 1977, p. 50.
31 Ivar Berg, *Education and Jobs: The Great Training Robbery*, New York: Praeger, 1970. See also Harry Braverman, *Labor and Monopoly Capitalism: The Degradation of Work in the Twentieth Century*, New York: Monthly Review Press, 1974.

32 'The content of discipline...is nothing but the consistently rationalised, methodically trained and exact execution of the received order, in which all personal criticism is unconditionally suspended and the actor is unswervingly and exclusively set for carrying out the command'. Max Weber quoted in H. H. Gerth and C. Wright Mills (eds) *From Max Weber*, Boston: Routledge and Kegan Paul, 1948, p. 254.

33 Henry Levin captures the essence of these aspects of the factory model of education in the following terms: 'Teachers supervise a work process that is relatively uniform and usually organised according to grade levels. The work process for teacher and student has been set out well in advance of the implementation of the schooling activity and without the involvement of the major participants. The design and planning of the curriculum, pedagogy, sequence of courses, selection of textbooks and methods of evaluation are usually set out by a political and administrative process with the help of specialists...Each course is generally divided into units and subunits which are followed sequentially and often learned by rote to enable success on standardized tests of the units. Students have little control over the use of their time and little input into the learning process'. See his 'Work and education', in G. Psacharopoulous (ed.) *Economics of Education: Research and Studies*, Oxford: Pergamon, 1987, 148.

34 Paul Willis, *Learning to Labour*, Farnborough: Saxon House, Teakfield, 1977, p. 199. See also Phillip Brown, *Schooling Ordinary Kids*, London: Tavistock, 1987.

35 Richard Sennett and Jonathan Cobb, *The Hidden Injuries of Class*, Cambridge: Cambridge University Press, 1977, p. 76.

36 ibid., p. 78.

37 Brian Jackson and Dennis Marsden, *Education and the Working Class*, London: Routledge and Kegan Paul, 1962, p. 241.

38 Barbara Ehrenreich, *Fear of Falling: The Inner life of the Middle Class*, New York: Harper Perennial, 1990, p. 76.

39 Quoted in Barbara Ehrenreich, *Fear of Falling* p. 62.

40 ibid., p. 81.

6 The End of Consensus

1 Sonia Orwell and Ian Angus (eds) *The Collected Essays, Journalism and Letters of George Orwell, Volume III*, London: Secker and Warburg, 1968, p. 119. The quote is from a review of F. A. Hayek's, apologia for the free market, *The Road to Serfdom*, Chicago: Chicago University Press, 1944.

2 Seymour E. Harris, (ed.) *Postwar Economic Problems*, New York: McGraw-Hill Book Company, 1943, p. 6.

3 Joseph Schumpeter, 'Capitalism in the postwar world', in Seymour E. Harris, (ed.) ibid., p. 120.

4 *The Economist*, 23rd June, 1945, pp. 837–8.

5 John Maynard Keynes, *The General Theory of Employment, Interest and Money*, London: Macmillan, 1936, p. 383.

6 Keynes' ideas impacted differently in different nations. In all cases any degree of acceptance involved a struggle between old orthodoxies and new ideas. It is useful to distinguish between the economics of Keynes and Keynesian economics. The former being Keynes specific theories and the latter the

predisposition of governments to take a hands on approach to economic policy, especially in the cause of maintaining full employment by organizing a nation's political economy including welfare state arrangements on the basis of negotiation between the state, employers and trade unions. Most post-war western nations regulated their economies and societies with a varying blend of all these notions of Keynesianism. For a discussion of the impact of Keynes' ideas on western societies see, Peter Hall (ed.) *The Political Power of Economic Ideas: Keynsianism Across Nations*, New Jersey: Princeton University Press, 1989.

7   See Robert Skidelsky, *John Maynard Keynes: The Economist As Saviour, 1920– 1937*, London: Macmillan, 1992, chapter 7.

8   By the War's end the aim of full employment was on the agenda of the advanced economies. A Full Employment Bill was introduced by the government in the United States immediately after the war, while in Britain, William Beveridge's unofficial report *Full Employment in a Free Society* formed the basis for a public policy which was to last until the 1980s.

One of the salient political consequences of full employment at the War's end was that unionized labour emerged stronger than when the War had started and was to prove essential to the success of economic nationalism. By the end of the war fourteen million American workers had been unionized and in 1946 the union movement flexed its muscles. In that year more Americans went out on strike than in any other year in the nation's history. The stakes were great because at issue were questions about the role of workers in production decisions and about the place of full employment in the post-war economy.

American business strongly opposed the Full Employment Bill arguing that it would destroy private enterprise and they achieved a partial victory. When the Bill was finally passed as the 1946 Employment Act full employment was rendered a pious intention rather than a legal commitment. It was not until 1978 that the Humphrey-Hawkins bill enforced a legal commitment to an unemployment rate of no higher than 4 per cent. By then the stable door was already open and control of low unemployment rates had escaped. In Britain, organised labour fared better. It had emerged from the War with over 45 per cent of the work force unionised and in 1945 it saw the return of an apparently sympathetic Labour government.

9   John Maynard Keynes, 'The end of *Laisser-Faire*', reprinted in *Essays in Persuasion*, London: Macmillan/Cambridge University Press, London, 1972.

10   See the paper by Peter Gourevitch, 'Keynesian politics: the political sources of economic policy choices', in P. Hall, (ed.) *The Political Power of Economic Ideas: Keynsianism Across Nations* (n. 6 above)

11   T. H. Marshall, *Sociology at the Crossroads*, London: Heinemann, 1963, p. 222.

12   ibid., p. 222.

13   The figures are taken from John Cornwall, *The Theory of Economic Breakdown*, Oxford: Basil Blackwell, 1991.

14   The figures are from the *Statistical Abstract for the United States, 1993*.

15   Quoted in Philip Armstrong, Andrew Glyn and John Harrison, *Capitalism Since World War II*, London: Fontana, 1984, p. 194.

16 The sentiment was expressed by Beveridge's wife Janet, in *Beveridge and his Plan*, London, 1954, which may account for the enthusiastic endorsement.

17 Keith Middlemass, *Politics in Industrial Society: The Experience of the British System since 1911*, London: Deutsch, 1979, p. 300.

18 Richard Titmuss, *War and Social Policy, Essays on the Welfare State*, Boston: Beacon Press, 1969, p. 85.

19 The figures for Britain are taken from Frank Gould and Barbara Roweth, 'Public spending and social policy: the United Kingdom, 1950–1977', *Journal of Social Policy*, 9, pp. 337–57. The figures for the United States are taken from *Statistical Abstracts for the United States*, 1993.

20 For a theoretical critique of the gender bias in welfare state arrangements see Carol Patemen, *The Disorder of Women: Democracy, Feminism and Political Theory*, Cambridge: Polity Press, 1989, Chapter 8.

21 Quoted in Alan Cochrane and John Clarke (eds) *Comparing Welfare States*, London: Sage/Open University Press, 1993, p. 21.

22 The significance of the distinction between welfare and social security is discussed in Theda Skocpol, 'America's incomplete welfare state: the limits of New Deal reforms and the origins of the present crisis', in Gosta Esping-Andersen, Martin Rein and Lee Rainwater (eds) *Stagnation and Renewal in Social Policy*, New York: M. E. Sharpe, 1987. For a discussion of the impact of the war on the development of the welfare state in America see, Edwin Amenta and Theda Skocpol, 'Redefining the New Deal: World War II and the development of social provision in the United States', in Margaret Weir, Ann Shola Orloff and Theda Skocpol (eds) *The Politics of Social Policy in the United States*, New Jersey: Princeton University Press, 1988.

23 For further development of these points see Gosta Esping-Andersen, *The Three Worlds of Welfare Capitalism*, Cambridge: Polity Press, 1990.

24 Peter Baldwin, *The Politics of Social Solidarity: Class Bases of the European Welfare States, 1875–1975*. Cambridge: Cambridge University Press, 1990, p. 121.

25 Beth Stevens, 'Blurring the boundaries: how the Federal government has influenced welfare benefits in the private sector', in Margaret Weir, Ann Shola Orloff and Theda Skocpol (eds) *The Politics of Social Policy in the United States* (n. 22 above).

26 Gosta Esping-Andersen, *The Three Worlds of Welfare Capitalism* (n. 23 above).

27 T. W. Hutchinson, *Economics and Economic Policy in Britain, 1946–1966*, London: Allen & Unwin, 1968.

28 Quoted in Alan Cochrane and John Clarke (eds) *Comparing Welfare States*, London: Sage/Open University Press, 1993, Chapter 9, Table 9 for the United States and Frank Gould and Barbara Roweth, 'Public spending and social policy: the United Kingdom, 1950–1977', *Journal of Social Policy*, 9, pp. 337–57.

29 Dexter Whitfield, *The Welfare State*, London: Pluto Press, 1992, pp. 114–115.

30 Assimilation should not be seen as an entirely 'innocent' policy. For example Theda Skocpol shows how the distinction between welfare and social security was based on racial (and racist) divisions. See her paper in Gosta Esping-Andersen, Martin Rein and Lee Rainwater (eds) *Stagnation and Renewal in Social Policy* (n. 22 above).

31 Frank Levy, *Dollars and Dreams: The Changing American Income Distribution*, New York: W. W. Norton, 1988, Tables 3.4 (p. 39) and 9.2 (n. 196)

32   John Burnett, *A History of the Cost of Living*, Harmondsworth: Penguin, 1969, p. 303.

33   Paul Krugman, *Peddling Prosperity: Economic Sense and Nonsense in An Age of Diminished Expectations*, New York: W. W. Norton, 1994, p. 131.

34   This is the view taken by the neo-Marxist Regulation theorists. See Alain Lipietz, 'New tendencies in the international division of labour: regimes of accumulation and modes of regulation', in Allen Scott and Michael Storper (eds) *Production, Work, Territory: The Geographical Anatomy of Industrial Capitalism*, Boston: Allen & Unwin, 1986: Michel Aglietta, *A Theory of Capitalist Regulation*, London: New Left Books, 1979.

35   Gosta Esping-Andersen, *The Three Worlds of Welfare Capitalism* (n. 23 above).

36   Beth Stevens, 'Blurring the boundaries: how the federal government has influenced welfare benefits in the private sector', in M. Weir, A. S. Orloff and T. Skocpol, (eds) *The Politics of Social Policy in the United States* (n. 22 above).

37   Gosta Esping-Andersen, *The Three Worlds of Welfare Capitalism* (n. 26 above).

38   Robert Skidelsky, 'The decline of Keynsian politic', in Colin Crouch (ed.) *State and Economy in Contemporary Capitalism*, London: Croom Helm, 1979.

39   Karl Marx and Friedrich Engels, 'The manifesto of the Communist Party' (1848) in L. S. Feuer (ed.) *Marx and Engels: Basic Writings on Politics and Philosophy*, New York: Anchor Books, 1959.

40   Daniel Bell, *The End of Ideology*, New York: Collier, 1961.

41   The province of experts because they were merely 'technical problems' to be addressed within a pre-determined framework – one in which there was an absence of ideological conflict.

42   The classic statement of this view is Harry Braverman's *Labour and Monopoly Capital*, New York: Monthly Review Press, 1974.

7   The New Global Competition

1   If capitalism has become the undisputed global champion it is because of its versatile character which allows it to adapt to diverse social, political and economic conditions. It can survive in the conditions of 'dark satanic mills' in nineteenth-century England and in the informational economy of twenty-first century Japan.

2   For data on the UK see Amanda Gosling, Stephen Machin and Costas Meghir, 'What has happened to the wages of men since 1966?', in J. Hills (ed.) *New Inequalities*, Cambridge: Cambridge University Press, 1996. For the US see Frank Levy, *Dollars and Dreams: The Changing American Income Distribution*, New York: Sage, 1987; Richard B. Freeman, *When Earnings Diverge: Causes, Consequences, and Cures for the New Inequality in the US*, Washington, DC: National Policy Association, 1997.

3   See Jared Bernstein, Edie Rasell, John Schmitt, and Robert Scott, *Tax Cut No Cure for Middle Class Economic Woes*, Washington DC: Economic Policy Institute, 1999.

4   Kenichi Ohmae 'Putting global logic first', *Harvard Business Review*, Jan/Feb 1995, 119–25, p. 120. See also his *The End of the Nation State: The Rise of the Regional Economies*, New York: Free Press, 1995; Richard Rosecrance, *The Rise of the Virtual State: Wealth and Power in the Coming Century*, New York: Basic

Books, 1999. An interesting comparison is Paul Hirst and Grahame Thompson, Globalization in Question, 2nd edn, Cambridge: Polity, 1999.

5 The Uruguay round of GATT completed in 1994, succeeded for the first time to gain agreement between the developed and developing counties aimed at giving fair access to all markets. Discussed in *Growth, Competitiveness, Employment: The Challenges and Ways Forward into the 21st Century,* White Paper, Brussels: Commission of the European Communities, 1993, p. 13.

6 Peter F. Drucker, *The New Realities,* London: Mandarin Paperbacks, 1990, p. 123.

7 Richard B. Freeman, 'Toward an apartheid economy?', *Harvard Business Review,* September–October 1996, 114–21, p. 117.

8 K. Shigehara, dep. sec. gen. of the OECD, *Globalization, Technology and Jobs,* pp. 8–9, 1997.

9 See Hans-Peter Martin and Harald Schuman, *The Global Trap: Globalization and the Assault on Democracy and Prosperity,* New York: Zed Books, 1997.

10 See 'US to act over Asian turmoil', *Financial Times,* 12 January, 1998.

11 Reported in Geoff Mulgan *Connexity: How to Live a Connected World,* London: Chatto & Windus 1997, p. 22.

12 Don Wilmott, 'The internet economy will take over', *PC Magazine,* June, 1999, p. 132.

13 Frank J. Derfler, 'Networks will be ubiquitous', *PC Magazine,* June, 1999, p. 114.

14 Reported in Katharine Campbell, 'The global company: the minnows' fight against the sharks', *Financial Times* 24 October, 1997.

15 Pete Richardson (ed.) *Globalization and Linkages: Macro-Structural Challenges and Opportunities,* Economics Department Working Paper No.181, Paris: OECD, 1997, p. 18. See http://www.oecd.org/eco/wp/onlinewp.htm

16 William Johnston, Global Workforce 2000, *Harvard Business Review,* March/April, 1991, 115–27.

17 Geoff Mulgan, *Connexity: How to Live a Connected World* (n. 11 above), p. 21.

18 These figures are taken from Martin Carnoy, Manuel Castells, Stephen Cohen, and Fernando H. Cardoso, *The New Global Economy in the Information Age,* University Park, PA: Penn State University Press, 1993 p. 49.

19 United Nations, *World Investment Report 1992: transnational corporations as engines of growth,* New York, United Nations, 1992; United Nations, World Investment Report 1993: *Transnational Corporations and Integrated International Production,* New York: United Nations, 1993 and World Investment Report 1994: Transnational Corporations, Employment and the Workplace, Geneva: UNCTAD. For an overview of the key issues see United Nations Conference of Trade and Development (UNCTAD) *Transnational Corporations and World Development,* Boston, Mass: International Thompson Business Press, 1996.

20 See Graham Vickery, 'Global industries and national policies', *OECD Observer,* January, 1993, 11–14, p. 12.

21 ibid.

22 See Stefan Wagstyl 'Japanese industry 1997: global investment has been at record levels', *Financial Times* 1612/97.

23   John H. Dunning and Karl P. Sauvant, 'Introduction: transnational corpora-
     tions in the world economy, in United Nations Conference of Trade and
     Development (UNCTAD) *Transnational Corporations and World Development*
     (n. 19 above), p. xi; United Nations Centre on Transnational Corporations
     (1988) *Transnational Corporations in World Development: Trends and Prospects*,
     New York: United Nations. See also Grazia Ietto-Gillies, *International Produc-
     tion: Trends, Theories, Effects*, Cambridge, Mass: Polity, 1994.

24   The figures on the extent of FDI is from United Nations, *World Investment
     Report 1993: Transnational Corporations and Integrated International Production*,
     and those on American exports are from Robert Reich, *The Work of Nations*,
     New York: Simon and Schuster, 1991, p. 114.

25   See *Financial Times* October 11, 1993.

26   OECD countries including the United States, Japan, European Union,
     and twelve other counties including Australia, Canada, Mexico, Korea and
     Switzerland.

27   See Pete Richardson (ed.) *Globalization and Linkages: Macro-Structural Chal-
     lenges and Opportunities*, (n. 15 above), p. 18.

28   ibid., p. 19.

29   ibid., p. 18.

30   These figures are derived from the table on p. 12 of *Growth, Competitiveness,
     Employment: The Challenges and Ways Forward into the 21st Century* (n. 5
     above).

31   M. Marckus, 'On the unholy word: competition', *Sunday Observer* September
     13, 1992.

32   See US Census Bureau, 'Household income at record high', Department
     of Commerce, 1999, at www.census.gov/press-release/www/1999/cb99–188.
     html

33   Richard B. Freeman 'Toward an apartheid economy?' *Harvard Business Review*,
     September–October 1996, 114–21, p. 114.

34   Amanda Gosling, Stephen Machin and Costas Meghir, 'What has happened
     to the wages of men since 1966?', in John Hills (ed.), *New Inequalities*, Cam-
     bridge: Cambridge University Press, 1996, p. 155.

35   See Paul Johnson, 'The assessment: inequality', *Oxford Review of Economic
     Policy*, vol. 12, 1996, 1–14, pp. 4–5.

36   The idea of the power to go abroad is described in Stephen H. Hymer's classic
     account of the multinational corporation. See *The International Operation of
     National Firms: A Study of Direct Foreign Investment*, Cambridge, Mass: MIT,
     1976. See also John H. Dunning, 'The nature of transnational corporations
     and their activities', in Nations Conference of Trade and Development
     (UNCTAD) *Transnational Corporations and World Development* (n. 19 above).

37   In the drive to reduce jobs, GM was following the example of many other big
     US corporations whose share of the labour force between 1975 and 1990 had
     declined from 17 per cent to less than 10 per cent. Reported in Robert Reich,
     The Work of Nations, p. 95.

38   Commission on the Skills of the American Workforce, *America's Choice: High
     Skills or Low Wages!* Rochester, NY: National Centre on Education and the
     Economy, 1990.

39   Paul Marglinson, 'Multinational Britain: Employment and Work in an Inter-
     nationized Economy, *Human Resources Management Journal*, 1994, 63–80, p. 64.

40 Reported in the *Financial Times*, October 29, 1993.

41 Interview with Graham Bowley 'The global company: corporate culture and a community contribution' *Financial Times*, October 31, 1997.

42 Tim Burt, 'Nissan stuns industry with £6bn revamp', *Financial Times*, October 19, 1999.

43 Peter Martin, 'The global company: the future depends on choice: global presence or local defense? Peter Martin sums up the lessons from the series, which included this quotation from Jack Welch, *Financial Times*, November 7, 1997.

44 There is legally no such thing as a global corporation, given that corporations continue to be subject to national legislation, tax regimes, etc. See Yao-Su Hu, 'Global or stateless corporations are national firms with international operations', *California Management Review*, 1992, Winter, 107–26.

45 For a discussion see Rosabeth Moss Kanter, *When Giants Learn to Dance*, London: Unwin Hyman, 1989; Charles Handey, *The Age of Unreason*, London: Century Hutchinson, 1989.

46 Robert Reich, *The Work of Nations* (n. 24 above), pp. 95–6.

47 'Foreign cars are best of British', *The Sunday Times*, July 25, 1993.

48 See Hans-Peter Martin and Harald Schumann, *The Global Trap: Globalization and the Assault on Democracy and Prosperity* (n. 9 above), pp. 99–101.

49 The costs involved in product innovation are discussed in B. Blackwell and S. Eilon *The Global Challenge of Innovation*, Oxford: Butterworth-Heinemann, 1991. See also Lester C. Thurow, *Building Wealth*, New York: Harper Collins, 1999.

50 For detail see Peter Dicken, *Global Shift: Transforming the World Economy*, (3rd edn), London: Paul Chapman, 1998.

51 Carol Levin, 'Little devices will think', *PC Magazine*, June, 1999, p. 123.

52 See Keith C. Cowling and Roger S. Sugden, *Beyond Capitalism: Towards a New World Economic Order*, London: Pinter, 1994, p. 37–40; Robin Murray 'Benetton Britain', in S. Hall and M. Jacques (eds) *New Times: The Changing Face of Politics in the 1990s*, London: Lawrence and Wishart, 1989; Manuel Castells, *The Rise of the Network Society*, Oxford: Blackwell, 1996, pp. 162 & 437; Bennett Harrison, *Lean and Mean: the Changing Landscape of Corporate Power in the Age of Flexibility*, New York: Basic Books, 1994.

53 Peter Acker, Chris Smith and Paul Smith (eds) *The New Workplace and the New Unionism*, London: Routledge 1996; John McIlroy, *Trade Unions in Britain Today*, (2nd edn), Manchester: Manchester University Press, 1995.

54 See Richard Rothstein, 'The global hiring hall: why we need worldwide labor standards', *The American Prospect*, 1994 Spring, 54–61.

55 Figures from *Financial Times Survey* 'North American business location' October 19, 1994.

56 See Barry Bluestone and Bennett Harrison, *The Deindustrialization of America*, New York: Basic Books, 1982 and *The Great American Job Machine: The Proliferation of Low-Wage Employment in the US Economy*, New York: Basic Books, 1988. They point out how profit making companies were closed because they failed to make corporate profit targets for branches and subsidiaries know as the 'hurdle rates of return'. Equally, they provide example of how 'mature' industrial subsidiaries or branches with high market share but low growth rates where defined as 'cash cows', milked in order to provide

investment funds for other forms of corporate activity. The alternative is to seek higher profits in niche markets for customized products. In this instance labour relations are democratized as profits become dependent upon the insights, knowledge and skills of individuals (as chapter 15 below).

57   Richard Rothstein, The global hiring hall: why we need worldwide labor standards', *The American Prospect*, 1994, p. 59.

58   From 'Managing low-skill jobs', *Bulletpoint*, sample issue, 1998.

59   See James Goldsmith's *The Response: GATT and Global Free Trade*, London: Macmillan, 1995, p. 125.

60   See Commission on the Skills of the American Workforce, *America's Choice: High Skills or Low Wages!* (n. 38 above); Bennett Harrison and Barry Bluestone, *The Great U-Turn: Corporate Restructuring and the Polarizing of America*, Basic Books: New York, 1988.

61   James, P. Womack, Daniel T. Jones and Daniel Roos, *The Machine that Changed the World*, New York: Rawson Associates, 1990, p. 277.

62   See Philip Garrahan and Paul Stewart, 'Work organisation in transition: the human resource management implications of the 'Nissan way'', *Human Resource Management Journal*, vol. 2, 1992, pp. 46–62.

63   See Joseph A. Schumpeter, *The Theory of Economic Development*, New York: Oxford University Press, 1961; Randall Collins, *Weberian Sociological Theory*, New York: Cambridge University Press, 1986; Basil Blackwell and Samuel Eilon, *The Global Challenge of Innovation* Oxford: Butterworth Heinemann, 1991. Moreover, the increasing costs of errors, demand for quality control, and for multi-skilled workers with a conceptual grasp of a large section of the production process or office activities has made the specialised division of labour in Fordism a source of organisational inefficiency (see chapter 15 below).

64   Reported in Anthony P. Carnevale and Jeffrey D. Porro, *Quality Education: School Reform for the New American Economy*, Washington DC: US Department of Education, 1994, p. 31.

65   Manuel Castells, 'The information economy and the new international division of labor, in M. Carnoy, M. Castell, S. Cohen, and F. H. Cardoso, *The New Global Economy in the Information Age*, Pennsylvania: Pennsylvania State University, 1994. See also his book, *The Rise of the Network Society*, Oxford: Blackwell, 1996.

66   See Anthony P. Carnevale and Jeffrey D. Porro, *Quality Education: School Reform for the New American Economy* (n. 64 above), p. 10.

67   See Commission on the Skills of the American Workforce, *America's Choice: High Skills or Low Wages!* (n. 38 above); James A. Auerbach and Richard S. Belous (eds) The *Inequality Paradox: Growth of Income Disparity*, Washington DC: National Policy Association, 1998.

68   Andrew Hacker, *Money: Who Has How Much and Why*, New York: Touchstone,1998, p. 214.

69   See Robert Reich, *The Work of Nations* (n. 24 above).

70   Alvin Toffler, *Power Shift: Knowledge, Wealth and Violence at the Edge of the Twenty-First Century*, New York: Bantam, 1990, p. 82.

71   US Department of Commerce, *21st Century Skills for 21st Century Jobs*, Washington, DC: Departments of Commerce, Education and Labor, 1999, p. iii.

72 See Lester C. Thurow, *Head-to-Head: The Coming Economic Battle Among Japan, Europe and America*, London: Nicholas Brealey, 1993; Peter F. Drucker *Post-Capitalist Society*, Oxford: Butterworth Heinemann, 1993.

73 Anthony P. Carnevale and Jeffrey D. Porro, *Quality Education: School Reform for the New American Economy*, (n. 64 above), p. 13.

74 Economists used to treat national economies as hermetically sealed units which limited international comparisons to rates of economic growth. Educational investment was important only in so far that it appeared to correlate to such differences in growth rates. There was little sense of an international labour market within which differences in the quality of education could have a decisive impact on the livelihoods of workers within different countries. See Phillip Brown, 'The globalization of positional competition', *Sociology*, spring 2001.

75 National Commission on Excellence in Education, *A Nation at Risk*, Washington, DC: NCEE, 1983, p. 6.

76 National Commission on Education, *Learning to Succeed*, London: Heinemann, 1993, p. 33.

77 Andy Green, 'Educational achievement in centralised and decentralised systems', in A. H. Halsey, H. Lauder, P. Brown and A. S. Wells (eds), *Education: Culture, Economy and Society*, Oxford: Oxford University Press, 1997.

8   Primitive Capitalism

1 Hugh Lauder 'The descent', in *Over the White Wall*, Christchurch: The Caxton Press, 1985.

2 Margaret Thatcher, 'The Brian Walden Interview' reported in the *Sunday Times*, May 8th, 1988.

3 Ronald Reagan quoted in M. Stephen Weatherford and Lorraine M. McDonnell 'Ideology and economic policy', in Larry Berman (ed.) *Looking Back at the Reagan Presidency*, Baltimore: John Hopkins University Press, 1990, p. 125.

4 Patricia Marchak, *The Integrated Circus: The Neo-liberal and the Restructuring of Global Markets*, Montreal & Kingston: McGill-Queen's University Press, 1990; John Gray, *False Dawn: The Delusion of Global Capitalism*, London: Granta Books, 1999.

5 These were all members of the Trilateral Commission in August 1975. See Michel J. Crozier, Samuel P. Huntington and Joji Watanuki, *The Crisis of Democracy: Report on the Governability of Democracies to the Trilateral Commission*, New York: The Trilateral Commission/New York University Press, 1975.

6 Thomas Ferguson and Joel Rogers 'Another trilateral election', *The Nation*, June 28, 1980, p. 785.

7 Michel J. Crozier, Samuel P. Huntington and Joji Watanuki, *The Crisis of Democracy: Report on the Governability of Democracies to the Trilateral Commission* (n. 5 above).

8 James Buchanan and Richard E. Wagner, *Democracy in Deficit*, New York: Academic Press, 1977.

9 See Bruce Cumings 'Chinatown: foreign policy and elite realignment' in Thomas Ferguson and Joel Rogers (eds) *The Hidden Election*, New York;

Pantheon Books, 1981, p. 129. In their introductory chapter 'The Reagan victory: corporate coalitions in the 1980 campaign', Ferguson and Rogers note that in America 'as in all advanced industrial democratic states, the major dynamics of domestic political and party competition are determined by two factors: the aggregate balance of power between business and labor within the domestic system, and the competition of industrial sectors within the world economy. But the operative significance of the first factor is limited in the American case by the "exceptionalism" of American politics, which features a weak and politically disorganized labor movement. As a consequence, business provides the driving force behind much of domestic politics, and political conflict is often best analyzed as derivative of conflict between different corporate sectors.' Ibid., p. 7.

10   The libertarians sought to reverse the state's encroachment into peoples' lives; the neo-conservatives wanted an end to the 'permissive' society through a return to traditional values of deference, authority and religious rectitude; and the corporate wing sought to free business from the grip of trade unions and to liberate their capital from national restrictions. What united these disparate groups was their common goal of dismantling the Keynesian welfare state. See M. Patricia Marchak *The Integrated Circus: The Neo-liberal and the Restructuring of Global Markets* (n. 4 above).

11   See Daniel Yergin and Joseph Stanislaw, *The Commanding Heights: The Battle Between Government and the Marketplace that is Remaking the Modern World*, New York: Simon and Schuster, 1998; James Buchanan and Richard E. Wagner, *Democracy in Deficit*(n. 8 above).

12   Ronald Reagan quoted in M. Stephen Weatherford and Lorraine M. McDonnell 'Ideology and economic policy', in Larry Berman (ed.) *Looking Back at the Reagan Presidency*, (n. 3 above), p. 125.

13   John Kenneth Galbraith, 'Up from monetarism and other wishful thinking', *New York Review of Books*, August 13, 1981.

14   Martin Gardner, 'The Laffer Curve and other laughs in current economics', *Scientific American*, December, 1981, 16–20.

15   Employment Policy Institute, *Tax and the Winner Takes All Society*, vol. 10, Jan/Feb., 1997.

16   Hugh Lauder and David Hughes, *Trading in Futures: Why Markets in Education Won't Work*, Buckingham: Open Univeristy Press, 1999.

17   Lawrence Mead, 'The new politics of the new poverty', *The Public Interest*, vol. 103, 1991, p. 12

18   ibid., p. 8.

19   ibid., p. 9. 'In dependency politics... the chief question is how far government should control the lives of dysfunctional people in their own interests. Do we require that people stay in school, obey the law, avoid drugs, and so on? Above all, do we require adults to work or prepare for work as a condition of receiving welfare? Proposals to do these things do not much change what government does for people. Rather, they demand that dependents do more for themselves in return.' Ibid., p. 9.

20   Lawrence Mead goes on the say 'The plight of the underclass suggests that the competence of many of the poor – their capacity to look after and take care of themselves – can no longer be taken for granted as it could in the past.' Ibid, p. 3. This is the clearest expression of a 'low-trust' society. That the state must

take over the running of peoples lives because they cannot be trusted to take the opportunities which are open to them, and so incompetent that they are unfit for everyday life.

21 Charles Murray proposed altering the 'incentives' by making it more difficult to receive welfare, and shaming (stigmatizing) those who seek welfare. See his book *Losing Ground*, New York: Basic Books, 1984. Mead (ibid.) opts for increasing the 'obligations' of welfare recipients through 'workfare': invigorating the work requirement with welfare.

22 The assuption here is that behaviour changes in line with incentives, especially when they appeal to individual self-interest. However, the connection between incentives and motivation is highly problematic. Its link with 'self-interest' and the assumption that this is the only, or the primary source of motivation is equally, if not more, so. Here we find a major flaw in their argument in relation to human capability. What turns most people on, more than anything else, is believing in something. Religous belief in some cases is enough for people to drive a car full of high-explosives into a army road block, belief in money is enough to make people commute over four hours a day or undertake the most mundane or dangerous tasks, but what most motivates most people is a belief in the intrinsic or social value of an activity, often in collaboration with others. The reason why most factory workers in Fordist plants would skip off whenever they have a chance is because they 'don't believe in it'. Here is the rub. Mead confesses that 'In today's social analysis, therefore, judgements of human nature play as great a role as any hard evidence'. Lawrence Mead, 'The new politics of the new poverty', *The Public Interest*, vol. 103, 1991, p. 12. Our view is that the Hobbsian view of 'all against all', and the appeal to self-interest is little more than an ideological justification for 'primitive capitalism'. The ideological battle over the question of human capability and motivation is a battle for 'human nature' (see Part III).

23 Charles Murray, *Losing Ground* (n. 21 above), p. 9.

24 ibid., p. 219.

25 Lawrence Mead, 'The new politics of the new poverty', *The Public Interest*, vol. 103, 1991, p. 11.

26 This legislation also covered comsumer protection along with new conservation and environmental regulations. See Paul, K. Conkin's *Big Daddy from the Pedernales: Lyndon Baines Johnson*, Boston: Twaynes, 1986, pp. 208–42.

27 This, in turn, has made the system suceptable to political interference and 'academic drift'. Such problems are evident, it is argued, in the teaching of anti-industrial attitudes and a disregard for the realities of economic life. Such arguments found substantial support from the popular press, which used it at local and national levels as a lever for educational reform, and as a scapegoat for youth unemployment and economic decline. Consequently, the New Right strenuously tried to undermine the ideology of meritocracy and to suggest that providing opportunities for working-class students was best achieved through market forces, rather than a state-regulated competition in a unified system. However, some state involvement in meritocratic competition is both necessary and desirable. The state must try to neutralise the impact of any social circumstances which may place students at an unfair disadvantage. This must involve limiting the opportunities for parents to buy

a better education than could be obtained by other children. This not only served to legitimate inequalities in adult life, but served to provide an efficient way of tapping into the supply of talent, given that this supply is consistently shown by social researchers to be randomly distributed. Therefore, in order for nations to tap this wealth of talent it is essential to nurture the growth potential of all students irrespective of social background, gender or race (see Part III).

28 Although education under primitive capitalism was presented as a 'big' idea, it harboured the same faith Lyndon Johnson's placed in the ability of the education system to resolve social and economic problems.

29 National Commission on Excellence in Education, *A Nation at Risk*, Washington DC: National Commission on Excellence in Education, 1983, p. 5.

30 Eric Hanushek, 'The economics of schooling: production and efficiency in public schools', *Journal of Economic Literature*, XVIV, Sept., 1141–77.

31 John Chubb and Terry Moe, *Politics, Markets and America's Schools*, Washington DC: The Brookings Institute, 1990.

32 Roger Scruton, *The Meaning of Conservatism*, London: Macmillan, 1984, p. 157

33 Charles Murray and R. J. Herrnstein, 'What's really behind the SAT-score decline', *The Public Interest*, No.106, 1992, 32–56, p. 56.

34 Theodore, W. Schulz, 'Investment in Human Capital', *American Economic Review*, vol. 51, 1961, 1–17, p. 15.

35 Hugh Lauder, 'Education, democracy and economy', in A. H. Halsey, H. Lauder, P. Brown and A. S. Wells, (eds) *Education: Culture, Economy and Society*, Oxford: Oxford University Press, 1997.

36 Phillip Brown, 'Cultural capital and social exclusion: some observations on recent trends in education, employment and the labour market', in A. H. Halsey, H. Lauder, P. Brown and A. S. Wells, (eds) *Education: Culture, Economy and Society*.

37 Michael W. Apple, *Cultural Politics and Education*, Buckingham: Open University Press, 1996; Stanley Aronowitz and Henry A. Giroux, *Education Under Siege*, London: Routledge and Keegan Paul, 1986; Stephen Ball, *Education Reform: A Critical and Post-Structuralist Approach*, Buckingham: Open University Press, 1994.

38 Mark Blaug, *An Introduction to the Economics of Education*, New York: Penguin, 1970, p. 4.

39 Phillip Brown 'Education and the ideology of parentocracy', *British Journal of the Sociology of Education*, 11, 1990, p. 65. See also Hugh Lauder, David Hughes and colleagues, *Trading in Futures*, Buckingham: Open University Press, 1999.

40 See Geoff Whitty, Sally Power and David Halpin, *Devolution and Choice in Education*, Buckingham: Open University Press, 1998.

41 Robert Reich *The Work of Nations*, London: Simon and Shuster, 1991.

42 Phillip Brown 'Education and the ideology of parentocracy', *British Journal of the Sociology of Education* (n. 39 above).

43 See Linda Darling-Hammond 'Restructuring schools for student success' and Harry Torrance, 'Assessment, accountability and standards: using assessment to control the reform of schooling', both in A. H. Halsey, H. Lauder, P. Brown and A. S.Wells, (eds) *Education: Culture, Economy and Society* (n. 35 above).

44 The die-hard Right will always protest that their reforms did not go far enough, that they were blocked by vested interests or sheer inertia. But

these are the last gambits of people who have seen their interpretation of the world fail when tested against reality. Proof, if ever it were needed, comes from New Zealand which has travelled further and faster down the Right path than any other nation. Here is a small country which discarded its highly protectionist economic policies in favour of an almost wholly open economy. Market principles were established in every corner of society. The consequence: a country socially divided with the most rapid polarization of income of any western society and after an initial spurt in economic growth after the introduction of the 'reforms' a return to a low growth path. So disaffected with these policies were the people of New Zealand that they voted for a new system of voting to block the further marketisation of their society. For an analysis of New Zealand see Jane Kelsey, *The New Zealand Experiment: A World Model for Structural Adjustment?* Auckland: Auckland University Press, 1995; John Quiggin, 'Social democracy and market reform in Australia and New Zealand', *Oxford Review of Economic Policy*, 14, 1998, 76–95.

9 Downsizing the Corporations

1 Rosabeth Moss Kanter, *When Giants Learn to Dance*, 1989, London: Unwin, p. 9–10.
2 Thomas K. McCraw, 'The trouble with Adam Smith', *The American Scholar*, 1992, Summer, p. 371. See also Chalmers Johnson, 'Comparative capitalism: the Japanese difference', *California Management Review*, 1993, Summer, pp. 51–67
3 Mahmou Ezzmel, Simon Lilley and Hugh Wilmo, 'Be wary of new waves' *Management Today*, 1993, October, 100–102.
4 David Harvey, *The Conditions of Post-Modernity: An Enquiry into the Origins of Cultural Change*, Oxford: Blackwell, 1989, p. 187.
5 John Hoerr, 'System crash: how workers at IBM learned that knowledge isn't power', *The American Prospect*, 1994, Winter, 68–77.
6 Robert Reich, *The Next American Frontier*, New York: Penguin Books, 1984, p. 141.
7 Robert Hayes and William Abernathy 'Managing our way to economic decline', *Harvard Business Review* 1980, July/August, 67–77, p. 68.
8 Simon Caulkin 'Manufacturing dead but not buried', *The Guardian*, March 27, 1993.
9 See *International Herald Tribune*, March 6, 1996, also reported in Hans-Peter Martin and Harald Schumann, *The Global Trap: Globalization and the Assult on Prosperity and Democracy*, trans. by Patrick Camiller, New York: Zed Books, 1997, p. 120.
10 See Harvey Robbins and Michael Finley, *TransCompetition: Moving Beyond Competition and Collaboration*, New York: BusinessWeek Books, 1998, p. 203. The referenced source of this figure is not given.
11 See Brendan J. Burchell, Diana Day, Maria Hudson, David Ladipo, Roy Mankelow, Jane P. Nolan, Hannah Reed, Ines C. Wichert and Frank Wilkinson, *Job Insecurity and Work Intensification: Flexibility and the Changing Boundaries of Work*, York: Joseph Rowntree Foundation, 1999, p. 21.

12   Michael Useem 'Business restructuring and the aging workforce', in J. A. Auerbach (ed.) *Through a Glass Darkly: Building the New Workplace for the 21st Century*, Washington, DC: National Policy Association, 1998, p. 27.

13   Reported in Aneil Mishra and Karen Mishra 'The role of mutual trust in effective downsizing strategies', *Human Resource Management*, 33, 1994, 261–79, p. 262.

14   *The Economist* 'The year downsizing grew up', December 21, 1996.

15   See Sue Dopson, Keith Ruddle and Rosemary Stewart, 'Mastering global business: from downsizing to revitalisation', *Financial Times*, February 27, 1998; also *The Economist*, 'The year downsizing grew up', December 21, 1996.

16   Roger Cohen 'The very model of efficiency, *The New York Times*, March 2, 1992.

17   ibid.; see also Aneil Mishra and Karen Mishra 'The role of mutual trust in effective downsizing strategies', *Human Resource Management* (n.13 above).

18   Reported in 'Public service, private profit', *Labour Research*, 1994, 13–14.

19   Reported in 'Business in Europe', *The Economist*, November 23, 1996, 3–22, p. 6.

20   Bruce Posner and Lawrence Rothstein 'Reinventing the business of government: an interview with change catalyst David Osborne', *Harvard Business Review*, 1994, May/June, 133–43, p. 134. See also Ted Gaebler and David Osborne, *Reinventing Government: How the Entrepreneurial Spirit is Transforming the Public Sector*, New York: Addison-Wesley, 1992.

21   Bruce Posner and Lawrence Rothstein 'Reinventing the business of government: an interview with change catalyst David Osborne', *Harvard Business Review*, p. 137.

22   Ian Johnson, 'Civil servants join the real world', *Management Today*, 1996, March. Also see 'Treasury seeks changed image', *The Guardian* October 20, 1994; 'Clark to slash back Treasury' October 18, *The Guardian* 1994; 'Essayist wins job as DTI's hit man', *The Guardian* January 27, 1994.

23   See John Atkinson, 'The changing corporation', in D. Clutterbuck (ed.) *New Patterns of Work*, Aldershot: Gower, 1985.

24   Bennett Harrison and Barry Bluestone, *The Great U-Turn: Corporate Restructuring and the Polarizing of America*, New York: Basic Books, 1988, p. 22.

25   See 'Sale of the century', *Fortune*, February 17, 1997, 42–8, p. 45.

26   All these figures are derived from Shaifali Puri's listing 'Deals of the year', *Fortune*, February 17, 1997, pp. 50–1.

27   See Alan Cane, Cathy Newman and Peter Thal Larsen, 'NTL wins fight to dominate UK cable industry', *Financial Times*, July 27, 1999.

28   Manfred, F. R. Kets de Vries and Katharina Balazs, 'The downside of downsizing', *Human Relations*, vol. 50, 11–50, p. 12.

29   Richard Waters, 'Return of the downsizers: corporate America is experiencing another wave of job cuts', *Financial Times*, December 19, 1997.

30   ibid.

31   In Kim Clark, 'These *are* the good old days', *Fortune*, June 9, 1997, 26–35, p. 28.

32   Reported in Hans-Peter Martin and Harald Schumann, *The Global Trap: Globalization and the Assult on Prosperity and Democracy* (n. 9 above).

33   ibid., pp. 104–7. There is no figure given for American insurance companies.

34   ibid., p. 103.

35 Lester C. Thurow, *Head to Head: The Coming Economic Battle among Japan, Europe and America*, London: Nicholas Brealey, 1993, p. 175.

36 John Hoerr, 'System crash: how workers at IBM learned that knowledge isn't power', *The American Prospect*, 1994, Winter, 68–77, pp. 76–7.

37 See 'Jobs: a survey', *Newsweek*, June 14, 1993, 10–25. Virginia L. duRivage, 'Flexibility trap: the proliferation of marginal jobs', *The American Prospect*, 1992, Spring, 84–93.

38 Nigel Nicholson and Michael West, *Managerial Job Change: Men and Women in Transition*, Cambridge: Cambridge University Press, 1988; Richard Scase and Rob Goffee, *Reluctant Managers: Their Work and Lifestyles*, London: Routledge, 1989; Richard Sennett, *The Corrosion of Character: The Personal Consequences of Work in the New Capitalism*, New York: W. W. Norton, 1998.

39 See Rosabeth Moss Kanter, *When Giants Learn to Dance*, London: Unwin, 1989; However, see Richard Sennett, *The Corrosion of Character: The Personal Consequences of Work in the New Capitalism*, New York: W. W. Norton, 1998; J.A. Auerbach (ed.) *Through a Glass Darkly: Building the New Workplace for the 21st Century*, Washington, DC: National Policy Association, 1998.

40 Manfred Kets de Vries and Katharina Balazs, 'The downside of downsizing', *Human Relations*, vol. 50, 11–50, p. 16.

41 See Phillip Brown and Richard Scase, *Higher Education and Corporate Realities*, London: University College London Press, 1994.

42 Wallace, C. Peterson, *Silent Depression: The Fate of the American Dream*, New York: W. W. Norton, 1994, p. 64.

43 See *Sunday Washington Post*, September 27, 1998, p. A06; Steve Macko, 'H1–B workers visa bill "wrong headed"', Emergency Response & Research Institute, at http://www.emergency.com.

44 See Brendan J. Burchell, Diana Day, Maria Hudson, David Ladipo, Roy Mankelow, Jane P. Nolan, Hannah Reed, Ines C. Wichert and Frank Wilkinson, *Job Insecurity and Work Intensification: Flexibility and the Changing Boundaries of Work*, York: Joseph Rowntree Foundation, 1999, p. 20; James, A. Auerbach and Richard S. Belous (eds) *The Inequality Paradox: Growth of Income Disparity*, Washington, DC: National Policy Association, 1998.

45 ibid., p. 20.

46 Barbara Ehrenreich, *Fear of Falling: The Inner Life of the Middle Class*, New York: Pantheon, 1989.

47 George Church in *Time*, November 22, 1993, 30–4, p. 31.

48 UK Department for Education and Employment (DfEE), *Labour Market and Skill Trends 1998/99*, London: Department of Education and Employment, 1998.

49 Kristina J. Shelley, 'The future of jobs for college graduates', *Monthly Labor Review*, 115, 1992, July, 13–21, p. 13.

50 Reported in Richard Waters 'Return of the downsizers: corporate America is experiencing another wave of job cuts', *Financial Times*, December 19, 1997; 'The year downsizing grew up', *The Economist*, December 21, 1996.

51 See also Richard W. Judy and Carol D'Amico, *Workforce 2020: Work and Workers in the 21st Century*, Indianapolis, Indiana, 1998, p. 78.

52 John Goldthorpe, with Catriona Llewellyn and Cllive Payne, *Social Mobility and Class Structure in Modern, Britain* (2nd edn), Oxford: Clarendon, 1987, p. 333.

53 Charles Heckscher, 'Can business beat bureaucracy?' *The American Prospect*, 1991, Spring, 114–28; Bennett Harrison and Maryellen R. Kelley, 'Outsourcing and the search for 'flexibility', *Work, Employment and Society*, 7, 1993, 213–35.

54 See Phillip Brown and Richard Scase, *Higher Education and Corporate Realities*, London: University College London Press, 1994; Phillip Brown, 'Cultural capital and social exclusion: some observations on recent trends in education, employment and the labour market', *Work, Employment and Society*, 9, 1995, 29–51.

55 'Coverstory', *Time*, November 22, 1993, 30–4, p. 31.

56 Katherine Newman, 'Uncertain seas: cultural turmoil and the domestic economy', in A. Wolfe (ed.) *America at Century's End*, Berkeley: University of California Press, 1991, p. 128.

57 Jeremy Myerson 'The end of 9 to 5?' *The Guardian*, December 3, 1993.

58 Mark Tran 'Digital shows a loss of $671m', *The Guardian*, July 26, 1991.

59 ibid.;Kim Cameron 'Guest editor's note: investigating organizational downsizing – fundamental issues', *Human Resource Management* , vol. 33, 1994, 183–8, p. 184.

60 ibid., p. 184.

61 ibid., p. 183

62 See Jane Martinson 'A hurrying sickness: fund managers love the fashion for global consolidation', *Financial Times,* December 10, 1997.

63 See Angela Briggins 'Perform or perish!' *Management Review*, vol. 86 1997. But most revealing was the short-term perspective of both sets of executives, with only 35 per cent of European executives planning to remain in their current position for only a year or two, although of course this does not necessarily mean that they will change companies, while the figure for US executives was 28 per cent.

64 See *Industry Week*, vol. 246, April 7, 1997.

65 Reported in George Church 'And it hurts: The US outruns the world, but some workers are left behind', Time Magazine, October 24, 1994, p. 56.

66 Tom Brown 'Sweatshops of the 1990s: employees who 'survived' downsizing are working harder and longer these days', *Management Review*, vol. 85, 1996. Brown states that 'Taken literally, the comment is absurd. 'Sweatshop' is 19th-century terminology describing workers forced to endure long hours at millstone work accompanied by wretched work conditions and low pay. In England in the 1850s, a "sweater" was an employer or middleman who hired cheap labor, then abused them with deadly, monotonous work.'

67 ibid.

68 Manfred Kets de Vries and Katharina Balazs 'The downside of downsizing', *Human Relations*, vol. 50, 11–50, p. 27.

69 Victor Keegan 'Economics notebook: special pleading cannot hide UK's industrial failure', *Sunday Observer*, June 27, 1994.

70 *Financial Times*, May 14, 1996.

71 See John Holusha, 'A softer 'neutron Jack' at G.E.' *The New York Times*, March 4, 1992.

72 Anne Fisher, 'The world's most admired companies', *Fortune*, 1997, 40–58. p. 52.

73 For a discussion of the difference between downsizing as a measure of workforce reduction and systemic cultural change, see Kim Cameron 'Strategies

for successful organisational downsizing', *Human Resource Management*, 33, 1994, 189–212; Peter Cappelli, Lauri Bassi, Harry C. Katz, David Knoke, Paul Osterman, and Michael Useem, *Change at Work*, New York: Oxford University Press, 1997.

74 P.A. Geroski and P. Gregg, *Coping with Recession: UK Company Performance in Adversity*, Cambridge: Cambridge University Press, 1997.

10   The Demise of Industrial Man

1 Robert Eisner, 'Damn the NAIRU – and full speed ahead', in J. J. Jasinowski (ed.) *The Rising Tide*, New York: John Wiley & Sons, 1998, p. 68.

2 Gordon Brown's speech at the Annual Labour Party Conference in Bournemouth, September 1999. See http://www.labour.org.uk/lp/new/labour/docs/

3 See *Social Trends 1998*, London: Central Statistical Office, 1998, p. 81; Frances Sly 'Women in the labour market: results from the spring 1995 labour force survey', *Labour Market Trends*, London: Government Statistical Service, 1996 March p. 94.

4 The scale of 'contingent' work in both America and Britain is underestimated given the criteria used to categorize workers. See Bureau of Labour Statistics, 'Contingent and alternative employment arrangements, February 1997 at http://stats.bls.gov/news.release/conemp.nws.htm. The BLS define 'on-call' workers are those who are called to work only as needed, although they can be scheduled to work for several days or weeks in a row.

5 Frances Sly, 'Women in the labour market: results from the spring 1995 labour force survey', (n. 3 above), p. 91.

6 See UK Department of Education and Employment (DfEE) report *Labour Market and Skills Trends 1998/9*, London: DfEE, 1998, p. 5.

7 Bureau of Labour Statistics (BLS) 'Employment by major industry division, 1986, 1996 and projected to 2006', at http://stats.bls.gov/news.release/ecopro.table2.htm. This category includes 'self-employed and unpaid family workers'. See also BLS *Monthly Labor Review*, November, 1997.

8 See John Hills, *Income and Wealth: Volume Two, A Summary of the Evidence*, York: Joseph Rowntree Foundation, 1995.

9 Department of Education and Employment (DfEE) *Labour Market and Skill Trends*, Sudbury, Suffolk: DfEE Publications, 1998, p. 5.

10 Institute for Employment Research, *Review of the Economy and Employment*, University of Warwick, 1999, p. 1.

11 US Bureau of Labor Statistics, Employment and Earnings, Table No.659 Statistical Abstracts of the United States, 1998, on-line at www.census.gov/stabab See also Labor Force Statistics from the Current Population Survey, Bureau of Labor Statistics, 'Work experience of the population during the year by sex and extent of employment, 1996–97' at http://stats.bls.gov/news.release/work.t01.htm. Part-time work is defined by BLS as usually 1–34 hours per week.

12 This figure is calculated by Charles Handy based on the assumption that the average worker in Northern Europe in the smokestack era worked on average 47 hours a week (including overtime) for 47 weeks of a year for 47 years of

their life from the age of 18–65, give or take a few! Charles Handy, *The Age of Unreason*, Hutchinson: London, 1989, p. 34–9.

13 ibid., p. 38. Handy also shows that half of the three 47s equates to 37 37 37   50 653.

14 ibid., p. 38.

15 These are based on seasonally adjusted, standardised International Labour Organisation (ILO) rates for the middle of 1999. See *Labour Market Trends*, Office of National Statistics, London: The Stationary Office, 1999.

16 Based on unemployment figures for the second quarter of 1995 when the total unemployment rate was 5.7 and the rate for youths was 17.2 per cent. See OECD *Economic Survey: United States 1995*, Paris: OECD.

17 Bureau of Labor Statistics (BLS) 'Employment situation summary – September 1999. The jobless rate for whites was 3.6 per cent, blacks 8.3 per cent and Hispanics 6.7 per cent: http://stats.bls.gov/news.release/empsit.nws.htm; 1999.

18 Cited by John Philpott, Employment Policy Institute (EPI), from the EPI Audit, Introductory Address to the In Search of Work Conference, London, June,1998.

19 John Hills, *The Future of Welfare*, York: Joseph Rowntree Foundation, 1993, p. 34.

20 These figures are taken from *OECD Economic Survey: United States 1995*, Paris: OECD, 1996, p. 206.

21 Editorial, 'Labour makets in the 1990s', *OECD Observer*, 1990, Oct/Nov.

22 Richard Freeman, 'The limits of wage flexibility to curing unemployment', *Oxford Review of Economic Policy*, vol. 11, 1995, 63–72; and also *When Earnings Diverge: Causes, Consequences, and Cures for the New Inequality in the US*, Washington, DC: National Policy Association, 1997.

23 See Paul Duggan, 'Youth feel the force of a vow kept', *The Washington Post*, November 9, 1999.

24 Criminal supervision is designed as parole or incarceration, *OECD Economic Report: United States 1995*, Paris: OECD, 1996, p. 149.

25 ibid., p. 150.

26 David Rose, 'Shattered dream of British justice', *The Observer*, November 17, 1996.

27 The US figures are take from '*Projections of Education Statistics to 2008*', at http://nces.ed.gov/pubs98/pj20008/p98c02.html, 1999. The British figures are from Department of Education and Employment (DfEE) *Labour Market and Skill Trends* (n. 9 above).

28 Sara S. McLanahan, 'The conseuqences of single motherhood, *American Prospect*, vol. 18, 1994, Summer, 48–58, p. 53.

29 Giving a total of 48.3 per cent. See Maya Federman et al. 'What does it mean to be poor in America?' *Monthly labour Review*, 1996 May, 3–17, p. 16.

30 Christopher Ogden, 'Bye-bye, American pie', *Time*, August 12, 1996, p. 19.

31 Sara S. McLanahan,'The consequences of single motherhood', *American Prospect* (n. 28 above), p. 57. Meanwhile it is estimated that the difference between what fathers could pay and do pay is about $34 billion.

32 Barry Hugill, 'Welfare hits state of crisis', *The Observer,* March 3, 1996. See also Alan Walker and Carol Walker, (eds) *Britain Divided: The Growth of Social Exclusion in the 1980s and 1990s*, London: Child Poverty Action Group, 1997.

33 See John Hills, *Income and Wealth: Volume Two, A Summary of the Evidence*, York: Joseph Rowntree Foundation, 1995, p. 22.

34 Paul Gregg and Jonathan Wadsworth, 'More work in fewer households?', in J. Hills (ed.) *New Inequalities*, Cambridge: Cambridge University Press, 1996, p. 182. Equally, in Britain only about half of families in the early 1990s included a full-time worker, compared to 65 per cent of families in 1979. This figure excludes those who were self-employed given the way the table was constructed. See Table 1 in Paul Johnson, 'The assessment: inequality', *Oxford Review of Economic Policy*, vol. 12, 1996, 1–14, p. 4.

35 See March 1999 Current Population Survey, United States Department of Commerce, http://www.census.gov/press-release/www/1999/cb99–188.html

36 Sara S. McLanahan, 'The consequences of single motherhood', *American Prospect*, (n. 28 above), p. 48.

37 Lawrence Mishel, Jared Bernstein and John Schmitt, *The State of Work in America*, Ithaca, NY: Cornell University Press, 1998, in Lester C. Thurow, *Building Wealth: The New Rules for Individuals, Companies, and Nations in a Knowledge-Based Economy*, New York: HarperCollins, 1999, pp. 42–3.

38 OECD *Employment Outlook*, Paris: OECD, 1996 July, see chart 3.3, p. 67. It should be remembered that the OECD is dependent on government statistical agencies providing the data it compiles. This should make the reader wary about the status of some of the data provided.

39 Amanda Gosling, Stephen Machin and Costas Meghir, 'What has happened to the wages of men since 1966?', in J.Hills (ed.) *New Inequalities*, Cambridge: Cambridge University Press, 1996.

40 Randy E. Llg, 'The nature of employment growth, 1989–95', *Monthly Labor Review*, 1996 June, 29–36. These figures are derived from Table one, p. 30.

41 Wolfgang Streeck, 'German capitalism: does it exist? can it survive?', *New Political Economy*, 2, 1997, 237–56; Income Data Servises (IDS) *New Unionism: Wither or Whither?*, No.91, 1999 September.

42 See Brendan J. Burchell, Diana Day, Maria Hudson, David Ladipo, Roy Mankelow, Jane P. Nolan, Hannah Reed, Ines C. Wichert and Frank Wilkinson, *Job Insecurity and Work Intensification*, York: Joseph Rowntree Foundation, 1999, pp. 34–6.

43 Andrew M. Sum, Neal Fogg and Robert Taggart, 'The economics of despair', *American Prospect*, vol. 27 1996 July/August, 83–8, p. 83.

44 ibid., p. 84. See also OECD *Employment Outlook*, Paris: OECD, 1996 July, especially chapter 4 'Growing into work: youth and the labour market over the 1980s and 1990s'.

45 Andrew M. Sum, Neal Fogg and Robert Taggart, 'The economics of despair', *American Prospect*, vol. 27 1996 July/August, 83–8, p. 84.

46 OECD *Employment Outlook*, Paris: OECD, 1996 July, especially chapter 4 (see n. 44 above), p. 139. The OECD however warn of the problems involved in compiling and interpreting these data.

47 See Department of Commerce, *21st Century Skills for 21st Century Jobs*, Washington, DC: Department of Commerce, 1999, p. 8, http://vpskillsummit.gov.

48 OECD, *Economic Survey: United States*, Paris: OECD, 1995, p. 114. see also See OECD *Lifelong Learning for All*, Paris: OECD, 1996, pp. 309–12.

49   Andrew M. Sum, Neal Fogg and Robert Taggart, 'The economics of despair', *American Prospect*, (n. 43 above), p. 83.

50   Lester C. Thurow, *Building Wealth*, (n. 37 above), p. 42.

51   See John Schmitt and Jonathan Wadsworth, 'The rise in economic inactivity' in Andrew Glyn and David Miliband (eds) *Paying for Inequality*, London: IPPR, 1994; Alan Walker and Carol Walker, (eds) *Britain Divided: The Growth of Social Exclusion in the 1980s and 1990s* (n. 32 above).

52   OECD *Lifelong Learning for All*, Paris: OECD, 1996, p. 310.

53   ibid., p. 226.

54   Lynn A. Karoly, 'Anatomy of the US income distribution: two decades of change', *Oxford Review of Economic Policy*, vol. 12, 76–94, 1996, p. 92.

55   See OECD *Economic Survey: United States*, Paris: OECD, 1995, p. 206.

56   See Randy E. Llg, 'The nature of employment growth, 1989–95', *Monthly Labor Review*, 1996 June, 29–36, p. 33.

57   Bureau of Labour Statistics '1996–2006 Employment Projections', http://stats.bls.gov/news.release/ecopro.nws.htm, 1999. They predict that professional specialty occupations will increase the fastest and add the most jobs – 4.8 million. Service workers are also expected to grow by 3.9 million jobs, 'These two groups – on opposite ends of the educational attainment and earnings spectrum – are expected to provide 46 percent of total projected job growth over the 1996–2006 period'.

58   Carole Pateman, *The Disorder of Women: Democracy, Feminism and Political Theory*, Cambridge: Polity Press, 1989.

59   ibid., p. 196.

60   Institute of Employment Research (IER), *Review of the Economy and Employment 1998/9*, University of Warwick, IER, 1999, p. 4.

61   Marilyn French, *The War Against Women*, New York: Summit Books, 1992, p. 13.

62   Joseph Rowntree Foundation, *Inquiry into Income and Wealth*, vol. 1, York: Joseph Rowntree Founation, 1995, p. 22.

63   Bureau of Labour Statistics '1996–2006 Employment Projections' (n. 57 above).

64   The British figures are from Department of Education and Employment (DfEE) *Labour Market and Skill Trends* (n. 9 above), p. 7.

65   Hilary Land, 'The demise of the male breadwinner – in practice but not in theory: a challenge for social security systems', in Sally Baldwin & Jane Falkingham (eds) *Social Security and Social Change*, London: Harvester Wheatsheaf, 1994, p. 110.

66   Andrew M. Sum, Neal Fogg and Robert Taggart, 'The economics of despair', *American Prospect*, vol. 27 1996 July/August, 83–8, p. 84.

67   Paul Johnson, 'The assessment: inequality', *Oxford Review of Economic Policy*, vol. 12, 1996, 1–14, p. 9; See also Alissa Goodman, Paul Johnson and Steven Webb, *Inequality in the UK*, Oxford: Oxford University Press, 1997. See also *Social Trends 1998*, London: Central Statistical Office, 1998.

68   Teresa Rees, *Mainstreaming Equality in the European Union: Education, Training and Labour Markets Policies*, London: Routledge, 1998.

69   Department of Education and Employment (DfEE) *Labour Market and Skill Trends* (n. 9 above), p. 11. The figures for clerical and secretarial jobs were 76.5 per cent in 1997 and 73.8 per cent in 2007. The comparable figures for women in managerial and administrative occupations were 34.8 per cent and 39 per cent respectively.

70 See OECD *Employment Outlook*, Paris: OECD, 1996 July, p. 192.

71 Arnlaug Leira, 'Combining work and family: working mothers in Scandinavia and the European Community', in P. Brown and R. Crompton (eds) *Economic Restructuring and Social Exclusion*, London: University College London Press, 1994.

72 Kathleen Gerson, 'Coping with commitment: dilemmas and conflicts of family life', in Alan Wolfe, (ed.) *America at Century's End*, Berkeley: University of California Press, 1991, p. 37.

73 Sara S. McLanahan, 'The consequence of single motherhood', *American Prospect* (n. 28 above), p. 55.

74 ibid., p. 53.

75 All these figures are taken from *Social Trends*, vol. 26, London: Central Statistical Office, 1996.

76 See Lynn A. Karoly, 'Anatomy of the US income distribution: two decades of change', *Oxford Review of Economic Policy*, vol. 12, 1996, 76–95, p. 77.

77 See US Census Bureau, Statistical Abstracts of the United States 1998, www.census.gov/stabab

78 Judith Stacey, 'Backward toward the postmodern family: reflections on gender, kinship, and class in the silicon valley', in Alan Wolfe (ed.) *America at Century's End*, Berkeley: University of California Press, 1991, p. 19. See also her *Brave New Families: Stories of Domestic Upheaval in Late Twentieth Century America*, New York: Basic Books, 1991.

79 This quotation from Delia Ephron is used as an epigraph in Judith Stacey's *Brave New Families*, p. 61.

80 Judith Stacey, 'Backward toward the postmodern family: reflections on gender, kinship, and class in the silicon valley', in Alan Wolfe (ed.) *America at Century's End*, p. 32.

81 ibid., p. 32.

82 Kathleen Gerson, 'Coping with commitment: dilemmas and conflicts of family life', in Alan Wolfe, (ed.) *America at Century's End* p. 40.

83 ibid., p. 42

84 Sara S. McLanahan, 'The consequences of single motherhood', *The American Prospect* (n. 28 above), p. 50.

85 ibid., p. 49.

86 Judith Stacey, 'Backward toward the postmodern family: reflections on gender, kinship, and class in the silicon valley', in Alan Wolfe (ed.) *America at Century's End* (n. 78 above), p. 26.

87 R. W. Connell, 'The big picture: masculinities in recent world history', *Theory and Society*, vol. 22, 1993, 597–623, p. 613.

11 A False Start

1 For a discussion of the 'third way' see Anthony Giddens, *The Third Way: The Renewal of Social Democracy*, Cambridge: Polity Press, 1998; See also Stephen Driver & Luke Martell, *New Labour: Politics after Thatcherism*, Cambridge: Polity Press, 1998; Joel Krieger, *British Politics in the Global Age*, Cambridge: Polity Press, 1999.

2   Gordon Brown, Chancellor of the Exchequer for New Labour in Britain. This is taken from a speech made at the Annual Party Conference in Bournemouth, September, 1999. See http://www.labour.org.uk

3   UK government White Paper: *Our Competitive Future: Building the Knowledge Driven Economy*, London: DTI, 1998, p. 11. See http://www.dti.gov.uk

4   'They are All Our Children' Speech delivered at East Los Angeles College, Los Angeles, May 14th, 1992.

5   Michael E. Porter, *The Competitive Advantage of Nations*, London: Macmillan, 1990; David S. Landes, *The Wealth and Poverty of Nations*, New York: W. W. Norton; Lester C. Thurow, *Head to Head: The Coming Economic Battle Among Japan, Europe and America*, London: Nicholas Brealey, 1993.

6   See for example David Ashton and Francis Green, *Education, Training and the Global Economy*, Cheltenham: Edward Elgar, 1996 and also Manuel Castells, *End of Millennium*, Oxford: Blackwell, 1998.

7   Manuel Castells, 'Information Technology and Global Capitalism', in Will Hutton and Anthony Giddens (eds) *On the Edge: Living with Global Capitalism*, London: Jonathan Cape, 2000; Jerry J. Jasinowski (ed.) *The Rising Tide*, New York: John Wiley, 1998; S. Weber, 'The end of the business cycle?' *Foreign Affairs*, July August, 74, 4, pp. 65–82.

8   See also Lester Thurow, *Building Wealth*, New York: HarperCollins, 1999.

9   These figures are cited in Stephen Bond and Tim Jenkinson, 'The assessment: investment performance and policy', *Oxford Review of Economic Policy*, 1996, 12, 1–29.

10   These figures are from Lester C. Thurow, *Head to Head: The Coming Economic Battle Amond Japan, Europe and America*, Nicolas Brealey: London,1993, p. 127, and the later figures from the International Federation of Robotics, reported in the *Financial Times* March 6, 1998. The leading countries are Japan, Singapore, Korea and Germany.

11   Here modest progress has been made in Britain where Gordon Brown the Chancellor of the Exchequer commissioned a review of the banking system 'to ensure that big institutions cannot hold back small business from investing, growing and creating jobs'. See his speech made at the Annual Party Conference in Bournemouth, September, 1999. See http://www.labour.org.uk

12   For a recent international analysis of this view see, *Gosta Esping-Anderen, Social Foundations of Postindustrial Economies*, New York: Oxford University Press, 1999.

13   Wiji Arulampalam and Alison Booth, *Labour Market Flexibility and Skills Acquisition: is There a Trade Off?*, Institute of Labour Research, University of Essex, UK, 1997.

14   ibid., p. 2.

15   F. Green, S. Machin and D. Wilkinson, *Trade Unions and Training Practices in British Workplaces*, mimeo, London: Centre for Economic Performance, London School of Economics, London, No. 278, 1996.

16   Michael J. Piore, 'Labor standards and business strategies', in S. Herzenberg and J. Perez-Lopez (eds) *Labor Standards and Development in the Global Economy*, Washington, DC: US Department of Labor, 1990.

17   Werner Sengenberger and Frank Wilkinson, 'Globalization and labour standards', in J. Michie and J.G. Smith (eds) *Managing the Global Economy*, Oxford: Oxford University Press, 1995.

18 OECD, *Employment Outlook*, Paris: OECD, 1994.

19 There has been a 21 per cent increase in the national minimum wage over 1996–1997 in the United States without loss of jobs: *The Guardian*, May 4, 1998. However this needs to set against the decline in the real minimum wages in the United States during the 1980s when it fell by 44 per cent. See Peter Gottschalk and Timothy M. Smeeding, 'cross-national comparisons of earnings and income inequality', *Journal of Economic Literature*, vol. xxxv, 1997, 633–87. The floor of the minimum wage and protective rights espoused by the Modernisers is likely to be too weak to act as an incentive to employers to upgrade the skill level of work. See Robert Kuttner's paper in D. Miliband (ed.) *Reinventing the Left*, Cambridge: Polity, 1994.

20 *Financial Times*, October 2, 1993.

21 Adrian Wood, *North-South Trade, Employment and Inequality: Changing Fortunes in a Skill-Driven World*, Oxford: Clarendon, 1994.

22 *The Economist*, October 18–24, 1997, p. 113.

23 It is argued, for example, that in a deregulated global finance market there is a shortage of investment funds, especially at times of growth. Now that there is the potential to invest in developing nations, as well as the developed nations, the competition for investment funds has increased dramatically. Also, in a global economy the business cycles of the developed and developing nations are likely to be more synchronised so that an economic upturn is likely to be met by a global demand for increased investment. See Robert Rowthorn, 'Capital formation and unemployment', *Oxford Review of Economic Policy*, 11, 1995, 26–39.

24 International Labour Organisation (ILO) *World Employment 1995*, Geneva: ILO, 1995.

25 ibid.; John Eatwell, 'The international origins of unemployment', in J. Michie & J.G. Smith (eds) *Managing the Global Economy* (n. 17 above).

26 Karen Gardiner, *A Survey of Income Inequality Over the Last Twenty Years – How Does the UK Compare?*, Welfare State Programme No. 100, Centre for Economics and Related Disciplines, London School of Economics, 1993; John Hills, *Income and Wealth – Volume Two A Summary of the Evidence*, York: Joseph Rowntree Foundation, 1995; OECD, *Employment Outlook*, Paris: OECD, 1993.

27 See Peter Gottschalk and Timothy Smeeding, 'Cross national comparisons of earnings and income inequality' (n. 19 above). Compare this account with Henry Levin and Carolyn Kelly, 'Can education do it alone?', in A. H. Halsey, Hugh Lauder, Phillip Brown and Amy Stuart Wells, (eds) *Education, Culture, Economy and Society*, Oxford: Oxford University Press, 1997. See also *Gosta Esping-Anderen, Social Foundations of Postindustrial Economies*, New York: Oxford University Press, 1999.

28 William Lazonick, 'Industry clusters versus global webs: organisational capabilities in the American economy', *Industrial and Corporate Change*, vol. 2, 1993, 1–24.

29 John Bound and George Johnson, 'What are the causes of rising wage inequality in the United States?' *Economic Policy Review*, Federal Reserve Bank of New York, vol. 1, 1995, 9–17.

30 Adrian Wood, *North-South Trade, Employment and Inequality: Changing Fortunes in a Skill-Driven World*, Oxford: Clarendon, 1994.

31 See Robert Reich, *The Next American Frontier*, New York: Penguin, 1984.

32   Employment Policy Institute, *Tax and the Winner Takes All Society*, vol. 10, Jan/Feb 1997, p. 2; Robert H. Frank and Philip J. Cook, *The Winner-Take-All Society*, New York: Penguin, 1996.

33   Amanda Gosling and Stephen Machin, *Trade Unions and the Dispersion of Earnings in UK Establishments, 1980–90*, Centre for Economic Performance Discussion Paper No. 140, London School of Economics, London, 1993. Mckinley L. Blackburn, David E. Bloom and Richard B. Freeman, 'The declining economic position of less skilled American men', in G. Burtless (ed.) *A Future of Lousy Jobs?* Washington, DC: Brookings Institute, 1990.

34   For a critical review of the school effectiveness literature see Hugh Lauder, Ian Jamieson and Felicity Wikeley, 'School effectiveness: limits and possibilities' in Roger Slee, Sally Tomlinson and Gaby Weiner, *Effective for Whom, Effective for What: Critical Perspectives on School Effectiveness Research*, London: Falmer Press, 1998.

35   Philip Brown, 'Cultural capital and social exclusion', in A. H. Halsey, Hugh Lauder, Phillip Brown and Amy Stuart Wells, (eds) *Education, Culture, Economy and Society*, Oxford University Press, Oxford, 1997; also 'The globalization of positional competition', *Sociology*, Spring 2001.

36   William Julius Wilson, *The Truly Disadvantaged*, Chicago: University of Chicago Press, 1990, p. 56.

37   Mike Davis, *City of Quartz*, New York: Verso, 1990.

38   See David Piachaud, 'Progress on poverty', *New Economy*, vol. 6, 1999, 154–60.

12   The Problem Restated

1   John Maynard Keynes, *Essays in Persuasion*, London: Macmillan, 1931, p. 369 then p. 372.The assumption that quality of life issues can only be attended to once the problem of wealth creation has been solved is an idea commonly found in the social sciences. For whereas Keynes believed that capitalism could deliver the good society, Karl Marx believed that this was only possible once capitalism had massively increased the wealth of nations and then been overthrown. But whereas Keynes was engaged in a Platonic 'noble lie' in the interests of future generations who will be delivered from the tunnel of economic necessity into daylight, Marx recognised 'commodity fetishism' as a grim con-trick deployed to maintain the exploitative interests of the ruling class.

2   Joseph Weizenbaum, *Computer Power and Human Reason: From Judgement to Calculation*, New York: Viking Penguin, 1984, p. 16. See also Hans Jonas, 'Technology and responsibility: reflections on the new tasks of ethics', *Social Research*, vol. 40, 1973, pp. 31–54.

Here we run into a fundamental problem which extends to how the quality of life itself is to be measured. The conventions relating to how paid work is rewarded conform to the accounting procedures of the economics profession. Although wiser heads understood very clearly the limitations of merely counting what was more easily measurable. 'The welfare of a nation can scarcely be inferred from a measurement of national income' wrote Simon Kuznets, one of the creators of national systems of accounting. The GNP and GDP are measured by the volume of goods and services bought and sold on the market but this is quite different from measuring the quality of life. Measures like GNP make no distinction between economic activities which may contribute to the overall quality of life and those which do not. The production of cigarettes and the treatment of cancer are both included in the calculation of economic health. This kind of social absurdity leads to the situation where the escalating costs involved in the treatment of pollution, whether it takes the form of chemical spills, measures to reduce air pollution in city centres, or the treatment of asthma sufferers, are all included as a contribution to economic growth. This led Krishan Kumar to surmise that we may not be far off the situation where what is counted as wealth creation is little more than a vast increase in pollution, environmental destruction and personal suffering, with the consequent expenditure of capital and labour to repair, maintain and renovate the physical, social and psychological fabric of the society. Thus 'if increases in productivity mean mainly the more and more intensive laundering of each other's dirty washing, we might reasonably begin to fear for the very survival of the clothes'. See Krishan Kumar, *The Rise of Modern Society*, Oxford: Blackwell, 1988, p. 66.

Research on the relationship between per capita income and quality of life, including environmental sustainability, show that in America and Britain measures of the quality of life tracked GDP until the mid-seventies and thereafter declined while GDP continued to rise (See T. Jackson, N. Marks, J. Ralls and S. Stymme, *Sustainable Economic Welfare in the UK, 1950–1996*, New Economic Foundation, Centre for Environmental Strategy, University of Surrey, 1997). This is hardly surprising given developments in the last two decades. For example, the secular decline in working hours throughout the twentieth century is now in reverse in the United States and Britain. Juliet Schor has suggested that there has been an 8 per cent increase in working hours over the last twenty years for both professional and service workers alike, as well as for both men and women. The increase in work pressures has not only been associated with problems of stress, anxiety and illness, but with a decline in the quality of family life. Between 1960 and 1986, for instance, the time per week parents had available to be with children fell between ten and twelve hours, a factor which has been linked to poor school performance, mental problems and drug abuse. See Juliet Schor, *The Overworked American*, New York: Basic Books, 1991.

3   Fred Block, *Postindustrial Possibilities: A Critique of Economic Discourse*, Berkeley: University of California, 1990, p. 3.
4   Richard Wilkinson, *Unhealthy Societies* London: Routledge, 1998, p. 226.
5   Smith, Adam, *An Inquiry into the Nature and Causes of the Wealth of Nations, Vol. 1*, edited by R. H. Campbell & W. B. Todd, Oxford: Clarendon Press, 1976, pp. 26–7.
6   Tony Blair, Reported in the *Financial Times*, May 22, 1995, p. 6.
7   Will Hutton, *The State to Come*, London: Vintage, 1997, p. 54
8   It is of course nonsensical to set the state and the market in oppositional terms as the market crucially depends on the significant state intervention to shape and maintain the viability of markets. See for example, Albert O. Hirschman, *Rival Views of Market Society and other Essays*, Cambridge, Mass.: Harvard University Press,1989; David Marquand, *The Unprincipled Society*, London: Jonathan Cape, 1988.

9   Anthony Smith, *Nations and Nationalism in a Global Era*, Cambridge: Polity, 1995, p. 147.

10 Paul Kennedy, *Preparing for the Twenty-First Century*, London: HarperCollins, 1993.

11 Anthony Smith, *Nations and Nationalism in a Global Era*, p. 150.

12 Naomi Klein, *No Logo*, New York: HarperCollins, 2000. See www.nologo.org

13 Paul Hirst, has an brief account of a federal structure of governance at the state level. See his *Associative Democracy*, Cambridge: Polity, 1994, p. 71. But as Mica Panic notes: 'The problem is, of course, that the day when nation states are ready to hand over sovereignty to a world authority, because it is much more likely to satisfy the economic and social aspirations of their citizens, belongs to a very distant future. Consequently, the critical issue in creating an effective supranational institutional framework is still the same as in 1944: how to make it worthwhile for a large number of countries at different levels of development, often with widely different problems and priorities, to collaborate in a way that makes all of them noticeably better off than they would have been otherwise.' Micra Panic, 'The Bretton Woods system: concept and practice', In N. Michie and J. Grieve Smith (eds) *Managing the Global Economy*, Oxford: Oxford University Press, 1995, p. 53.

14 Susan, Strange, 'The defective state', *Daedalus*, vol. 124, pp. 55–74.

15 Emile Durkheim, *The Division of Labour in Society*, trans. George Simpson, New York: Macmillan, 1933, Preface to the first edition, p. 37.

16 ibid., p. xlii.

17 ibid., p. 377.

18 ibid., p. 377

19 For a discussion of 'community of fate' see Tomas Matiesen, *Law, Society and Political Action: Towards a Strategy Under Late Capitalism*, London: Academic Press, 1980; Benedict Anderson, *Imagined Communities: Reflections on the Origins and Spread of Nationalism*, London: Verso, 1983.

20 Fred Block, *Postindustrial Possibilities: A Critique of Economic Discourse*, Berkeley: University of California, 1990, p. 75.

21 Alan Fox, *Beyond Contract* , London: Faber & Faber, 1974, p. 362–3

22 R. H. Tawney, in Norman Dennis and A. H. Halsey's *English Ethical Socialism*, Oxford: Oxford University Press, 1988, p. 223. Likewise, Charles, F. Sabel notes 'mistrust freezes technological progress while trust fosters it', see *Work and Politics*, Cambridge: Cambridge University Press, 1982, p. 226.

23 Giddens, Anthony, *Beyond Left and Right: The Future of Radical Politics*, Cambridge: Polity Press, 1994, p. 86.

13   Collective Intelligence

1   Robert Bellah et al., *Habits of the Heart*, Berkeley: University of California Press, 1985, p. 290.

2   See Charles F. Sabel, *Work and Politics*, Cambridge: Cambridge University Press, p. 244; a similar position is taken by Douglas McGregor in *The Human Side of Enterprise*, New York: McGraw-Hill, 1960.

3   'In this society of free competition the individual appears free from the bonds of nature, etc., which in former epochs of history made him a part of a definite, limited human conglomeration. To the prophets of the eighteenth century, on whose shoulders Smith and Ricardo are still standing, this eighteenth-century individual, constituting the joint product of the dissolution of the feudal form of society and of the new forces of production which had developed since the sixteenth century, appears as an ideal whose existence belongs to the past; not as a result of history, but as its starting point.
    Since the individual appeared to be in conformity with nature and [corresponded] to their conception of human nature, [he was regarded] not as a product of history, but of nature'. Karl Marx, 'A Contribution to the Critique of Political Economy', in T. Parsons et al. (eds) *Theories of Society*, Glencoe: Free Press, 1961, Vol. 1, p. 136–7.

4   Stephen Jay Gould, *The Mismeasure of Man*, London: Pelican, 1981.

5   This is known as the Flynn effect after James Flynn of the University of Otago in New Zealand. See his 'Massive IQ gains in 14 nations: what IQ tests really measure', *Psychological Bulletin*, pp. 171–91, 1987.

6   The scale of 'wastage' is in reality impossible to measure because 'talents' need to be cultivated as we will explain below, but clearly there is a huge untapped pool of visible and 'hidden' talent.

7   Samuel Bowles and Herbert Gintis, *Schooling in Capitalist America*, New York: Routledge, 1976.

8   Hugh Lauder and David Hughes, 'Social origins, destinations and educational inequality', in John Codd, Richard Harker and Roy Nash (eds) *Political Issues in New Zealand Education*, Dunmore Press: Palmerston North, 1990.

9   Claude Fischer, Michael Hout, Martin Sanchez Jankowski, Samuel Lucas, Ann Swidler and Kim Voss, *Inequality by Design: Cracking the Bell Curve Myth*, Princeton University Press: Princeton, 1996.

10 Of course, as these researchers point out, such calculations only tell half the story because they fail to explain the way that income, wealth and life-chances are embedded in the social structure.

11 See Michael Apple, *Cultural Politics and Education*, Buckingham: Open University Press, 1996; Martin Carnoy, *Faded Dreams: The Politics and Economics of Race in America*, Cambridge: Cambridge University Press, 1994; Phillip Brown, A. H. Halsey, Hugh Lauder and Amy Stuart Wells, 'The transformation of education and society: an introduction', in A. H. Halsey et al. (eds) *Education: Culture, Economy and Society*, Oxford: Oxford University Press, 1997.

12 Stephen Jay Gould, *The Mismeasure of Man*, London: Pelican, 1981.

13 Christopher Lasch, *The Revolt of the Elites: and the Betrayal of Democracy*, W. W. Norton: New York, 1995, p. 39.

14 John Dewey, '*Democracy and Education*', New York: Free Press, 1916, p. 344.

15 Perhaps the most telling point about the way our ability to develop more powerful mental capacities has evolved socially comes from the work of Ian Hacking who has shown how styles of reasoning have developed at specific times in history. He illustrates this through his study of the idea of probability in the nineteenth century. See *The Emergence of Probability*, Cambridge: Cambridge University Press, 1975 and *The Taming of Chance*, Cambridge: Cambridge University Press, 1990.

16 See Ulrich Beck, *Risk Society*, London: Sage, 1992; also his book *The Reinvention of Politics*, Cambridge: Polity, 1997; Anthony Giddens *Modernity and Self-Identity: Self and Society in the Late Modern Age*, Cambridge: Polity, 1991.

17 Conservative critics of Gardner's view will claim that the various multiple manifestations of 'intelligence' are derived from a general ability which can be measured by IQ. In other words, people with high IQs will be better at all expressions of intelligence. However, as Robert Sternberg, a leading authority on intelligence has argued, 'The weight of the evidence at the present time is that intelligence is multimimensional, and that the full range of these dimensions is not completely captured by any single general ability', in 'Myths, countermyths, and truths about intelligence', *Educational Research*, March, 1996, pp. 11–16.

18 Phillip Brown and Richard Scase, *Higher Education and Corporate Realities*, University College London, 1994.

19 Daniel Goleman, *Emotional Intelligence*, London: Bloomsbury, 1996, p. xii.

20 Colin Lacey, 'The idea of a socialist education', in H. Lauder and P. Brown (eds) *Education: In Search of a Future*, London: Falmer Press, 1988, p. 94. Lacey also states that 'Intelligence has to do with understanding the relationships between complex systems and making judgements about when it is appropriate to create new courses of action or avenues of thought. Most fundamental, intelligence entails the understanding of the relationship between the internal characteristics of the person and external systems': p. 94.

21 Alan Ryan, *John Dewey and the high tide of American liberalism*, New York: W. W. Norton, 1995, p. 28.

22 Arguments about human nature and capability will never be resolved, because nature quite literally unfolds in history. However, to hang on to the assumption that only a few are capable of social injustice.

23 See William K. Cummings, *Education and Equality in Japan*, New Jersey: Princeton University Press, 1980.

24 Lawrence Steinberg, *Beyond the Classroom: Why School Reform has Failed and What Parents Need to Do*, New York: Simon and Schuster, 1996.

25 Erich Fromm, *Fear of Freedom*, London: Routledge and Kegan Paul, 1942, p. 207.

26 The classic statement of the difference between private troubles and public issues is in C. Wright Mills, 1959 *The Sociological Imagination*, New York: Oxford University Press.

27 This emphasis on problem solving may appear to some readers as too instrumental, leaving insufficient space for forms of collective activities which are analogous to 'art for art sake', but it is better to see our approach as experimental rather than instrumental, because it involves entering into a dialogue with others which is likely to involve differences in political beliefs or interests about what should be seen as the problem to be solved and also different views about the best solutions.

28 Our definition also highlights the fact that the acquisition of intelligence and the ability to use it depends on the learning potential of individuals (and institutions) in all spheres of life and is not restricted to the formal learning which goes on in our schools, offices or factories.

29 See Phillip Brown, 'The globalization of positional competition', *Sociology*, Spring, 2001.

30 R. H. Tawney, *The Acquisitive Society*, Brighton: Wheatsheaf, 1982, p. 10.

31 Hence, in speaking about these embedded relations of trust we are referring to the perception people have of the trust reposed in their behaviour as it is expressed and embodied in the rules and relations which others seek to impose on them, or they seek to impose on others. See Alan Fox, *Beyond Contract*, London: Faber & Faber, 1974, p. 15; pp. 67–9.

32 James S. Coleman, 'Social capital in the creation of human capital', *American Journal of Sociology*, 94, Supplement, 1988, S95–S120.

33 James Coleman and Thomas Hoffer, *Public and Private Schools: The Impact of Communities*, New York: Basic Books, 1987.

34 US General Accounting Office, *Elementary School Children: Many Change School Frequently, Harming Their Eduction*, Report to the Hon. Marcy Kaptur, House of Representatives, Washington, DC, 1994.

35 William Julius Wilson, *The Truly Disadvantaged: The Inner City, The Underclass and Public Policy*, Chicago: Chicago University Press, 1987.

36 Dewey, *Democracy and Education*, New York: Free Press, 1916, p. 141.

37 ibid., p. 101.

38 ibid., p. 98.

39 ibid., p. 87.

40 See the discussion on Emile Durkheim in the previous chapter.

41 Karl Marx, *Capital Volume 1*, Harmondsworth: Penguin, 1976, p. 452.

42 ibid., p. 451. For a classic study of the development of industrial time, see E. P. Thompson, 'Time, work-discipline, and industrial capitalism', *Past and Present*, vol. 38, 1967.

43 For an interesting and controversial account see Peter. F. Drucker's account of the 'productivity revolution', in his *Post-Capitalist Society*, London: Butterworth-Heinemann, 1993.

44 For an excellent study of postwar industrial relations, see Alan Fox, *Beyond Contract: Work, Power and Trust Relations*, London: Faber & Faber, 1974.

45 This was certainly the practice at the British Leyland plant as Cowley, Oxford in England during the mid-1970s. The Cowley plant has since lost over half its workforce and British Leyland was taken-over by the Rover Group which became part of the German car company BMW, before it was then sold on for £10.00.

46 Emotional Intelligence (see n. 19 above), p. 160.

47 A. H. Halsey, *Change in British Society*, 3rd edn, Oxford: Oxford University Press, 1986, p. 173; See also A. H. Halsey with Josephine Webb, (eds) *British Social Trends: The Twentieth Century*, Basingstoke: Macmillan, 2000.

48 What is equally clear is the need for an holistic approach to social change. It must reject the tendency, for instance, to treat questions of productivity and redistribution as separate realms of policy. This may be administratively convenient but it encourages segmental thinking which downplays their interrelationship in the desire to improve the quality of life for all. Zsuzsa Ferge has made the useful distinction between societal policy and social policy in her study of Hungarian society in the post-war period: 'The concept of societal policy...is used in a special sense. It encompasses the sphere of social policy (the organisation of social services or the redistribution of income), but also includes systematic social intervention at all points of the cycle of the reproduction of social life, with the aim of changing the structure

of society'. See T. H. Marshall and Tom Bottomore, *Citizenship and Social Class*, London: Pluto Press, 1992, pp. 60–3.

14   The Learning State

1   Richard G. Wilkinson, *Unhealthy Societies: The Afflictions of Inequality*, London: Routledge, 1996. Ichiro Kawachi, Bruce Kennedy, Richard Wilkinson (eds) *The Society and Population Health Reader: Income Inequality and Health*, New York: New Press, 1999.
2   This phrase was first coined, to our knowledge, by Seaun Hargreaves-Heap. See his *Rationality in Economics*, Blackwell: Oxford, 1989.
3   Marilyn Waring, *If Women Counted: A New Feminist Economics*, London: Mac-Millan Press, 1989.
4   These figures are taken from Andrew Hacker, *Money, Who Has How Much and Why*, New York: Scribners, 1997.
5   This of course did not always mean acceptance of middle-class norms of society. See Paul Willis, *Learning to Labour*, Farnborough: Saxon House, 1977; Michael Buroway, *Manufacturing Consent: Changes in the Labour Process of Monopoly Capitalism*, Chicago: University of Chicago Press, 1979.
6   George Gilder, *Wealth and Poverty*, New York: Basic Books, 1981.
7   Richard Wilkinson, *Unhealthy Societies* (n.1 above); Andrew Oswald, *The Missing Piece of the Unemployment Puzzle*, An Inaugural Lecture, Department of Economics, University of Warwick, November, 1997.
8   Andrew Oswald, ibid.
9   Ian Gough, 'Justifying basic income?' *Imprints*, vol. 1, 1996, pp. 82–3.
10   This phrase is taken from Michael Ignatieff, *The Needs of Strangers*, London: Chatto & Windus, 1984.
11   This is slightly unfair to Bill Clinton who did raise taxes for the upper income bracket in 1993 so that the top 10 per cent paid about 59 per cent of taxes. However, the point stands in relation to the argument below.
12   The common use of the terms 'consumer' and 'consumer choice' are an interesting linguistic symptom of this fundamental shift in the way we interact with one another.
13   The major criticisms of the welfare state from the Right have been developed by public choice theorists and their fellow travellers. See Charles Murray, *Losing Ground: American Social Policy 1950–1980*, New York: Basic Books, 1984, for a critique of social policies and Eric Hanushek, 'The economics of schooling: production and efficiency in public schools', *Journal of Economic Literature*, vol. 24, 1986, 1141–77 for the application of this theory to education. For a review of Marxist critiques of the welfare state, see Ian Gough, *The Political Economy of the Welfare State*, London: MacMillan Press, 1979.
14   Claus Offe, *Contradictions of the Welfare State*, London: Hutchinson, 1984.
15   Although we have characterized this distinction between income and motivation as that between Left and Right, this is only so as a matter of history, rather than principle. In the post-war era, when there was full employment and there was little 'down time' between jobs, income support was all that was required. It was only when unemployment rose to high and persisting levels did the issue of motivation rise.

16 See Jane Millar, *Making Work Pay: Integration of Family Payments in Australia*, Centre for the Analysis of Social Policy, University of Bath, UK, 1998. There is clearly a problem of gender and power within family dynamics with such a scheme but it is also confronted by programmes relating to child support now such as that in Australia.

17 Paul Johnson and Howard Reed, 'Intergenerational mobility among the rich and the poor: results from the National Child Development Survey', *Oxford Review of Economic Policy*, vol. 12, 1996, 127–42.

18 Peter Gottschalk, 'Inequality, income growth and mobility: the basic facts', *Journal of Economic Perspectives*, vol. 11, 1997, 21–40; Stephen Raudenbush and Rafa Kasim, 'Cognitive skill and economic inequality: findings from the National Adult Literacy Survey', *Harvard Educational Review*, vol. 68, 1998, 33–79. John Bynner, *New Routes to Employment: Integration and Exclusion*, Social Statistics Research Unit, City University, London, April, 1996.

19 Williams Julius Wilson, *The Truly Disadvantaged: The Inner City, The Underclass and Public Policy*, Chicago: University of Chicago Press, 1987.

20 For easily understood discussions of these issues see Alissa Goodman, Paul Johnson and Steven Webb, *Inequality in the United Kingdom*, Oxford: Oxford University Press, 1997; Andrew Hacker, *Money, Who Has How Much and Why*, New York: Scribners, 1997; Frank Levy, *The New Dollars and Dreams*, New York: Russell Sage, 1998.

21 Given that the system will certainly mean higher taxes for the top 20 per cent – see the following discussion on Andrew Hacker's calculations.

22 Andrew Hacker, *Money, Who Has How Much and Why* (n. 20 above), ch.10.

23 Betsy Morris, 'Is your family wrecking your career? (and vice versa)', *Fortune*, March 17, 1997, pp. 41–9.

24 Betsy Morris, ibid.

25 Andrew Hacker, *Money, Who Has How Much and Why* (n. 20 above), p. 56.

26 ibid., p. 40. Raising the revenue for either a carers or citizens wage need not be done simply by taxing the wealthier more. However, given Frank Wilkinson's (ibid.) argument for the benefits of a society moving towards a greater equality of incomes a significant part of the revenue should be raised through progressive income tax. Nevertheless, alongside the desirability of greater overall equality in society there is also a need to develop policies of environmental sustainability. Here James Robertson has made an interesting case for linking a citizen's income to eco-tax reform strategies. See, for example, his 'Towards a new social compact: citizen's income and radical tax reform', in *The Political Quarterly*, vol. 67, 1996, pp. 54–8.

27 Jeremy Rifkin, *The End of Work*, New York: Tarcher/Putnam, 1996, p. 294.

28 ibid., p. XV

29 There is a considerable body of writing on the citizen's wage. See for example Philippe Van Parijs, (ed.) *Arguing for Basic Income*, New York: Verso, 1992. The symposium in *The Political Quarterly*, vol. 67, 1996. Interestingly the championing of a citizen's wage has come not only from traditional Left but also from the Right.

30 Philippe Van Parijs, 'Basic income and the two dilemmas of the welfare state', *The Political Quarterly*, vol. 67, 1996, 63–6.

31 Ian Gough, 'Social welfare and competitiveness', *New Political Economy*, vol. 1, 1996, 209–32.

32   Ann Orloff, 'Is one man's ceiling another woman's floor?' women and BIG (basic income guarantee)', paper given at the conference on *Basic Income Guarantees: A New Welfare Strategy*, University of Wisconsin, April, 1990; Andre Gorz, 'On the difference between society and community and why basic income cannot confer full membership of either', in Philippe Van Parijs, (ed.) *Arguing for Basic Income*, New York: Verso, 1992, p. 181.

33   Carol Pateman, *The Disorder of Women*, Cambridge: Polity Press, 1989, p. 202.

34   See Bob Connell, 'The big picture: masculinities in recent world history', in A. H. Halsey, H. Lauder, P. Brown, and A. S. Wells, A. (eds) *Education: Culture, Economy and Society*, Oxford: Oxford University Press, 1997.

35   Martin Carnoy, *Faded Dreams: The Politics and Economics of Race in America*, Cambridge: Cambridge University Press, 1994.

36   Lawrence Steinberg, *Beyond the Classroom: Why School Reform Has Failed and What Parents Need to Do*, New York: Simon and Schuster, 1996, pp. 92–3.

37   On the contrast between Japanese and American views of ability and motivation see, Susan Holloway, 'Concepts of ability and effort in Japan and the United States', *Review of Educational Research*, vol. 58, no. 3, 1988, 327–45.

38   See Robert Bhaerman and Rick Spill, 'A dialogue on employability skills: how can they be taught?', *Journal of Careers Development*, vol. 15, no. 1, 1988, 341–53; and the OECD Report, *Prepared for Life*, Centre for Educational Research and Innovation, Paris: OECD, 1997 which discusses how skills of this kind can be measured.

39   For a discussion of this issue see A. H. Halsey, Hugh Lauder, Phillip Brown, and Amy Stuart Wells, (eds) *Education: Culture, Economy and Society*, (n. 34 above), especially their introductory chapter.

40   The pioneering research into group work was done by David W. Johnson and Roger T. Johnson, *Learning Together and Alone: Cooperation, Competition, Individualism*, New Jersey: Prentice Hall, 1975.

41   On the notion of compensatory education see A. H. Halsey 'Sociology and the equality debate', *Oxford Review of Education*, vol. 9, 1975, 9–23. See also Pierre Bourdieu and Jean-Claude Passeron, *The Inheritors: French Students and their Relation to Culture*, Chicago: University of Chicago Press, 1964; Phillip Brown and Richard Scase, *Higher Education and Corporate Realities: Class culture and the Decline of Graduate Careers*, London: University College London Press, 1994.

42   E. Said 'Orientalism Reconsidered', in F. Barker et al. (eds) *Literature, Politics and Theory*, New York: Methven, 1986, p. 153.

43   There is an important link to be made between socially situated learning as the key social psychology of collective intelligence. See Lauren Resnick, John Levine and Stephanice Teasley, (eds) *Perspectives on Socially Shared Cognition*, Washington, DC.: American Psychological Association, 1991; Jean Lave, *Cognition in Practice*, Cambridge: Cambridge University Press, 1988; and Jean Lave and Etienne Wenger, *Situated Learning*, Cambridge: Cambridge University Press, 1991; Harry Daniels (ed.) *In Introduction to Vygotsky*, New York: Routledge, 1996.

44   See Howard S. Becker, 'Schools and Systems of Stratification' in A. H. Halsey et al. (eds) *Education, Economy and Society*, New York: Free Press, 1961.

45   OCED Economic Surveys, *The United States* Paris: OECD, 1999. See http://www.oecd.org/eco/surv/esu-usa.htm

46 James Coleman, 'The concept of equality of educational opportunity', *Harvard Educational Review*, vol. 38, 1968, pp. 7–22.

47 See Martin Thrupp, *Do Schools make a Difference?: Let's Get Real*, Milton Keynes: Open University Press, 1999.

48 Paul Hirst, *Associative Democracy: New Forms of Economic and Social Governance*, Cambridge: Polity Press, p. 66 & p. 61.

49 See Andy Green, Tom Leney and Alison Wolf, *Convergences and Divergences in European Education and Training Systems*, EC Directorate General XXII Education, Training and Youth. Available from the Institute of Education, University of London, 1997.

50 A learning bank for lifelong learning is discussed in *Social Justice: Strategies for National Renewal*, The Report on the Commission of Social Justice, London: Vintage, 1994, pp. 141–47. The introduction of a 'lifetime learning' tax credit of 20 per cent of all educational costs up to $10,000 after 2000 by Al Gore in the US is clearly a step forward. See http://vpskillsummit.gov/speeches.asp

51 See Michael Young, *The Curriculum of the Future*, London: Taylor & Francis, 1998.

52 Zsuzsa Ferge, *A Society in the Making: Hungarian Social and Societal Policy, 1945–1975*, Harmondsworth: Penguin, 1979, p. 13. See also Tom Bottomore 'Citizenship and social class: forty years on', in T. H. Marshall and Tom Bottomore, *Citizenship and Social Class*, London: Pluto Press, 1979.

53 The provision of a carer's wage and subsequently a citizen's wage will provide a material foundation for a multicultural society in which difference is celebrated. One of the fundamental questions concerning such a society is: what holds such a society together if the emphasis is on difference? See Mark Olsen's 'Citizenship and Education: From Alfred Marshall to Iris Marion Young' forthcoming in *Education, Philosophy and Theory*. This is a sympathetic critique of the latter's excellent *Justice and the Politics of Difference*, Princeton, New Jersey: Princeton University Press, 1990. See also Nancy Fraser, 'Rethinking the Public Sphere: A Contribution to the Critique of Actually Existing Democracy' in Craig Calhoun (ed.) *Habermas and the Public Sphere*, Cambridge, Mass.: MIT Press, 1992.

15   A High-Skills Economy

1 A high skills route is an essential pre-condition for the introduction of the citizen's wage. It is only if a nation can compete in at least some of the high value added mass and niche markets within the global economy that there is any prospect of creating the prosperity to fund a citizen's wage. However, a high-skills policy based on a citizen's wage cannot solve unemployment and underemployment as discussed in chapter ten. What is can do is provide a solid raft of employment stability in a highly uncertain world.

2 Peter F. Drucker, *Post-Capitalist Society*, London: Butterworth-Heinemann, 1993, p. 176.

3 The personification of knowledge is clearly recognized in Peter F. Drucker's account of the productivity of knowledge. See his *Post-Capitalist Society*, ch. 12.

4 See Douglas McGregor, *The Human Side of Enterprise*, New York: McGraw-Hill, 1960.

5   See Antonio Gramsci, 'Americanism and fordism', in Q. Hoare and G. Howell-Smith (eds) *Selections From the Prison Notes of Antonio Gramsci*, London: Lawrence & Wishart, 1971.

6   Collins, Randell, *Weberian Sociological Theory*, Cambridge: Cambridge University Press, 1986, p. 115.

7   See Charles Leadbetter, *Britain: The California of Europe? What the UK Can Learn from the West Coast*, London: Demos.

8   This was discussed in chapter 9 'Downsizing the Corporation'.

9   Dan Rasher and Claire Brown, *The Competitive Semi-Conductor Human Resources Project: Second Interim Report*, The Institute of Industrial Relations, Berkeley, University of California, 1997.

10   Lester C. Thurow, *Building Wealth: The New Rules for Individuals, Companies, and Nations in a Knowledge-Based Economy*, New York: HarperCollins, 1999, p. 133.

11   Fred Hirsch has observed while the collective actions of workers who organise in unions are asked to restrain their use of disruptive economic power 'individuals who are able to exert greater acquisitive power without recourse to disruptive power remain free to do so' Fred Hirsch, *Social Limits to Growth*, London: Routledge & Kegan Paul, 1977, p. 155.

12   Shoshana Zuboff, *In the Age of the Smart Machine*, New York: Basic Books, 1989, p. 414.

13   ibid., p. 395.

14   Michael H. Best, *The New Competition: Institutions of Industrial Restructuring*, Cambridge: Polity Press, 1990, p. 235.

15   Workers in low-trust organizations are assumed not be capable of initiative or to share the goals of management 'They are neither trained to show nor rewarded for initiative. And they know it.' Charles Sabel, *Work and Politics: The Division of Labour in Industry*, Cambridge: Cambridge University Press, 1984, p. 210.

16   Heckscher's review of the literature found that over 50 per cent of large companies had introduced policies to improve the level of employee involvement. Charles Hechscher, 'Can business beat bureaucracy?' *American Prospect*, Spring, 1991, 114–28. Also see his book *White-Collar Blues: Management Loyalties in an Age of Corporate Restructuring*, New York: Basic Books, 1995.

17   See Max Weber, *Economy and Society*, G. Roth and C. Wittich (eds) Berkeley: University of California, 1978; Edward Shils, 'Charisma, order and status', *American Sociological Review*, 30, 1965, 199–213; Phillip Brown, 'Cultural capital and social exclusion: some observations on recent trends in education, employment and the labour market', *Work, Employment and Society*, 9, 1995, 29–51.

18   Max Weber's formulation of the charasmatic leadership was reserved for a minority of 'extraordinary' individuals among the religious prophets, military heroes, political leaders and social reformers such as Adolf Hitler, Martin Luther King and Ronald Reegan. The use of the term applied here follows Edward Shils' (ibid.) distinction between this form of 'extraordinary' charisma based on intense and concentrated action, from what Shils views as its 'normal' form which is more attenuated and dispersed.

19   Stanley Davis, *Future Perfect*, New York: Addison Wesley, 1987, p. 197–8.

20   H. Rush and J. Bessant 1990 'The diffusion of manufacturing technology, OECD Observer, Oct/Nov. p. 21.

21 ibid p. 22.
22 Paul Strassman, *Information Payoff: The Transformation of Work in the Electronic Age*, New York: Free Press. Quoted in Fred Block, *Post-Industrial Possibilities*, Berkeley: University of California, 1990, p. 106.
23 This model draws on the work of Douglas McGregor, *The Human Side of Enterprise*, New York: McGraw-Hill, 1960.
24 See US Department of Commerce, *Twenty-First Century Skills for Twenty-First Century Jobs*, Washington, DC: US Government Printing Office, 1999, p. 19 or at http://vpskillsummit.gov
25 'A letter from ASTD's president', in Laurie, J. Bassi and Mark E. Van Buren, *The 1999 ASTD State of the Industry Report*, Washington, DC: ASTD, 1999, p. 2.
26 See Department of Commerce, *Twenty-First Century Skills for Twenty-First Century Jobs* (n. 24 above).
27 Robert Wade, *Governing the Market: Economic Theory and the Role of Government in East Asian Industrialization*, Princeton: Princeton University Press, 1990, p. 380–1.
28 See Melvin Kohn and Cami Schooler, *Work and Personality: An Inquiry into the Impact of Social Stratification*, New Jersey: Ablex Publishing Company, 1983; See also Melvin Kohn, *Class and Conformity*, Chicago: University of Chicago Press, 1977.
29 The classic statement of this distinction is to be found in the work of Friedrich A. Hayek. See *The Road to Serfdom*, Chicago: University of Chicago Press, 1944; *The Constitution of Liberty*, Chicago: University of Chicago Press, 1960; For a recent example of a similar argument see Daniel Yergin and Joseph Stanislaw, *The Commanding Heights: The Battle Between Government and the Marketplace that is Remaking the Modern World*, New York: Simon and Schuster, 1998.
30 The key stakeholders in Germany now realize that their bottom-up approach to skill formation can not fulfil the task of economic intelligence in the context of a global economy. Greater co-ordination at the federal level is now seen to be required. Exactly who will be responsible for the co-ordination of economic intelligence is yet to be decided, but it will probably be the BIBB. This has recently been researched by the authors in collaboration with Professor Andy Green at the Institute of Education, University of London: The 'High Skill Project' is funded by the Economic and Social Research Council of Great Britain. See the special issue of the *Journal of Education and Work*, devoted to the High Skills Project, vol. 12, 1999 October; Phillip Brown, Andy Green and Hugh Lauder, *High Skills*, Oxford: Oxford University Press, 2001.
31 For an interesting discussion of these issues see Anthony Gidden, *Beyond Left and Right*, Cambridge: Polity Press, 1994; *The Third Way: The Renewal of Social Democracy*, Cambridge: Polity Press, 1998.
32 This interview was part of the High Skills Project (see n. 30 above).
33 Rosabeth Moss Kanter, 'Small business and economic growth', in Jerry J. Jasinowski (ed.) *The Rising Tide*, New York: John Wiley & Son, 1998, p. 95.
34 ibid., p. 99.
35 See Lester C. Thurow, *Building Wealth: The New Rules for Individuals, Companies, and Nations in a Knowledge-Based Economy*, New York: HarperCollins, 1999, pp. 99–116.
36 ibid., p. 109.

37   Martin Fransman, 'Is national technology policy obsolete in a globalised world?' in Daniele Archibugi and Jonathan Michie (eds) *Technology, Globalisation and Economic Performance*, Cambridge: Cambridge University Press, 1997, p. 66.

38   Pari Patel, 'Localised production of technology for global markets', in Daniele Archibugi and Jonathan Michie (eds) *Technology, Globalisation and Economic Performance*, p. 213.

39   See Martin Fransman, 'Is national technology policy obsolete in a globalised world?' in Daniele Archibugi and Jonathan Michie (eds) *Technology, Globalisation and Economic Performance* (n. 37 above).

40   Rosabeth Moss Kanter, 'Small business and economic growth', in Jerry, J. Jasinowski (ed.) *The Rising Tide* (n. 33 above), p. 93.

41   ibid., p. 93.

42   Reported by Peter Koenig in the *Independent on Sunday*, May 15, 1998.

43   See Robert Wade and Frank Veneros, 'The Asain crisis: the high debt model versus the Wall Street–Treasury–IMF complex', *New Left Review*, No. 228, 1998, 3–23; Chalmers Johnson, 'Economic crisis in East Asia: the clash of capitalisms', *Cambridge Journal of Economics*, vol. 22, 1998, pp. 653–61.

44   Will Hutton, *The State We're In*, London: Jonathan Cape, 1995, p. 176.

16   Conclusion

1   Edward Luttwak, an interview in *Le Monde*, June 5, 1995; see also *Turbo Capitalism: Winners and Losers in the Global Economy*, New York: Harper Collins, 1998.

2   George Soros, 'The capitalist threat', *Atlantic Review*, February 1997 and *The Crisis of Global Capitalism*, London: Little, Brown and Company, 1998.

3   We should not be content simply to patch up what is an indefensible global economic system. It manifestly needs to be changed. There have been several suggestions as to how this could be done. See Larry Elliott and Dan Atkinson, *The Age of Insecurity*, London: Verso, 1998; David Foden and Peter Morris (eds) *The Search for Equity: Welfare and Security in the Global Economy*, London: Lawrence and Wishart, 1998; Daniele Archibugi, David Held and Martin Kohler, (eds) *Re-imagining Political Community*, Cambridge: Polity Press, 1998.

4   John K. Galbraith *The Politics of Contentment*, New York: Houghton Mifflin, 1992, p. 16–17.

5   John, K. Galbraith is also correct in the suggestion that the Republican and Conservative governments in America and Britain during the 1980s reflected the sentiments of the contented. Conservative 'statecraft', that is the 'art of willing elections and . . . achieving a necessary degree of governing competence in office,' has been based around an appeal to the self-interests of the contented. See Jim Bulpitt, 'the discipline of the new democracy: Mrs Thatcher's domestic statecraft', *Political Studies*, 34, 1986, pp. 19–39.

6   Robert Reich, *The Work of Nations*, New York: Simon and Schuster, 1991, p. 268.

7   Norman Dennis and A. H. Halsey, *English Ethical Socialism: Thomas More to R. H. Tawney* Oxford: Clarendon Press, 1988, p. 203

8   Reported in J.Carlin, 'What makes US women voters cross', *Independent on Sunday*, August 27, 1995.

9   Gender divisions in welfare provision are not restricted to the 'liberal' welfare states of USA and Britain. See Gosta Esping-Anderson, *The Three Worlds of Welfare Capitalism*, Cambridge: Polity Press, 1990, and *Social Foundations of Postindustrial Economies*, Oxford: Oxford University Press, 1999; Carole Pateman, *The Sexual Contract*, Cambridge: Polity Press, 1988, and Arnlaug Leira, *Welfare States and Working Mothers: The Scandanavian Experience*, Cambridge: Cambridge University Press, 1992.

10 Naomi Wolf, *Fire with Fire: The New Female Power and How it will Change the 21st Century*, London: Chatto & Windus, 1993, p. 17.

11 ibid., p. 322.

12 David Marquand, *The Unprincipled Society*, London: Johathan Cape, 1988, p. 226; see also his book *The New Reckoning: Capitalism, States and Citizens*, Cambridge: Polity Press, 1997.

13 See Norman Dennis and A. H. Halsey, *English Ethical Socialism: Thomas More to R. H. Tawney*; John Dewey, *Democracy and Education*, New York: Macmillan, 1916; R. H. Tawney, *Equality*, London: Unwin Books, 1931.

14 Jeremy Rifkin, *The End of Work*, New York: Tarcher/Putnam, 1996, p. 267.

15 Anthony Giddens, *Beyond Left and Right*, Cambridge: Polity Press, 1994, p. 112

16 Emile Durkheim, *The Evolution of Educational Thought*, London: Routledge, 1977, p. 5.

Index